9-20-2013

To Donna,

In gratitude for the gift of your friendship —

Affectionately,
Mary and Norm

TOOLS FOR UNDERSTANDING

The Historical Series of the Reformed Church in America
no. 60

TOOLS FOR UNDERSTANDING
ESSAYS IN HONOR OF DONALD J. BRUGGINK

James Hart Brumm, Editor

© 2008 Reformed Church Press
All rights reserved

Wm. B. Eerdmans Publishing Co.
2140 Oak Industrial Drive S.E., Grand Rapids, Michigan 49503 /
P.O. Box 163, Cambridge CB3 9PU U.K.
www.eerdmans.com

Printed in the United States of America

Library of Congress Cataloging-in-Publication Data

Tools for understanding : essays in honor of Donald J. Bruggink / James Hart Brumm, editor.
    p. cm. -- (The historical series of the Reformed Church in America ; no. 60)
  Includes index.
  ISBN 978-0-8028-6483-3 (cloth : alk. paper) 1. Reformed Church in America--Doctrines. 2. Theology. I. Brumm, James Hart.
  BX9521.T66 2008
  230'.57--dc22
                            2009010640

The Rev. Dr. Donald J. Bruggink
(photograph, Carla Plumert)

The Historical Series of the Reformed Church in America

The series was inaugurated in 1968 by the General Synod of the Reformed Church in America acting through the Commission on History to communicate the church's heritage and collective memory and to reflect on our identity and mission, encouraging historical scholarship which informs both church and academy.

General Editor
    Rev. Donald J. Bruggink, Ph.D., D.D.
    Western Theological Seminary
    Van Raalte Institute, Hope College

Associate Editor
    Rev. George Brown, Jr., Ph.D.
    Western Theological Seminary

Copy Editor
    Laurie Baron

Production Editor
    Russell L. Gasero

Commission on History
    Douglas Carlson, Ph.D., Northwestern College, Orange City, Iowa
    Mary L. Kansfield, M.A., East Stroudsburg, Pennsylvania
    Hartmut Kramer-Mills, M.Div., Ph.D., New Brunswick, New Jersey
    Jeffery Tyler, Ph.D., Hope College, Holland, Michigan
    Audrey Vermilyea, Bloomington, Minnesota
    Lori Witt, Ph.D., Central College, Pella, Iowa

Contents

Preface	xi
Foreword	xv
A Tribute to Donald J. Brugink	
Jack E. Nyenhuis	xix
Contributors	xxiii
Introduction:	
Tools for Understanding Donald J. Bruggink	xxvii

Part 1: Tools for Understanding Western Theological
    Seminary   1

1 From Dosker to Bruggink: Teaching Historical
    Theology at Western Theological Seminary,
    1884-1999
        Eugene Heideman   3

2 Finding a Place at the Table
        George Brown, Jr.   31

3 Frances Davis Beardslee and the Leading Ladies
    of Holland, Michigan, 1912-1917
        Mary L. Kansfield   67

Part 2: Tools for Understanding Historiography   111

4 The Story of the Archives of the
    Reformed Church in America
        Russell L. Gasero   113

5 Bottoms Up—A Copy Editor's Perspective on
    the Historical Series of the Reformed
    Church in America
        Laurie Z. Baron   127

Part 3: Tools for Understanding Theological Education   139
   6   Teacher of the Church: The Office of Professor
          of Theology in the Reformed Church in America
            Norman J. Kansfield   141
   7   John Henry Livingston as Professor of Theology
            John W. Coakley   189
   8   When East Meets West: Theological Education
          and the Unity of the Reformed Church in America
            Dennis Voskuil   201

Part 4: Tools for Understanding God and God's Church   229
   9   Human Diversity and Christianity Imagined:
          Past, Present, Eternal
            J. Jeffery Tyler   231
  10   The Ministry of the State: A Reformed Approach
          to Public Theology
            Allan J. Janssen   247
  11   Not Only for Necessity: The Problem of Aesthetics
          in Reformed Worship
            James Hart Brumm   263
  12   Calvin on the Atonement: A Reexamination
            I. John Hesselink   295

       A New Hymn
          James Hart Brumm
          Kathleen Hart Brumm   321

       Published Works of Donald J. Bruggink
          Compiled by George Brown, Jr.   325

       Index   341

Illustrations

Elaine and Edward Lubbers	41
The Lubbers family shortly after Ed's death	42
Elaine Lubbers, 1958 graduation picture	45
Professor Elaine Lubbers	52

Preface

"History is a tool for understanding."

George Brown tells me that this was a favorite phrase of Donald Bruggink's when he was teaching,[1] a reminder that understanding history helps us understand the church, and our churches, and the scriptures. As many people around the Reformed Church began to discuss how best to honor him on the occasion of his eightieth birthday, a few things became obvious. First of all, the general editor of the Historical Series had to be honored with a volume in the series. Second, his interests, passions, and areas of knowledge are wide and varied: teacher, pastor, theologian, historian, liturgist, ecumenist, advocate for social justice, architect, father, husband, editor, and, of course, historical tour guide. Third, all of these varied subjects could be subsumed into one overriding pursuit: understanding his world and his God and helping others to understand.

Bruggink has been helping people understand for over half a century—fifty-five years, if you count from his ordination as a minister of the Word.[2] While he referred to his ministry in the past

---

[1] Quoted (from memory) in a conversation with the author Thursday, October 2, 2008, at Western Theological Seminary, Holland, Michigan.

[2] Donald J. Bruggink was licensed and ordained by the Classis of Wisconsin in 1954. Russell L. Gasero, *Historical Directory of the Reformed Church in America 1628-2000*, Historical Series of the Reformed Church in America, no. 37 (Grand Rapids: Eerdmans, 2001).

tense when speaking with this editor—in an oral interview that will be cited extensively in the introduction to this volume[3]—that was a rare misunderstanding on his part. While he was declared a professor of theology emeritus in 1999, his ministry has continued through the increased activity of the Historical Series,[4] his regular presence at Western Theological Seminary, where he maintains an office and participates in the life of the school, his work with the Van Raalte Institute, and, of course, the tours in the footsteps of apostles and other saints that he continues to lead. Even as his ninth decade of life, not to mention his second decade of retirement, begins, he continues to give tools for understanding to anyone who will read or listen. Looking at this and examining how he spent his life, the title and structure of this book became obvious.

Structure is especially important for this book. Donald Bruggink's gifts for architecture, liturgy, and history, as well as his editorial skills, suggest a mind that thinks structurally, a mind that wants things to fit together and wants to make connections. A mind that thinks structurally sees meaning in how things are put together and will be looking for meaning, intended or inadvertent, in the way these pages have been ordered. That puts a particular pressure on this editor. Therefore, not having any conscious control over the accidental meanings that may be found here, allow me to take a moment to review my intent.

Beginning with Bruggink's own notion that "history is a tool for understanding," the dozen essays in this volume are tools for understanding four areas of his life and ministry: Western Seminary, where he has spent a significant amount of time for half his life; the study of history, which has been a passion of his since his days at Central College; theological education, the primary vocation for most of his ministry; and the nature of God and the church. Lest it seem that architecture has been forgotten, it is integral to an essay in the final section, all the more appropriate because the architecture of worship spaces has been his primary interest in this area. While all the contributors to this volume have benefited from Bruggink's friendship, teaching, and ministry, the first and last essays are by the contributors he has known longest, who had a formative role in his life: Eugene Heideman and I. John Hesselink.

[3] James Hart Brumm, interview with Donald J. Bruggink at Western Theological Seminary, October 1, 2008.
[4] Twenty-nine of the sixty-one volumes have been published in the last ten years. Cf. George Brown, Jr., "Published Works of Donald J. Bruggink," p.323.

This is not only Donald Bruggink's eightieth birthday year; it is also the 225th anniversary of the theological professorate. This is noted historically in the chapter from Norman Kansfield and celebrated artistically with a new hymn in honor of the theological professorate and the ministry of teaching. It is hoped that our honoree will even appreciate the tune name.

Volumes in the Historical Series are always community efforts, and collections of essays even more so. Those whose essays are included here are the most obvious. They have given gifts to Donald Bruggink and the whole church by freely sharing their knowledge and expertise and, in the process, have opened up new areas for study and discussion that can produce many fruitful conversations in the church wise enough to use them. The Van Raalte Institute, which supports Don's research, has generously supported the creation of this book, as well.

The members of the Commission on History and Jeff Tyler, its moderator, conceived of this volume and honored me with its trust in asking me to prepare it and, of necessity, bypass some of the usual avenues in the production process. Laurie Baron, copy editor for the series; Russell Gasero, production editor; and George Brown, Jr., assistant general editor, have all taken on more than double duty with this book. First, they each authored essays in this book, in addition to the usual work they do to make any volume in the series possible. On top of those two roles, the three of them, along with the commission members and the staff at William B. Eerdmans Publishing Company, have participated in a grand, intricate scheme designed to surprise the general editor of the Historical Series with this book. My wife, Kathleen, and son, Christopher, have once again given me to the church at large, that I might take time away from them and do this work.

Even though he doesn't yet know anything about this book, Donald Bruggink, who has taught me so much in my two previous forays editing volumes for this series, and who has put so many resources and procedures in place to make the Historical Series of the Reformed Church in America a reality, has left his imprint here. His teaching and ministry not only inspired this festschrift, but he gave us the tools to build it. All of us who have labored in his footsteps hope he appreciates these efforts.

Soli Deo Gloria!
James Hart Brumm,
Epiphanytide, 2009

Foreword

To celebrate the eightieth birthday of Donald J. Bruggink and to mark this occasion with the publication of the sixtieth volume in Historical Series of the Reformed Church in America, the members of the Commission on History wish to honor our colleague, mentor, and friend.

Since the creation of the Historical Series over four decades ago, the Reverend Dr. Donald J. Bruggink has served with distinction as general editor. Indeed, since 1966 Bruggink has championed the preservation and ongoing discovery of the denomination's history through the series. This he has done by encouraging hesitant authors, vetting hundreds of manuscripts, engaging in the demanding task of editing, and fiercely promoting the Historical Series—all to reveal that the stories of the past are important and useful to the future of the church. Thanks to Bruggink and his judicious oversight of the financial resources of the series, new books will continue to be published for future generations to use and to enjoy.

It is with great admiration that members of the Historical Commission express appreciation to the following:

To William B. Eerdmans, Jr., and the William B. Eerdmans Publishing Company we are indebted for their belief in the value and the future of a Reformed Church historical series. Without such kindness and generosity, it is unlikely there would be what is now the longest-lived and most distinguished series of historical volumes ever produced by an American denomination.

To the Reverend James Hart Brumm who, along with Dr. J. Jeffery Tyler, conceived the idea of honoring Bruggink by means of a festschrift. Brumm has labored graciously and winsomely as editor of this volume. Although not currently sitting on the Commission on History, he has previously served therein with distinction and continues to be engaged with the ongoing work of the commission.

To Laurie Baron, who has excelled as copy editor of the Historical Series for nearly twenty years. Laurie's commitment to making the volumes in the Historical Series editorially noteworthy is a gift to Bruggink, the commission, and the Reformed Church.

To Russell L. Gasero, archivist for the Reformed Church, who has worked over the years as production editor of the Historical Series and staff support to the Historical Commission. Without fanfare or pretense, Gasero has labored on behalf of the entire denomination to collect archival materials, make these resources available, and encourage the work of scholarly research.

To the Reverend Dr. George Brown, Jr., the associate general editor of the Historical Series, whose efforts have been indispensable in moving this book forward. He has made it possible for the commission and James Hart Brumm to operate deftly behind the scenes and beneath Bruggink's radar as this volume has developed.

During the last forty years, many generations of scholars, pastors, and lay people have served on the Commission on History. All have been given the rare opportunity of working with Bruggink to encourage research, review manuscripts, and promote the Historical Series. His efforts have generated a spirit of cooperation, thoughtfulness, and open exchange among commission members. We have learned from one another. This latest volume reflects this steady collaboration and celebrates Bruggink's gifted leadership.

On behalf of all members of the Commission on History, past and present, we offer this volume to Donald J. Bruggink, a festschrift born of the commission and penned by friends, colleagues, and former students—a labor of steadfast admiration and enduring affection.

    The Reformed Church in America Commission on History
        Douglas Carlson   J. Jeffery Tyler
        Mary L. Kansfield   Lori Witt
        Hartmut Kramer-Mills Audrey Vermilyea
                                Epiphany, 2009

Whereas the Rev. Dr. Donald J. Bruggink has contributed to the education of clergy and laity at New Brunswick Theological Seminary in 1960 and at Western Theological Seminary from 1962 until his retirement in 1999, and,

Whereas the Rev. Dr. Donald J. Bruggink has faithfully served as the general editor of the Historical Series of the Reformed Church in America from its inception in 1968 and has developed the series to include more than sixty volumes and has been a faithful steward of the resources needed to publish that series, and,

Whereas the Rev. Dr. Donald J. Bruggink has represented the Reformed Church in America on ecumenical bodies and agencies, in many and diverse ways enriching our worship life, enhancing our theological understanding, and strengthening our ecumenical commitments,

Therefore, be it resolved that on this eighth day of June, in the year of our Lord 2009, the Reformed Church in America's Commission on History, along with his friends and family, present the Rev. Dr. Donald J. Bruggink with this festschrift in honor of his contributions to the life and ministry of the church and in celebration of his eightieth birthday and gratefully thank him for his persistent, diligent service to the church and praise God for the gifts given to and shared by the Rev. Dr. Donald J. Bruggink.

A Tribute to Donald J. Bruggink

I consider it a special privilege to offer a tribute to my good friend and colleague, Don Bruggink. By the time I arrived at Hope College in 1975, Don was already very well established at Western Theological Seminary. My initial contacts with him were casual, at college or seminary events and at lunch in the Kletz, but I soon developed a very healthy respect for him—not only because of what others were saying about him, but also because my wife, who was a student in an art history course at Hope College that Don cotaught with Professor John M. Wilson, often enthused about Don's teaching and about his textbook, *Christ and Architecture*. During the six years that Don has been a senior research fellow at the Van Raalte Institute that respect has deepened, and our acquaintance has grown into a warm friendship.

Don and I share a number of passions, including a love for Greece and the larger Mediterranean region and delight in introducing students, alumni, and friends to the ancient world through travel to important archaeological sites and museums. Since establishing his Western Christendom Travel Seminar in 1967, he has organized and conducted some fifty travel seminars—over a dozen of them focused on art and architecture, with some designed specifically for AIA architects. We also share an enthusiasm for haute cuisine, for the bouquet of a fine vintage, and for the elegant design of classic automobiles. Over the past five years, I have enjoyed his photographs of Ferraris, the Bugatti Veyron, the Mercedes Benz SCL 600 (controlled by a joy-stick!), and other magnificent automobiles from the latest *Concours d'Elegance*.

When Don retired in 1999 from his endowed professorship at Western Theological Seminary, he was honored with a special issue of *Reformed Review: A Theological Journal of Western Theological Seminary* (vol. 52, no. 3, Spring 1999) to celebrate his thirty-seven years on the faculty. In an introductory essay, "The Committed Self: The Public Career of Donald J. Bruggink," Norman J. Kansfield, former student, former colleague, and long-time friend, aptly described Don as "a man of fervent commitments." He has succinctly and skillfully articulated Don's commitments to teaching, to history, to worship, and to justice.

To these commitments I would add the virtue of courage. After the Reformed Church in America's General Synod of 2005—while dealing with charges brought against Kansfield, who had until recently been president of New Brunswick Theological Seminary—sought to insert an extracanonical test for church membership and ministry into the *Book of Church Order*, Don wrote a strong challenge to that attempt in an essay published in a 2007 festschrift honoring Dr. Elton J. Bruins. Don's commitment to justice, previously lauded by Kansfield in 1999, led him to challenge his own church, just as he had challenged support for the Vietnam War in the 1960s.

These commitments indeed deserve to be celebrated and emulated. Equally worthy of celebration and emulation are both Don's dedication to scholarship and his selfless support for the scholarship of others. Professor Kansfield recognized Don's scholarly achievements within the context of the four categories cited above, but I single them out for separate recognition, because the past decade has provided even greater evidence for doing so.

If Don had published nothing more than the two books he wrote with his architect cousin, Carl H. Droppers—*Christ and Architecture* (1965) and *When Faith Takes Form: Contemporary Churches of Architectural Integrity in America* (1971)—his scholarly reputation would have been secure. But of course he wrote more, much more, as can be seen in his bibliography published in the *Reformed Review* (Spring, 1999) and in this current festschrift. His is a fertile mind, and his knowledge of church history, church architecture, and Christian worship is both broad and deep. One can only guess at how many more books he would have published, if he had limited himself to his own research interests.

Instead, he devoted a great deal of his energy to advancing the scholarly careers of others. In his role as founding general editor of the Historical Series of the Reformed Church in America, Don has shepherded sixty books into print since 1968. Whereas the series grew, on average, by one volume per year for the first three decades, Don has produced nearly twenty volumes in the past decade. It is such a pleasure to see Don's delight at presenting yet another volume in the series: his enthusiasm nearly rivals the exuberance that he expresses when talking about his beloved grandchildren, who live in Marquette, Michigan. When he recently brought me Number 59 in the series, he was about as excited as if he had written the book himself: he truly is a devoted and enthusiastic proponent of every one of his authors and editors.

The Van Raalte Institute consists of a number of us retired professors who continue to take delight in doing research and writing, drawing upon the rich resources of the Joint Archives of Holland and of the institute's own library and archives. Now in our sixteenth year, we have a long-standing tradition established by our founding director, Elton J. Bruins, of gathering daily for coffee. Our conversations are free-wheeling and wide-ranging, from our current research to religion to politics to music and theater to family and friends. Don brings to our coffee times not only his wit and his wisdom, but also his already mentioned passion and commitments (to which one might add opera, theater, and music in general). As a result, we can be sure that our conversations are never dull, always stimulating, often arousing hearty laughter.

The small farming towns of mid-America, such as Cedar Grove, Wisconsin, where Don grew up, have produced a remarkable number of outstanding teachers and scholars. Among them all, Don stands out as wonderfully unique and richly accomplished. We are all blessed to know him as teacher, colleague, mentor, editor, and friend.

Jacob E. Nyenhuis
Director, Van Raalte Institute

Contributors

Jacob E. Nyenhuis is professor of classics and provost, emeritus, and director of the Van Raalte Institute at Hope College. He is the author or editor of eight books, including *Latin Via Ovid*, *Myth and the Creative Process*, *A Goodly Heritage*, and, most recently, *Dutch-American Arts and Letters in Historical Perspective*.

Eugene Heideman is retired after serving as secretary for program and world mission for the Reformed Church in America. He served on the faculty of Western Theological Seminary from 1976-1982. His book, *The Practice of Piety: A History of Theology in the Midwestern Reformed Church in America, 1866-1966*, is forthcoming in the Historical Series of the Reformed Church in America in 2009.

George Brown, Jr. is G.W. and Eddie Haworth Professor of Christian Education and associate dean at Western Theological Seminary in Holland, Michigan. He serves as associate editor of the Historical Series of the Reformed Church in America and edited for the series *Herman J. Ridder: Contextual Preacher and President*.

Mary L. Kansfield is an independent scholar and the author of *Letters to Hazel: Ministry within the Woman's Board of Foreign Missions of the Reformed Church in America*, for the Reformed Church's Historical Series. She resides with her husband, Norman, in East Stroudsburg, Pennsylvania.

Laurie Z. Baron is a freelance editor and writer living in Holland, Michigan. She serves as copy editor for the Historical Series of the Reformed Church in America.

Russell L. Gasero has served as the archivist of the Reformed Church in America since the archives' formal establishment in 1978. He is editor of the *Historical Directory of the Reformed Church in America* and coeditor of *Servant Gladly*, both in the Reformed Church's Historical Series. He also serves as the co-chair of the Lone Arrangers Roundtable in the Society of American Archivists.

Norman Kansfield has served the church as a pastor, a seminary librarian, and a seminary president, and was a member of the editorial committee for the hymnbook, *Rejoice in the Lord*. In retirement he continues to teach, to research, and to write. Norman lives with his wife, Mary, in East Stroudsburg, Pennsylvania.

John W. Coakley is L. Russell Feakes Professor of Church History at New Brunswick Theological Seminary. He has edited, among other volumes, the Historical Series volume *Concord Makes Strength: Essays in Reformed Ecumenism* and is the author of *Women, Men, and Spiritual Power*.

Dennis Voskuil is Marvin and Jerene DeWitt Professor of Church History at Western Theological Seminary, where he also served as president. He is the author of *Mountains into Gold Mines: Robert Schuller and the Gospel of Success*.

J. Jeffery Tyler is professor of religion and director of the Senior Seminar Program at Hope College. He is the author of *Lord of the Sacred City: the Episcopus Exclusus in Late Medieval and Early Modern Germany*.

Allan Janssen is the pastor and teacher of the Community Church of Glen Rock and assistant professor of theological studies at New Brunswick Theological Seminary. He is the author of the Historical Series volumes *Constitutional Theology: Kingdom, Office and Church*; and *Gathered at Albany*.

James Hart Brumm is pastor and teacher of the Blooming Grove Reformed Church, DeFreestville, New York. He has edited the Historical Series volumes *Equipping the Saints: the Synod of New York 1800-2000* and *Liturgy Among the Thorns: Essays on Worship in the Reformed Church in America*, and he is author of *Singing the Lord's Song: the English Language Hymnals of the Reformed Church in America*; *Out of the Ordinary: Hymns and Worship Songs by James Hart Brumm*; and *Rhythms of Praises: Hymns by James Hart Brumm 2001-2007*.

I. John Hesselink is the Albertus C. Van Raalte Professor of Systematic Theology Emeritus at Western Theological Seminary, Holland, Michigan. Hesselink lectures frequently at conferences in the United States and around the world and continues to do some work at the seminary, particularly with graduate students from overseas.

Kathleen Hart Brumm is pastor and teacher of the First Reformed Church in Athens, New York, and a composer of numerous hymn tunes and musicals for children.

Introduction:
Tools for Understanding Donald J. Bruggink

James Hart Brumm

Bruggink, Donald J. b Kalamazoo, MI, Jun 39, 1929. s of Dirk & Gertrude. AB, Central, 1951; BD, WTS, 1954; PhD, UEdinburgh, 1956; American Acad, Rome, 1970-71. Lic & Ord Cl Wisconsin, 1954. Pas, Fordham Manor, Bronx, NY, 1957-62; lect, NBTS, 1960; vis prof, WTS, Holland, MI, 1962-63; asst prof, 1963-66; James A.H. Cornell Prof of Hist Theol, 1966-99; adj prof, HopeC, 1982; SanFranciscoTS, 1984-87; dir, Overseas CONnECTS, WTS, 1999-; st clk, CL New York, 1959-62, Ret.[1]

This is the listing for Donald J. Bruggink in the latest *Historical Directory of the Reformed Church in America*, with data that is now nine years old. It is very much like the listings for all of the approximately six thousand ministers of Word and sacrament whose names appear on those pages. It tells us that he was born in Kalamazoo, graduated from Central College, Western Seminary, and the University of Edinburgh,

---

[1] Russell L. Gasero, *Historical Directory of the Reformed Church in America 1628-2000*, Historical Series of the Reformed Church in America (HS) no. 37 (Grand Rapids: Eerdmans, 2001), 54.

along with pursuing studies at the American Academy in Rome, Italy. He was licensed and ordained by the Classis of Wisconsin, pastored Fordham Manor Reformed Church in the Bronx, New York, and taught at Western for thirty-seven years, as well as teaching some at New Brunswick Seminary, Hope College, and San Francisco Theological Seminary. He was even a stated clerk for a while.

But, all in all, it is a rather dry bit of business. In Corwin's *Manual of the Reformed Church in America*,[2] we get much more expansive discussions and even pleasant stories—without citation and apparently part of the oral tradition—about many of the ministers. That was, of course, written in a different time: standards of documentation were different, publishing costs as a percentage of everything else were lower, and there weren't as many ministers or churches. But the very fact that a festschrift is being published to celebrate Bruggink means that there is probably more to his life than the dry entry above. A more complete biography is not only standard operating procedure for a book like this, it is a necessary tool for understanding Donald Bruggink.

It is then a matter of getting a history of one of the Reformed Church's leading historians. Such a matter is hardly simple, however, when the biography is being prepared in secret, and when said historian will be perusing the finished product. Furthermore, since said historian comes from good, reticent Dutch stock, he would be, as Norman Kansfield once wrote, "embarrassed if much of his private life were used to celebrate the importance of his career."[3] As a result, there was but one logical choice for author of a biography of Donald J. Bruggink: Bruggink himself. Using a bit of subterfuge—he was indeed the first professor of theology to be the subject of an oral interview on behalf of the Reformed Church Archives—this author sat down with our honoree and gave him the opportunity to tell his own life story,[4] in effect coauthoring this essay. Even so, we will leave out what Kansfield would call "the really savory stuff."

---

[2] Edward Tanjore Corwin, *Manual of the Reformed Church in America, fourth edition* (New York: Board of Publication of the Reformed Church in America, 1902).

[3] Norman J. Kansfield, "The Committed Self: the Public Career of Donald J. Bruggink," *Reformed Review* 52, no. 3 (Spring, 1999): 189.

[4] James Hart Brumm, oral interview with Donald J. Bruggink at Western Theological Seminary, October 1, 2008. Unless otherwise noted, all of the Bruggink quotations in this essay come from this interview.

Growing Up

While Bruggink was born in Kalamazoo, his childhood was spent primarily on the other side of what many locals call "the big lake."

> We lived on the outskirts of the village of Cedar Grove. My father had been born, raised on a farm, loved farming, and, while he was gainfully employed as county treasurer, he still kept two cows and a bunch of chickens on our four acres, all of which I learned to hate with great enthusiasm.
>
> Our church was the First Reformed Church of Cedar Grove, which was a very supportive institution. The first pastor that I remember was Gary De Jong.[5] Gary De Jong and his wife, Eberdine, had been stranded by the Depression; they were missionaries to the Arabian Gulf, but the board did not have money to send them back, and Gary's father-in-law was a retiring pastor of First, Cedar Grove,[6] if I remember correctly, so it was natural that Gary just filled in as a pastor until the board could send them back to the Arabian Gulf.
>
> In those days, of course, woman ministers were not even thought of. On the other hand, whenever Eberdine, his wife, spoke, she spoke from the pulpit and delivered a much better sermon than Gary, with a lot more vim and verve, and the entire congregation much preferred Eberdine "speaking" from behind the pulpit than they did Gary "preaching" from behind the pulpit. So, that was an early lesson in the acceptance of women who could both teach and preach.
>
> So, I also had lots of cousins, both on my father's side and on my mother's side. On my mother's side, they lived closer, a family that eventually numbered six girls, and they were always great fun and great companions. And Uncle Chester was a good uncle, albeit my wife blames Uncle Chester for my bucolic sense of humor, which is something akin to Garrison Keillor's, albeit not as good.[7]

---

[5] DeJong was pastor at Cedar Grove 1933-1938. Gasero, *Historical Directory*, 92.

[6] This would be Cornelius Kuyper, pastor at Cedar Grove 1911-1933. Ibid., 510.

[7] Out of respect for Erma Bruggink, an example of this humor, found in the interview transcript, will be saved for future generations of scholars.

> When I was in high school I fully intended to be an architect, because my cousin Carl was an architect. His father was the Reverend Oliver Droppers,[8] who was a fine example of an excellent minister. But I subscribed to the *Architectural Forum* when I was in high school and read books by William Lescaze and followed the career and buildings of Frank Lloyd Wright and had intended to go to the University of Wisconsin until Erma's father recruited me for Central, playing on the fact that it was a Christian college, rather than a godless institution like the University of Wisconsin where they even sold beer to students.

Learning

Gerritt VanRoekel was a recruiter for Central College in Pella, Iowa. Because of the good work he did on a visit to Cedar Grove, he would become Don Bruggink's father-in-law, an example of what Bruggink would call "unintended consequences." But Don and Erma met in Pella, where "she was also a student at Central and also a member of Third Church, which I attended frequently when I was in college." It was also in Pella that Bruggink first recognized his callings as minister and historian.

> Central was a very good experience. In those days, Central was a bit more down-home than Hope, a bit less sophisticated, and it was an excellent, excellent education. Perhaps one of my finest professors was Dr. Laura Nanes,[9] who taught me everything I needed to know to do a Ph.D. thesis. In her history classes—I became a history major—basically, for every semester class we had to turn in three term papers, ranging in length anywhere from ten to twenty pages, and I must say that I started out rather low on the totem pole, having gone to a high school that did not have overly rigorous academic standards and, while I was good for memorizing data, Dr. Nanes taught me, gradually, how to "Point up the facts, Mr. Bruggink. Point up your facts!" and I managed to move from "C"s to "B"s to straight "A"s by pointing up my facts. And that was training for doing a doctoral thesis

---

[8] A native of Cedar Grove, Droppers was pastor of various Reformed Church congregations over a career of forty-two years. Gasero, *Historical Directory*, 112.

[9] Laura M. Nanes was professor of history at Central College 1939-1969. Central College *Bulletin 1968-69*, vol. 68, no. 4 (Pella, Iowa: Central College, 1968), 129.

that needed no additions, amendments, or anything else. It went through as it was presented, which was somewhat unusual at the University of Edinburgh....

I went to Central, and there I fell in with a group of sinister preseminarians like John Hesselink and Eugene Heideman and Ed Mulder,[10] and one thing led to another and Uncle Oliver urged me: if I could get out of going into the ministry, I certainly should! Well, that was enough to convince me that I really should [go]. So that's how I got into seminary.

Upon graduation from Central College, Bruggink moved to Holland, Michigan, to study at Western Theological Seminary.

[There were] six professors, which included the president and the dean. Dr. Mulder,[11] who was president, also taught homiletics at the time. George Mennenga,[12] who was dean, taught English Bible. Gene Osterhaven[13] was the new kid on the block and taught systematic theology.

But, in my book, the two stars of the seminary, from whom I learned most, were Dr. Oudersluys[14] and Dr. Kuyper.[15] They taught me biblical exegesis. And they tried desperately to teach me Greek and Hebrew, and I learned enough to use critical commentaries to advantage. Never became fluent in those languages; even that statement is hyperbole. But, be that as it may, they taught me how to read the Bible within historical context, and to examine what it had to say from the perspective of the historical context in which

---

[10] Hesselink and Heideman have essays in this festschrift and are listed among the contributors. Edwin Mulder was ordained in 1954 and served various parishes, as minister for evangelism for the Board of North American missions (1964-1968), as president of the General Synod (1979-1980), and as general secretary of the Reformed Church in America (1983-1994).

[11] John R. Mulder was on the faculty of Western 1928-1960 and was president of the school the final eighteen years of that tenure. Gasero, *Historical Directory*, 279.

[12] George H. Mennenga was on the faculty of Western 1939-1961. Ibid., 263-64.

[13] M. Eugene Osterhaven was on the faculty at Western 1953-1986. Ibid., 295.

[14] Richard C. Oudersluys was on the Western faculty 1942-1977 and then taught as an adjunct at Western and Hope 1978-1988. Ibid., 296.

[15] Lester Jacob Kuyper was on the Western faculty 1939-1974 and interim president of both Western and New Brunswick Seminaries 1971-1973. Ibid., 225.

it was written, rather than an a-historical, a-temporal, a-original languages, literalistic way. They taught me to eschew the attitude of one branch of the Princeton School, represented, I think, by Charles Hodge, that, if you had a Webster's Dictionary and an English Bible, you could find out what God had to say to you. They taught me a far more sophisticated way of reading scripture. They were good. And, on that base, I suppose, in addition to Dr. Nanes's tutelage, they also helped me do historical-critical work when I got to Edinburgh....

I inherited selling books from "Old Book" Holbrook[16] who, up until his death, still ran around with treasured books in his trunk to sell to unsuspecting ministers. And he was good at it and taught me everything I knew, and he ran a bookstore out of his dorm room, which was not the bookstore of the seminary, which sold seminary textbooks. But instead, it was a matter of knowing what you had and convincing students that what you had they needed, essentially commentaries. And while we managed to import some commentaries, like the series from T&T Clark, surreptitiously through British book dealers, we specialized in used books and poured over the used book catalogues from Britain and imported classic commentaries by the English pastor and bishop theologian exegetes which were far more friendly than the higher critical stuff coming out of Germany, and it was a good fit....

In seminary I was no good in languages, that sort of ruled out the foreign mission field. However, my conviction was that I could teach church history a lot better than it was being done at the time. So, as soon as I was done in seminary I toddled off to Edinburgh for a degree in historical theology....

So I had a good, good solid education, you know, nothing to complain about whatsoever in terms of what Western did for me or what Central did for me. I don't think I could have gotten a better education, probably, anywhere, in terms of my ability to receive. You know, perhaps Harvard or Yale could have done better, but I don't think I would have been able to manage that

---

[16] Joseph Holbrook graduated from Western in 1952 and served as pastor of various Reformed Church congregations over a thirty-seven year career. Ibid., 183.

cultural milieu. I was from Cedar Grove; a hundred and seven, half the size of Lake Wobegon.[17]

[Upon graduation from Western] Gene Heideman and I both left the country at the same time for darker worlds. And the rationale was we had no furniture, we sort of had the clothes on our back and whatever gifts we'd been given when we got married, which we could store at our parents homes, and this was the time to do it. And so we did. On the basis of Erma's one-year teaching salary and my income from having sold books during seminary, we toddled off to Edinburgh for doctoral work....

[Scotland] was a real...learning experience in quite a different way. After having been given syllabi and course work and due dates and all that sort of stuff, I got to Edinburgh and asked around New College as to when things started and they said, "Well look at the bulletin board as you enter the Rectangle." And so I did. And so I found, yeah, they were having a luncheon at such-and-such a date, and they were registering for classes at such-and-such a date. O.K. Well, nobody told me that. So I went to the luncheon—there was a luncheon for all the students—and then I found my way, later, to where we registered for classes and asked the question, "Well, if I find that there's another class that I'd rather go to, who do I tell that I've stopped going to the class that I've registered for and would like to go to. Is there a drop-add period?" And they looked at me rather strangely and said, "No." They said, "Nobody takes attendance. Just come and go as you please. If you don't want to attend any classes, you really don't have to. But then you'd waste your two pounds, six, for having registered." Two pounds, six, all the classes you wanted to take were two pounds, six. Roughly, in those days, that would be about, oh, about eight dollars, at most, for a semester.

I sort of scattered myself thin the first semester, but then sort of focused on the classes taught by my advisors and by Tom Torrance. I wanted to work with Torrance, but Torrance wouldn't have me, because any of the things I suggested he didn't think were worth a doctoral thesis, and so, instead, I approached principal emeritus Hugh Watt, who was still teaching, who was only emeritus from

[17] The fictional Minnesota community featured in stories on Garrison Keillor's National Public Radio program, "A Prairie Home Companion."

having gotten stuck with the principal's job. And he said, "Why don't you write on Thomas Boston. Thomas Boston was a good theologian," he said. "There's a lot to learn from him. The last thesis we had on him wasn't much good. You're from the States, you're Reformed, you know your theology, I think you could do a better job." And so, I did Thomas Boston, morning, noon, and night. Well, mostly noon and night, because mornings I was frequently in class. And didn't have much money for traveling, which is probably a blessing, because it meant that I spent more time working.

Recreation consisted primarily of going out and preaching on Sunday. Didn't do much of that the first year. Billy Graham—William Graham, at the Church of Scotland offices—did assignments for preaching, and, basically, you had to prove your oats with William Graham; mainly, I suspect that he didn't want too many complaints coming back. But most of all he didn't want to call you and ask you to preach and have you say no. He wanted to be able to fill a pulpit with one call. I think that was the real criterion. Well, during the first year, he learned that [with me] he only had to make one call, and so the second year I went out preaching maybe every other but certainly every third Sunday and got to see much of Scotland that way, and learned a great deal about not only the Scottish Church but also the Anglican Church.

Not that I ever preached in an Anglican Church, but one of my great revelations came at noon, after services, in a little hotel, where an Anglican cleric who was also filling the Anglican pulpit that Sunday beckoned me over to his table....Somehow we got on the Prayer Book and, having come out of a totally free-prayer tradition, I somehow made what I suspect was an unwitting but mild aspersion against read prayers. And the Anglican cleric looked at me earnestly and said, "Y'know, I've often wondered how you people in the free prayer tradition can really pray when you're thinking of what to say." Well, that was a revelation to me! So here's a tradition where what I...regarded as a positive—the fact that we were thinking of what we were going to say to God—was actually getting in the way of prayer! And just a whole new world of prayer opened to me in one conversation....

So it was a good experience. And, we were very, very lucky. We had

> a coterie of friends who were already there: Bastian Kruithof,[18] who wrote in the *Sunday School Guide*, who late in life was doing a doctorate; Harold Englund,[19] who early in life was doing a doctorate; and Bill Jellema, a classmate one year in advance of me, was also in Edinburgh doing a doctorate. When we got there, Bill and Lo Jellema said, "Well, to find a place to live, you go to Jenner's department store and you go up to the fourth floor, and there they have a—I forget the British term for it, but—a realty office, and you tell them who you are and that you're at the university and that you've got a family and a wife and you're looking for an apartment. So, I did that. And the girl looked at me and said, "Bruggink. I have just the place for you....At 17 Abercrombie Place: he has an apartment to let. You'll like him." I said, "Don't you think I should have a few others to look at, to compare?" She said, "No! This is the one for you!" So I went home and got my wife and we traipsed off to 17 Abercrombie Place and—wow!—it was in the new town on a street which has a gentle arc; all of the houses matched; they were all one unit, the whole two blocks. Across the street were the Queen Street Gardens—a fenced garden—and here, at 17 Abercrombie Place, was the *Consulate te Nederlanden*....
>
> Well, the Consul General came in after we had a chance to look around and he said, "Well, I hope you'll come." And he looked at Erma and said, "And I want you to know that with the apartment comes the job of second secretary." And Erma said, "I'm no secretary." "Oh no!" he said. "You'll do fine." And she said "But I don't type well." He said, "That doesn't make any difference! You won't have a lot of typing to do. It's settled! You'll be second secretary!"

After two years in Edinburgh, the Brugginks returned to the United States, where Don was called to be pastor and teacher of the Fordham Manor Reformed Church in the Bronx, New York. This was, in many ways, another learning experience for him.

> I left Cedar Grove—which was homogeneous ethnically and religiously—and I came to Holland, Michigan—which was homogeneous religiously and ethnically—and then I went to

---

[18] Kruithof would go on to pastor three Reformed Church congregations, then spend seventeen years on the faculty of Hope College. Gasero, *Historical Directory*, 223.

[19] Englund would pastor two Reformed Church congregations and then go on to be acting president of Western, 1960-1962. Ibid., 126.

Edinburgh—which was still, essentially, pretty homogeneous ethnically and religiously—and then I got a call to the Bronx, to Fordham Manor, where my real education began. American pluralism with a vengeance!...

I followed a very successful...young man[20] who was doing a degree at Union. And he did a superb job of attracting a number of young couples to the church. Basically, we had 120 people on the rolls, the real live people that we could locate. If we hit 100 in worship attendance, that was par for the course. We didn't always make par, but that was par for the course. If we had 100, that was a good Sunday.

The problem with all those young couples that he brought in was that most of them were in business, most of them were working on MBAs, and, the moment they got their MBAs, they got a raise, which was enough to move out to the suburbs. And so, basically, I had to replenish 10 percent of the congregation every year. One year, in fact, we lost half the Sunday school in one fell swoop when three couples got their MBAs at once. And the Bronx at that time was 60 percent Jewish, 35 percent Roman Catholic, and Protestants and pagans split the five percent that were left, and, of the Protestants that were left, quite a large percentage of those still had their membership in downtown churches [they'd attended] before they or their families had moved up to the Bronx. So it was slim pickings, and every night I wasn't at a church meeting I was pounding the pavement, visiting the families of people who had been there on Sunday or people who had been referred to me and it was being out every night, and during the day it was also calling on the sick and whoever wasn't working.

The church grew modestly while I was there; it held its own, installed a new organ, put in the new Reformed Church hymnal, and it was repainted, it was...a certain amount of repair that was done and basically I think I left it a bit stronger than when I found it. But it was hard work!...

I can remember the first Sunday that I was there. This woman that I had never seen before came up to me at the door after the service,

---

[20] George Hinsdale Winn, III, came to the Reformed Church from the Presbyterian Church; he left Fordham Manor after three years to pastor the Ellenville, New York, Reformed Church for fifteen years. Ibid., 469.

threw her arms around me, and flattened herself up against me. And I came from Cedar Grove, where you shook hands at arm's length, and, well, that was a part of the culture I must confess that I adapted to rather readily. Having card parties in the church basement on Saturday night, that was a lot harder to swallow, and I sort of absented myself from those, which wasn't very bright. I called on people alphabetically, which was dumb; I didn't know enough to start off with the power brokers, so that kept me in trouble for some time until I could mend fences....

One of the bright things that I realized, after doing a bit of calling and a bit of listening, is that I could either empty the church by trying to disabuse people of all their wrong ideas and bad theology, or I could just preach the gospel and hope that it fell on good soil and grew. Had I told people, of all things, about all of their theology that was wrong, gee, the place would have been vacant in no time. By preaching the gospel, I think it built up the congregation and built a lot of friends, and I also learned that theology isn't the only game alive...! I learned all sorts of things about people who were not in my mold but who were just wonderful, wonderful Christians, of such tremendous depth.

Teaching

After living at a great physical distance from the Midwest in Scotland, and at a great cultural and demographic distance in New York City, Erma and Don and their two young sons moved back to Holland, Michigan, in 1962. Don had been asked to come teach at Western Seminary. At first, it was only to be for a year, as a sabbatical replacement for Eugene Osterhaven. Though Don didn't leave New York behind entirely.

My wife came kicking and screaming. She liked the Bronx, wanted to stay there. I told her it was only for a year. But, lo and behold, here we still are. But we do get away now and then. And the first few years were made easier by the fact that I was on the Executive Committee of the Board of Education. I was a very cheap hire when I was in the Bronx and it was just a fifteen-cent subway ride down to the Interchurch Center. But, Bernie Mulder[21] was very gracious and, after I moved out to the Midwest, he kept me on

---

[21] Bernard J. Mulder was secretary for the Board of Education of the Reformed Church in America 1945-1966. Ibid., 278.

for the remainder of my term. And so I don't know how I did it, but, teaching three three-hour courses every term, all brand new, and, whenever a Friday afternoon Executive Committee meeting would come up, we would pile in the car on Thursday, drive to New York, go to the meeting, stay through Sunday, and somehow maneuver the classes so I didn't have to be back until Tuesday, and drive back. And we did that several times. I don't know how I did it. Later on, I started to fly, which made a lot more sense, but then Erma didn't get to go along. But one of the great things of flying out is I could fly out on Thursday, sometimes Thursday morning, but that would mean an afternoon Executive Committee meeting, an opera in the evening, a matinee on Saturday, another opera on Saturday evening, and then flying home after services on Sunday. Yeah. Sometimes I could work in a ballet in the afternoon on Sunday afternoon, as well. So that really paid off....

I was invited to become a sabbatical replacement for Dr. Osterhaven, and life became somewhat easier [than at Fordham Manor]. I only had three new courses to teach in each of three terms, which meant I taught nine new courses the first [year] I was here. And then, when Gene came back, Eenigenburg[22] was moved into ethics and I was tapped for church history. And so I had nine more new courses to teach. That was a pretty rough beginning....

You really teach some rotten classes that way. I mean, you know, you skim the text a night ahead and....Theology was easy because you could always play the system, and you could always explain to students how a belief here affected a belief there. And you could do a lot of good education simply explaining the system. I think some of the most effective theological teaching I ever did—in fact, Gordy Dragt[23] will attest to it—was working through the Heidelberg Catechism and showing how things related within the catechism. And you could find a good solid body of theology out of that catechism, and—union with Christ! I mean, how many kids who had to memorize that catechism ever realized that the doctrine of union with Christ was integral to the doctrine of the sacraments, and to the doctrine of grace, and how it all fit

---

[22] Elton Marshall Eenigenburg was on the faculty at Western 1954-1985 and academic dean 1969-1977. Ibid., 122.

[23] Gordon R. Dragt, Western Seminary Class of 1965. Ibid., 111.

together?...

But...in the second term I got off a whiz-bang course in Reformation history. I devoted all my real time to putting together that course. And that drew applause at the end, really saved my job, because, first term, I got awful marks from the students. Which were richly deserved. They were absolutely right. But a Methodist student who I had that first term was a Godsend to me. He took me aside one day and said, "I've got to tell you this: I think you've got good stuff, but you're shooting yourself in the foot. Don't sit when you lecture. It takes away all of your dynamic. Stand when you lecture. Secondly, don't try to be profound. You just confuse people. Don't put your lead sentence in the middle of the paragraph; they never catch it. Put your lead sentence at the beginning of the paragraph so that students know what you're trying to say."Ah! I didn't have to be profound, I just had to be simple; that was a lot easier. And, basically, that's what I did in that second-term Reformation class, and it saved my job.

[When I arrived, Western] had gone into a whole new paradigm of faculty. In the old days, my predecessor, John Piet, taught in the old system. The old system was that you were on probation, essentially, for two years. If, after two years, they decided you were worthy and a good fit, then you became full professor, full pay, just like everybody else who had been there for ten, twenty, or thirty years. All were at a par. The president was on a par; the president got the same salary as the rest of the faculty; he just had to teach fewer hours. That was it. Harold Englund, as president, instituted a system which is much more in line with general academia, where you had four levels of the professorate: adjunct, assistant, associate, and a full professor, with a different range of pay for all. You also had a president who was on a different level than faculty, both in terms of perks and in terms of salary, which is, perhaps, the biggest perk. So that was different. So there was a much more risky existence than had been prior.

Also, there were people who were being added to the faculty. I think it was in my second year that Elaine Lubbers came, the first woman on the faculty. After she left Hugh Koops came in, and while Christian Ed. was not his main major, he sort of covered Christian Ed. and ethics, which was his major, until he went to New Brunswick. Then Bob Nykamp came in counseling. When he left, then Stan Rock came. Bud Ridder coaxed Norm Kansfield into changing his Old Testament track towards a doctorate into that of librarian. He succeeded Millie Schuppert, which meant that for the first time we had a fully accredited librarian, although nobody got more work done than Millie. Not before and not since. The library was her family, and she worked hard and she did good....

My career here at Western was...a career of winning some, losing some, and, if confession is good for the soul, why, this will do my soul at least a little good....I fell in love with Jaroslav Pelikan,[24] who, it seemed to me, was writing a text on a graduate level, a level which would be a challenge to students who had already had church history in college, who had had Williston Walker, who knew the broad outlines of the history of the church, which I assumed that anybody heading for seminary would have the good sense to do. And I also assumed that, perhaps, if students couldn't read, then maybe they shouldn't be in seminary, since being a pastor should entail a good deal of reading. And so, I felt that Pelikan—I mean, he was one of the ten most important theological books published in the decade, according to *Christian Century*, and that's not a bad recommendation—and so I started using Pelikan.

Well, Pelikan was everything I intended it to be for the top third of the class. For the middle third, it was a struggle from which they learned something. For the bottom third of the class, who did not read well, who didn't know anything about theology and nothing about the history of the church, it was a total disaster. I mean, you know, they didn't know the people involved, they didn't know the timeline, they didn't know the history of the church, Pelikan's sentences were far too long and involved, and I became clearly aware of this when I was teaching...this senior colloquium in interfacing the media with theology. How do we read theology in relation to the media? And this particular day, we were on cartoons, and the one student said he never read "Doonesbury"; too many words. Well, with that, I went home and did a *mea culpa, mea culpa, mea culpa* for all those students upon whom I had visited Pelikan who couldn't read.

---

[24] *The Christian Tradition: A History of the Development of Doctrine* (Chicago: Univ. of Chicago Press, 1971).

And, of course, that didn't win me any friends in the bottom third or even the middle third of the class, but it prepared the top third for first-class doctoral work where they got into some pretty impressive schools. It prepared others for first-class preaching and thinking and ability to relate the biblical message to the present age rather than reading sociological conservatism into the Bible.

So, would I do it over again? Gee, I'd probably try to convince the administration that there should be a double track, something for the bottom third, with the middle third able to make a choice....

I made a number of career mistakes. One career mistake was not sticking with church architecture as an avocation. I should have stuck with contemporary church architecture and kept publishing in that field. Instead, I did my first sabbatical, and....what I wanted to do was laudable: I wanted to do a history of the development of church architecture from a theological perspective. Well, I didn't pace myself adequately and spent just too much time reading the first five, six, seven centuries. That's all the farther I got.

When I got back to Western, instead of being able to continue research and writing, I fell right in the midst of a horrible political mess. Bud Ridder,[25] my patron saint, really, had resigned and left to be minister of Central Reformed. The Bi-Level Multi-Site was still struggling to survive. There was the matter of whether or not the two seminaries would continue on their road to combining. There was the question of whether or not the seminaries were to continue to have one president for both seminaries. There was the question of, well, since we didn't have a president for either seminary, whether we were going to have one or two. And what did the faculty do? They elected me as their representative on this committee. Well, this just sucked up all of my time for the next several years, and by the time that was settled and the dust settled, the Bi-Level Multi-Site had bit the dust, we had two presidents rather than one, and by that time I was far more interested in continuing doing overseas seminars each year than I was in continuing to write another book.

[25] Herman J. "Bud" Ridder was president of Western Theological Seminary 1963-1969 and president of both Western and New Brunswick Theological Seminaries 1969-1971. Gasero, *Historical Directory*, 324. See also *Herman J. Ridder: Contextual Preacher and President*, Historical Series of the Reformed Church in America, no. 59 (Grand Rapids: Eerdmans, 2008).

In 1967, a series of overseas travel seminars began which have continued, in one form or another, to the present day. They were the brainchild of Don Bruggink, with some crucial help.

I'd seen this marvelous film by Charles and Ray Eames on the [Basilika] Vierzehnheiligen...in Bavaria, which was done by [Balthasar Neumann], a great Baroque church. And they had put slides, which they turned into a film, just to music, Baroque music with this Baroque church. It was sensational....And I thought, "Gee! I'd like to go to Ravenna and take pictures so that I could use the photographs in teaching church history." So, basically, what I wanted was a paid trip to photograph...

And so I approached Herm Ridder with the idea, "Wouldn't it be great to have a seminar on church history and teach it where it was, where it happened?" To give, you know, a sense of place, to make it real, and not only that, but I would have the students each do a paper on one day's site, so that we would have the students fully invested in this project. And he thought that it was a wonderful idea. The only thing he didn't like was that I had planned a twelve-week tour, and he thought that that was pretty much and I should cut it in half. So I did....

It was terribly successful. Bud Ridder had gone along and thought it was wonderful. In fact, he went along on the next one I did, two years later, in '69. And then there was a hiatus while I did my sabbatical in '70-'71, but by '73 I was back on the road again, and then started doing them every other year, and then it got to be every year, and they were becoming more and more ecumenical, 'til finally I started to have my Roman Catholic summer in Rome and my Orthodox summer in Greece. I just kept moving them back and forth. Then, when things got a bit dicey in Greece, when you had to get off the plane in the midst of guys with machine guns and had to go to the bank to get cash with the guy with the machine gun standing behind you at the door, I thought, "No I'm going to do a Reformation tour." Did a Huguenot tour for a summer or two. And that was fun. But, basically, these were great opportunities that enriched my teaching and, I think, enriched the lives of the students who went on them.

Editing

The third phase of Donald Bruggink's ministry, which has overlapped the second, must be the editorial phase, as a historiographer of the Reformed Church in America. Elton Bruins wrote a marvelous account of how this all began.[26] What follows are some of Don's own reflections.

> [For] the four hundredth anniversary of the Heidelberg Catechism, I edited a book of essays which was done under the sponsorship of the Theological Commission, on which I was at the time: *Guilt, Grace, and Gratitude*,[27] and that got, I think that was finished in '64. And then in '65, I completed our magnum opus, *Christ and Architecture*.[28] I got all that done while I was teaching those nine courses every year....
>
> Well, I guess I got my feet wet with *Guilt, Grace, and Gratitude*. And there was a feeling that, yeah, wouldn't it be great if we had a historical series, a place where people could publish the history of the church, because we really didn't have anything like that. And so, on the basis of having been editor of *Guilt, Grace, and Gratitude*, I got stuck with being editor of *Ecumenism in the Reformed Church in America*, by Herman Harmelink, III,[29] which we published just in time for the battle of union with the Southern Presbyterians, and Winfield Burggraaff sat on the thing long enough so that it didn't really play a part in that discussion, because he didn't want it in the mix, for whatever reason.
>
> But it ultimately got published, and then the next offering was Elton's book on *The Americanization of a Congregation*,[30] and this went through rather easily and then, you know, there was a year in between, and then there was *Pioneers in the Arab World* by...Dorothy Van Ess.[31] Dorothy and John Van Ess, fifty years in the Arab world together as super-duper missionaries. Well, Dorothy had written the book twice, and it sort of overlapped, and so one summer I...laid out this manuscript on multiple tables in the Commons of the seminary, so that I could visually see where they overlapped and put the overlapping together and then rewrote the chapters

---

[26] "Donald J. Bruggink's Contribution to Reformed Church in America Historiography," *Reformed Review* 52, no. 3 (Spring 1999): 213-24.
[27] (New York: Half Moon Press, 1963).
[28] Donald J. Bruggink and Carl H. Droppers, *Christ and Architecture: Building Presbyterian/Reformed Churches* (Grand Rapids: Eerdmans, 1965).
[29] HS no. 1(Grand Rapids: Eerdmans, 1968).
[30] HS no.2 (Grand Rapids: Eerdmans, 1970).
[31] HS no.3 (Grand Rapids: Eerdmans, 1974).

so that they meshed nicely and oh boy, was that a job of editing, but it turned out to be a great book.

It's Marv Hoff[32] who deserves the credit for the Revolving Fund. After our second or third volume, Marv recognized that we could spend the denomination into oblivion by publishing if we didn't have to get our money back. And so he set up a revolving fund and said, "O.K. This is it. If you run out of money, tough! That's the end of the Historical Series." Now, at the same time, Marv was very generous with subventions when it came to specifically General Synod items like the *Historical Directory*,[33] like the *Digest and the Index*[34] of the synodical minutes. Those had generous subventions from Marv, which meant that, together with their sales, we were able to start building the Revolving Fund. When we had institutions like Northwestern College that wanted a centenary volume, we could say, "Well, you're going to pay for having this thing printed anyway. You're going to pay for having it copy edited anyway. Why not do it with us and get international exposure through Eerdmans?" And so they'd do it, but, by the fact that they were footing the bill and we sold a few copies as well, it augmented the fund.

And, of course, in the good old days, when we could do our pitch at General Synod, we could sell several hundred volumes and collect a couple thousand dollars at a single synod. In fact, even this past synod, our quarterly sales through Faith Alive, which includes General Synod: the first quarter of the year, we netted $555; second quarter of the year, which includes General Synod, with the little bit of from-the-podium promotion that we were able to do, two thousand plus dollars net, four times as much just from that little bit of pitch to a willing audience.

---

[32] In addition to pastoral work and serving as executive director of the Foundation for Theological Education in South East Asia, Marvin D. Hoff was in charge of operations and finance for the General Program Council of the Reformed Church in America, 1971-1981, and president of Western Theological Seminary, 1985-1994. Gasero, *Historical Directory*, 179-80.

[33] Vandenberge, Peter N., *Historical Directory of the Reformed Church in America, 1628-1978*, HS no. 6 (Grand Rapids: Eerdmans, 1978).

[34] Schuppert, Mildred W., *A Digest and Index of the Minutes of the General Synod of the Reformed Church in America, 1958-1977*, HS no. 8 (Grand Rapids: Eerdmans, 1979).

How did [the Commission on History] react to it? Well, the way you usually react to Marv: you're presented with something that is a fact, a *fait accompli*, if you will. Got him into trouble with faculty at the seminary, but Marv usually had things pretty well thought out. Didn't always hit a home run, but, in this case, we were happy to have a fund, we were happy to have something, and I had enough confidence that we could make this thing work. And Marv's initial generosity with some basic books put us on a sound footing. The financial establishment—that is to say the people who invest the money of the church—were getting us great interest rates during the Carter years, and, in other years, they've done well in terms of equities. So there were some years when we made more money in interest than we did selling books. Those were years when we didn't have any new books to sell, but it's still indicative of how the fund grew. And so. No, it was generally well received. There were some people who were anxious, but I thought we could make it go and it's gone.

Conclusions: Identifying the Tools

When we look at the life of Donald J. Bruggink, we see pieces being put into place that have made his ministry possible. There was the nurture of his community growing up, including a strong identification with his church, and early exposure (thanks to Eberdine De Jong and her occasional presence in the Cedar Grove pulpit) to the possibility of things not yet considered by the church, which he would later call the church to consider. The work of Laura Nanes, Richard Oudersluys, Lester Kuyper, Thomas Torrance, Hugh Watt, and others shaped his critical thinking. Ministry at Fordham Manor exposed him to the idea that there was a larger world out there and shaped his pastoral thinking; Fordham Manor, along with his dorm-room bookstore at Western, helped build the entrepreneurial spirit that decades of Commission on History members have come to know and which has built the Historical Series and its Revolving Fund. And, every step of the way, there have been relationships, relationships that brought him to Central and then Western, that helped him and Erma make a home in Scotland, then in the Bronx, then in Michigan, relationships that constantly exposed him to new horizons and shaped his vision of the church which he has done so much to shape.

I think the best things that happen are the small things. The big things, if you will look at the…Reformed Church, you will find that most of the big campaigns, except for a few right after World War II, have not fully accomplished their goals. I think the most significant things...happen...quietly in classes where people who are moderators work to get pastors who will be good fits with congregations. I think significant things happen in congregations, great and small. I think that in little congregations that are hanging on by their fingernails in depopulated areas or areas that have ethnically changed, but who are ministering to people who need the comfort of the gospel, and who are hanging on until either better days or a larger population or a more ethnically attuned pastor can get there, I think these are great. I think Bob Schuller, at the other end of the scale, a Reformed Church minister, has put together an incredible empire and has done it without succumbing to either monetary or sexual greed. I mean, he has led a clean, upright life, and is a model of a creative evangelist rather than simply an old-style Bible-thumper, of whom there are plenty on the airwaves already. And to minister to the churches in-between and to keep them on track, doing what they do best, whether that's a church like Third [Holland] or whether it is a church that is strictly for people who listen to bluegrass and western during the week and want the same on Sunday. I think these are the important things that are going on....

I came to the conclusion near the end of my ministry that Christians needed to hear what they were doing as Christians, where they were mirroring the Bible. They didn't need to hear how bad they were; most people know how bad they are, it's just that they're not telling other people. But they don't have to be told from the pulpit; they already know that. I find Christians tremendously obtuse in not realizing how Christian their lives are. Good ol' Stacia Whistler, our chiropractor, who when she saw somebody slumped in a position that indicated a bad back, would lay them down in the church pew after service and give them a free treatment to help straighten them out. And when her neighbors in the apartment building were sick, if she didn't know them, that was all right, she'd bring them chicken soup anyway. Now those were Christ-like acts, and when I shared those with the congregation, Stacia just glowed; she was even brighter than her brightly colored hats. And I think we should do more of that, and do more of that with congregations, as well. Well, that's what I think is most significant about the Reformed Church, and if it lasts another hundred or two hundred years, it will be because of those faithful pastors and parishioners by the hundreds who keep acting like Christians.

Donald Bruggink has done his best to live a Christian life, to help other people find Christ's presence in their lives, and to tell those stories to the Reformed Church and the world. In the chapters that follow, people who have been witnesses to this life and work venture out a little further into areas of story, beauty, justice, and gospel that he has pointed out to all of us.

PART 1

Tools for Understanding Western Theological Seminary

Donald J. Bruggink taught at Western Theological Seminary from 1962 until his retirement in 1999. He has maintained an office there in his retirement, and, of course, was there as a student, making for five decades—well over half his life—that he has spent at this school in Holland, Michigan. Celebrating the life of Donald Bruggink includes understanding Western Seminary.

The first three essays in this volume give us insights into Western Seminary. Eugene Heideman examines how church history has been taught from the school's beginnings. George Brown, Jr., tells the story of the seminary's first Christian education teacher and first female faculty member, Elaine Lubbers, who joined the faculty the same year Bruggink did. And Mary L. Kansfield helps us understand the town of Holland, an important part of Western's context, with her discussion of Frances Beardslee, wife of a distinguished faculty member at Western who would also serve at New Brunswick Seminary.

As Western approaches its sesquicentennial, what we have here is not a complete critical history by any means. But these chapters do important spadework, and they offer critical tools for understanding how Western Theological Seminary has developed into the institution it is today.

CHAPTER 1

From Dosker to Bruggink: Teaching Historical Theology at Western Theological Seminary, 1884-1999

Eugene Heideman

The Professors of Historical Theology at Western Theological Seminary

In this festschrift produced in honor of the Reverend Dr. Donald J. Bruggink, it is appropriate that we trace the history of teaching historical theology at Western Theological Seminary. Bruggink taught at the seminary beginning in 1962 and was installed as the James A. H. Cornell Professor of Historical Theology and Church History in 1966. He retired in 1999. His tenure in the chair surpasses by far that of any of his predecessors:

The Rev. Henry E. Dosker, D.D.	1894-1903
The Rev. Nicholas M. Steffens D.D.	1903-1911
The Rev. Matthew Kolyn, D.D.	1911-1918
The Rev. Siebe C. Nettinga, D.D.	1918-1938
The Rev. William Goulooze, Th.D., D.D.	1939-1952
The Rev. Elton M. Eenigenberg, Ph.D.	1952-1963[1]

[1] It was the custom for Hope College to confer the honorary Doctor of Divinity degree on men who had not earned a doctor's degree previously in

The Rev. Donald J. Bruggink, Ph.D.   1966-1999[2]

Historical theology has been taught at the seminary by a linkage of five generations of church historians. In fact, there are six in the line, because the progenitor of the five was Samuel M. Woodbridge, professor of historical theology at New Brunswick Theological Seminary. He was the teacher of Henry Dosker in 1878 and of Matthew Kolyn, who graduated from New Brunswick in 1880. Dosker in turn was the teacher of the second-generation professor, Seibe C. Nettinga, who graduated from Western in 1903. Nettinga was the teacher of the third-generation William Goulooze, who graduated in 1928. Goulooze in turn taught the fourth-generation teacher, Elton Eenigenberg, a 1940 graduate. Donald Bruggink took one course from Goulooze and then, as the fifth generation in the linkage, completed his church history studies in his final two years at the seminary under the teaching of Eenigenberg in 1954.[3]

The line of succession in the professors of historical theology is an indication of how seriously the seminary desired to fulfill its purpose of preparing men (and, eventually, women) for the pastoral ministry. Their goal as instructors of church history was to enable their students to grasp the essentials of church history that are necessary for the practice of the ordained ministry. Each of those who held the office was an ordained minister with intellectual gifts who had manifested the ability to preach and to serve well in pastoral ministry in one or more congregations. Prior to World War II, the seminary gave priority

---

recognition of their attainments prior to their being elected to the office of professor of theology.

[2] Donald J. Bruggink is the James A.H. Cornell Professor of Historical Theology and Church History, Emeritus. Responsibility for teaching church history since 1999 has been assumed by Christopher B. Kaiser, professor of Historical and Systematic Theology; Steven Chase, associate professor of Christian spirituality; and Dennis N. Voskuil, who served both as president of the seminary and professor of church history.

[3] William Goulooze entered into treatment for a recurrence of cancer at the end of the fall term, 1951, and no longer taught after that. Dennis Voskuil retired as president of the seminary at the end of the 2007-2008 academic year and has served full-time as professor of church history beginning in the 2008-2009 academic year. Donald Bruggink was his teacher, so he is actually the sixth generation in the linkage. Voskuil is the first person in the history of the seminary to have earned his Ph.D. specifically in the field of church history rather than historical theology.

to ministerial and intellectual gifts without searching for a teacher with a Ph.D. degree in church history or any other theological discipline.[4]

The professors worked in less than ideal conditions during the nineteenth and early twentieth century. The Reverend Dr. Albertus Pieters, who graduated in 1890, described the seminary's facilities as follows:

> *What there was in my student days is easily described; grounds, none; recitation hall, none; maps, none; library, none.* This is a complete and accurate inventory of the equipment of the Western Theological Seminary at that time.[5]

In that context, the professors relied on a textbook, lecture, and recitation method of teaching. Nicholas Steffens, who was called in 1883 to be the first professor at Western Theological Seminary, taught church history as well as systematic theology. He used Johan Kurtz, *Sacred History*, for the junior year's historical theology course and Kurtz's *Church History* for the middler and senior years.[6] The first professor of historical theology, Henry Dosker, continued to use the textbooks by Kurtz and also prepared for himself a set of outlines that he used as his

---

[4] William Goulooze earned his Th.D. in the field of pastoral counseling in 1950 with the intention of eventually moving into the chair of practical theology. He was appointed to that position beginning in 1952, following the retirement of the Rev. Dr. Simon Blocker, but his illness at the end of 1951 prevented him from serving.

[5] Albertus Pieters, "Let Us Remember...: A Historical Address delivered by Albertus Pieters, Dosker-Hulswith Professor of English Bible and Missions, at the Semi-Centennial of the Re-opening of Theological Instruction at Holland, Michigan," located in box 1, Albertus Pieters file in Western Theological Seminary/Joint Archives of Holland, located at Hope College, Holland, Michigan (WTS/JAH), 17-18.

[6] John Henry Kurtz, *Manual of Sacred History*, Charles F. Schaeffer, tran., 6th ed. (Philadelphia: J.B. Lippincott, 1895); *Text-book of Church History*, J.H.A. Bomberger, tran., from 7th ed. (Philadelphia: Smith, English, 1875). Kurtz studied at Halle under the Lutheran orthodox pietists Ullman and Tholuck. Kurtz's church history was recommended consistently for use by students until World War II, even when no longer used as a textbook. Kurtz taught, "The goal of church history is to describe the development which the church has undergone through the reciprocal influences of divine guidance and human freedom. This development is, however, seldom wholly pure but moves under the influence of human errors and sins. The history of the church therefore must set forth not only the normal development of the church, but also keep before our eyes the ways the church has strayed away and allowed its life blood to sour and coagulate" (John Henry Kurtz,

lecture notes. At the request of his students, he reluctantly had a printer in Milwaukee publish his notes.[7]

Little direct evidence remains about the precise methods used by Dosker's successors prior to World War II. Although Steffens wrote a vast number of lengthy articles for the Dutch religious paper *De Hope*, he was essentially a systematic theologian[8] and pastor rather than a historian. After serving at the Presbyterian seminary in Dubuque and the First Reformed Church in Orange City, Iowa, between 1895 and 1903, he returned to Western Theological Seminary to be professor of ecclesiastical history.[9] He used the textbooks by Kurtz as reference

---

Beknopt Leerboek der Kerkgeschiedenis, J.E. Toorenenbergen, tran. [Utrecht: Kemink & Zoon, 1884], 1 [translation mine]). Dosker's copy of this book is filled with his marginal notes and heavy underscoring. It is housed in the special collection in Western Theological Seminary.

[7] Henry Dosker, *Topical Outline Studies in Ecclesiastical History* (Milwaukee: Houtkamp & Cannon, 1901), 1. Dosker wrote in his preface that he had prepared for the press the outline studies that he had used in the classroom. The book was clearly designed for use in the classroom. It consists of short paragraphs, often containing incomplete sentences or phrases to refer to an event or person. It has three parts, with each part being perhaps the material covered in a three-hour course. He also wrote, "The magnificent 'Manual' of Dr. Kurtz is followed, in the main, and without its use, these Outlines will be of little value" ("Preface"). Dosker's *Topical Outline Studies in Ecclesiastical History* to be found in the Henry E. Dosker file, WTS/JAH.

[8] M. Eugene Osterhaven, professor of systematic theology from 1950 to 1986, defined systematic theology as follows: "Theology, we have said, is systematized knowledge of God and of his relation to mankind. Every science is an accumulation of systematized knowledge. Theology's peculiar interest is the living God and his self-disclosure. Theology begins with the apprehension of God and an attempt to make the experience with him rationally meaningful. It goes on to attempt to understand comprehensively the entire biblical record of his coming to men through prophets, apostles, other chosen instruments, and Jesus Christ. Its firm belief is that its labor is second to none in importance" ("The Theological Field," *Reformed Review* 19, no.4 [May 1966], 47) Osterhaven's definition would have been accepted by all of the professors of systematic theology at the seminary from the time of its origin.

[9] That Steffens preferred teaching theology rather than the chronology that plays so important a part in church history came to the surface in his remarks in the *Catalog 1906-07* regarding his junior course in sacred theology in the 1906-07:

Special attention is given to the character of Sacred History as compared with universal history, the history of the people of Israel and the history of the Jewish people. To a certain extent the study of chronology, this most unsatisfactory of the sciences, is taken up,

books. Steffens's successor, Matthew Kolyn, used two textbooks, one by John W. Moncrief and the other by Henry C. Sheldon. The notes in the margins of the books in the file indicate that Kolyn's points of emphasis may have served for his use in the lecture and discussion periods.[10] It is not clear which years he used each of the textbooks, but in view of the dates of purchase written in the inside covers of each it would appear that he used Sheldon's book most of the time.

After Matthew Kolyn's arrival in 1911, the junior four-hour course was entitled, "Sacred History." It was "a careful study of the history of God's revelation to Israel during the period of the Old Dispensation; a brief course in Intertestamentary History; the study of the life of Christ, and the founding of the Christian Church. Text-book, lecture, and theses."[11] The inclusion of biblical history in the field of historical theology was consistent with the doctrine of the church as stated in the Heidelberg Catechism, which reads:

> I believe that the Son of God through his Spirit and Word, out of the entire human race, from the beginning of the world to its end, gathers, protects, and preserves for himself a community chosen for eternal life and united in true faith. Moreover, I believe that I am and forever will remain a living member of it.[12]

Sacred History was later changed to a one-semester course named "The English Bible," but it was not moved to the Biblical Field until 1926-27.

The textbook and lecture method continued to be used by Kolyn's successor, Siebe Nettinga, but no information is available concerning which book or books served as his textbook during the years he taught, 1918 to 1938. A seven-year-long weekly series of articles in *De Hope*, covering the whole nineteen centuries of church history, provides information about Nettinga's approach to the

---

while geography and other branches of study, of a similar kind, are relegated to Biblical Antiquities. Although the historical view of the development of the people of Israel is not neglected, special attention is given to the history of revelation (*Catalog, 1906-07*, 9).

[10] The textbooks were John W. Moncrief, *A Short History of the Christian Church* (Chicago: Revell, 1902), and Henry C. Sheldon, *History of the Christian Church* (New York: Thomas Y. Crowell, 1894). These two books are included in the Matthew Kolyn file, WTS/JAH.

[11] *Catalog, 1911-1912*, 12-13.

[12] Question and Answer 53, translation adopted by the Reformed Church in America in 1988 (as found on www.rca.org).

discipline of church history.[13] His successor, William Goulooze, used the two-volume textbook by Albert Henry Newman, *A Manual of Church History*.[14] Goulooze's notes for the middler course on church history give information about his approach to the subject and the usefulness of church history for his students.[15]

In contrast to the practice of professors of systematic theology, who relied almost exclusively on Reformed theologians, the professors of church history felt free to encourage students to use texts prepared by teachers in several different traditions, since church history textbooks were supposed to be objective in the presentation of facts. They relied heavily on translations of books by German church historians that were placed on reserve in the library. German Lutheran historians John Lawrence von Mosheim[16] and Johann Heinrich Kurtz, Charles Hase,[17] and the Reformed pietist Augustus Neander[18] were usually included. Textbooks by American writers included the Congregationalists

---

[13] The series ended in June 1932. Each article contained approximately 1,400-1,500 words, adding up to the equivalent of a four-volume church history in volumes of four hundred pages each.

[14] (Philadelphia: American Baptist Publication Society, 1904). Newman received degrees from Rochester Baptist Theological Seminary and Southern Baptist Theology Seminary. He taught at six Baptist universities and seminaries during his career, which lasted from 1877 to 1928.

[15] The notes are in the file of William Goulooze in WTS/JAH.

[16] Mosheim is often called "the father of [modern] church history." John Lawrence von Mosheim, the eighteenth-century Lutheran historian and chancellor of the University of Gutingen, emphasized the need for an accurate portrayal of the facts and their causes. He wrote in the introduction to his three-volume work, "In treating of both the external and the internal history of the church, the writer who would be useful, must trace events to their *causes*; that is, he must tell not only *what* happened, but likewise *how* and *why*. He who narrates the naked facts, only enriches our memory and amuses us; but he who at the same time states the operative causes of events, profits us, for he both strengthens our judgment and increases our wisdom. Yet it must be confessed that caution is here necessary, let we should fabricate causes, and palm our own waking dreams upon men long since dead" (John Lawrence von Mosheim, *Institutes of Ecclesiastical History, Ancient and Modern*, James Mudock, tran., vol. 1 [New York: Harper & Brothers, 1839], xvii).

[17] Charles Hase, *A History of the Christian Church*, Charles E. Blumenthal and Conway P. Wing, trans. (New York: D. Appleton, 1855).

[18] Augustus Neander, *General History of the Christian Religion and Church*, Joseph Torrey, tran. (Boston: Crocker and Brewster, 1872). Neander had been influenced by Schleiermacher and was a teacher of Philip Schaff.

Williston Walker[19] and George Park Fisher,[20] the Methodist Henry Sheldon, the Baptist Albert Henry Newman, and the German Reformed Philip Schaff.[21]

The materials available to us do not indicate any attempt to encourage the students to consult primary sources, such as the writings of the church fathers or reformers such as Zwingli, Luther, and Calvin. The rationale for the way church history was taught was given by Dosker in his inaugural address in Louisville in 1904. He stated that the three years a student studied at the seminary were but an introduction to the whole range of theological studies. It was a time to lay foundations.

> From the nature of the case the work of the Seminary historian must be generic and general, rather than specific and exhaustive. The Seminary student is a discoverer rather than an explorer, he deals with continents rather than with limited areas, he builds foundations rather than superstructures; but even thus the glimpses of the field before him are a warning and a comfort and an inspiration.[22]

The fact that the professors of church history at Western Theological Seminary recommended consistently that students consult this broad range of the standard textbooks written by a denominationally diverse number of respected church historians shows that the seminary's church history courses were not taught in a sectarian or denominationally confining manner. The students were working in the mainstream of American theological studies and had opportunity to become aware of denominational differences in

---

[19] Williston Walker, *A History of the Christian Church*, has gone through a number of editions and has been fully revised from time to time. It probably has been used by more church history teachers than any other textbook since it was first published in 1918 and is still in print for use as a textbook. Williston Walker was professor of ecclesiastical history at Yale University, 1901-1922.

[20] George Park Fisher, *History of the Christian Church* (New York: Scribner's, 1887). Fisher served as professor of historical theology at Yale University.

[21] Phillip Schaff, *History of the Christian Church* (New York: Scribner's, 1882-1912).

[22] Dosker, *Inauguration*, 22. It was not only the church historians who neglected to encourage students to read primary sources. The lecture notes of the systematic theologians available in the Western Seminary Archives also demonstrate that students were expected to master material presented in the textbook and lectures, without being encouraged to read primary sources.

understanding the faith. Moreover, in spite of the limitations of the seminary's facilities and number of books in the library, it was possible for the students to achieve a broad knowledge of the facts of church history that rivals and perhaps even surpasses that of current American students, in view of the much wider scope of courses necessary for their ministerial preparation.

The Great Subjects in the Study of Church History

Prior to 1894 there were only two installed professors at Western Theological Seminary, Nicholas Steffens, professor of didactic and polemical theology,[23] and John Walter Beardslee, professor of biblical languages and literature (1888-1917), plus Peter Moerdyk, a local pastor who served as an instructor where needed.[24] After giving priority to chairs of systematic theology and biblical exegesis, the General Synod of the Reformed Church in America agreed to add the chair of church history on the condition that an adequate financial base could be raised to support it.[25] The relationship between systematic theology, biblical exegesis, and the history of theology had already been set forth by Steffens in the address delivered on the occasion of his inauguration into the chair of dogmatic and polemical theology in 1884. Concerning systematic theologians he said,

> We go to the Bible, for there we find the source of all truth; but we listen also to the voices of those men that have gone before us seeking after the truth of God and the God of truth. And we verily believe that they were crowned in their search, with rich results.[26]

---

[23] The name of this position was later changed to professor of systematic theology.

[24] Peter Moerdyk was pastor of the First Reformed Church in Grand Rapids at that time.

[25] In his 2003 presidential address to the American Society for Church History, E. Brooks D. Holifield reported that as late as 1884, when there were more than four hundred institutions of higher learning in the United States, there were no more than fifteen professors and five assistant professors assigned exclusively to teaching history. In waiting until 1893 to appoint a professor of historical theology the seminary was not lagging significantly behind other institutions ("On Teaching the History of Christianity: Traditions and Presuppositions," *Church History*, 72, no.2 [June 2003]: 238).

[26] Nicholas Steffens, "Inaugural Address" (Grand Rapids: D.J. Doornink, printer) 1885, 22-23. Dosker also recognized that, historically, systematic theology proper "as a scholastic discipline, for centuries occupied the

In that statement, Steffens distanced himself from the Roman Catholic Church, which had placed tradition above the scriptures, and from the sectarians, who ignored historical theology in their emphasis on the Bible alone. He went on, however, to indicate that, while the church historian has much to offer the systematic theologian, systematic theology is bound by the supreme authority of the Bible alone.

> It is our privilege to go to the Word of God, as His free children, who are willing to be His servants, but who decline to be enslaved either by theories or by men. Bound and free at the same time; bound, where we ought to be bound, by our Lord and Master, freed where we ought to be free from all human fetters—behold the platform of a truly Reformed Theologian, who is determined to be guided alone by the *formal principle of the Reformation, the supreme authority of the Bible in matters of faith.*[27]

Steffens's statement about the relationship of systematic theology to the scriptures made it clear that the duty of church history was to assist in the development of systematic theology.[28]

---

front rank, for Theology dominated the sciences and was their queen" in comparison with "Ecclesia, Biblia, Rhetorica" (Henry Dosker, "Inauguration," Lecture at Presbyterian Theological Seminary of Kentucky, May 2, 1904, 16.)

[27] Steffens, "Inaugural Address," 23-24. Steffens accepted a call to teach at the Presbyterian seminary in Dubuque, Iowa, in 1895. He was called to return to Western Theological Seminary in 1903, where he continued to teach until his death in 1912. By 1903, Gerrit Dubbink had been called to be the professor of didactic and polemical theology, so Steffens occupied the office of professor of historical theology during his second term. He had received his theological education at Kampen in the Netherlands, so he is the exception to the line of linkage that goes back to Woodbridge in New Brunswick. I have not found any information about how he taught courses in historical theology or church history, but his voluminous articles printed in *De Hope* during that period provide strong evidence that he was far more interested in Reformed confessional and theological issues than in teaching the facts of church history.

[28] In 1966, Eugene Osterhaven, professor of systematic theology stated plainly his understanding of the relationship of historical theology to systematic theology: "Historical theology benefits other branches of theology which, in turn, give it fresh materials for study in the work and witness of the church today" (Osterhaven, "The Theological Field," 47).

Dosker's teacher at New Brunswick, Samuel Woodbridge, wrote that "Church History might justly be called a history of the conflicts of the Church of Jesus Christ."[29]

Woodbridge taught that the "great subjects" in the study of church history are (1) the extension of Christianity including missions and persecutions; (2) the history of doctrines, including dogmas and heresies; (3) the cultus, or history of worship, including architecture, sacraments and government, and (4) life and morals.[30] Although the title used at Western Theological Seminary was "Professor of Historical Theology," which is the second of the "great subjects," the professors spent most of their time teaching the facts of the expansion of Christianity in a course on church history.

In Woodbridge's classification of the subjects of church history, historical theology (the second great subject) is the discipline that studies the history of dogma and doctrines. Historical theology's focus is on the development of doctrines rather than the historical facts of the institutional, political and social life of the church.

> But while there is not development in revelation, there is an advance by the Church, not in more distinct apprehension of the doctrines, yet in the enunciation of them in scientific forms, usually in opposition to the assaults of enemies; here it is that historical theology differs from dogmatic; in the latter the direct appeal is to the Scripture, the settlement of dogma specially by exegesis, not excluding Christian experience; in the former, doctrine is regarded in its relation to human history, its position in time and in the current of events, its influence on mankind, its bearing on the life and work of the Church, and also of the deliverance of the world.[31]

Although Dosker had been installed as "Professor of Historical Theology," his actual teaching can be more properly called "church

---

[29] Samuel M. Woodbridge, *A Manual of Church History* (Jersey City: Press of J.H. Pilson, 1895), 85. Although this book was published almost twenty years after Dosker had studied there, it is safe to assume that Woodbridge had taken the same approach to church history two decades before he published *Manual* that gives evidence of having been based on his lecture notes used in class.

[30] Woodbridge, *Manual*, 24. Materials for the fourth great subject, life and morals, was incorporated in courses of the extension of Christianity and in courses in ethics taught in systematic theology.

[31] Woodbridge, *Manual*, 86.

history," the first "great subject." His definition of church history is to be found in his book, *Outline Studies in Ecclesiastical History.*

> CHURCH HISTORY is the systematic narration, in the order of their sequence, of the events, which indicate the organic development of the Kingdom of God, its difference from Sacred History. Church history records both the *normal* and *abnormal* developments in the organism of the Church.[32]

Dosker's successors through World War II understood the discipline of church history very much as Dosker did. His definition of church history distinguished between (a) sacred history and church history and (b) the church as institute and the church as organism, and he spoke of (c) the development of the church as organic, with the pluriformity of the church and American denominations. Each of these will be explored in turn.

Sacred History and Church History

At the time Dosker began to teach at Western Seminary, church historians were regarded with suspicion by other academic historians, who believed that religious and confessional commitments made it impossible for church historians to be scientific and objective in their methodology. Nevertheless, church historians insisted that they could use the same methodology as historians in general, claiming that "the study of church history was a scientific enterprise, an objective science, that could take its rightful methodological place alongside the other sciences, such as chemistry, mathematics, or physics."[33] They objected, however, to a positivistic view that ruled out any relation of history to the acts of God. They maintained that there is sacred history as well as church history. Albert Henry Newman defined the difference in his textbook, which William Goulooze used to teach at the seminary. Newman wrote:

> Sacred history is the setting forth of the known facts of man's development as it has been affected by the providential, inspiring, and self-revealing presence of God.[34]

---

[32] Henry Dosker, *Topical Outline Studies in Ecclesiastical History* (Milwaukee: Houtkamp & Cannon, 1901), 1.
[33] Hans J. Hillerbrand, "Church History as Vocation and Moral Discipline," *Church History*, 70, no.1 (March 2001): 7.
[34] *Church History*, I, 4.

> Church history is the narration of all that is known of the founding and the development of the kingdom of Christ on earth. The term church history is commonly used to designate not merely the record of the organized Christian life of our era, but also the record of the career of the Christian religion itself.[35]

Nicholas Steffens, Dosker's successor as professor of historical theology, vigorously defended the role of sacred history in a 1907 address given under the title, "Sacred History a Bulwark of our Christian World." It was a powerful attack against the hegemony of the scientific methodology as used by secular historians. He complained about

> the era of hegemony of natural science which has ushered in a new order of things. The mechanical view of the world in connection with evolution has captured and enslaved the minds of many of our contemporaries. The universe, according to this view, is an immense machine, most accurate in its movements and manner of working, needing no *Deus ex machina*, because it is subject to law, which is inexorable, excluding the possibility of miracles and the efficacy of prayer.[36]

Steffens insisted on a sacred history worldview that must govern our understanding of a scientific approach to church history. He declared:

> History is the development of God's glory and the end of it will be its consummation. God predestined this world to be a manifestation of His glory, therefore He created and redeemed it and will bring it to a state of perfection notwithstanding all the ravages of sin and misery, using for His purpose even the passions of men and the devices of the evil one.[37]

He went on to attack the view that cosmic and human history is the story of the evolution of things from dead matter.

---

[35] *Church History*, I, 4.

[36] Nicholas Steffens, "Sacred History, A Bulwark of our Christian Worldview" (lecture given in 1907), on file in the WTS/JAH, Holland, Michigan, 2-3. Steffens used Kurtz's *Sacred History* as the textbook for his introductory course in church history (*WTS Bulletin & Catalog, 1906-1907*). Kurtz wrote, "The distinguishing feature of Sacred History is God's progressive revelation of himself, when he deposits a divine form, power and intelligence in the creature, for the purpose of enabling it to reach the end assigned to it by the divine counsel" (Kurtz, *Sacred History*, 31).

[37] Steffens, "Sacred History," 2.

Our idea of progress has to take into account man's state of integrity in paradise, his fall and God's grace, watching over mankind in general and over His Kingdom in a special manner.... Sacred History may not be an explanation of all the details of historical development, and much may have to be left to painstaking historical research, but the grand lines along which the hosts of the Lord are inworking to victory are clearly pointed out to all, who have an eye for the divine side of history.[38]

The defense of the legitimacy of teaching sacred history along with church history was linked at Western Seminary to the doctrine of providence. Siebe Nettinga taught that the doctrine of providence provided an incentive to the study of church history. He wrote,

Historie is His Story, God's story. It is the narrative of what God has brought about the execution of his decree in the course of centuries. He marches with majestic footsteps through the centuries. He usually works slowly and undisturbed by virtue of what we usually call the law of cause and effect. As a consequence there usually are many years of preparation in the evolution of each great movement.[39]

Dosker stated that in the providence of God there is an organic development of the kingdom of God. Church history records the normal and abnormal developments in the organism of the church.[40] In tracing the development, he included chapters devoted to the missionary activities and numerical growth of the church through the centuries.[41] It is crucial for students and ministers of the church to be informed about the progress of dogma in the history of the church. In his inaugural address at Louisville, he affirmed:

In this discipline we trace the gradual development of the various doctrinal systems of the Church, all springing from the same original root, but diverging, as the centre of gravity is shifted from one doctrine to another and as the truth is differentiated in

---

[38] Steffens, "Sacred History," 20.
[39] Nettinga, "Het Leding Blad in de Geschiedenis," *De Hope*, September 29, 1925. (Italics are a mixture of Dutch and English in the original; translation of paragraph is mine).
[40] Dosker, *Outline Studies*, 1.
[41] Dosker, *Outline Studies*, especially part 1, chapter 11; part 2 chapter 2, part 3, chapter 14.

the minds of men. History teaches us the laborious process of this evolution; it enables us to view the present in the light of the past; it warns us against the danger of complacency...[42]

Dosker's rhetoric soared in his enthusiasm for the usefulness of church history in confirmation of the providence of God. Church history, he urged,

> will keep you from that jaundiced pessimism, which sees no good in the present and which looks for the momentary collapse of the Kingdom of God. At the same time, it will safeguard you against an inane optimism, which sees no danger ahead and whose horizon is bounded by its immediate environment. It will make you steady and self possessed under fire, sure of yourselves, strong in your convictions, yet broad and deep in your sympathies. It will quicken your imaginations and it will give you an inexhaustible field of rich homiletical illustrations.[43]

The Church as Organism and the Church as Institute

In *Outline Studies in Ecclesiastical History*, published in 1901, Dosker defined church history as "the systematic narration, in the order of their sequence, of the events, which indicate the organic development of the Kingdom of God."[44] By placing church history within the context of the organic development of the kingdom of God, he not only recognized the providential dimension of church history, but he also left open the possibility that church history should include the study of the whole range of activities of Christian believers, including Christian institutions such as hospitals, schools, and various social agencies as well as Christian governments.

In his inaugural lecture at Louisville in 1904, he defined the task of church history more narrowly. He said that in teaching church history it is necessary to eliminate all extraneous matter.

> We must consider the Church as an institute, as an independent organization, and thus treat it historically. Church history then becomes the systematic narration of the events of the life of the Church as an institution, logically and chronologically considered.[45]

---

[42] Dosker, *Inaugural Address*, 25-26.
[43] Dosker, *Inaugural Address*, 26.
[44] Dosker, *Outline Studies*, 1; see note 7 above.
[45] Dosker, *Inaugural Lecture*, 21.

In contrast to the church as an institution, the church as an organism includes all that believers do in their daily lives as well as in the organized church. It is what the New Testament calls the "body of Christ" as it lives in the world. The church as institute exists in the institutional form that includes the governance through the office bearers of the church, the preaching of the Word and the celebration of the sacraments, as well as the creeds and confessions that have been formed in the course of history. As institute, the church functions in relation to the state. The church as institute exists for the edification of the believers in Christ and for the extension of the church as an organism in the world.[46]

In teaching church history, the distinction between the church as organism and the church as institute was useful in two ways. First, the distinction made it possible to limit the range of history that had to be taught in the classroom. Dosker, like Kuyper, maintained that the church historian's task is to teach the history of the church as an institution without seeking to unfold the whole range of activities of believers since the time of Christ. The church historian must therefore concentrate on the extension of the spread of Christianity through the missionary activity of the church, on the governance and official ministerial offices, on church doctrine and dogma, on the liturgy, and on its moral teachings within the context of secular history. When one examines the tables of contents of the textbooks recommended for student use, it becomes clear that it is the historical church as institute that is described in them even when the authors do not make that distinction.[47]

---

[46] In distinguishing between the church as organism and the church as institute, Dosker and his successors at Western Seminary were indebted to Abraham Kuyper in the Netherlands. For a full discussion of the ramifications of the distinction, see Abraham Kuyper, *Encyclopedie der Heilige Godgeleerdheid*, vol. 3 (Kampen: J.H. Kok, 1909), 260-93. Copies of correspondence between Dosker and Kuyper are on file in WTS/JAH. For a brief exposition of the distinction, see Louis Berkhof, *Systematic Theology* (Grand Rapids: Eerdmans, 1941), 567.

Although Dosker and several of his successors accepted the distinction between the church as institute and the church as organism and also made a distinction between common grace and special grace, they did not follow Kuyper in advocating the establishment of separate Christian organizations for schools, labor unions, and other social organizations for the sake of building up a Christian culture.

[47] In recent years, it is the focus on the church as institute that has led to the complaint that "history has been written by the winners," while leaving out of consideration the role of the women and all others who have been

The Pluriformity of the Church and American Denominations

Along with the distinction between the church as institute and the church as organism, Dosker accepted the doctrine of the pluriformity of the church. By this he meant that the growth of the church can be compared to the growth of a tree that begins with a single seed, grows a trunk, and then spreads out in many branches. He also compared the growth of the church to a stream where "the current of ecclesiastical life spreads itself before us like a many armed delta."[48]

The doctrine of the pluriformity of the church as institute fit well with the way post-Reformation and American church history was taught in Protestant seminaries in the nineteenth and early twentieth centuries. Most of the standard church history textbooks closed with a description of each of the major Protestant churches in Western Europe and Great Britain, followed by a brief objective portrait of the American denominations in what Newman called "the Era of Modern Denominationalism (1648-1903)."[49] Such objective teaching about the denominations left students with the impression that American denominationalism was a form of the church as institute that was a natural development of the one organic church to suit modern conditions.

Professors at Western Theological Seminary favored cooperation among the denominations while remaining hesitant about the prospects of church union. Church union required confessional unity prior to the merger of governmental structures. In the 1890s, when the Reformed Church in America was debating whether to move forward into a Federal Union with the (German) Reformed Church in the United States and a wider Federal Union with several Protestant denominations, Nicholas Steffens stated firmly that church unity must be based on confessional unity. Without confessional agreement, new tensions can arise that lead to conflict and schism.[50]

---

marginalized in the life of the church. It led historians in America to focus on describing the history of American white Protestant denominations while ignoring black churches and the churches of other new immigrant populations. See for example, Gonzales, *The Changing Shape of Church History* (St. Louis: Chalis, 2002), 10-11.

[48] *Inaugural Lecture*, 23.
[49] Newman, *Church History*, II, ix-xi, 519-717. See also for examples, Kurtz, *Church History*, III, 271-458; Woodbridge, *Manual*, 393-406; Dosker, *Outlines*, 263-322.
[50] Steffens, Wekelijksch Budget, *De Hope*, January 13, 1892, 6.

Teaching American Church History

After World War II the teaching of American church history began to shift away from the study of the major denominations alongside each other to a broader study of what church historian William Warren Sweet at the University of Chicago called "the story of religion in America." Sweet objected to the denominational approach to the subject. He insisted that many other influences must be taken into account. He wrote:

> Taken by themselves, all the incidents which go to make up the life of a denomination do not mean much in gaining an understanding of the total religious life of the nation. Indeed, the history of one church, taken by itself, may actually be misleading. To gain a complete understanding it is needful to take into consideration what all the churches have done, as well as every other influence which has entered into the moral and religious life of the people.[51]

The new approach to American church history was adopted at Western Theological Seminary in the 1950s when Elton Eenigenberg used Sweet's textbook in his course on the subject. Sweet influenced a number of church historians in the "Chicago school" to write textbooks and other works that avoided the denominational approach in favor of the broader study of the story of religion in America.[52]

When Sydney E. Ahlstrom's book, *A Religious History of the America People*, was first published in 1972, Bruggink immediately adopted it as his textbook for the course in American church history. Ahlstrom recognized that it was crucial that the study of religious history in America move beyond its previous denominational ethnocentricity to include a more adequate history of the Roman Catholic Church

---

[51] William Warren Sweet, *The Story of Religion in America* (New York: Harper & Brothers, 1939), 2.

[52] For a brief survey of important books on American religious history that appeared between 1950 and 1970, see Sydney E. Ahlstrom, *A Religious History of the American People* (New Haven: Yale Univ. Press, 1974), 10. Other textbooks on American and Canadian church history used from time to time by Bruggink were Jerald C. Brauer, *Protestantism in America* (Philadelphia: Westminster, 1953); Martin E. Marty, *Pilgrims in their own Land: 500 Years of Religion in America* (Boston: Little, Brown, 1984); and Mark Noll, *A History of Christianity in the United States and Canada* (Grand Rapids: Eerdmans, 1991).

and the black churches and black religion in America in the context of the broad social movements throughout the history of the United States. He also included a brief survey of other religious movements in America.[53]

In moving away from the older textbooks that listed and described the history of denominations one after another, there came a new emphasis upon the diversity of religious movements in American life. The focus of attention was not so much on the churches as it was on the wider religious life of the American people. As a result, the distinction set forth by Dosker between the church as institute and the church as organism faded into the background as greater attention was paid to social, humanitarian, and political issues on matters such as race, discrimination, and economic justice for all. The nineteenth-century emphasis upon the organic development of the church as compared to a tree branching or a stream issuing out in a delta also faded into the background. In the late twentieth century, the various denominations continued to play an important role in American religious life, but Ahlstrom believed that a broader focus was required in the teaching of church history. His book was written "in the firm conviction that the moral and spiritual development of the American people is one of the most intensely relevant subjects on the face of the earth."[54]

Teaching the History of the Reformed Church in America

Professors of historical theology bear the heavy responsibility of preserving, teaching, and critically examining the great tradition of the Christian faith through the course of the centuries. Those who teach in a denominational seminary have a particular responsibility to help their students and their denomination learn about and reflect upon the denomination's collective memory. From Steffens and Dosker through

---

[53] Ahlstrom was conscious of the limitations of what he had written. He wrote, "I exist in the middle of things and inherit the limitations of my situation. Not only the inadequacy of my knowledge, but also my hidden presuppositions and my unexamined major premises will in due course be exposed" (*A Religious History of the American People*, 4th printing, 1974, xv). For an evaluation of Ahlstrom's volume, see Henry Warner Bowden, *Church History in an Age of Uncertainty*, 179-83. See also the critical comments of Justo Gonzales, *The Changing Shape of Church History*, 31-32. He noted, "When the story is told by Hispanic Americans the West gains a prominence that it did not have when the story was told almost exclusively by Anglo-Saxon males. Similarly, when the same story is told by African Americans, it is the South that gains new prominence" (32).

[54] Ahlstrom, *Religious History*, xiii.

the generations to Bruggink and his successors, there has always been a course of instruction that includes teaching the history of the Reformed Church in America.

Under the leadership of Donald Bruggink, that responsibility has been carried out on a broader scale since the establishment of the Historical Series of the Reformed Church in America in 1967.[55] Every book in the series, which now includes sixty volumes and counting, has been published by the Wm. B. Eerdmans Publishing Company under the editorship of Bruggink, who has served without remuneration from 1967 to the present. Bruins stated, "Don's accomplishments have greatly advanced the understanding of the RCA's history, and place him on a par with Corwin, the first great light in the denomination's historiography."[56]

Teaching the History of Doctrine

The second great subject of church history, according to Dosker and his teacher, Woodbridge, was that of the history of doctrine. There were church historians who agreed with the fourth-century church historian, Eusebius, who, in his *Ecclesiastical History*, taught that only heresy has a history, while orthodox teaching has been maintained from the days of the apostles.[57] John von Mosheim, the father of modern church history, agreed that all doctrines were present from the beginning, so in fact there was no real development. Joseph Berg, who taught at New Brunswick Theological Seminary from 1861 to 1871, opposed vigorously the Roman Catholic Church's emphasis on tradition. He held to the "Waldensian theory" of church history, according to which the doctrines inherited by the Reformation churches had been preserved through the Waldensian church and not through the Roman Catholic Church. The doctrine had been preserved intact since the second century.[58]

---

[55] A history of the first thirty years has been published in an article by Elton J. Bruins, "Donald J. Bruggink's Contribution to Reformed Church in America Historiography," *Reformed Review*, 52, no. 3 (Spring 1999): 213-24. Bruggink's history of the denomination is no. 44 in the series: Donald J. Bruggink and Kim N. Baker, *By Grace Alone: Stories of the Reformed Church in America* (Grand Rapids: Eerdmans, 2004).

[56] Bruins, "Bruggink's Contribution," 218.

[57] Jaroslav Pelikan, The *Christian Tradition: A History of the Development of Doctrine*, vol. 1 (Chicago: Univ. of Chicago Press, 1971), 7-8.

[58] Joseph Berg had been a pastor in the German Reformed Church in America prior to accepting the call to teach in New Brunswick Theological Seminary. After Philip Shaff had given his lecture on "Das Princip des

With the growing interest in geological evolution and the prominence of the philosophy of Hegel, historians in the nineteenth century also began to pay more attention to the process of development in the history of the church. Augustus Neander wrote in 1825 that the gospel works like yeast in the course of the centuries.

> Looking back on the period of eighteen centuries, we would survey a process...moving onward, though not in a direct line, but through various windings, yet in the end furthered by whatever has attempted to arrest its course; a process having its issue in eternity, but constantly following the same laws, so that in the past, as it unfolds itself to our view, we may see the germ of the future, which is coming to meet us.[59]

John Henry Newman shocked the Protestant world in 1845 with *An Essay on the Development of Christian Doctrine*. After pointing out that in the early centuries there had been much disagreement among the church fathers about central doctrines of the faith, it proved necessary that "as the Church grew into form, so did the power of the Pope develop; and wherever the Pope has been renounced, decay and division have been the consequence."[60] Moreover, it must be insisted that

> doctrine cannot but develop as time proceeds and need arises, and that its developments are parts of the Divine system, and that therefore it is lawful, or rather necessary, to interpret the words

---

Protestantismus" at his inaugural lecture for being installed as professor of biblical literature and ecclesiastical theology at the Theological Seminary in Mercersburg October 18, 1844, Berg brought heresy charges against Schaff, contending that Schaff had "Romanizing tendencies" as well as a view of the intermediate state that was not in conformity with Reformed doctrine. Schaff was exonerated of the charges and Berg left the German church to enter the Reformed Church in America in 1852. For a review of the controversy and Berg's "Waldensian" interpretation of church history, see John W. Nevin, ed., "Editor's Preface," in Philip Schaff, *The Principle of Protestantism*, (Philadelphia: United Church Press, 1964), 2-17; George H. Shriver, *Philip Schaff: Christian Scholar and Ecumenical Prophet* (Macon, Georgia: Mercer Univ. Press, 1987), 21-28.

[59] Neander, *Christian Religion and Church*, vol. 1, 1. Neander's textbook was listed consistently as a book to be consulted by Western Theological Seminary students, in spite of the fact that he had been a student of the great German theologian Schleiermacher, who was regarded with suspicion by teachers at the seminary.

[60] John Henry Cardinal Newman, *An Essay in the Development of Christian Doctrine*, 10th ed. (London: Longmans, Green, 1987), 154.

and deeds of the earlier Church, by the determinate teaching of the later.[61]

As a result of his conclusions, Newman took the logical step of joining the Catholic church.[62] Within a few decades, Protestants also recognized that the promulgation of the dogmas of the immaculate conception (1854) and the infallibility of the pope (1870) flowed from the position of John Henry Cardinal Newman.

In the same decade that Newman's essay was published, Philip Schaff and John Nevin were beginning to teach a doctrine of organic development in what became known as Mercersburg Theology.[63] John Nevin wrote:

> Christianity is organic. This implies, in the nature of the case, development, evolution, progress. The law of its life moreover in this form includes its whole life. It is not as though the knowledge of some truths had been absolutely complete, and so stationary from the beginning, while the knowledge of other truths has been numerically added to it from time to time....It assumes that the system is complete in its own nature from the beginning, and that the whole of it too is comprehended in the life of the church, at all points in its history. But the contents of this life need to be unfolded, theoretically and practically, in the consciousness of the church.[64]

By 1894, when Dosker was installed as professor of historical theology at Western Theological Seminary, the fear that the teaching of Nevin and Schaff would lead to Rome no longer existed. Teachers

---

[61] Newman, *Essay*, 155.
[62] Newman, *Essay*, x.
[63] For an article on the impact of the Mercersburg Theology on two Reformed denominations, see Gregg Mast, "A Decade of Hope and Despair: Mercersburg Theology's Impact on Two Reformed Denominations," in Jacob E. Nyenhuis, ed., *A Goodly Heritage: Essays in Honor of the Reverend Dr. Elton J. Bruins* (Grand Rapids: Eerdmans, 2007), 163-80. For a full discussion, see James Hastings Nichols, *Romanticism in American Theology* (Chicago: Univ. of Chicago, 1961). For an evaluation of the contribution of Schaff, see Stephen R. Graham, "Philip Schaff," in Michael Bauman and Martin I. Klauber, *Historians of the Christian Tradition*, 273-304.
[64] John W. Nevin, "Introduction," in Bard Thompson and George H. Bricker, eds., *Philip Schaff, The Principle of Protestantism*, John W. Nevin, trans. (Philadelphia: United Church Press, 1964), 44-45. The date of Nevin's introduction is 1845.

agreed with Schaff: the Bible as the Word of God is the *formal principle* of Protestantism. It, not tradition, is *"the pure and proper source as well as the only measure of all saving truth."*[65]

The position of Western Theological Seminary professors concerning the progress of dogma was enunciated briefly by Gerrit H. Dubbink in his inaugural lecture on the occasion of his becoming professor of didactic and polemical theology in 1904. He said, "There must be a starting point if there is to be progress; there must be a Living One if life is to be originated, and God must be powerful and wise if He is to create and govern." [66] Dubbink referred twice to the book by James Orr, *The Progress of Dogma*.[67] He agreed with Orr who wrote, "All I am contending for is, that such a development [of dogma] shall be *within* Christianity and not *away* from it, that it shall recognize its connection with the past, and unite itself organically with it."[68]

Orr's thesis was that the temporal order of the fixing of dogma corrsponded to the logical order that is set forth in textbooks on systematic theology. Thus, the temporal order of the development of the doctrines of the Trinity, Christology, soteriology (atonement), and application of redemption (justification, regeneration, etc.) is the order followed in the teaching of systematic theology.[69] The progress of dogma is "organic, a continuation of the developments of the past, not a reversal of them....The test of a sound theological development is not its independence of what has gone before, but the degree of its respect

---

[65] Schaff, *Principle of Protestantism*, 98. (Schaff's italics in the quote above). Professors at Western Seminary hesitated about whether to accept what Schaff called the *material principle* of Protestantism, "the doctrine of the *justification of the sinner before God by the merit of Christ alone through faith*" (80, Schaff's italics). For example, while Nicholas Steffens agreed that justification of the sinner before God is a crucial doctrine in the Christian faith, it does not give adequate attention to sanctification. The Reformed have emphasized the sanctification of the sinner, looking to holiness and perseverance to the end (Nicholas Steffens, "Beginselen, en Wat er mede in Verband Staat," *De Hope*, January 19, 1898; Steffens, *Inaugural Address delivered on the occasion of his installation as Professor of Didactic and Polemic Theology*, December 4, 1884 [printed in Grand Rapids: D.J. Doornink], 1895, 6-13; located in Steffens's file, WTS/JAH).

[66] Gerritt H. Dubbink, *Inauguration* (printed lecture in Dubbink file, WTS/JAH), 23.

[67] Ibid., 24, 27.

[68] Ibid., 27.

[69] James Orr, *The Progress of Dogma* (Grand Rapids: Eerdmans, 1952), 21. The original date of publication of the book was 1901, three years before Dubbink gave his 1904 lecture.

for it."⁷⁰ "The clock never goes back. It never returns upon itself to take up as part of its creed what it has formally, and with full consciousness, rejected at some bygone stage."⁷¹

Although Dubbink agreed with Orr on the progress of dogma, he used Orr's thesis to attack innovations and defend the permanent achievement of Calvinism. Regarding innovations such as modern views of the incidental misfortune of sin, universal salvation, or the universal fatherhood of God, Dubbink reminded his audience, "It is characteristic of a living organism that it can endure nothing save what it can digest, absorb, assimilate. A sliver or malignant growth will cause pain or disturbance until it is removed."⁷²

Regarding Calvinism that has been built on the foundation of Reformed principles, he affirmed, "No higher commendation of Calvinism is conceivable than that it lends itself to being made the basis of a structure of truth so universally and comprehensively Christian in all its lines and proportions."⁷³

Dubbink and his colleagues at the seminary actually applied Orr's theory only to the period leading up to the era of the Protestant Reformation and the decisions of the Synod of Dort.⁷⁴ In their antagonism to Rome, they were suspicious that tradition would again take its place alongside scripture. In practice, then, they were not far from Eusebius's position after all.

Teaching Historical Theology in a Wider World

Western Theological Seminary was entering a new phase of its existence in 1962, the year that Donald Bruggink began to teach there. The country and the Reformed Church in America were changing as racial and social justice and peace issues came to the fore. Ecumenical relationships in the National and World Councils of Churches, as well as with churches related to the National Association of Evangelicals, had to be addressed. The Second Vatican Council (1962-1965) opened the way to new relationships between the Roman Catholic Church

---

70 Orr, *Progress of Dogma*, 19-20.
71 Orr, *Progress of Dogma*, 17.
72 *Inaugural*, 26.
73 Ibid., 28.
74 For example, his teacher and colleague Nicholas Steffens opposed vigorously the movement in the Presbyterian Church to consider a revision of the Westminster Confession; see "Wekelijksch Budget," *De Hope*, October 30, 1889; November 13, 1889; December 18, 1889; March 12, 1890; March 19, 1890.

and Protestant churches, with the result that church historians were faced with the need to re-evaluate the conclusions set forth in the older textbooks. New Reformed congregations began to have members who had little or no Dutch or German ethnicity and little background in the Reformed tradition. The seminary was broadening its historic purpose from educating Reformed Church men for ministry in the Reformed Church in America toward one that eventually would seek to "equip men and women for Christ-centered, biblically based, theologically integrated, culturally sensitive, mission-oriented Christian leadership."[75]

In a seminary with a broadening mandate, the teaching of historical theology also had to change. It was important that students become better acquainted with the actual words in the documents of previous centuries and that the ecumenical nature of historical theology come more to the fore. When the new church history textbooks published by Prentice-Hall, Inc., *A History of Christianity: Readings in the History of the Early and Medieval Church* (Ray C. Petry, ed. 1962), and *A History of Christianity: Readings in the History of the Church from the Reformation to the Present* (Clyde L. Manschreck, ed. 1964), became available, Bruggink used them as basic texts. These two textbooks differed from their predecessors in that they included brief excerpts from documents and leaders of the church through the centuries alongside the descriptive narrative history of the church. For the period from the Reformation to the present, they provided readings from and commentary about the activities of the Reformers. They provided readings and commentary for broad movements in the time following the Reformation, including the Counter Reformation, the Age of Reason, evangelicalism, modernism, the social gospel, and the ecumenical movement. The Prentice-Hall texts provided more balance between church history and historical theology than did other texts.

A deficiency was that in making choices about what could be included in the two Prentice-Hall textbooks, the editors chose to give only a limited amount of space to the Trinitarian and Christological controversies and creedal formulations of the fourth and fifth centuries. They almost totally ignored the Eastern churches.

---

[75] Printed annually on the inside front cover of Western Theological Seminary's catalog for the past decade. The original purpose for establishing Western was to educate men for ministry in the Reformed Church in America, particularly in its Midwestern congregations; see Albertus Pieters, "What Western Theological Seminary Seeks to do," *Intelligencer-Leader*, May 25, 1937, 17.

However, Bruggink's predecessor as professor of church history, Dr. Elton M. Eenigenberg, had already opened up the students to a more ecumenical understanding of historical theology. In his last year of teaching church history prior to his appointment as Professor of Christian Ethics and Philosophy of Religion, he offered a broad range of elective courses entitled "The Ecumenical Movement and its Theology," "The History and Doctrine of Roman Catholicism in the Modern Period," "Contemporary Cults," and "Theological Developments in American Protestantism,"[76] in addition to the basic required courses.

The deficiency was addressed further when Bruggink used Jaroslav Pelikan's *The Christian Tradition: A History of the Development of Doctrine* as soon as it was published in 1971. Although it proved to be a difficult textbook for students, it had the advantage of providing a solid grounding in historical theology with a deep ecumenical dimension, including the Eastern church. By using Pelikan's history of the development of doctrine, students were led to a more nuanced understanding of the nature of doctrinal continuity than was the case in Dubbink's acceptance of James Orr's theory of the progress of dogma. Pelikan proposed:

> The history of Christian doctrine is the most effective means available of exposing the artificial theories of continuity that have often assumed normative status in the churches, and at the same time it is an avenue into the authentic continuity of Christian believing, teaching and confessing. Tradition is the living faith of the dead; traditionalism is the dead faith of the living.[77]

Donald Bruggink found *The Christian Tradition* particularly suited to what he believed to be of crucial importance in the teaching of historical theology. In its ecumenical approach to the teaching of historical theology, it included an extensive study of the theological developments of the Eastern churches. In an article that Pelikan offered to the *Reformed Review* issue dedicated to Donald Bruggink in the year that he retired, Pelikan used the opportunity to write a critique of the work of the great German Lutheran church historian, Adolf Harnack. He objected to Harnack's strong bias that maintained that the three most alien elements in Christian history were ritualism,

---

[76] Western Theological Seminary, *Catalog and Bulletin*, 1962-63, 23, 24.
[77] Pelikan, *The Christian Tradition*, vol. 1, 9. For an evaluation of Pelikan as a historian, see W. David Buschart, "Jaroslav Pelikan," in Michael Bauman and Martin, eds., *Historians of the Christian Tradition*, 551-77.

institutionalism, and dogmatism.⁷⁸ In opposition to Harnack, Pelikan emphasized the close and positive relation of liturgy to dogma in the history of the church. He appreciated the role of ecclesiastical offices and ecumenical councils in the governance of the church.⁷⁹ Through the use of Pelikan's text, Bruggink sought to encourage a greater understanding of the relation of theology and worship in his students, many of whom had grown up in Protestant congregations where there was little experience of the great traditions of the church's liturgy and the ecumenical history of Reformed theology.

The History of Christian Worship: the Third Great Subject of Church History

According to Woodbridge, the teacher of Dosker, the history of Christian worship is the third great subject of study in church history.⁸⁰ However, in the Western Theological Seminary curriculum, the subject of worship had been the responsibility of the practical theology professor and was related closely to the teaching of homiletics. There was considerable resistance to an emphasis on "liturgy," except for the use of the liturgical forms required for the celebration of the sacraments. Sunday worship in Midwestern Reformed congregations was centered in the plain preaching of the Word. The use of written prayers, vestments, candles, and crosses was regarded as more suitable to the Roman Catholic Church. Henry Dosker wrote that the pulpit must occupy the central place in the Reformed Church liturgy and architecture. Everything else, organ, music, Lord's Table, and baptismal font, must remain subordinate to the preaching of the Word.⁸¹ By 1911, Nicholas Steffens was lamenting that liturgy was taking more and more time away from the sermon. He bemoaned the new situation in which the music with choir and organ was becoming a "concert," and sermons lasting fifteen minutes were becoming a "talk."⁸²

During the 1950s and 1960s, the Reformed Church in America went through a long process of rewriting its *Liturgy*. The new liturgical

---

78 Jareslav Pelikan, "The Predicament of the Christian Historian: A Case Study" *Reformed Review*, 52, no. 3 (Spring 1999): 202.
79 Pelikan, "The Predicament of the Christian Historian," 199.
80 Woodbridge, *Manual*, 24.
81 Henry Dosker, "Wekelijksch Budget," *De Hope*, July 21, 1897.
82 Steffens, "Liturgiek en Homiletiek," *De Hope*, September 26, 1911; see also his "Het Nut der Middelmatige Dingen in de Godsdienst," *De Hope*, September 22, 1897, and "Wekelijksch Budget," *De Hope*, August 21, 1889.

forms for worship were written with a deep awareness of long ecumenical liturgical traditions dating back to the New Testament and the church fathers, as well as to the forms of worship developed in Reformed churches in Europe, especially under Martin Bucer in Strassburg during the period when John Calvin was also residing there. In 1966-67, the course on the history of worship was being taught by Bruggink. The "History of Christian Worship" course description read, "The development of worship from the time of the apostolic church, seeking to distinguish legitimate development from distorting accretions, with special attention to the period of the Reformation."[83] Along with the course on the history of worship, he served for a number of years on the seminary's chapel committee, which gave direction to the morning worship five days a week. In the daily chapel services led by faculty and students, the liturgy often followed the order suggested in the *Liturgy* of the Reformed Church in America, but those who led worship were free to experiment with new forms of worship as well. In an article in the *Reformed Review,* the chapel committee wrote:

> For each season of the church year the Chapel Committee suggests a theme or general approach which can give direction or emphasis to worship. Last year the God-directed nature of worship was emphasized as well as the fact that worship is the *action* of the people of God. While for most of the year each student is free to choose his own scripture lessons, during special seasons of the church year (Advent, Epiphany, and Lent) lessons from the lectionary are used.[84]

Theological Education Travel Seminars

European travel seminars in church history broadened the seminary's offerings and outlook. In 1967, Donald Bruggink led the first Western Christendom Travel Seminar, offered for academic credit during three weeks in the summer. The tour moved from Rome through Switzerland and Germany and concluded in the Netherlands. Students and other participants in the seminar prepared papers and visited historical sites with the purpose of gaining greater appreciation and knowledge about Europe's religious history, its architecture and its art, as well as the opportunity to speak personally with Roman Catholic

---

[83] *Western Theological Seminary Catalog,* 1966- 67, 24.
[84] Donald J. Bruggink and Norman J. Kansfield, "Worship: The Chapel Committee," *Reformed Review*, 27, no. 2 (Winter, 1974): 67.

and Protestant leaders in the new era of ecumenical understanding. Bruggink continues to lead travel seminars even in his retirement. In recent years, there have been seminars and tours in areas of Russia and the Lower Danube to help students and other participants become better acquainted with Eastern Orthodox Christianity. Journeys in Turkey have included study of first-century Christianity in the area of the seven cities of the Book of Revelation; in Cappadocia, an area that was especially significant in the fourth and fifth centuries; and in the city of Istanbul, which has been so significant in the history of both Christianity and Islam. All together, Bruggink has led approximately forty-five travel seminars.

Throughout the century that elapsed between the installation of Henry J. Dosker and the retirement of Donald J. Bruggink as professors of historical theology at Western Theological Seminary, five generations of church history teachers have fulfilled faithfully the purpose of the seminary that began with a vision to prepare Reformed Church men for ministry in the Reformed Church in America. At the end of the century, the vision and purpose had broadened with a vision to be not simply a denominational seminary but one that was "catholic, evangelical, and Reformed," with a purpose that included equipping women as well as men to lead the church in ministry. They were engaged not only in teaching the facts and the doctrine, but in strengthening the Christian and professional identity of those enrolled. The first professor of historical theology, Henry Dosker, after ten years of teaching at the seminary, spoke words which set forth not only his, but also the dedication of his successors to their calling:

> With all my soul, I love the engrossing task and, God willing, I would inspire my students with a little of that love. And above all would I kindle in their hearts some sense of the grandeur of our own confessional faith, in its historic interpretation; so that in loving its past, they shall fervently believe in its future; so that they shall know themselves and shall be able intelligently to answer the questions—*"what am I, why am I what am I, and what for?"*[85]

---

[85] Dosker, *Inaugural*, 28.

CHAPTER 2

Finding a Place at the Table

George Brown, Jr.

Introduction

Picture a long, wooden conference table, with a top of green inlaid leather squares and gold leaf trim. In the 1950s, one could find tables like this in boardrooms across the country. This particular table, however, was part of the furnishings of Western Theological Seminary's new home in 1955. A dozen or so wooden captain's chairs with cushioned green leather backrests surrounded the table. It was around this table that Western's faculty assembled for its meetings.[1]

The number of faculty members at Western Theological Seminary in 1962 was small enough to sit comfortably around this single table. Seated around the table during the 1961-1962 academic year would be the familiar faces of the president, Harold N. Englund; the dean of students, Henry J. Ten Clay; and professors Henry Bast (preaching), Elton M. Eenigenburg (church history), Lester J. Kuyper

---

[1] The table, now found in the second floor conference room of the Cook Center for Theological Research, was originally located in a conference room across from the Commons.

(Old Testament), Richard C. Oudersluys (New Testament), M. Eugene Osterhaven (systematic theology), and John H. Piet (English Bible and missions). When the faculty met in the summer of 1962, there were two new faces at the table: Donald J. Bruggink and Elaine E. Lubbers.

Donald Bruggink, a thirty-three-year-old father of two, came to Holland from the Bronx, where he had served as pastor at Fordham Manor from 1957 to 1962. He had received a doctorate from the University of Edinburgh in 1956 and was a logical choice for Professor Osterhaven's sabbatical replacement during the 1962-1963 academic year.

Elaine Lubbers was a thirty-six-year-old widow with four children who had come to Holland from Richmond, Virginia, where she had served on the staff of the Board of Christian Education of the Presbyterian Church in the United States (PCUS). She had just received a two-year appointment as assistant professor of Christian education at Western.[2]

Bruggink's presence at the table would not have surprised anyone passing by the conference room on an afternoon when the faculty was meeting. Until 1962, all those attending faculty meetings had been men. However, Lubbers's presence would likely have prompted a double-take, and not only because Elaine Lubbers was an attractive woman. It was, rather, the presence of any woman at this table that would have been surprising. For the first time in Western's history, a woman was a member of the faculty.

Other women would follow Elaine Lubbers's lead: Sonja M. Stewart, Robin D. Mattison, Diane Maodush-Pitzer, Dianne Bertolino, Carol Bechtel, Leanne Van Dyk, Meri MacLeod, Cynthia Holder Rich, Theresa Latini, and Dawn Boelkins would, eventually, all find places at this table.

---

[2] In 1962, the Executive Committee of the Board of Trustees of Western Theological Seminary recommended that Elaine E. Lubbers receive a two-year appointment as an instructor or assistant professor of Christian education (Minutes of the Annual Meeting of the Board of Trustees of Western Theological Seminary, 1962, 33). President Harold N. Englund welcomed Lubbers at her first meeting with the faculty in the summer of 1962. The minutes of that meeting read: "The President welcomed into our fellowship, Mrs. Elaine Lubbers, who will be professor of courses in Christian Education." The word "professor" is stricken out and the word "instructor" written above it in blue ink (Faculty Minutes, August 13, 1962). Lubbers was appointed assistant professor of Christian education starting in 1963 (Minutes of the Annual Meeting of the Board of Trustees of Western Theological Seminary, 1963, 3).

Elaine Lubbers is the focus of this chapter. She taught courses in the field of Christian education, a field which has been described as marginalized. In finding a place at the table through this field she was not unlike other women who found in this field a point of entry into leadership positions in the church.

Bruggink's teaching ministry at Western coincided with Lubbers's teaching ministry. As Norman J. Kansfield has pointed out, Bruggink's commitment to justice included the advocacy of women in ministry:

> Don was equally outspoken in justification of a role for women equal to that of men within the church. Western Seminary had enrolled its first woman student even before Don arrived as a faculty member. Elaine Lubbers was hired as the seminary's first woman professor at the same time Don was hired. Don provided early and important support for both women students and faculty. When, finally, the RCA took up the constitutional issue of women in the ordained offices of denomination, Don was vocal in their support.[3]

Lubbers would find in Bruggink a sympathetic and supportive colleague.

The Context

In order to understand more clearly what it meant for Elaine Lubbers to find a place at the faculty table as a professor of religious education, it is important to understand the historical and cultural context in which the event happened. Two factors stand out in this regard: the state of Christian education in the curriculum of Western Theological Seminary and in the educational practice of the church in the late 1950s and early 1960s; and the status of women as leaders in the church, particularly the Reformed Church in America, and in the wider society.

Christian Education in the Seminary and the Church

Prior to Elaine Lubbers's arrival at Western Theological Seminary, courses in Christian education were taught by William Goulooze (1903-1955) and Henry Bast (1906-1983). Goulooze was a native of Pella, Iowa, and a graduate of Central College and Western

---

[3] Norman J. Kansfield, "The Committed Self: The Public Career of Donald J. Bruggink," *Reformed Review*, 52, no. 3 (Spring, 1999): 194.

Theological Seminary, and he had earned a Th.D. from the Free University in Amsterdam. He had served churches in Iowa and Grand Rapids, Michigan, before joining Western's faculty in 1939.[4] At first he taught historical theology and church history. From 1952 to 1955, Goulooze held the chair in pastoral theology and Christian education.[5] Henry Bast occupied this chair from 1956 until 1960.[6] Prior to joining Western's faculty, Bast had served as pastor of the Richmond Reformed and Bethany Reformed churches in Grand Rapids and had taught Bible at Hope College from 1939 to 1944. Bast brought considerable pastoral experience to his teaching at the seminary, but unlike Goulooze, he did not have a doctorate.[7] In addition to courses in preaching, Henry Bast taught courses in Christian education and administration.

In the late 1950s, Western Seminary offered only three courses in Christian education. CE 202 "Orientation in Christian Education" and CM302 "Organization and Administration of Christian Education" were required of all students, while CM403 "Teaching the Bible" was offered as an elective.[8] The description for CE 202 "Orientation in Christian Education," a three-credit course, read:

> Introduction to Christian Education as a function of the Church. Lectures and assigned reading in the principles of educational psychology. Study and demonstration of audio-visual aids.[9]

CM302 "Organization and Administration of Christian Education" covered:

> The history and principles of catechetical instruction in the Reformed Churches. Methods of teaching the Heidelberg Catechism. Curriculum and the organization of a weekday Bible school. The history of the Sunday School movement, and the administration of the Sunday School program in a contemporary

---

[4] Russell L. Gasero, ed., *Historical Directory of the Reformed Church in America 1628-2000*, Historical Series of the Reformed Church in America, no. 37 (Grand Rapids: Eerdmans, 2001), 149.
[5] Western Theological Seminary, *Calendar and Bulletin, 1963-1964*, 37.
[6] Western Theological Seminary, *Calendar and Bulletin, 1964-1965*, 35. The *Annual Catalogue 1956-1957* and *Announcements 1957-1958* lists Bast as the Seine Bolks Professor of Pastoral Theology and Christian Education, 6.
[7] Gasero, *Historical Directory*, 18.
[8] Western Theological Seminary, *Annual Catalogue 1958-1959* and *Announcements 1959-1960*, 25-26.
[9] Ibid., 25.

church situation. Students are required to do actual Sunday School observation with written reports. The youth program in the local church.[10]

In the elective course CM403 "Teaching the Bible," the emphasis was on "...the pedagogical use of the Bible as distinguished from the homiletical use." Lecture and discussion were the teaching methods used in the class. Students were expected to make lesson plans and to discuss them in class.[11]

Dorothy Jean Furnish has characterized the period from 1945 to 1965 in the history of the professionalization of Christian education as one of "Recovery and Growth." During this period, most churches reported an increase in Sunday school attendance. Renovation of existing Christian education facilities and construction of new buildings gave evidence of economic recovery after WWII. New curricula were developed. During this period, the number of those employed by churches as directors of Christian education in North America grew from an estimated one thousand to nearly eleven thousand.[12]

As demand for directors of Christian education grew, theological schools and seminaries across North America began to explore adding degrees in religious education to their academic programs. Western Seminary was among those schools considering the addition of a Master of Religious Education degree.

There were no uniformly recognized standards for a master's degree in theological education at the time, but proposed standards were to be presented by the American Association of Theological Schools (AATS)—precursor to the present Association of Theological Schools (ATS), the accrediting agency for seminaries—at the association's meeting at Richmond in June of 1960.

The AATS issued a report on advanced studies that further informed conversations about a master's degree program. Drawing on this report, Elton Eenigenburg identified two requirements: a master's degree for the practical field, and a master's degree for the teaching ministry. The faculty adopted a motion by Eenigenburg that

> ...we as a seminary move forward into a master's degree program in the biblical and theological fields in the fall of 1961 and that

---

[10] Ibid.
[11] Ibid., 26.
[12] Dorothy Jean Furnish, *DRE/DCE—the History of a Profession* (Nashville: Christian Educators Fellowship, United Methodist Church, 1976), 43-45.

the curriculum committee present details to the faculty for carrying out this program.[13]

At the next faculty meeting, Eenigenburg submitted requirements based on a survey of other seminaries. These were discussed and approved without a formal motion, final action being deferred until a later time.[14]

Following the Second World War, the church experienced a period of expansion and creativity in Christian education. The *Annual Report of the Board of Education, R.C.A.* to the 144th General Synod meeting at Buck Hill Falls, Pennsylvania, heralded 1950 as "a signal year in the field of Christian Education."[15] That year the church celebrated the 170th anniversary of the Sunday school, an educational institution that continued to play a significant role in faith formation. By the mid-1950s the Board of Education employed an executive secretary and nine directors and managers to staff the various departments.[16]

"The 1950s was the great decade for curricular innovation and renovation," according to Robert W. Lynn and Elliott Wright.[17] The Reformed Church in America, while producing its own educational resources for use in the church, partnered with the Moravian Church, the Presbyterian Church U.S., and the United Presbyterian Church of North America in the production of educational materials. In 1955, the Board of Christian Education of the Presbyterian Church U.S. appointed a special Curriculum Study Committee "to study afresh questions related to the communication of Christian faith through the educational work of the Church." The committee, chaired by Charles E.S. Kraemer, president of the Presbyterian School of Christian Education in Richmond, included two outstanding Christian educators: Rachel Hendelite and C. Ellis Nelson. The other partner denominations were invited to appoint representatives to this committee. The Reformed Church was represented by Bernard J. Mulder, Winfield Burggraff, and Elsie Stryker. After two years of intensive work, the study committee presented its report, which was adopted by the Boards of Christian Education of the PCUS and RCA in 1959. The presuppositions and

---

[13] Western Theological Seminary, *Faculty Minutes*, January 6, 1961.
[14] Western Theological Seminary, *Faculty Minutes*, January 13, 1961.
[15] *Annual Report of the Board of Education, R.C.A. May 1, 1949 to April 30, 1950*, 1.
[16] *Annual Report of the Board of Education, R.C.A.* 1956, 19.
[17] Robert W. Lynn and Elliott Wright, *The Big Little School: Sunday Child of American Protestantism* (New York: Harper and Row, 1971), 91.

guiding principles provided the basic design for the Covenant Life Curriculum.[18]

The Covenant Life Curriculum was introduced in 1963. It was organized around a three-year cycle of year-long themes (Bible, church, and Christian life) studied by all ages in ways appropriate to each age group's developmental level.[19]

> In Covenant Life, as in *Faith and Life*, the Bible is central in two fundamental ways: first, as *witness* to God's revelation; and secondly, as *means* for contemporary men, women, and children to experience God's coming to the world to invite them into covenant relationship.[20]

The organizing principle of the Covenant Life Curriculum, as C. Ellis Nelson pointed out, was "...the local church in its worship, study, and work rather than a certain configuration of content of experience that can be devised for the classroom."[21] Nelson identified three emphases that were distinctive features of the curriculum: adult education, home and family, and congregational life. He wrote, "In practical terms, this curriculum gives more attention to adult education than any contemporary curriculum, because adults form and fashion the local church."[22] The church as God's covenant community was the hermeneutical key in the Covenant Life Curriculum.[23] David C. Hester wrote:

> Covenant Life Curriculum was visionary, designed to provide an educational approach that saw the whole life of the covenant community as the true setting for learning. This vision, however, was never successfully communicated to churches, which seemed unable to move past the schooling model of systematic study to decision making that engaged the social issues of the day.[24]

[18] "Foreword," *Basic Presuppositions and Guiding Principles for the Educational Work of the Church* (Richmond: Marshall C. Dendy, 1960), 2.

[19] David C. Hester, "The Use of the Bible in Presbyterian Curricula, 1923-1985," in Milton J. Coalter, John M. Mulder, and Louis B. Weeks, eds., *The Pluralistic Vision: Presbyterians and Mainstream Protestant Education and Leadership* (Louisville: Westminster/John Knox, 1992), 219-21.

[20] Hester, 221.

[21] C. Ellis Nelson, "The Curriculum of Christian Education," in Marvin J. Taylor, ed., *An Introduction to Christian Education* (Nashville: Abingdon, 1966), 167.

[22] Nelson, "Curriculum," 167.

[23] Hester, "Use of the Bible," 221.

[24] Ibid., 222-23.

Women in Society and Church

Writing about the origin of the Reformed Church's Woman's Board of Foreign Mission in the nineteenth century, Mary L. Kansfield uses the term "separate spheres" to describe the place of women in society at large as well as in the church.

> Women and men lived in "separate spheres." Here, clear lines of authority marked the boundaries between the sexes and delineated the behavioral expectations of both women and men. Living in separate spheres was also reflected in church life and architecture. In many Reformed congregations, women and men were seated separately. Since church sanctuaries often had no central aisle, women and children were seated in a large central section of pews, and men were seated in smaller sections on either side of the nave.[25]

Due to several factors, including the women's rights movement in the twentieth century and the changing role of women in the aftermath of World War II, the boundary between these spheres was breaking down by the middle of the twentieth century.[26]

Leadership roles for women in the church were still limited in the 1960s. While it was acceptable for women to play a supportive role in relation to ministry and mission, it was not until the 1970s that ordination of women to the offices of elder, deacon, and minister of Word and sacrament became a possibility for women in the Reformed Church in America.

The question of the ordination of women had first been raised in the Reformed Church in a 1918 overture from the Particular Synod of Albany and the Classis of Montgomery. Between 1918 and 1951, the issue was the subject from time to time of a number of overtures from classes. But in 1951, there were thirteen overtures—six in favor of changing the *Constitution* by deleting the word "male" from Article IV, Section 42, and seven opposing any change.

---

[25] Mary L. Kansfield, *Letters to Hazel: Ministry within the Women's Board of Foreign Missions of the Reformed Church in America*, Historical Series of the Reformed Church in America, no. 46 (Grand Rapids: Eerdmans, 2004), 17.

[26] For other treatments of the role of women in the church see Renee S. House and John W. Coakley, eds., *Patterns and Portraits: Women in the History of the Reformed Church in America*, Historical Series of the Reformed Church in America, no. 31 (Grand Rapids: Eerdmans, 1999) and Una Ratmeyer, *Hands, Hearts, and Voices: Women Who Followed God's Call* (New York: Reformed Church Press, 1995).

The issue of the ordination of women was addressed in the late 1950s in a series of reports prepared by members of a Committee on the Ordination of Women. The committee had been appointed by the General Synod of 1955. The committee, composed of the Reverend Dr. Vernon Kooy, a professor at New Brunswick Theological Seminary; Andrew Meyer, an elder at the North Park Church in Kalamazoo, Michigan; the Reverend Dr. Richard Oudersluys, a professor at Western Theological Seminary, and the Reverend Lambert Ponstein, a professor at Hope College; was chaired by Gerrit T. Vander Lugt, president of Central College. "The Practice of other Churches in the Ordination of Women" was written by Meyer and Ponstein. Kooy wrote two papers: "Ordination of Women and the Old Testament" and "The Ordination of Women: Practices in the Early and Post-Apostolic Church." Oudersluys wrote, "The Ordination of Women and the Teaching of the New Testament." Two study papers, "Ordination of Women in the Reformed Church" and "The Offices and the Ordination of Women," were written by Vander Lugt. Four of the six study papers appeared in the *Church Herald* in January and March of 1957.[27] The six study papers were not printed in the *Acts and Proceedings* of General Synod but were distributed to the churches for review and comment. They were later published in a collection of official ecclesiastical statements on the subject of women's ordination.[28]

In the Reformed Church in America, as in several other Protestant churches and in North American society generally, women found increasing opportunities for service in education. Only later were they able to gain access to the ordained offices of the church. In the Presbyterian Church in the United States, the offices of elder, deacon, and minister of Word and sacrament were opened to women in 1964.[29] The Reformed Church in America did not open these offices to women until later. The offices of elder and deacon were opened to women

---

[27] The Kooy paper, "The Ordination of Women: Practices in the Early and Post-Apostolic Church," and the Vander Lugt paper, "The Offices and the Ordination of Women," were not published in the *Church Herald*.

[28] Melton, J. Gordon, ed., *The Churches Speak on Women's Ordination: Official Statements from Religious Bodies and Ecumenical Organizations* (Detroit: Gale Research, 1991), cf. 189-219. This collection mistakenly divides Oudersluys's study paper in two. The confusion may arise from the fact that the paper was published in two parts in the *Church Herald* in March of 1957.

[29] Estelle Rountree McCarthy, "Rachel Henderlite," *20th Century Christian Educators*, at http://www.talbot.edu/ce20/educators/view.cfm?n=rachel_henderlite, accessed June 2, 2008.

officially in 1972, even though some congregations had ordained women to these offices as early as 1970. Although the ordination of the first woman to the office of minister of Word and sacrament in the Reformed Church took place in 1973, the office would not be open to women officially until 1979.

In 1981, Susan Thistlethwaite wrote:

> The relationship of the Sunday school to the church is, in many respects, a microcosm of the problems women face in the whole church today. Many women seminarians who consider themselves feminists avoid courses and careers in religious education because of the identification of religious education as stereotypically "woman's" work in the church. When a clergywoman joins a multiple-staff ministry, it is often assumed that she will most "naturally" be able to handle the Sunday School. Men who pursue religious education often face skepticism regarding the seriousness of their career choice.[30]

Passivity, self-sacrifice, privatization, and dependency are traits often attributed to women. Contrast these with another set of traits: active, productive, public, and independent.[31] For Thistlethwaite, the marginalization of religion and women carries over into religious education, resulting in what she calls the "feminization of religious education." Like women, religious education has been marginalized in the life of the church. She asserts, "Religious education is the wife of the church."[32] Thus, women in the field of Christian education, whether in a church or a seminary, were typically regarded as marginalized.

Glenn T. Miller has also written about the feminization of the profession in the first half of the twentieth century. Noting the erosion of the "political position of religious education professors on many faculties," Miller writes:

> If the professor was a male, he was regarded as teaching in a "female" profession; if a woman, she was disregarded because of gender. Common gender stereotypes drifted from women in general to religious educators in particular.[33]

---

[30] Susan Thistlethwaite, "The Feminization of American Religious Education," *Religious Education*, 76, no. 4 (July-August, 1981): 391.
[31] Ibid., 399-402.
[32] Ibid., 397.
[33] Glenn T. Miller, *Piety and Profession: American Protestant Theological Education, 1870-1970* (Grand Rapids and Cambridge, U.K.: Eerdmans, 2007), 581.

Elaine and Edward Lubbers
(Family photograph courtesy of Douglas Lubbers)

In this context, finding a place at the table in theological education was not easy for a woman in the sixth decade of the twentieth century. Having identified critical elements of the historical and cultural context, attention can now be directed to the life and ministry of the first woman to serve on Western's faculty.

Elaine Elizabeth Lubbers

Elaine Elizabeth Kanis was born in Orange City, Iowa, October 16, 1921, to Arie and Jeanette Kanis. Elaine was the oldest of their three children.[34] Elaine graduated from Northwestern Junior College in 1940 and taught in public schools in Iowa and Michigan for four years. She began her teaching career in Center Township in Sioux County, Iowa.[35]

Egbert Edward Lubbers (1941-1955) was born in Grand Rapids, Michigan, in 1914. The son of Dutch immigrants—Nick and Anna Lubbers—Ed (his preferred name) earned A.B. and A.M. degrees from Calvin College.

Elaine Kanis had come to know Edward Lubbers at Northwestern Junior College. They were married in the American Reformed Church in Orange City March 10, 1941, and moved to Booneville, Missouri, where Ed was teaching at Kemper Military College.[36]

---

[34] Elaine had a younger brother, Herman, and sister, Patty. Douglas Lubbers, e-mail to George Brown, Jr., May 7, 2008.
[35] *Harwarden Independent*, February 13, 1941.
[36] Alton, Iowa, *Democrat*, Friday, March 21, 1941.

The Lubbers family shortly after Ed's death
(Family photograph courtesy of Douglas Lubbers)

Ed began doctoral studies at the University of Chicago. Recognizing his gifts for ministry, Elaine encouraged him to enroll in seminary. He enrolled at Western Theological Seminary in Holland, Michigan, and graduated with a B.D. in 1945. Ed was licensed and ordained by the Classis of Holland in that same year. While enrolled at Western, he continued his doctoral studies at the University of Chicago, commuting to Chicago for classes, and received a Ph.D. in economics in 1946.[37]

The Lubbers went to Egypt, serving as missionaries under the sponsorship of the Reformed Church in America. Ed served as a professor at the American University in Cairo from 1945 until 1949. Elaine studied Arabic and Near Eastern Studies at the university for a year. During their stay, the couple traveled extensively in Upper Egypt, Palestine, and Syria.[38] Their two oldest children were born during this time: Clark Edward in July of 1946 and Jill Claire in October of the following year.

On their return to the United States in 1949, the Lubbers moved to Sherman, Texas. Ed was dismissed to the Presbyterian Church.[39] For six years he taught economics at Austin College and then served as pastor of the First Presbyterian Church in Sherman, Texas. Elaine worked as an advisor with campus groups, was involved in programs at the church, active in civic projects, and substituted as a teacher in the public schools. The Lubbers had two more children: Paul Jeffrey, born in December of 1951, and Brent Douglas, born in April of 1953.

---

[37] Gasero, *Historical Directory*, 242.
[38] Elaine Lubbers, letter to Harold N. Englund, president of Western Theological Seminary, March 19, 1962.
[39] Gasero, *Historical Directory*, 242.

Ed died of polio, November 21, 1955,[40] leaving thirty-four-year-old Elaine to raise their four children—nine-year-old Clark, eight-year-old Jill, four-year-old Paul, and two-year-old Douglas—on her own.[41]

In order to provide more adequately for the needs of her family, Elaine equipped herself for a career in education, completing an A.B. degree in Bible and education at Austin College in 1956 and then enrolling in the M.C.E. degree program at Austin Presbyterian Theological Seminary. In the 1950s, churches were looking for qualified candidates to lead their Christian education programs.[42]

The Presbyterian seminary in Austin was among a number of seminaries around the country that were gearing up to meet the growing demand for Christian educators. The two-year M.C.E. degree program at Austin had been approved by the seminary's board of trustees in 1955, so the program was in its initial stage when Elaine started taking courses in 1956. The program was designed for lay workers. Some of the education courses were to be taken in the graduate school of the University of Texas in Austin. There were enough elective hours in the sixty semester hours required for the M.C.E. degree to allow for some specialization, depending on the student's vocational interests.[43] The seminary catalog for 1956-1957 identified four church vocations for which the M.C.E. degree program could equip students: director of Christian education, student or youth worker, kindergarten teacher, and public school Bible teacher. Students had to declare their vocational goals before matriculating. Regardless of their vocational goals, all students in the M.C.E. program at Austin took courses in Bible, theology, and church history in addition to courses in education, Christian education, and educational psychology.[44]

At Austin Presbyterian Theological Seminary, Elaine Lubbers would have taken C.E. 349 "Curriculum of Christian Education" in the fall semester of her first year and C.E. 353 "Supervision of Christian Education" in the spring semester of the second year. In the spring semester of the first year she would have been able to choose between C.E. 322 "The Christian Nurture of Children," C.E. 324 "The Christian Nurture of Youth," and C.E. 350 "Student Work." Her course of study would have included a course in psychology and a course in educational

---

[40] Texas Death Index, 1903-2000—Ancestry.com, accessed March 18, 2008.
[41] *Colorado Springs Gazette Telegraph*, January 21, 1981, A:4:1.
[42] Furnish, *DRE/DCE*, 45.
[43] Austin Presbyterian Theological Seminary, *Catalogue*, 1956-1957, 29.
[44] Ibid., 32.

psychology. For electives, she could have chosen courses like C.E. 247 "Audio-Visual Aids" or C.E. 351 "Christianity and Personality," as well as education courses at the University of Texas. Along with other students, she would have been required to take P.T. 246 "Church Program and Presbyterian Polity."

Lubbers majored in theology with a minor in education. She said that courses in theology and Bible were the "most beneficial part" of her training. Lubbers took courses in theology with James I. McCord, who had a significant influence on her thought.[45] Since M.C.E. students at Austin Seminary took some education courses at the University of Texas, Lubbers studied personality development and group dynamics there. She had a summer assignment as director of Christian education at a large church in Fort Worth and did her year-long field work in a new church being established in suburban Austin as a part-time director of Christian education. In addition, Lubbers was also a student assistant to James Wharton, a professor of Old Testament.[46]

The courses in Christian education at Austin Presbyterian Theological Seminary during Lubber's first year in the M.C.E. program were taught by C. Ellis Nelson, a leading figure in the field. Nelson was responsible for expanding the religious education program at Austin.[47] He had taught courses at Austin Presbyterian Seminary in the early 1940s before going to Richmond, Virginia, in 1945 to serve as the director of youth work for the Board of Christian Education of the Presbyterian Church U.S. Nelson returned to Austin in 1948 and taught there until leaving to become Skinner and McAlpin Professor of Practical Theology at Union Theological Seminary in New York in 1957. While at Austin, he earned a doctorate in the joint Union Seminary-Columbia University program that produced several leading Christian educators including Mary Boys, Thomas Groome, and John H. Westerhoff.[48]

After graduating from Austin Presbyterian Theological Seminary in 1958, Lubbers became director of Christian education at the Parkway Presbyterian Church in Corpus Christi, Texas. Many adults in this congregation of 670 communicant members had college educations

---

[45] In her letter to Western Seminary president Harold Englund, Lubbers listed McCord as a reference. Lubbers, letter to Harold N. Englund, March 19, 1962, 3.
[46] Lubbers, letter to Harold N. Englund, March 19, 1962, 1-2.
[47] Ronnie Prevost, "C. Ellis Nelson," *20th Century Christian Educators*, at http://www.biola.edu/ceacademic/nelsonc.cfm, accessed August 14, 2003.
[48] Prevost, "C. Ellis Nelson."

Elaine Lubbers when she graduated from the Austin Presbyterian Theological Seminary, 1958
(Courtesy Austin Presbyterian Theological Seminary Archives)

and some had graduate degrees. Lubbers described the congregation's teaching ministry with adults in an article published in the *International Journal of Religious Education*. In that article, Lubbers expressed the belief that "a strong adult educational program can change the entire tone of a congregation's life."[49]

The "high-level adult educational program" at Parkway Presbyterian Church—then in its second year—featured a spring retreat on the meaning of human existence that resulted in participants following up by reading articles by well-known philosophers and theologians and committing themselves to a three- to four-hour evening discussion every other week. Parkway's program of adult education offered three-month-long elective classes Sunday mornings and evenings, providing adults with up to seven courses a year. Lubbers reported that, in the fall of 1959, enrollment in the evening courses was four times what Sunday school enrollment had been in the past. Moreover, Lubbers reported a deeper level of discipleship and growth in leadership as a result of this high-commitment approach to adult Christian education.[50]

Marjorie Nelson, a member of Parkway Presbyterian Church, recalled Lubbers in an interview.

> So things were going along pretty well. And it was in about 1958, or something like that. I can't remember, 1957 or 1958. This woman came to our church–Elaine Lubbers–to be an assistant minister. I'm not sure she called herself a feminist but she was the first real feminist I'd seen. Her husband had died, leaving her with four children, and she'd gone to seminary. She was a liberation theologian and she was brilliant. She wanted to bring that to us.

[49] Elaine Lubbers, "A Serious Approach to Adult Education," *International Journal of Religious Education*, 36, no. 5 (January, 1960): 11.
[50] Lubbers, "A Serious Approach to Adult Education," 11, 12.

> So she started setting us up to go up to the Christian Faith and Life Community in Austin, Texas. She started talking in ways about demanding-she wanted to be a minister but she couldn't get the job. But we were all immensely impressed with Elaine. She had a huge influence in my life. So we started going up there, to Austin, Texas, and they were introducing us to Paul Tillich and to-what they talked about was remythologizing Christianity. In other words, you say you're a Christian. You go to church. But what does it mean? And they were really challenging us. I loved it. I ate it up because it began to make sense to me. It got me really to talk about things in a very different way. It was a profound influence on my life.[51]

As was true throughout her life, Lubbers was actively involved in various community activities in addition to her professional responsibilities at the church. In Corpus Christi, she served on the Youth Board of the Y.W.C.A., participated in an interdenominational pastors' study group, and was a leader for presbytery and synod conferences.[52]

Sometime in late 1960 Lubbers returned to Austin, leaving the Parkway Presbyterian Church in order to become a member of the Christian Faith and Life Community. Combining elements of a lay renewal institute with an experimental alternative to conventional campus ministries, the Christian Faith and Life Community at the University of Texas resonated with Lubber's vision for adult Christian education in the church.

Writing in 1962 about the Christian Faith and Life Community in Austin, Texas, Parker Rossman, then associate professor of religion in higher education at Yale Divinity School, described the community in terms of controversy and challenge.

> The Christian faith and life community at Austin, Texas, is the center of controversy precisely because of the challenge it presents to the conventional efforts at Christian work in American universities. This center represents a challenge from the intellectual world of today to the work of the churches of Texas, as well as the thrust of the Church into the university at

---

[51] Marjorie Nelson, interviewed by Kate Weigand, May 18-19, 2005, North Hampton, Mass. Transcript: Tape 1 of 5, p. 18. © Sophia Smith Collection 2006.

[52] Lubbers, letter to Harold N. Englund, March 19, 1962, 2.

a moment when many of the conventional patterns of campus Christian life appear to be sterile.[53]

The passion with which staff and student members of the community embraced an existentialist ideology was a source of some of the controversy. According to Rossman, some critics described the community's commitment to an existentialist ideology as "brainwashing."

The Christian Faith and Life Community must be understood in the context of changes in campus ministry after the Second World War. Rossman observed that

> Between 1944 and 1949 campus Christian movements began to develop a new sense of intellectual responsibility. Through much of the history of voluntary student religious activities university Christian movements and organizations had been concerned for personal evangelism, for nurturing personal and group spirit to life, for social action and for instruction to overcome the "religious illiteracy" of students; yet, the intellectual concern expressed in these activities and even in credit courses of religion left something to be desired. Following World War II the American student Christian movements were stirred by two new currents: the theological revival and the World Student Christian Federation's materials on the "university question"—that is, the theological examination and critique of the university itself.[54]

The Reverend W. Jack Lewis (1915-2002), a Presbyterian minister, had become director of the Presbyterian Westminster foundation at the University of Texas in 1946. Dissatisfied with the state of religious programs for students, Lewis looked for an alternative that would nurture "mature, responsible, intelligent Christian laymen."[55] In 1952, the Christian Faith and Life Community was formed in response to the need for a different kind of campus ministry.

> From the beginning Lewis viewed the Community as an experimental center where a curriculum could be developed, i.e., a course of study by which students might examine the Christian faith in depth. It is significant to note at this point

---

[53] Parker Rossman, "The Austin Community: Challenge and Controversy," *Christian Scholar*, 16, no. 1 (Spring, 1962): 44.
[54] Rossman, "The Austin Community," 45.
[55] Ibid.

that while American Protestant churches have spent years developing curricula for church schools (cradle to grave) and for other aspects of church program, there is no ecumenical curriculum recommended for voluntary study during the four college years. Further, the staff of the Community came to feel a growing changing course of study, rooted in worship and a sense of mission, was essential to give new power to the lay man. Continuing experimentation has sought the sort of study of Christian faith which is basic for a more adequate adult program of a lay training center. Different ideas, new methods of teaching, unique approaches to content are tried; imaginative teaching methods and curriculum are being developed for use in a larger program of lay training with adults across the state.[56]

The idea was to create a learning community "as a pioneering age of the Christian mission of our time." Lewis envisioned thirty students living together for an academic year in a house.[57] In addition to seminars, lectures, and worship, mealtime conversations were to provide "a stimulating intellectual Christian atmosphere."[58] Joe Slicker offers this description of life together in the community:

> The life together included what was usually called "waste time" that included morning worship, structured conversations at meals and one night a week for lecture and seminars. In addition, he and the students built a stone chapel behind the living quarters for daily worship. Also included in the student commitment was attending the Friday lecture series after dinner where key professors of the University of Texas were invited to come and share the edge of their work and engage in questions and answers with the students. It became a winner among the students.[59]

In 1956, Lewis brought Joe Matthews, professor of ethics at Perkins School of Theology, to Austin to serve as dean at the community.[60]

---

[56] Ibid., 46.
[57] According to Joe Slicker, the house was "a cooperative style apartment building." Cf. Joe Slicker, "Waves that Built the Order," (September, 2007), http://www.ica-usa.org/livinglegacyevent/greetings/slicker.htm
[58] Rossman, "The Austin Community," 45.
[59] Joe Slicker, "Waves that Built the Order," (September, 2007), http://www.ica-sa.org/livinglegacyevent/greetings/slicker.htm
[60] Joe Slicker, "Waves that Built the Order," (September, 2007), http://www.icausa.org/livinglegacyevent/greetings/slicker.htm

According to Rossman, in 1960-1961 the faculty consisted of ten theologically trained instructors.[61]

As dean, Matthews held responsibility for developing the curriculum of the Christian Faith and Life Community at Austin.[62] The curriculum consisted of two terms each semester (a total of four terms). Courses covered theology, biblical studies, church history, and ethics. The curriculum represented an effort to answer the question, "What is it that every layman should know?"[63]

Students were exposed to the writing of theologians such as Niebuhr, Bultmann, Herbert, Knox, and Kierkegaard. Time constraints prevented students from reading very long books, so selected portions were chosen for reading and discussion.[64]

It is important to note the emphasis on mission in this experiment in Christian community and learning.

> True, the Community is concerned with theological study as a means to overcome "religious illiteracy" and to clarify the nature and meaning of the Christian mission in the world. Yet, the aim of Christian work is not merely to study the Christian faith, but to focus upon mission![65]

Mission and the education of the laity are significant themes in the life and witness of Elaine Lubbers. She later wrote of the value of this experience:

> This was a very valuable experience, for here I came to a deeper awareness of the hunger for laymen to be treated as responsible church members, wanting an intellectual and relevant faith that would equip them to fulfill this role of being servant in and to the world. I served as a member of the faculty at the community. Since this was a corporate ministry, I learned much of the meaning of corporate discipline and corporate study. The methods of adult education, week-end seminars and retreats, and the dialogue between faith and culture through a program of discussions with faculty members of the University of Texas, have been exceedingly valuable in giving me new insights into Christian education.[66]

---

[61] Rossman, "The Austin Community," 47.
[62] Joe Slicker, "Waves that Built the Order," (September, 2007), http://www.icausa.org/livinglegacyevent/greetings/slicker.htm
[63] Rossman, "The Austin Community," 47.
[64] Ibid., 48.
[65] Ibid.
[66] Lubbers, letter to Harold N. Englund, March 19, 1962, 2-3.

She did not remain a member of the Christian Faith and Life Community for long, however. Differences over ecclesiology and Christology were too great for her Calvinist theological roots.

No doubt Lubbers's effectiveness as a Christian educator in the local church and her experience at the Christian Faith and Life Community helped her secure a staff position with the Board of Christian Education of the Presbyterian Church in the United States. Lubbers served on the staff of the Board of Christian Education in Richmond from January of 1961 until the summer of 1962. Working under the leadership of Marshall C. Dendy, executive director of the board, Lubbers served as family editor and administrative assistant to Rachel Henderlite (1905-1991).

Henderlite, the first woman to be ordained to the office of minister of Word and sacrament in the Presbyterian Church U.S., was a driving force behind the Covenant Life Curriculum discussed earlier. The new curriculum was developed by the PCUS in collaboration with several other denominations, including the Reformed Church in America. Family life and adult education were Lubbers's primary areas of responsibility. She also contributed to presbytery leadership schools and seminars, introducing the Covenant Life Curriculum, as well as teaching classes in local churches.[67] Lubbers later wrote a resource for the curriculum, *Families within the Family* (1963).[68]

Like Austin Presbyterian Theological Seminary and other seminaries around the country, Western Theological Seminary was also looking at the possibility of expanding its academic programs to include a master's degree in religious education. The seminary sought the advice and counsel of D. Campbell Wyckoff (1918-2005), Thomas W. Synnott professor of Christian Education at Princeton Theological Seminary, regarding the establishment of a master's degree in religious education. Excerpts from a letter written by D. Campbell Wyckoff, a prominent figure in Christian education, were read at the January 9, 1960, faculty meeting. Based on ideas presented in his letter, he was invited to campus to discuss courses in Christian education with the faculty.[69]

---

[67] Ibid., 3.
[68] Western Theological Seminary, *Faculty Minutes*, April 6, 1962.
[69] Western Theological Seminary, *Faculty Minutes*, January 9, 1960. There is no mention of Wyckoff's response or reference to any subsequent faculty discussion with him in later faculty minutes. No copy of Wyckoff's letter was found in the seminary's papers at the Western Theological Seminary/Joint Archives of Holland.

The seminary's curriculum study concluded that a master's program in religious education would require Western to expand the faculty by adding a full-time professor in the field of Christian education. In November of 1960, the instruction committee requested information about the kind of courses and work that a faculty position in Christian education would entail.[70] A faculty search was begun following Eenigenburg's reports to the faculty early in January of 1961.[71]

Lester Kuyper, who presided at the March 23, 1962, meeting of the faculty in the absence of the president, Harold N. Englund, announced that Englund had gone to Richmond, Virginia, to interview Lubbers "relative to her training in Christian education."[72] On April 6, Englund reported to the faculty on his interview with Lubbers. Other members of the faculty, it was noted, "spoke with appreciation of her ability."[73]

Arrangements were made for her to come to Holland. Englund, Henry J. Ten Clay (the dean), and Elton M. Eenigenburg were appointed to meet with Lubbers to discuss curriculum and courses.[74] It is not clear whether Ten Clay actually met with Lubbers, as the minutes of the April 20, 1962, faculty meeting indicate that Englund and Eenigenburg had met with Lubbers and that "both of them were well pleased with the gifts of Mrs. Lubbers in the teaching and understanding of Christian education."[75] The executive committee recommended that Lubbers receive a two-year appointment as either an instructor or assistant professor, leaving the final decision regarding her rank to the president.[76]

In addition to adding a Master of Religious Education degree to its offerings, Western also wanted to expand the offerings in the Master of Theology (Th.M.) degree in the early 1960s. The size and configuration of the faculty limited offerings in this program to biblical studies and theology. With the appointment of Lubbers, Western was finally in a position both to add an M.R.E. degree and to expand the offerings of the Th.M. degree. In July, the faculty recommended to the executive committee that the Th.M. degree offer work in the practical field as

---

[70] Western Theological Seminary, *Faculty Minutes*, November 4, 1960.
[71] Ibid., January 6 and January 13, 1961.
[72] Ibid., March 13, 1962.
[73] Ibid., April 6, 1962.
[74] Ibid., April 13, 1962.
[75] Ibid., April 20, 1962.
[76] Annual Meeting of the Board of Trustees of the Western Theological Seminary, 1962, 33.

Professor Elaine Lubbers

well as in the biblical and theological fields. The executive committee approved, in principle, the offering of courses for a Master of Religious Education degree pending the development of course descriptions.[77]

Thus it was that on August 13, 1962, Elaine Elizabeth Lubbers found herself seated at the faculty table as instructor of Christian education. Seated with her at the table were President Englund; Dean Ten Clay; and professors Bast, Eenigenburg, Kuyper, Oudersluys, and Piet. Donald Bruggink was also at the table in Eugene Osterhaven's place while the latter was on sabbatical.

Lubbers's appointment was historic in several ways. First, she was the first woman to serve on the faculty of Western Theological Seminary. Second, hers was the first full-time faculty position in the field of Christian education. Third, she was the first nonordained person to be appointed to the faculty. Fourth, she was the first non-RCA member of the faculty. The last point is debatable. While it might be argued that Lubbers was the first faculty member to come from outside of the Reformed Church because of her continuing Presbyterian affiliation, in another sense it could also be argued that since she had started out within the RCA, she was only returning home. Still, she kept her affiliation with the Presbyterian Church and joined the recently established Presbyterian congregation in Holland.

Developing a master's degree in religious education was the first order of business for Lubbers at Western. The faculty had already done

---

[77] Western Theological Seminary, *Faculty Minutes*, July 5, 1962, and July 16, 1962.

some preliminary work, following ideas first suggested by Wyckoff. At the August 13, 1962, faculty meeting, Eenigenburg submitted a schedule of courses for the first year of the proposed Master of Religious Education (M.R.E.) degree. A plan for the second year was to be developed once specific courses had been identified.

Eenigenburg questioned the title for the new degree program. Until then the program had been referred to as a Master of Religious Education (M.R.E.) degree. Would it be appropriate, he wondered, to call the degree a Master of Christian Education (M.C.E.)? Lubbers was asked to study the matter and report back to the faculty.[78] After communicating with Dr. Jesse Ziegler, associate director of AATS, and based on Austin Seminary's nomenclature for the degree, Lubbers moved that the degree program at Western be renamed Master of Christian Education. Supported by John Piet, the motion was carried.[79]

Work on the new degree program proceeded, with Lubbers presenting a report to the faculty at its February 13, 1963, meeting. The relation of M.C.E. candidates to B.D. candidates in matters such as chapel leadership, student council leadership, and financial aid were discussed. There was considerable discussion about junior M.C.E. candidates engaging in catechetical instruction before they had received instruction in method and theology. Lubbers proposed that junior M.C.E. candidates spend a year observing pedagogical practices before teaching in churches. In the end, Piet, supported by Oudersluys, moved adoption of Lubbers's recommendation. It was carried. Bruggink then moved that implementation details be studied by the Practical Department and reported back to the faculty. The M.C.E. program was endorsed by the faculty with a starting date in September 1963.[80]

Western's two-year M.C.E. curriculum consisted of ninety hours of academic work, twelve of which were taken as elective courses in the Practical Department. The emphasis on biblical (thirty hours) and theological (thirty-three hours) courses was consistent with Lubbers's belief that "...one cannot separate preparation for the ministry of education from preparation for the ministry of the Word, for they are both approaches to the same goal, the proclamation of the gospel."[81]

There were two required Christian education courses for M.C.E. students: CE221 "History and Theology of Christian Education" and

---

[78] Western Theological Seminary, *Faculty Minutes*, August 13, 1962.
[79] Ibid., September 4, 1962.
[80] Ibid., February 13, 1963.
[81] Lubbers, letter to President Harold N. Englund, March 19, 1962, 2.

CE331 "Curriculum Analysis and Organizing Principles." In addition, M.C.E. students took five elective courses, four of which were to be chosen from among Christian education elective courses. These included courses in ministry with the three basic age groups (adults, youth, and children) and families, communication, drama, the role of the Bible, educational aspects of worship, administering a church's education program, the work of a director of Christian education, and the church and higher education.[82]

Apart from her leadership role in the development of Western's M.C.E. degree, Lubbers also helped shape the first-year experience for Bachelor of Divinity (now Master of Divinity) students. First-year students were often expected to perform ministerial duties as part of their part-time field work, even though they lacked preparation for these responsibilities. As a result of conversations with Henry Quinius at Austin Seminary, Lubbers developed an expanded year-long program of observation in congregations and in the community. First-year students were required to observe church life in different congregations for two quarters and observe aspects of community life in the third quarter. Students were assigned to visit a hospital emergency room, ride in a police car, and meet with court officers and social workers. These experiences took place in Grand Rapids (outside the seminary's Holland and Ottawa County context) at St. Mary's Hospital, with the Grand Rapids Police Department, the Kent County Department of Social Welfare, and the Kent County Juvenile Court.[83]

Students responded to Lubbers in a variety of ways. For some students Lubbers was too liberal, while others thought her too conservative.[84] Recalling his positive experience in Lubbers's class, Bruce Laverman (B.D., 1965) said, "She pushed the envelope a little for us, but that's what all professors are supposed to do." Laverman added that he "learned a good deal from her about the origin of the Sunday school movement and Christian education in general."[85] Another student, Karl Overbeek (B.D., 1966), found her to be "a good teacher." Reflecting on his experience, he wrote:

> Maybe she had a bit of an edge to her—kind of enjoyed being in a "cutting-edge" position as a woman. It seems to me she didn't put

---

[82] Western Seminary *Calendar and Bulletin, 1963-1964*, 19-20.
[83] Western Theological Seminary, *Faculty Minutes*, August 19, 1964.
[84] This perception was shared with the author by Stanley A. Rock (Class of 1966) April 1, 2008.
[85] Bruce Laverman, in e-mail correspondence with the author, April 26, 2008.

up with a lot of nonsense stuff in regards to old school thinking and behaving.[86]

The adjective "cutting-edge" is one that appears frequently in comments about Lubbers.

Charlotte M. Heinen, the first and only woman student on campus at the time, offered a description that summarizes Lubbers's qualities as a teacher:

> Mrs. Lubbers was the kind of professor who was very interested in getting to know the students in her class. She was also available to talk with me and the other students on campus at any time during the school hours when she was not teaching a class. She was a wonderful teacher, always ready to review, and to help us with any questions we had—about our classwork, or just to talk with us as individuals! She was always ready to encourage us to be the best STUDENT that we could be! She also challenged us to stretch our minds and to be interested in subjects that were beyond what we were studying in our classes![87]

In a petition to president-elect Ridder, the class of 1963 wrote:

> As seniors we want to take this opportunity to express to you our high regard for Professor E. Lubbers. She has been a great help to us in seeing the possibilities of Christian education. We hope that you will appreciate our enthusiasm for the help and instruction she has given us this year. In terms of our practical preparation for the parish ministry we feel that her course has been one of the most helpful in our seminary training.[88]

While not all Western students may have appreciated Lubbers's teaching, the majority resonated with the sentiments of the class of 1963.

Lubbers's impact on graduates of Western Seminary was observed by one Reformed Church in America staff member. In a memorandum to then president Herman J. Ridder, Arthur O. Van Eck, who was

---

[86] Karl Overbeek, in e-mail correspondence with the author, April 29, 2008.
[87] Charlotte M. Heinen, in personal correspondence with George Brown, Jr., September 17, 2008. Later ordained as a minister of Word and sacrament in the Reformed Church in America, Heinen was the first graduate of Western's new M.C.E. degree in 1965.
[88] Quoted in H.J. Ridder and E.M. Eenigenburg, Recommendation Relative to Professor Elaine Lubbers, January, 1964.

director of adult education with the Board of Education from 1963-1968, wrote, "Believe me, as I have gone through the church, the boys who had her for Christian education, for the most part, were deeply involved and committed to the kind of Christian education which wrestles with the nature and the mission of the church."[89]

Reformed Church in America staff members who were responsible for Christian education at the denominational level appreciated Lubbers's contributions to the field in her position as a seminary professor. Arthur O. Van Eck remembers her as "a breath of fresh air." He reports that she was very bright and tended to rub conservatives the wrong way.[90] Upon learning that the seminary board had approved a recommendation to reappoint Lubbers in 1964, Bernard J. Mulder, executive secretary of the RCA's Board of Education, wrote in a congratulatory letter to Ridder: "This is what we need at Western and for the Church, and no more suitable or competent person could be found anywhere."

Mulder underlined the importance of Lubbers's position at the seminary for the denomination's program of Christian education:

> With the inception of the Covenant Life Curriculum the training of seminary students in its nature and use is most necessary. You are opening the door to this possibility, and in this respect the Board of Education and the Theological Seminary will be walking along together in a very beautiful way.[91]

Of course, not everyone shared Mulder's appreciation for this new curriculum.

Lubbers's contributions to the field of Christian education while she was at Western extend beyond curriculum and classroom. The aforementioned article on adult education published in the *International Journal of Religious Education* is not the only example of Lubbers's writing. Shortly after arriving at Western, Lubbers wrote an article for the *Church Herald*. "Test Your Teaching" appeared in a regular feature entitled, "Tested Techniques for Teachers."[92] In this article, Lubbers sought to make a case for testing as a means of program

---

[89] Arthur O. Van Eck, memorandum to Herman J. Ridder following Lubbers's resignation, July 6, 1965.
[90] Arthur O. Van Eck, in a conversation over lunch with the author at the Association of Presbyterian Church Educators meeting in San Diego, February 12, 2008.
[91] Bernard J. Mulder, letter to President Herman Ridder, January 13, 1964.
[92] Elaine Lubbers, "Test Your Teaching," *Church Herald*, January 4, 1963, 8-9.

evaluation, noting both the value and inevitability of evaluation. She identified some common objections to testing and described three types of testing: testing for *"factual information,"* for *"understanding,"* and *"changes in attitudes or Christian growth."*

In addition to the article written for the *Church Herald* and the Covenant Life Curriculum resource, *Families within the Family*, during her time at Western Seminary, Lubbers wrote three articles on Christian education for the *Reformed Review*.[93] If the *Church Herald* article was written in a popular style for a general audience of lay volunteers, the three articles in the *Reformed Review* were more scholarly in character. In her 1964 article, "The Education of the Christian Layman," she saw educating for mission as the greatest challenge for adult education. The article reflected convictions that grew out of Lubbers's experience with adult education at the Parkway Presbyterian Church and her engagement with the Faith and Life Community in Austin. In the article, "On Learning Forgiveness from the Perspective of Christian Education" (September, 1965), she explored the role that a forgiving community plays in how people learn a theology of forgiveness. Forgiveness was a topic addressed by Rachel Henderlite, her mentor and former colleague at the Board of Christian Education in Richmond.[94] Lubbers wrote about the importance of relationships for learning in "The Dynamics of Learning in Christian Education," her third and last article for the *Reformed Review* (December, 1965).

There is some evidence that Lubbers's place at the faculty table was changing in early 1965. During the 1962-1963 academic year, she served on three faculty committees: Curriculum, Public Relations, and Student Council. She is not listed as serving on any faculty committee in the 1964-1965 academic year, although in the fall of 1964 she served on the Academic Events Committee for the seminary's centennial celebration.

Lubbers resigned in the summer of 1965 and took a position as director of Christian education at the Eastminster Presbyterian Church in Grand Rapids, Michigan.[95] Her resignation seems unexpected

[93] "The Education of the Christian Layman," 18, no. 1 (September, 1964): 3-15; "On Learning Forgiveness from the Perspective of Christian Education," 19, no. 1 (September, 1965): 18-24; and "The Dynamics of Learning in Christian Education," 19, no. 2 (December, 1965): 27-36.
[94] Cf. Rachel Henderlite, *Forgiveness and Hope: A Theological Basis for Christian Education* (Richmond: John Knox, 1961).
[95] Western Theological Seminary, *Faculty Minutes*, July 2, 1965; Minutes of the Annual Meeting of the Board of Trustees of Western Theological Seminary, 1966, 41.

and abrupt. At the end of March, she had written President Ridder, confirming her intention to take her "summer vacation" in the fall quarter of the 1965-1966 academic year in order to take courses at either Western Michigan University or Michigan State University. In the same letter, she related plans to join Roy Fairchild, J.C. Wynn., and Bill Genne, members of the adult education staff of the PCUS Board of Christian Education at a workshop in June at Montreat in order to do some "creative thinking in regard to the Home and Family Nurture Program in the Covenant Life Curriculum."[96] In a letter dated April 5, 1965, Ridder responded, confirming these arrangements.

In January of 1964, the seminary's board had received a recommendation from Ridder and Eenigenburg, the acting academic dean, urging the board to retain Lubbers as assistant professor. The recommendation cited Lubbers's "high intelligence," her role in developing and implementing the new M.C.E. degree, her teaching, teamwork, her commitment to the Reformed faith, and her place on the "growing edge" of theological education as reasons for extending her appointment.[97]

The suddenness of Lubbers's resignation gave rise to speculation that she had been forced out by more conservative elements on the seminary board and in the church. There was some resistance to being taught by a woman on the part of some students. However, Lubbers's views on the interpretation of scripture and her association with the Covenant Life Curriculum were also sources of tension and conflict. Lubbers's advocacy for the curriculum, along with her Presbyterian affiliation, was linked in the minds of some with the tension across the denomination over conversations about a proposed merger of the RCA with the PCUS and with criticism of the new curriculum. The latter, as Bruce Laverman observed, was "a hot button issue at the time."[98]

Many in the Reformed Church believed the Covenant Life Curriculum to be liberal in its theological and biblical content and difficult for teachers to use. In a letter to the editor of the *Church Herald*, a Zeeland church member wrote,

> We have been very disturbed by the use of the Covenant Life Curriculum in our Reformed Church and by the recommendation

---

[96] Elaine Lubbers, letter to Herman J. Ridder, March 31, 1965.
[97] H.J. Ridder and E.M. Eenigenburg, Recommendation Relative to Professor Elaine Lubbers, January, 1964.
[98] Bruce Laverman, in e-mail correspondence with the author, April 26, 2008.

for its use by the General Synod. The teachings do not all hold to the Bible as the perfect and infallible Word of God, and therefore should not be considered as proper instruction.[99]

The Classis of South Grand Rapids instructed its agent on education, the Reverend Warren Burgess, to write the *Church Herald* about *Into Covenant Life,* a Covenant Life Curriculum resource used in a study session prior to a meeting of the classis. In a letter to the editor, Burgess expressed both appreciation and criticism of this resource. Several positive things were noted:

> The use of this study book has led many of our people to ask more specifically, "What does the Reformed Church believe?"; it has, because of its catechetical basis, been a welcome review for families long in the Reformed Church, and a new study to those who have come to us from other communions; it has been appreciated, because of its systematic arrangement and presentation; it has made for larger class preparation and new-found interest in Bible study; and it has been found to be very useful where the class was led by a well-qualified teacher.

At the same time, Burgess noted, "On the other hand, we deprecate the study book's neo-orthodox orientation."

There were other signs that stress was taking a toll on Lubbers. Members of the class of 1965 had come to Western at the same time as Lubbers and had experienced a kind of bond with her. One member of the class recalled a light-hearted moment in a course with Lubbers in which the mood shifted suddenly as she began to cry.[100] At some point that spring she was also hospitalized briefly for exhaustion.[101]

While it is undoubtedly true that the climate at Western in the early 1960s was stressful for Lubbers, the reasons for her resignation are to be found as much in her basic commitment to her family as in any institutional factors. Two factors in particular weighed heavily in her decision: the needs of her four children, then nineteen, eighteen, fourteen, and twelve years of age; and the needs of Ed's aging parents.

On Saturday, October 5, 1963, a head-on collision on Riley Street, a two-lane road leading toward Lake Michigan on Holland's

---

[99] P.R.Van Eenenaam, letter to the editor, *Church Herald*, 21, no. 45:20.
[100] The incident was related to the author by a member of the class of 1965 in a telephone conversation May 8, 2008.
[101] Douglas Lubbers in a phone conversation with George Brown, Jr., May 7, 2008.

north side, took the lives of five young people: West Ottawa high school seniors Todd Hilbink and Thomas Fairbanks and Fairbanks's thirteen-year-old sister Jeanne, Pamela Bradley, also thirteen years old, and David Van Overloop, a college freshman.[102] All five were riding in a convertible driven by Thomas Fairbanks. The deaths had a deep impact on the entire Holland community and were keenly felt in the Lubbers household, especially by Jill—a classmate of Fairbanks and Hilbink—and by Paul.

In addition to tending to the emotional needs of her children as they mourned the loss of their friends, Ed's parents were becoming increasingly dependent on her. Ed had been the only child of Nick and Anna Lubbers, an immigrant couple, and they looked to their daughter-in-law for support. There were frequent trips to Grand Rapids to tend to their needs. Lubbers began to experience what today would be recognized as "compassion fatigue."[103]

Given the churches' demand for staff to direct their programs of Christian education, it is not surprising that Lubbers would receive inquiries about her availability. When there was an opening at Eastminster Presbyterian Church in Grand Rapids, Lubbers saw an opportunity to meet her family's needs more adequately. With Clark a sophomore at the University of Michigan in Ann Arbor and Jill about to enter her freshman year at Western Michigan University in Kalamazoo, Grand Rapids seemed like an ideal central location from which to coordinate the care of her children and her aging in-laws.

Lubbers's ministry at Eastminster was short. In February of 1966, she informed the congregation that she was accepting an invitation to become director of Christian education at the Grosse Pointe Memorial Church, a 3,500-member Presbyterian Church in suburban Detroit. This move, after serving only a few months as director of Christian education at Eastminster, was grounded in Lubbers's continuing concern to provide for her family. There were increased financial pressures with Clark now in his second year at the University of Michigan and Jill in her first year at Western Michigan University, so the better salary offered by Grosse Pointe Memorial was a significant factor in her decision.[104]

---

[102] "Five Killed in Two-Car Crash," *Holland Evening Sentinel*, Monday, October 7, 1963, 1.

[103] Douglas Lubbers in a phone conversation with George Brown, Jr., May 7, 2008.

[104] Elaine Lubbers, letter to the congregation at Eastminster Presbyterian Church, February 9, 1966.

In late 1967, Lubbers moved from Grosse Pointe, Michigan, to Colorado Springs, Colorado. She had suffered a heart attack and decided it was best to live near her brother, Herman.[105] The move provided important support for her and stability for her children.

Lubbers earned an M.A. degree in education and sociology from Western State College in Gunnison, Colorado, in 1967 and returned to teaching. She taught sixth grade at Roosevelt School in District 11 of the Colorado Springs public schools until 1975, when she was hired by the Colorado Springs Police Department, first as director of the volunteer program and then as director of youth counseling. Lubbers worked for the police department until 1980.[106]

Lubbers's decision to seek employment outside the institutional church may be explained in part by a comment in a 1972 interview with Cyd Shewchuk, a staff writer for the *Colorado Springs Sun* newspaper. Lubbers told Shewchuk that her experience as an assistant pastor at Grosse Pointe led her to the conclusion that she could "do more for people as a layman than as a pastor." Lubbers was disturbed by the inconsistency between the congregation's preaching about integration and its actual practice. Lubbers said, "The mark of a professional churchman cut me off from the world....I can work more creatively outside of the traditional institution."[107]

While earning a living through employment outside the church, Lubbers was involved in a number of volunteer activities and part-time church-related work in Colorado Springs. She planned and led workshops and seminars at the local church, presbytery, and synod levels and served on the General Council of the Presbytery of Pueblo and chaired the Presbytery's Christian Education Committee. From 1968 to 1970, Lubbers was a paid consultant to LOGOS, an ecumenical center in Colorado Springs. She was a consultant to the chaplain at the Air Force Academy for their church school program.[108] A Presbytery Leadership Development Grant funded a position that Lubbers filled for three years. From 1970 to 1973, she worked with twenty-six mountain churches under the provisions of the grant.[109] Lubbers

---

[105] Douglas Lubbers, e-mail to George Brown, Jr., May 5, 2008.
[106] Presbyterian Church U.S.A. Personal Information Form for Elaine Lubbers, September 26, 1980, 2.
[107] Cyd Shewchuk, "Teacher and preacher becomes articulate critic of churches," *Colorado Springs Sun*, January 13, 1972, 11.
[108] Cyd Shewchuk, 11.
[109] Presbyterian Church U.S.A. Personal Information Form for Elaine Lubbers, 2.

served as a ruling elder at the Gateway United Presbyterian Church in Colorado Springs.[110]

In contrast to the view she expressed in the 1972 newspaper interview, Lubbers's involvement at the congregational and Presbytery levels was moving her closer toward ordained ministry. In 1976, she took twelve hours of graduate courses at Iliff School of Theology in Denver.[111] In 1979, Lubbers decided to seek ordination in the Presbyterian Church U.S.A. and in September of 1980 completed the denomination's Personal Information Form as part of the process for ordination.[112]

If death had not intervened, Lubbers and her son, Brent Douglas— a senior M.Div. candidate at Princeton Theological Seminary—would have appeared before the Presbytery of Pueblo for ordination. On January 21, 1981, Elaine Elizabeth Lubbers died during surgery to replace an artificial valve in her heart.

Teaching, mission, the ministry of the laity, and the importance of families were four important themes in Lubbers's life and ministry. Teaching in public schools served as a set of book ends that bracketed her teaching in churches and in the seminary. She started as a public school teacher in Iowa and Michigan, and, after serving as a director of Christian education for churches and as a seminary professor, returned to the public school classroom in Colorado Springs. Whether in seminary or church or public school, first and foremost Lubbers was a teacher.

The purpose of Christian education, in Lubbers's thought, was mission. "If the church is defined by her mission, which is to declare the good news of God's redemption in Jesus Christ," she wrote, "then the primary task of education is equipment for mission."[113] As Lubbers saw it, the problem with the church was that it focused more on membership than on discipleship. She pointed out:

> The call to discipleship continues to be a call to mission. Christian education is the education of the Christian for his reason for being. As Israel was elected for service, so we are called out only to be "sent back in." *Worship* in [sic.] our response; *Nurture* our responsibility; and *Mission* our reasonable service.[114]

---

[110] *Colorado Springs Gazette Telegraph*, January 23, 1981, A:4:1.
[111] Presbyterian Church U.S.A. Personal Information Form for Elaine Lubbers, 2.
[112] Ibid., 1.
[113] Lubbers, "The Education of the Christian Layman," 3.
[114] Ibid., 15.

Lubbers's interest in mission can be traced back to the period she spent in Cairo under the auspices of the Reformed Church's Board of World Mission. It is further reflected in the resource she wrote for Friendship Press, *A Guide for Early Teens on Mission: The Christian's Calling* (1965).

For Lubbers, the missional thrust of Christian education had to be linked closely to the role of the laity. Her efforts in adult education at the Parkway Presbyterian Church were aimed at equipping laity for mission. In relation to the adult education program at Parkway, Lubbers wrote: "If the doctrine of the priesthood of all believers is to become a reality in their lives, lay people must be given an opportunity to fulfill their rightful role as disciples of the living Lord."[115] Her brief involvement with the Faith and Life Community in Austin reflects her commitment to the ministry of the laity. She articulated this theme most clearly in "The Education of the Christian Layman," in which she wrote, "Laymen are called to the vocation of ministry and discipleship which is fulfilled basically in the arena of their occupation."[116]

An interest in families was a constant theme throughout Lubbers's life and ministry. It appears in her work for the Board of Christian Education of the PCUS and in the family life resource she wrote for the Covenant Life Curriculum. Her interest in families is also found in her work with Colorado Springs Police Department. Recognizing the effect of stress on the marriages of police officers, Lubbers helped organize a workshop for police wives.[117]

In appointing Lubbers, Western Theological Seminary brought to the teaching of Christian education courses someone with formal training in Christian education, experience directing the program of Christian education in a local church, and the expertise of a denominational staff person familiar with curriculum design and development. The seminary also created a place at the table for a woman. Lubbers recognized herself as a pioneer and realized that the role of pioneer evoked resistance. Lubbers told her son Brent Douglas, "I broke the ground. Sometimes that's the critical task."[118]

---

[115] Elaine Lubbers, "A Serious Approach to Adult Education," 12.
[116] Elaine Lubbers, "The Education of the Christian Layman," 4.
[117] Gene Birkhead, "Police Wives Coping with Stress," *Colorado Springs Sun*, Thursday, September 15, 1977, 9.
[118] Brent Douglas Lubbers, in a telephone conversation with George Brown, Jr., May 7, 2008.

Conclusion

Finding a place at the faculty table at Western Theological Seminary was not easy for Elaine Lubbers. There were not only the challenges of being the first woman to serve on what had been an all male faculty teaching only men. She was also a single parent, with four children to raise on her own. Her ties to the Presbyterian Church and her involvement with the Covenant Life Curriculum were not viewed with enthusiasm in some quarters of the Reformed Church. And while some of Western's faculty lacked the requisite doctorate, for a woman to serve with only a master's degree was not quite regarded in the same light.

As Marjorie Nelson noted in an interview, after graduating from Austin Presbyterian Theological Seminary, Lubbers had wanted to be a minister but was unable to do so.[119] Shortly after her arrival at Western Seminary, Lubbers applied for admission to the Bachelor of Divinity program. Dean Ten Clay presented her application to a special meeting of the faculty September 4, 1962. His recommendation that she be a candidate for the B.D. degree was supported by Lester J. Kuyper and approved by vote of the faculty.[120] While Lubbers did not complete the B.D. degree, in 1962 she took the three-course sequence in biblical Hebrew, courses in homiletics and principles of preaching, and a course on the pastor as family counselor.

It is clear that Lubbers helped create a place for women at Western Theological Seminary. While enduring learner resistance, she helped change student attitudes and expectations. While experiencing the limitations of being the woman in a community of scholars where men where in the majority, she demonstrated a level of competence that instilled respect and brought recognition.

Lubbers also made significant contributions to the field of Christian education. Among these were contributions to the family life emphasis of the Covenant Life Curriculum and the implementation of the first professional degree in Christian religious education at an RCA seminary. As a result of her teaching, many seminarians entered parish ministry with a deeper appreciation for the church's teaching ministry.

Elaine Lubbers left her imprint on theological education. It was Lubbers who first recognized that first-year students were better served

---

[119] Marjorie Nelson, interviewed by Kate Weigand, May 18-19, 2005, North Hampton, Mass. Transcript: Tape 1 of 5, 18. © Sophia Smith Collection 2006.

[120] Western Theological Seminary, *Faculty Minutes*, September 4, 1962.

by observing ministry in the church and the community context than by engaging directly in ministry in congregational settings before being introduced to the basic skills of preaching, teaching, and caring. This was an important contribution to Western's B.D. curriculum in the 1960s. One can only wonder what else Lubbers might have accomplished had she been given more time to develop as a seminary professor.

Perhaps most important of all, Elaine Lubbers accomplished the critical task of breaking the ground by becoming the first woman professor to find a place at Western Seminary's faculty table.

CHAPTER 3

Frances Davis Beardslee and the Leading Ladies of Holland, Michigan, 1912-1917

Mary L. Kansfield

To most outside observers, Holland, Michigan, in 1912 would have seemed quaint, flourishing, and unassuming. Strategically located on the eastern shore of Lake Michigan at the mouth of the Black River, the Dutch immigrant city boasted a population of 11,800. Most of its residents had migrated to the United States from the Netherlands in 1847 and the years immediately following under the leadership of the Reverend Albertus C. Van Raalte. These residents took pride in their city's thriving industrial life and in the central role that their churches played in the life of the community. Their commitment to education and to the training of pastors and missionaries was reflected in the founding of Hope College and Western Theological Seminary, both institutions of the Reformed Church in America. Social and intellectual life for city residents, especially women, revolved around the church, these two educational institutions, and a number of interlocking social and community-service organizations.[1] But by 1912, the residents of

---
[1] For a broad overview of the interrelatedness of women's church, educational, service, and social organizations, especially the home and foreign mission societies, the Women's Christian Temperance Union

this pious, Dutch-Calvinist enclave had begun to feel a tension between two powerful but divergent forces. On the one hand, they wished fervently to enter the mainstream of American life. On the other, they sought to maintain their Dutch culture and values.

Within the interplay of this tension, the announcement of John W. Beardslee, Jr.'s intention to marry Frances Davis came as shocking news to the Holland community and a bitter disappointment to many mothers who had hoped to see their marriageable daughters wed to the community's most eligible bachelor. That "most eligible" bachelor, John Walter Beardslee, Jr., was a professor at Hope College[2]—a classics scholar, theologian, and icon of scholarly and cultural refinement. And that bachelor had chosen a bride. The bride he chose was not like most of the young women of Holland. She was not ethnically Dutch, nor had she grown up within the Dutch Reformed church tradition. Having been raised in Connecticut and Massachusetts, she was an "outsider" in almost every way.[3]

(WCTU), and the Young Men's/Women's Christian Associations, see Anne Firor Scott, *Natural Allies: Women's Associations in American History* (Urbana and Chicago: Univ. of Illinois Press, 1992). See also Barbara Brown Zikmund, "Women's Organizations: Centers of Denominational Loyalty and Expressions of Christian Unity," in Jackson Carroll and Wade Clark Roof, eds. *Beyond Establishment: Protestant Identity in a Post-Protestant Age* (Louisville: Westminster John Knox, 1993), 116-56.

[2] According to the *2002 Hope College Alumni Directory*, John Walter Beardslee, Jr., began teaching Latin at Hope College in 1900. He became instructor in ethics and evidences and Christianity in 1903, professor in 1905, professor of ethics in 1909, and Rodman Professor of Latin in 1912. In 1913, he resigned from the Hope faculty to become professor of biblical languages and literature at Western Theological Seminary. There he became professor of New Testament in 1916. In 1917 he was elected Thomas DeWitt Professor of Hellenic Greek and New Testament Exegesis at New Brunswick Theological Seminary, where he served through 1949. He served as president of New Brunswick from 1936-1947.

[3] John Beardslee's bride was raised in Connecticut and Massachusetts. Her mother, Ellen Rigby Davis (1850-1943), was an 1871 graduate of Cornell College in Mount Vernon, Iowa, a frontier, Methodist, coeducational college. She was involved in the work of the church her entire life. When the bride started high school in 1900, the family moved to Wellesley Hills, Massachusetts. Because the closest church within walking distance from their home was the Wellesley Hills Congregational Church, it became their church home. The bride was a member of that church before she met John Walter Beardslee, Jr., in Chicago.

The young professor had been in his final year of graduate study at the University of Chicago when he met Davis.[4] She had come to Chicago as a doctoral student in classics, and for two academic quarters in 1909 Beardslee and Davis had taken the same required classes in Greek tragedy. Davis was a graduate of Wellesley College, a women's college in Massachusetts. As a result of her stellar academic record in classics, Davis had been admitted to the University of Chicago's graduate school with no deficiencies. Beardslee, on the other hand, a graduate of Hope College, had entered the University of Chicago with four deficiencies. No doubt this difference was the result of the limited number of course offerings in classics at Hope College at that time. Following completion of her master's degree and after taking two additional quarters of graduate study, Davis abruptly dropped out of the Chicago doctoral program[5] and pursued a master's degree in library science at Simmons College in Massachusetts.

---

[4] My interest in the life and work of Frances Davis Beardslee began shortly after my husband became president of New Brunswick Theological Seminary in 1993 and our family moved into the President's House at 25 Seminary Place. For thirty-three years the house had been the home of Frances and John Walter Beardslee, Jr., and their five children, the oldest of whom, John Walter Beardslee III, served on the New Brunswick faculty as an emeritus faculty member. Stories about Frances Beardslee were legion.

For forty-seven years of her life in New Brunswick (1917-1975), Frances Beardslee enjoyed membership in the Travelers' Club. This club continues today as a women's literary club, where thirty women gather twice a month during the academic year to present research papers on a given theme. Meetings are held in members' homes, and during Frances Beardslee's years as a member, many club meetings took place at "number twenty-five." My own life has been enriched by membership in the Travelers' Club. When members arrived for the first club meeting at our home, older club members expressed delight to be back in familiar surroundings. Without so much as batting an eye, one older club member turned to me and asked how it felt "to be living in Frances Beardslee's house?" And so I began to investigate this remarkable woman's life in the hope of one day writing her biography.

[5] For a more complete analysis of Frances Davis's educational experience at the University of Chicago and possible reasons for her failure to complete the doctoral program, see "Chicago 1892: Frances Davis and the University of Chicago," a paper prepared and presented by Mary Kansfield to the Travelers' Club of New Brunswick, New Jersey, March 21, 2000. Papers of the Travelers' Club are available in the archives of Rutgers University, Alexander Library, Rutgers the State University, New Brunswick, New Jersey.

This return to the East appears not to have dimmed the courtship. On August 8, 1912, John Walter Beardslee, Jr., and Frances Eunice Davis were married in Boston in a modest ceremony in the bride's home,[6] conducted by the groom's father. Shortly thereafter, the new Mrs. Beardslee arrived in Holland.

Once she had moved into the elegant Beardslee family home at 26 East 12th Street, Frances Beardslee took up housekeeping responsibilities for her new husband and her widowed father-in-law, the Reverend Dr. John Walter Beardslee, Sr. The senior Beardslee had served on the faculty of Western Theological Seminary since 1888 as professor of biblical literature, and over the years his presence in the affairs of church, school, and community was widely recognized and deeply respected. His beloved wife, Sarah, had died in 1909,[7] preceded in death by their older son, the Reverend William Armitage Beardslee.[8] After Sarah Beardslee's death, John Sr. and John Jr. had lived together alone until the new Mrs. Beardslee arrived to begin married life and to take up her responsibilities as wife and daughter-in-law.

Beginning in the 1880s, a term had been coined that generally described middle-class, college-educated women who were independent-minded and sought to work outside the home or to volunteer for myriad charitable and civic causes. These women were called "new women," and Frances Davis Beardslee certainly qualified for that designation. Author Betty A. DeBerg describes the new women this way:

> This new generation of women activists, the New Women, had been born and reared within the limits set by the separate-spheres ideology of the Victorian middle class. They based their work and arguments on the assumptions of gender-specific spheres and character. Women's leadership in the public realm, from temperance to suffrage to church ministry, was desirable and necessary, they argued, because women were uniquely qualified to protect the home and all the virtues associated with it. Late nineteen-century women's rights activity had wider appeal than

---

[6] As reported in the *Holland Daily Sentinel* (*HDS*), August 9, 1912, 8.
[7] Sarah Eliza Armitage was born February 25, 1838, and married John Walter Beardslee in Constantine, Michigan, February 22, 1866. Sarah Beardslee died in Holland, Michigan, April 17, 1909, at age seventy-one.
[8] William Armitage Beardslee was born April 4, 1867, in Constantine, Michigan. He graduated from Rutgers College in 1888 and New Brunswick Theological Seminary in 1891. He served three RCA churches in New York State and died Oct 19, 1897, in Holland, Michigan, presumably from tuberculosis.

its earlier counterpart. And, although it never directly refuted the prevailing notions of male and female gender roles and identity, it was, on the basis of numbers alone, much more startling and obvious evidence that conventional middle-class gender ideology, so fragile and important to American men, was beginning to crumble.[9]

From 1912 to 1917, Frances Beardslee made the city of Holland her home. To the residents of Holland, Michigan, she clearly was a Yankee outsider and a new woman.[10] How was it possible for this new woman, this outsider, to find acceptance in the tightly knit, socially conservative Dutch community? In what organizations would she seek acceptance, and who were the women leaders in the community from whom she would find welcome?

[9] Betty A. DeBerg, *Ungodly Women: Gender and the First Wave of American Fundamentalism* (Minneapolis: Augsburg Fortress, 1990), 28.

Such an understanding of New Women found expression in the *Annual Report of the Board of Foreign Missions* to the General Synod of 1896, where the Woman's Board of Foreign Missions described their work in India thus:

Woman's work for women is being actively extended. If the preaching columns do show the *minus* sign, those relating to "Zenana and Bible Women's Work" show the opposite very largely. Nearly every station is making special efforts in this direction, and the "shut-ins" are hearing new and wonderful things from their more free sisters. Of course, our Hindu Girls' Schools are the great aids in opening doors to our workers. The girls get a taste for education and advance in these schools, and insist on further opportunity for improvement in their own houses. We already begin to see the "new woman" here and there. Not the objectionable type we hear of, but one emerging from centuries of darkness into new light and new privileges. An instance in point is that of a well-educated young girl who absolutely refused to marry an ignorant man appointed for her, until he should pass a certain literary examination which would make him a fitter companion. The young man "went away sorrowful," but with a new purpose, and wonder to relate, studied, passed the prescribed test and now rejoices in the immediate prospect of realized hope: and this *in India!* Such new women are worth while.

[10] Sara Winter Zwemer (Mrs. Theodore F. Zwemer) graduated from Hope College in 1916. She had taken John W. Beardslee, Jr.'s course in ethics in her senior year, and during that year she boarded with an aunt who lived on 12th Street, next door to the Beardslee family. In an interview in 1996 with the Rev. Dr. William Armitage Beardslee, Frances Beardslee's son, Sara Zwemer, at one hundred years of age, recalled "with a sparkle" when the new Mrs. Beardslee arrived in town. Said Zwemer, "There was a lot of talk about this foreign woman in this Holland Dutch community." Letter from William A. Beardslee to Mary Kansfield dated June 22, 1996, in the possession of the author.

To answer these questions, an analysis has been made of the following organizations to which Frances Beardslee belonged and for which some historical documents or newspaper accounts are available[11]: Hope Church Ladies' Aid Society, Hope Church Ladies' Missionary Society, the Holland Classical Union, the Woman's Literary Club, the Century Club, the Daughters of the American Revolution, and the Holland Chapter of the Michigan Equal Suffrage Association. Within this essay, first, the character of these organizations will be identified. Second, their membership lists will be analyzed to learn who the women were who figured most prominently in leadership roles in Holland during the period 1912-1917. Third, Frances Beardslee's relationship with these leaders will be detailed.

The Ladies' Aid Society

When Frances Beardslee arrived in Holland in 1912, sixteen churches, representing six different church traditions, served the religious life of the community.[12] Until the conclusion of World War I, the use of the Dutch language figured prominently in the life of the community. In homes, in shops, and in worship, Dutch was often the preferred language at the time of Frances Beardslee's arrival. It was for English-speaking residents of the community (especially the members of the college faculty and their families from the East) that Hope Church had been established in 1862, as an English-language

---

[11] It is lamentable that archival materials needed to document the civic involvements and reform efforts of Holland's women have either not been saved or have yet to attract the attention of scholars to tell about the heroic efforts of these women. For example, no records have been collected for the Holland or Ottawa County chapters of the Equal Suffrage Club. The story of Holland's Women's Christian Temperance Union, the largest of Holland's reform groups, has yet to be told. Both of these women's reform groups exerted immense influence in the community. Historical records for Hope College's Susan B. Anthony Chapter of the Collegiate Suffrage Association and the Hope College Young Women's Christian Association likewise need to be collected if the stories of college women are to be told.

[12] According to the *Holland Michigan City Directory 1913-1914*, these churches included one Episcopal church, one Evangelical Lutheran church, two Methodist churches, five Reformed and five Christian Reformed churches, one Roman Catholic church, and one Church of God. *Holland Michigan City Directory 1913-1914*, published by Wilkinson-Ryan Co., Holland, Mich., and found in the Joint Archives of Holland, located at Hope College, Holland, Michigan (JAH).

congregation. Hope Church was the second Reformed congregation founded in Holland.[13]

Frances Beardslee was received into the membership of Hope Church October 6, 1912. She immediately became a member of the Ladies' Aid Society. From the founding of this congregation,[14] women had worked collectively to contribute materially to the church's welfare, to evangelize, and to show pastoral care to those both within and beyond the congregation. The Ladies' Aid Society raised funds routinely for items beyond the reach of the congregation's general budget and exercised physical care to keep the church building "Dutch clean."[15]

According to its Constitution of 1883,[16] two standing committees existed within the Ladies' Aid organization—a Visiting Committee and a

[13] In his essay "The Classis of Holland: A brief History," which appears in *In Christ's Service: The Classis of Holland and Its Congregations 1847-1997* (Holland: the Classis of Holland Reformed Church in America), 1997, 6, Elton Bruins points out:

> In a report of the Particular Synod of Chicago in 1906, it was noted that two congregations of the Classis of Holland used only English in worship, three had an English service every Sunday, six had an English service monthly, and five had English services "occasionally." So sixteen congregations had English in worship to a greater or lesser extent. But six of the twenty-two congregations in the Classis at that time used (only) Dutch solely [sic.] in worship. Not until the World War I era did the use of Dutch diminish—in large part because the American public, which despised the German nation and anything German, often confused Dutch with German. However, Dutch was in continuous use much longer. In a very unusual move, the Seventh Reformed Church was organized in 1924 by Holland Classis to serve Dutch-speaking people exclusively; the congregation was disbanded after the death of its pastor, Paul Van Eerden, in 1947.

[14] It is interesting to note that when Hope Church was formally organized within the Classis of Michigan on July 20, 1862, its ten charter members formed a gender-balanced group of five men and five women. They included "Bernardus Ledeboer, M.D. and his wife Alide Goetschius, Bernardus Grotenhuis, Margaret Ann Jordan Phelps, wife of Dr. Philip Phelps, William B. Gilmore, Henry D. Post and his wife, Ann Coatsworth, Charles F. Post, Mrs. James Lipp nee Elizabeth Welcher, and Mrs. Brodmore, a widow." This list was taken from the *Hope Church Eightieth Anniversary Booklet*, May 3, 1942, 6.

[15] Hope Church, Minutes, Ladies' Aid Society, May 19, 1897, and September 15, 1897, W91-1034, JAH.

[16] The Great Holland Fire of 1871 destroyed early church records. The Ladies' Aid Constitution of 1883 is the earliest constitutional document extant, although references to the work of "the ladies" do appear. One such reference included the gift of a malodeon made to the church by "the

Social Committee. Assigning two ladies to each of three congregational districts, the task of Visiting Committee members was "to call upon families not in attendance upon any Church, invite them to our Church and endeavor to make them feel at home among us." These early efforts to evangelize were coupled with the commitment "to call upon families in sickness or sorrow and extend to them, in the name of the Church, Christian sympathy and attention."[17] In practical terms, such pastoral care assumed myriad forms, and for families in need, especially widows and their children, the women of the Ladies' Aid Society were compassionately present from birth to death. The Social Committee, according to this constitution, consisted of five members whose task was "to have charge of whatever social gatherings may be arranged by the Society." The minutes record a steady stream of socials and suppers, of celebrations and dinners, all focused on enriching the bonds of friendship and making meaningful the social lives and work of the saints.[18]

The Ladies' Missionary Society

In addition to joining the Ladies' Aid Society, Frances Beardslee also became a member of the Ladies' Missionary Society. It was the Hope Church Missionary Society that had claimed the heart and energy of Sarah Armitage Beardslee (1838-1909), Frances Beardslee's mother-in-law. From March 1889 until her death in April 1909, Sarah Beardslee served as president of the Ladies' Missionary Society. Frances Beardslee continued this family involvement. Although never serving as president, Frances studied Reformed Church foreign missions and made presentations to the group.[19] Her interest in foreign missions would continue to be a focus throughout her life.

For women in mainline Protestant denominations, the call to missions began in the early nineteenth century.[20] What began as

---

ladies" near the time the first church building was erected in 1864. For its earliest years, Minutes of the Ladies' Aid Society beginning 1896 serve as the earliest records available in addition to the constitution adopted May 8, 1883.

[17] Found in Hope Church Collection, W91-1034, Box 5, JAH.
[18] See pp. 21-23 in the *Hope Church Eightieth Anniversary Booklet*, May 3, 1942, for a sample listing of the projects and relief aid undertaken by the Ladies' Aid Society.
[19] See Minutes of March, 1915. Hope Church Collection, W91-1034, Box 6, JAH.
[20] See Russell L. Gasero "The Rise of the Woman's Board of Foreign Missions," in Reneé House and John Coakley, eds., *Patterns and Portraits, Women in the*

a plea for women to come to the aid of other women and children in foreign lands in fulfillment of the Great Commission developed into a world mission movement that changed the course of history for women. For Reformed Church women, the organizational roots began January 7, 1875, when "twelve or thirteen" women met in a raging snowstorm at the Marble Collegiate Church in New York City to establish the Woman's Board of Foreign Missions. To say these women were determined, committed, and dedicated is understatement. These women were on fire for the Lord, and their understanding of the task to which God was calling them was absolutely clear. In a dramatically organized way, the leaders of the Woman's Board established auxiliaries first in New York and New Jersey. In 1880 an auxiliary was organized in Constantine, Michigan,[21] and in the *1880 Annual Report of the Woman's Board of Foreign Missions*, it reports:

> Mrs. M.S. Van Olinda from Hope Church, Holland, Michigan, a lady inspired with zeal for the cause of Christ and ardent love for our branch of Zion has made a successful effort in this direction by a union of the three Dutch speaking Churches with the Hope Church which is English, in forming an Auxiliary. Our correspondent called on these ladies and found them much interested in the missionary cause and ready to enter into the work. Three weeks were spent in visiting the different congregations; and after obtaining the approval and co-operation of the ministers, a meeting was held which resulted in the formation of an Auxiliary by the married ladies, one also by the young ladies, and a Mission "Band" and "Circle" by the children and youth. The exercises were conducted in both the Dutch and English languages, as many of the ladies present could not take part in the English.[22]

History of the Reformed Church in America, Historical Series of the Reformed Church in America, no. 31 (Grand Rapids: Eerdmans, 1999), 98.

[21] From 1864-1884, the senior Beardslee served as pastor of the Reformed Church in Constantine, Michigan. During this time Sarah Armitage Beardslee worked to establish a women's missionary society there. When the Beardslee family moved to Holland and joined Hope Church in 1884, Sarah Beardslee joined immediately in the work of the Hope Church Ladies' Aid and the Ladies' Missionary Societies.

[22] *Annual Report of the Woman's Board of Foreign Missions* (ARWBFM), 1880, 19, as found in Mary L. Kansfield, *Letters to Hazel: Ministry within the Woman's Board of Foreign Missions of the Reformed Church in America*, Historical Series of the Reformed Church in America, no. 46 (Grand Rapids: Eerdmans, 2004),

To mark the first anniversary of the Holland Auxiliary of the Woman's Foreign Missionary Society, members gathered March 1, 1881, at the First Reformed Church (a Dutch-language congregation). The order of their service is as follows:

> Prayer, in the Hollandish language, Rev. Dirk Broek
> Singing, "O'er the gloomy hills of darkness."
> Scripture Reading, (Isaiah lx: in Hollandish.)
> Singing – Selection, (Isaiah lii: 7, 8.) "How beautiful upon the mountains."

59-60.

The story of M.S. Van Olinda has yet to be told. The board's fifty-year history, published in 1925, notes:

> It was in November 1879 that the attention of the Woman's Board was first drawn to the plan of organizing auxiliaries in the Western Church. Mrs. M.S. Van Olinda of Holland, Michigan, an energetic worker for missions and temperance, wrote to Mrs. Cumming urging the importance of beginning women's work for women and children in Eastern lands among the women in her section of the Dutch Church. The new Woman's Board had as yet scarcely found its footing in the Eastern branch of the Church and Mrs. Cumming was instructed to reply that the time was hardly propitious for entering on this more distant work. But Mrs. Van Olinda, burning with energy and enthusiasm for the great cause, called together the women of Hope Church and the other Holland-speaking churches in February 1880 to consider with them the question of forming an auxiliary. Her appeal met with hearty response from them and in March, 1880, a large number met in the spacious parlors of Mrs. J.W. Bosman, a fine Christian woman, interested in every good work, and there organized as a society auxiliary to the Woman's Board of Foreign Missions, the Holland Woman's Foreign Missionary Society. In 1884 there existed societies in Pella, Iowa, Constantine and Zeeland, Michigan, and three in the town of Holland, Michigan. Thus was begun that large and beneficent work for foreign missions among the women of the Western Church which has grown to such proportions that today the Woman's Board can ask them for $25,000 for its Amoy Girls' High School.

Mrs. W.I. Chamberlain, *Fifty Years in Foreign Fields China, Japan, India, Arabia: A History of Five Decades of the Woman's Board of Foreign Missions Reformed Church in America* (New York: The Woman's Board of Foreign Missions Reformed Church in America, 1925), 36-37.

In December 1914, Mrs. J.C. Post was honored by being given a life membership in the Women's Christian Temperance Union. At this time it was noted in the *Holland Daily Sentinel* that "the only other member so honored was the late Mrs. M.S. Van Olinda," *HDS*, December 19, 1914, 5.

> Reading the Annual Report, Rev. Daniel Van Pelt
> Singing – 14th Stanza, Psalm 22nd, (Hollandish.)
> Address,.. by Rev. Philip Phelps, Jr. D. D.
> Singing – "From Greenland's icy mountains."
> Address, (in Hollandish,) Rev. Nicholas M. Steffens
> Singing, – "Wake Isles of the South."
> Address,... Rev. Charles Scott, D.D.
> Singing, 8th Stanza, 72nd Psalm, (Hollandish.)
> Prayer,... Rev. T. Romeyn Beck, D.D.
> Singing, "Jesus shall reign where'er the Sun."
> Collection, Doxology, Benediction.[23]

Only men provided leadership, as women generally did not speak in public.[24] At the urging of the board[25] (not to mention contending with the length of meetings caused by the need to conduct meetings in both Dutch and English), separate auxiliaries were soon formed in the First, Hope, and Third Reformed churches.[26]

For Hope Church women, the constitution and founding documents dated February 7, 1886, spell out the purpose of their missionary society and its dual auxiliary relationship to the Woman's Board of Foreign Missions and to the Women's Executive Committee of the denomination's Board of Domestic Missions.[27] Conducted by an

---

[23] *ARWBFM*, 1881, 30.
[24] Gerda Lerner, *The Grimke Sisters from South Carolina: Pioneers for Woman's Rights and Abolition* (New York: Houghton Mifflin, 1967), 5.
[25] WBFM board members were very intentional in creating a process for the formation of auxiliaries. For a fuller explanation of this process see Kansfield, *Letters to Hazel*, 56.
[26] It is interesting to note that when the WBFM published its fifty-year history in 1925, a Dutch summary translation was made available, although "this was the last attempt of the Board to publish missionary information in their own tongue for the diminishing generation of Holland women who do not understand English—those staunch supporters of the Mission cause, whose homes have sent many sons and daughters to the Mission Field and exerted an inestimable influence on future generations." Sarella Te Winkel, *The Sixth Decade of the Woman's Board of Foreign Missions Reformed Church in America* (New York: Woman's Board of Foreign Missions, 1935), 9.
[27] Founded in 1882, as the Women's Executive Committee of the denomination's Board of Domestic Missions, the women's domestic mission organization became incorporated as The Women's Board of Domestic Missions December 14, 1909. See *Golden Years in Miniature: A History of the Women's Board of Domestic Missions of the Reformed Church in America* (New York: Women's Board of Domestic Missions, 1932).

executive committee of annually elected officers, Hope Church women met the first Wednesday of each month, "the object of which shall be prayer and conference, on missionary subjects and labors; giving and receiving information respecting the work and needs of the Mission fields and the gathering of monthly offerings."

The society's commitment "to give and receive information respecting the work and needs of the Mission fields" represented a paradigm shift for Hope Church women and for all churchwomen everywhere at that time. Prayer had been an intimate part of women's lives for centuries. What was different involved the engagement of churchwomen's minds. To inquire studiously about the lives and cultures of women and children living in distant places had the transforming effect of lifting churchwomen beyond their circumscribed lives in their local communities and exposing them to new ideas and different ways of living. The drive for "missionary intelligence"[28] paved the way. Coming to the aid of other women and children in faraway places in the name of Jesus Christ had the dramatic effect of changing women "at home" as much as it did the lives of women and children in distant places.

The Classical Union

It didn't take long for the leaders of the Woman's Board of Foreign Mission to recognize that, indeed, *Eendracht Maakt Macht*. For years this broadly used motto of the Reformed Church in America (translated "in unity is strength") provided strength and direction for the denomination. Churchwomen found similar strength in the formation of classical unions. As women's missionary societies sprang rapidly into existence, a classis-wide network of these societies was established. These would serve to strengthen the work of individual societies and bind them together in tightly knit regional organizations called classical unions that were dedicated to the great work of missions.[29] As with other classical unions within the network, the work

---

[28] This was a commonly used term referring to any and all information common to the lives and work of missionaries and those to whom missionaries were sent.

[29] The work of organizing auxiliaries began in 1881, after a woman named Mrs. E. Troop Martin from Auburn, New York, suggested to the WBFM board that "classical meetings for women be held in connection with the Church meetings of Classes, similar meetings having been successful in a sister Church held in connection with Presbyterial meetings." Martin suggested a plan in which "two women were to be appointed in each

of the classical union of Michigan revolved around bringing auxiliary women together to worship and to share "missionary intelligence." Like her church friends, Frances Beardslee participated in the work of the classical union and attended mission festivals and evangelistic rallies. Here the art of hospitality was practiced by extending a warm welcome to missionary guests, who shared with area women stories and insights about the mission work they were doing on behalf of all churchwomen. The church commitments Frances Beardslee made at Hope Church, Holland, remained passions for her throughout her life.

The Woman's Literary Club

For many Holland women, including Frances Beardslee, the Woman's Literary Club became the center of intellectual and social activity.[30] The club had its origin as a reading group within the local Women's Christian Temperance Union (WCTU). Derived from the Chautauqua[31] established by Michigan Methodists at Bay View (a revival retreat near Petoskey, Michigan), the group soon became the Bay View Reading Club. The purpose of the four-year Bay View reading curriculum was "the study of literature, history and science."[32] Events

---

Classis who were to endeavor to arouse a missionary spirit and to establish societies auxiliary to the Woman's Board in all the churches in the Classis in which they did not already exist." Given the hard work of each of the two women who volunteered as classical agents or representatives in each classis, this plan eventually resulted in a unified network of local auxiliaries held together by classical unions and two strong national women's organizations. Chamberlain, *Fifty Years in Foreign Fields*, 35.

[30] Appreciation for the written history of the Holland Woman's Literary Club is extended to Marie N. Zingle, who chronicled the club's history in 1989 in *The Story of the Woman's Literary Club 1898-1989*. It is the first major history of Holland women to be written (Holland: Woman's Literary Club, 1989).

[31] The word Chautauqua refers to a late nineteenth-century movement grounded in a combination of religious revivals and education. Summer camp meetings that stimulated the Christian faith, challenged the mind through study, and used the arts to inform and inspire found favor among families as a vacation place, often during the summer months, to hear outstanding preachers, to be inspired by engaging teachers, and to enjoy the delight of gifted musicians and entertainers. Inspired by the Methodists, the first Chautauqua, the New York Chautauqua Assembly, was organized in 1874 in upstate New York and continues today. Thought to be a successor to the Lyceum movement, Chautauquas flourished and reached the height of their popularity in the 1920s.

[32] According to Marie Zingle's history, this course "was part of an educational program that resembled the Chautauqua Institution's in New York state,

such as an annual picnic added a social component to the group. Anna Coatsworth Post (Mrs. Henry Post) is credited with founding the Bay View Reading Club in 1894 in Holland. Of its early members, "most circle members belonged to the WCTU as well as Hope Church, and several were D.A.R. members from New England roots."[33]

Following the completion of the four-year reading course, the reading club members organized Holland's Woman's Literary Club in October 1898. Seeking to draw attention to women as individuals, the club was named the *Woman*'s Literary Club. Its collective purpose included the following: "Believing that our happiness as individuals and our usefulness as citizens depends upon our intelligence, we women of Holland unite our efforts to further intellectual improvement, and to diffuse useful knowledge."[34]

In its first year, the club borrowed and circulated among its members fifty books from the state library. This practice continued in each of the next thirteen years. Committees on history, art-literature, science-education-miscellaneous, and music were established.[35] Weekly programs included book reports, study papers, poetry, dramatic readings, and musical renditions given by club members. Plays and pageants were soon added to the club's programs.

In 1905, the literary club became a member of the Michigan Federation and the General Federation of Women's Clubs, which moved club members to broaden their focus to include social concerns

---

with university courses and a four-week Assembly offered each summer at the resort community of Bay View, near Petoskey, Michigan. Subscribers to the home studies course composed the Bay View Reading Circle, and the $3.00 annual cost per member covered examination fees, the *Bay View Magazine* published monthly from November through June, and three textbooks." Zingle, *Woman's Literary Club*, 3.

[33] According to Marie Zingle's history, nineteen active charter members and nine associate charter members formed the group. The difference in memberships involved the payment of $1.00 or $2.00 in club dues and consent by associate members to have their names printed in the annual printed program. Among the active charter members is listed Mrs. J.J. [sic] Beardslee, Frances Beardslee's mother-in-law, who, with her husband and family, arrived in Holland in 1884. Ibid., 4.

[34] It must be remembered that although these women had intellectual curiosity and a sense of civic duty, they also had to have the luxury of their availability one afternoon a week and homes sufficiently large to host meetings. Meetings were timed to begin at 3:00 in the afternoon and to end with the blowing of the 5:00 city whistle.

[35] Ibid, 9.

and community problems.³⁶ Community health and community improvement received the attention of club members, and, as Marie Zingle points out, "These were not women concerned with women's issues, although they <u>were</u> denied the right to vote. The members were primarily interested in issues involving children and youth—child labor laws, orphanages, schools, and health care."³⁷

Following the legal incorporation of the club in 1908, members proceeded in an entrepreneurial way to purchase property on Tenth Street and Central Avenue.³⁸ There they had built a "club home." Constructed at a cost of $12,500, the carefully designed, red brick, classic revival building was dedicated February 6, 1914, with 170 club members represented on the membership roll. J.W. Beardslee, Sr., took part in the dedication ceremony, and we can only assume that Frances Beardslee was present to join that celebration.

Frances Beardslee had joined the Woman's Literary Club shortly after her arrival in Holland. She was an active club member and made a number of program presentations. On April 15, 1913, she presented a paper on Daniel Webster, and on April 28 that same year she gave a reading of Bryant's "The Forest Hymn." She gave a reading December 8, 1914, on *Up from Slavery* by Booker T. Washington, and on April 7, 1917, Frances joined her friend Katherine Post in presenting a program described by the *Holland Daily Sentinel* as "devoted to the interests of the superior sex." Frances's paper, "Women's Work in the World Today,"

> dwelt chiefly on the work of women as brot [sic] out by the present war, and proved her efficiency in field, dairy, factory, mine, railway station and even amunition [sic] plant, not to mention the spheres where she has always proved indispensable, namely in the hospital and Red Cross work. The Women of England, say the English statesmen, will have the ballot because by their work during this

---

36 At the beginning of the 1907-08 club year four committees were named to oversee new branches of the club's work: Anti-Tuberculosis Committee (later became the Civic Health Committee), Library Extension Committee, Civic Improvement Committee, and the Public Schools Committee. Ibid., 15.
37 Ibid., 12. Emphasis is Zingle's.
38 The club had to follow a circuitous route to obtain ownership of the exact property they desired for a club house. After their incorporation in the State of Michigan May 2, 1908, club members purchased a lot on West Eleventh St. near River Ave. for a cost of $650. This lot was subsequently sold at a profit, and on July 18, 1910, they purchased land on the northeast corner of Ninth Street and College Avenue for $1,200.

war they have earned it. "Man is more dense than ungrateful." Women of wealth and leisure too have not been idle and have done most excellent service in free kitchens and nurseries. The paper closed with a stirring appeal to the women of America, more indolent and pleasure-loving perhaps than their European sisters, to rise now in what threatens to be their country's need of them, especially to deeds of helpfulness and mercy.[39]

Katherine Post's paper focused on the life and work of Anna Howard Shaw, onetime Michigan resident and a leader in the suffrage movement. According to the local newspaper:

> Miss Post also took the leadership in a brief discussion of the success of suffrage in those states where it has been tried, and the work of [sic] that it has accomplished in prohibition, raising the "age of consent," better laws for babies, and for health, mother's rights of guardianship, censorship of "movies," mother's pensions, milk inspection, women as factory inspectors, and in many other laws for moral uplift.[40]

The common interests of Katherine Post and Frances Beardslee as college educated women[41] and their commitment to passage of the suffrage for women found many expressions during Frances Beardslee's Holland years. Their friendship continued long after the Beardslee family departed Holland in 1917. Frances's participation in the life of the mind, complete with presenting a scholarly paper annually and enjoying the company of a close circle of women friends, continued after she moved to New Brunswick, New Jersey. There she became a member of the Travelers' Club, a women's literary society, where for forty-six years she prepared and presented papers just as she had for the Woman's Literary Club.

The Century Club

If self improvement and social enjoyment motivated the early formation of the Bay View Reading Club and the Woman's Literary Club, the Century Club of Holland was created as a private social

---

[39] *HDS,* April 7, 1917, JAH.
[40] Ibid.
[41] Katherine Post was awarded an AB degree from the University of Michigan in 1909 and a master's degree in 1910. Frances Beardslee received an AB degree from Wellesley College in 1908 and a master's degree from the University of Chicago in 1910.

club. Established in 1897 by Hope College faculty members and the city's leading citizens (many of whose families were related to the city's founders), Century Club membership was limited to one hundred, as its name suggests. Entry to club membership was by invitation only, and most meetings were held in members' homes, which necessarily implied a commodious space for these biweekly gatherings. Members included both men and women, single persons as well as couples. The Century Club Constitution stated the purpose of the club to "be the literary, musical and social entertainment of its members." Over the years, annual club programs included presentations by numerous authors, famous guest lecturers, statesmen, foreign diplomats, and concert artists. Members themselves made literary and musical presentations. Plays, pageants, and skits, written and enacted by club members, often enlightened and/or entertained the group. Names of club members were well known in the community inasmuch as club programs and social hosts were routinely reported in the local newspapers. Given the limited nature of its membership, this press coverage helped create an unwritten understanding that members of the Century Club generally represented the city's arbiters of cultural taste and social refinement.

Among the charter members of the Century Club were Sarah and John W. Beardslee, Sr., and John W. Beardslee, Jr.[42] Meetings were frequently held in the Beardslee home on Twelfth Street. John W. Beardslee, Sr., served as president of the club in 1901-1902, and John W. Beardslee, Jr., continued this tradition.[43] Frances Beardslee joined the Century Club shortly after her arrival in Holland.[44] She participated as a hostess on various occasions, and at the October 19, 1914, meeting, she reviewed a popular book entitled *Thinking Black*, by Dan Crawford.[45] This must have been an honor for Frances and for her husband, John.

---

[42] Charter member list, Holland Century Club, T95-1402, Holland (Michigan) Museum Archives (HMA).

[43] In 1914 John W. Beardslee, Jr., served as vice-president of the club as well as a member of the Executive Committee, the Nominating Committee and the Program Committee. In 1915 he became president of the club with continuing responsibilities on the Executive Committee and the Program Committee. Holland Century Club record of the secretary/treasurer, pages 4 and 33, T95-1402, HMA.

[44] Member listing for 1912-1913, p. 199, T95-1402, HMA.

[45] Subtitled *22 Years without a Break in the Long Grass of Central Africa*, and published in New York by George H. Doran, 1912, the text covers the author's expeditions in Angola, the Congo, Rhodesia, and Mozambique. Frances's interest in books of exploration and discovery continued through her life.

At this same club meeting, the Nominating Committee recommended the name of Katharine Post, who was duly elected to membership in the club.

The National Society, Daughters of the American Revolution (DAR)

The drive among Holland's residents to become Americanized was consistent with a growing patriotic spirit throughout the nation. It was this sense of patriotic pride, plus the refusal of the Sons of the American Revolution to admit women, that motivated the founding of the Daughters of the American Revolution in Washington, D.C., in 1890. Membership was and continues today to be based on documenting one's lineal bloodline to a descendant who aided in the American War for Independence.[46] Chartered by Congress in 1896, the organization's objectives have remained the same since its founding. These objectives focus on history, education, and patriotism.

The organization's membership grew quickly, and, in 1900, the Michigan State DAR Society was founded. In 1907, a group of women in Holland, Michigan, under the leadership of Ida Sears McLean, began the work of organizing a local chapter. As they considered a name for their chapter, they felt it appropriate to underscore the Dutch connection by naming their chapter for Elizabeth Schuyler Hamilton (1757-1854), who was a member of the prominent Dutch Schuyler family in New York[47] and the wife of Alexander Hamilton.[48] A charter was granted to the Elizabeth Schuyler Hamilton Chapter of the DAR February 15, 1908. Of the sixteen charter members in this local chapter,[49] only three bore Dutch-sounding family names.[50] Over half of the charter members

---

[46] Membership is also by invitation, and women had to be at least eighteen years of age to be considered.

[47] Elizabeth Schuyler Hamilton's parents were Catherine Van Rensselaer Schuyler and Philip Schuyler, both of whom came from prominent Dutch families in the East. Philip Schuyler served as a general under General George Washington.

[48] As a brilliant military strategist, Alexander Hamilton (1757-1894) had served under General George Washington and distinguished himself in the War for Independence. He co-wrote the *Federalist Papers*, signed the Constitution, and served as the first secretary of the treasury.

[49] These women included Myrtle Beach, Florence M. Boot, Ada Duffy, Ruby Gerrod, Anna M. Hall, Lilla Maria Harrington, Alice M. Kramer, Georgia Hinman Kramer, Laura McBride, Ida Sears McLean, Katherine Post, Martha Sherwood, Adeline Hinkley Swift, Anna Wheeler, Avis Yates, Gertrude Yates.

[50] Both Boot and Kramer are Dutch names. Two of the women were named Kramer.

were members of Hope Church, and one only wonders at the capacity of these women to speak Dutch and to appreciate the Dutch connection.

Once resident in Holland, Frances Beardslee applied for DAR membership. The membership and involvement of her husband in the local chapter of the Sons of the American Revolution, the elite patriotic organization for men, must have encouraged Frances to consider DAR membership.[51] According to her application, which was approved October 30, 1914, Frances traced her lineal descent through her paternal great-grandmother, who was the daughter of Private Benjamin Palmer (1757-1849) of Connecticut, who served in Providence, Rhode Island.[52] In 1915, Frances Beardslee's name appears on the membership list of the Elizabeth Schuyler Hamilton Chapter, where she was an active member. At the November 11, 1915, meeting, she presented a paper entitled, "Amusements and Industries of Colonial Children." And on December 14, 1916, Frances presented a program, "Christmas Story," at which meeting her husband John also made an address.

Frances had spent her childhood years growing up on a farm outside the small town of Jewett City, Connecticut. Anna Wheeler, who was a DAR charter member and active at Hope Church, was born in Norwich, Connecticut, a comparatively large city located not too distant from Jewett City. This bond helped make Frances feel that she was not entirely outside her element. Although considerably older than Frances, Anna Wheeler became her friend, and that relationship

---

[51] Social occasions were often shared by the Sons and Daughters of the Revolution. On Ladies Night in January, 1913, the Sons hosted the DAR women, and as reported in the *Holland Daily Sentinel*, costumes, decorations, and program collectively resonated with a colonial theme, complete with five couples dancing the minuet. This particular occasion was made festive by the use of a gavel made of the wood of the old Ship *Constitution*, which played an important part in the War of 1812. On this particular occasion, John Beardslee presented a paper on "The Naval Battle of the War of 1812," which "was repeated last night by request." Such were the elaborate social occasions often celebrated by both the DAR and SAR. *HDS*, January 11, 1913, l.

[52] In 1921, Frances transferred her membership from the Elizabeth Schuyler Hamilton chapter to the Jersey Blue Chapter of the New Jersey Society of the National Society of the DAR, from which she resigned in 1933. Although there was speculation by her family in later years that Frances's resignation was prompted by the failure of the DAR to grant concert space to famed contralto Marian Anderson in 1939 due to Miss Anderson's African American heritage, the date of Frances's resignation, October 20, 1933, precludes this possible explanation. It would not be out of character, however, for Frances to have been so motivated.

endured (according to the memories of Frances's children), even after the Beardslees moved to New Brunswick.[53]

The work of the Elizabeth Schuyler Hamilton chapter received inspiration from the State and National DAR organizations. Local delegates were sent to state and national meetings, and members received information from visiting DAR dignitaries, who spoke at their monthly meetings. While "not seeking social distinction, but aspiring to keep burning the sacred fire of true patriotism," the chapter undertook a number of activities. Among the activities reported to the state chapter in 1914[54] was the annual oratory contest held among high school students with a prize awarded for the best oration on a patriotic theme.[55] Two prizes were also awarded to the students with the highest standing in history.[56] During that year, members of the chapter undertook historical research on the early settlement of Ottawa County and forwarded that research to the state historian and the historian general in Washington, D.C. Christmas gifts were given to ladies in the county infirmity. Flag Day was celebrated with a picnic at Castle Park, with members of the board of directors of the Grand Rapids chapter as guests.

As the shadow of war crept over the nation, members of the Elizabeth Schuyler Hamilton Chapter initiated a major effort for war preparedness. Working through the Red Cross and in conjunction with the Women's Christian Temperance Union and the Woman's Literary Club, DAR members called upon all the women of the city to sew bandages and fracture pillows, pads, binders, compresses, etc., for the soldiers. The literary club graciously made its clubhouse available, and all day every Tuesday and Saturday all women of the city were asked

[53] Note from John W. Beardslee, III, to the author, December 12, 1996. Note is in the possession of the author.

[54] As reported in the *Holland Daily Sentinel*, "Yesterday in connection with the big D.A.R. gathering in Kalamazoo, *The Kalamazoo Telegraph Press* printed a special D.A.R. edition. In it appeared the cuts [engraved picture plates] of prominent D.A.R. workers throughout the state, among them that of Mrs. F.C. Hall, regent of the Elizabeth Schuyler Hamilton Chapter of this city. In the same issue appeared an article written by Mrs. Hall describing the work of the local chapter...." September 30, 1914, 2.

[55] For the best oration on a patriotic theme a prize of a $5.00 gold piece was awarded, with a $2.50 gold piece being awarded to the second place speaker. The amount of this award is spelled out in *HDS*, February 26, 1917, 1.

[56] The prize awarded each history student "was an appropriately marked bronze tablet, bearing the name of the pupil or class and the donor, and became the property of the school." *HDS*, September 30, 1914, 2.

to come and help. It was a massive effort, and, as it was noted in the newspaper, "the ladies of the city are not backward when it comes to loyalty to the Flag and the country, and the men will have to 'go some' to keep up with the ladies."[57]

The Equal Suffrage Club

The story of the struggle for the woman's franchise and how those efforts played out in Holland, Michigan, over the years 1912-1917 suffers from the absence of any records for the Holland Equal Suffrage Club. The story of these local efforts, however, begs to be told in any form. What follows is an effort to piece together from secondary sources a sense of how the story unfolded for Frances Beardslee during the years of her residence in Holland. Because the documents needed fully to tell the story are incomplete, a simple chronological order will be used as a backdrop for pinpointing Frances's involvement in the Equal Suffrage Club.

From the one relevant document that does exist, which is Frances Beardslee's contribution to the 1918 Wellesley College *Record Book*, we are informed that she was "one of the founders of the Equal Suffrage Club and custodian of its funds." Within the story of three referenda attempts to change the Michigan State Constitution,[58] three separate suffrage campaigns were carried out in Holland. The first campaign occurred in 1912, the second in 1913, and the last in 1918. Although a local Equal Suffrage Club had been formed to advance the suffrage cause in 1912, it was in preparation for the 1918 referendum that a successor Holland Equal Suffrage Club was formed in October 1915. It is of this successor organization, founded in 1915, that Frances Beardslee ascribes herself as a cofounder. Other unnamed women might also have served as cofounders of this club, but surely its driving force, as we shall see, was Frances's close friend Katherine C. Post.

On November 4, 1912, Holland's all-male voters would elect a new president. They would also decide whether or not to change the Michigan State Constitution to allow women the privilege of

---

[57] *HDS*, April 11, 1917, 1.
[58] According to Virginia Caruso, Michigan legislative data began to be collected and published in the 1880s in the *Michigan Manual*. In it are recorded woman suffrage results for four referenda votes: 1874, 1912, 1913, and 1918. For the purposes of this essay, only the referenda for 1912, 1913, and 1918 are considered. Virginia Ann Paganelli Caruso, "A History of Woman Suffrage in Michigan," unpub. diss., Michigan State University, 1986, xviii.

voting.⁵⁹ For Holland's residents, the suffrage issue seems to have been a particularly uncomfortable one, for it represented a challenge to the traditional role and place of women in society—a society understood to be defined clearly in the pages of the Bible.

Although Frances may not have seen the *Grand Haven Daily* for August 21, 1912, that paper reported, in small print, that "Ottawa County in comparison with other counties in Michigan, has not done her share of the work in this movement." In response to this situation, Mrs. C.C. Coburn of Grand Haven, who represented the Michigan Equal Suffrage Association, called a meeting to organize suffrage efforts in Ottawa County.⁶⁰ Such an undertaking evolved from the growing resolve and strength of the Michigan Equal Suffrage Association, which was founded in 1884 and functioned as a member of the National American Equal Suffrage Association.⁶¹ The success of Coburn's efforts was revealed when a notice in the September 12 issue of the *Holland Daily Sentinel* reported:

> There will be a meeting of the officers and committee members of the Equal Suffrage association of this city this evening at 8 o'clock at the home of Mrs. J.C. Post. One of the purposes of the meeting is to make arrangements for prominent speakers to make addresses in Holland before the November election.⁶²

A flurry of campaign activity followed. The city was divided into sections, and suffrage literature in Dutch and English was distributed.⁶³

---

⁵⁹ In addition to Michigan, referenda on the woman's suffrage question would also be voted on in Arizona, Kansas, Oregon, Ohio, and Wisconsin in 1912. It passed in Arizona, Kansas and Oregon, but failed in Michigan, Ohio, and Wisconsin.

⁶⁰ As the county leader, Coburn organized Ottawa County into sixteen suffrage associations of which Holland was one. As reported in the Oct. 4, 1912, issue of the *Holland Daily Sentinel* (1): "The object of this county wide organization is principally to post the voters on the true issue of woman suffrage, and thus far the workers are meeting with every encouragement.... The women of Ottawa county are responding with enthusiasm to the call for the workers, and every member of every organization is working like a beaver for the cause."

⁶¹ The histories of the National Equal Suffrage Association and the American Equal Suffrage Association are detailed in numerous sources. Although originally published in 1959, an excellent general account of the suffrage movement continues to be Eleanor Flexner's *Century of Struggle: The Woman's Rights Movement in the United States* (Cambridge, Mass.: 1959).

⁶² *HDS*, September 12, 1912, 8.

⁶³ Among the brochures was *Michigan Laws Relating to Women and Girls*. This frequently updated little brochure, copyrighted by the Michigan Equal

Local suffragists were encouraged, as a number of men spoke out on behalf of their enfranchisement.⁶⁴

On September 27 it was announced that suffragists in Ottawa County would canvass the county, and members of Holland's Equal Suffrage Club would "block out" the city and conduct a systematic canvass "with a view of determining how the city is likely to vote on the woman suffrage amendment in November. The outcome proved encouraging. The *Holland Daily Sentinel* reported:

> All indications seem to point to the fact that equal suffrage sentiment has been growing in this city and the chances are that it will grow still more between now and election day. A few years ago the man who favored suffrage for women was the exception here while now there are many of them. Among the women too, the sentiment seems to be growing.⁶⁵

Suffrage Association, effectively identifies those Michigan state laws pertaining to women and girls based on the Acts of the Michigan State Legislature of 1899, 1901, 1903, 1905, 1907, 1909, and 1911. Grand Rapids Public Library, Collection #127.

Although the Michigan State Equal Suffrage Association had its headquarters in Detroit, Grand Rapids became the center for the 1912 campaign. In the October 4, 1912 issue of the *Holland Daily Sentinel* (1) it was reported that "Grand Rapids has sent out three tons of literature since the campaign opened....Literature is being issued from the Grand Rapids headquarters published in English, Holland, German and all foreign languages."

⁶⁴ One such voice came from a "favorite son" of the community. A graduate of Hope College and professor of economics at the University of Michigan, Henry Rottschaefer had published in the *Holland Daily Sentinel* a detailed argument in favor of woman's suffrage. Titled "Why I Am a Suffragist," Rottschaefer put forth a searing argument against "the natural prejudice against the cause that exists throughout the state. And it would undoubtedly be not at all unfair to this city to say that a good deal of this exists in the minds of the local voters. Indeed it would be a strange thing if the contrary were the fact. There are some who seem to feel that it would be an invasion of man's sphere. But there seems to be no logical reason why a woman should not be as much interested in a clean and pure government as any man since it is responsible for laws under which she and her children must live. A woman has as much business in taking an interest in politics as any man, if not more. Nor need we fear that the women of Michigan and especially of this city will become masulinized [sic] by this step....Nor need we fear that she will be corrupted by mingling in the political life of the community, for to admit such a fear is to admit that one of the greatest businesses of the citizen is degrading in its effects." *HDS*, September 3, 1912.

⁶⁵ *HDS*, September 27, 1912.

"Let Women Vote; They Will Know How to Use Ballot for Civic Housekeeping"[66] served as the rallying cry of the suffragists, and the number of organizations supporting the suffragist cause in Michigan continued to grow.[67] As Election Day drew nearer, suffrage activity increased.[68] Speakers used automobiles (which were still new to the general population), and eventually local suffragists hired a hall.[69] The outlook was invigorating.

On Election Day, however, the suffragists' hopes were dashed. They were disappointed on two fronts. On the one hand it was reported, "Muskegon and Ottawa counties voted against the measure by larger votes than any counties heard from and are dubbed the 'worst' counties of the state."[70] On the other hand it was reported, "The Suffragists are now of the belief that they will win out. The older counties of the state and the so-called 'Yankee' counties polled big votes favorable to the measure."[71] But such was not the case. Ballot irregularities and "blatant fraud" resulted in defeat.[72] The defeat of this hard-fought fight inspired

---

[66] *HDS*, September 30, 1912, 4.

[67] One advertisement appearing in the *Holland Daily Sentinel*, October 16, 1912, showed organizational support of the suffrage cause to include the Grange, the Farmers' Clubs, the Gleaners, the Lady Maccabees, the Women's Christian Temperance Union, the Nurses' Association, the Federation of Labor, and the State Federation of Women's Clubs. Their combined membership was identified to be 287,300.

[68] One insightful advertising claim by local suffragists involved the number of tax dollars paid by women based on property valuation. In the article, "Women of Holland Pay Taxes on Million Dollar Valuation," it was noted, "'The women of Holland pay taxes on a property valuation of very nearly a million dollars,' said a prominent Holland woman who has given this matter some study: 'and yet the women have nothing to say about the selection of the men whose salaries they help pay and who expend for the city and the county this money.'

"The estimate of this Holland woman does not seem very wide of the mark, judging from a comparison with other cities in Ottawa County. The total amount of assessment in Ottawa County on property owned by women is $3,433,360. This property is owned by 1,784 women and the amount paid in actual taxes is about $107,638." *HDS,* October 29, 1912.

[69] "Suffragists Are Busy These Days: Many Meetings and Speeches During Last Days of Campaign," *HDS,* October 23, 1912, 8.

[70] *Grand Haven Daily Tribune*, November 7, 1912, 1.

[71] Ibid. For national interest in the upcoming Michigan election, see "All Michigan Torn by Suffrage Fight," *New York Times*, April 6, 1913.

[72] The Michigan defeat was described this way by Carrie Chapman Catt and Nettie Rogers Schuler:

The early returns showed favorable figures and the suffrage majority

Governor Ferris of Michigan in January, 1913, to call for a new election. The date was set for April 1913, and in spite of continued campaigning, the vote for women was defeated this time by a margin of just under 100,000 votes.[73] This was devastating to Michigan suffragists.

Although only men could vote on the suffrage question, the election of 1913 did permit the women of Holland to vote on a bond issue to allow the city to purchase the fair grounds for $10,000. Beginning with the 1908 Michigan State Constitution, women were permitted to vote on "direct expenditures of public funds or the issue of bonds"—provided they owned property or paid property taxes jointly with their husbands and were registered to vote.[74]

As a local option, the question of the sale and consumption of liquor also appeared on the 1913 ballot. Once again only men were allowed to vote. When election was over, and a recount of the ballots was completed, prohibition won by a vote of 1,114 for and 1,093 against. The ordinance had passed—but only by a margin of 21 votes.[75]

---

climbed steadily to 8,000. But many scattered precincts mysteriously withheld their returns, without explanation. One by one these were released, cutting the majority to 5,000, where it seemed established and Michigan was announced to the world as another suffrage state. Then the delayed precincts began sifting in their returns, each with a suspiciously large adverse majority, until the favorable majority became a slightly adverse one. Many weeks had been consumed in the process and nerve-racked suffragists, knowing precisely what was taking place, stood helpless before the deliberate theft of an election.

Carrie Chapman Catt and Nettie Rogers Schuler, *Woman Suffrage and Politics* (New York: Scribner's, 1923), 180-81 as found in Eleanor Flexner, *Century of Struggle*, 260.

For an excellent review of the election fraud, see The Grange's "Report of the Equal Suffrage Campaign for 1912" by Ida L. Chittenden, manager. This report was included in the Education packet titled "How the Suffragists Changed Michigan" made available through the Grand Rapids Public Library.

[73] The vote was actually 168,738 to 264,882. This is taken from the "Time Line for Michigan Women's History," http://www.michiganwomenshalloffame.org/pages/timeline.htm

[74] School suffrage was granted to Michigan women beginning in 1875. Between 1838 and 1910, eighteen states permitted school suffrage. Between 1894 and 1908, four states approved limited suffrage that involved voting on taxation or bonding issues. *Michigan Suffragist* 4, nb. 2 (February, 1917): 12.

[75] See "'Antis' Lose Two Votes; Recount Shows 'Drys' Win by a Margin of 21 Instead of 23," *HDS*, April 11, 1913, 1.

In November, 1916, prohibition was again on the ballot in the form

Temperance was an issue of long standing, and Holland's WCTU organization was at one time the largest and the oldest women's reform group in Holland.[76] Leaders of the WCTU assumed similar leadership positions in the Equal Suffrage Club and the Woman's Literary Club.[77] The ideological origins of the temperance and suffrage issues derived from very different democratic concepts,[78] but taken together these concepts blurred when played out on a local level. According to WCTU membership lists, however, Frances Beardslee was not a member.

At this point the attention of the nation began to focus on Washington, D.C., where, the day before Woodrow Wilson's inauguration in 1913, a suffrage parade of some five thousand

of an amendment to the Michigan constitution. It passed. In Holland the amendment passed by a majority of 557. "Holland Votes Dry By 557 Majority," *HDS*, November 7, 1916.

[76] According to the overview for the WCTU collection, which is now housed at the Holland Museum, "During the time of Prohibition, in the 1920's, the union reached full fruition gaining more than 300 members and becoming Michigan's largest chapter of the WCTU." For the year 1916-17, the WCTU membership list notes a total of 100 members. Membership lists, WCTU, T90-1134, HMA.

Established in May, 1877, the Holland chapter of the Women's Christian Temperance Union was predated by the Holland City Temperance Society. As of October 28, 1876, The Holland City Temperance Society was meeting and discussing "the proposed Amendment to the Constitution, repealing the Anti-License clause." *Holland City News*, October 18, 1876, 5.

[77] In 1913, for example, Mrs. J.C. Post served both as president of the WCTU and the Equal Suffrage Club. In December, 1914, Mrs. J.C. Post was honored by being made a life time membership in the WCTU. *HDS*, December 19, 1914, 5.

[78] One of the finest analyses of voting patterns in referenda voting, especially in Michigan, was articulated by Eileen L. McDonagh and H. Douglas Price. In it these ideological differences are articulated this way:

Temperance and prohibition were a response to a social problem—drunkenness and alcoholism—viewed as threatening a democratic conception of community and society. Temperance—the movement in which women were most actively involved—advocated voluntary abstinence or self-control, with the primary goal the restoration of the family unit threatened by increasing drinking problems....By contrast, woman suffrage was part of a feminist movement viewed as radical and based on arguments of rights and principles necessitating such a new vision of women and women's relationship to society that some place it with transformations as major as the Reformation. In the name of the equality asserted by the Declaration of Independence, suffrage leaders protested the "contradiction between [democratic] principle and practice."

participants was organized by two young women named Alice Paul and Lucy Burns. Alice Paul had arrived recently from England, where she had worked with the more militant English suffragists. She and Lucy Burns were committed to working solely for a federal amendment to the constitution. They rejected the state referenda approach of the National American Equal Suffrage Association, eventually formed their own political party called the Congressional Union, and immediately set to work advancing the cause of a federal constitutional amendment.

Although the 1913 Michigan referendum vote was defeated, Michigan suffragists became increasingly organized, using a plan adopted in January 1913.[79] By establishing and implementing this organizational plan, Michigan suffragists shifted into a grassroots organizational and educational mode. In February, 1914, the *Michigan Suffragist*, a monthly publication, published its first issue. This communication effort proved to be a significant strategic move, and reports of the work by county organizations, including Ottawa County, began regularly to appear in the *Suffragist* starting in February 1915.

In 1910, the Michigan Federation of Women's Clubs endorsed suffrage for women,[80] and by 1914 members of the Holland Woman's Literary Club, a member of the Michigan Federation, as well as members of the local WCTU, were engaged seriously in debating the suffrage issue. On September 28, 1914, the question, "Is the Ballot a Wise and Safe Gift to Women?" was debated before the women of the

---

[79] Titled "Plan of Work for Campaign," the congressional district was determined to be the unit through which organizational work was to take place, and each district would oversee the work of organizing the counties in that district. Specific strategies were identified, along with the means to be used for enhancing communication among the county organizations. Additionally, the plan called for raising $6,000 to be used to meet organization expenses. This Michigan Equal Suffrage Association 1913 publication is available in "How the Suffragists Changed Michigan," an educational resource packet, 1989, made available from the Michigan Women's Historical Center and Hall of Fame, Lansing, Mich.

[80] Virginia Caruso notes: "The struggle for the endorsement of woman suffrage by the General Federation of Woman's Clubs (GFWC) had begun at the 1906 biennial meeting where the issue was quietly mentioned. At the biennial meeting in 1908, woman suffrage had been openly discussed and strong sentiment had existed in the 1912 biennial meeting. In 1914 the federation endorsed suffrage. The Michigan Federation endorsed suffrage in 1910." Virginia Ann Paganelli Caruso, "A History of Woman Suffrage in Michigan," 167.

See also Karen J. Blair, *The Clubwoman as Feminist: True Womanhood Redefined, 1868-1914* (New York, Holmes and Meier, 1980), 113.

WCTU with Mrs. F.T. Miles presenting a paper in the affirmative and Maud Zwemer arguing in the negative. Both papers reflected immense research, tightly reasoned arguments, and careful articulation, and both papers were published in their entireties in the *Holland Daily Sentinel*.[81]

In November 1914, Mrs. Charles McBride presented a paper entitled "Suffrage for Women" to members of the Woman's Literary Club. This presentation was described at length in the *Holland Daily Sentinel*. The article concluded with the reporter saying, "The discussion which followed this paper indicated that many of the club members are in favor of woman's suffrage. At least, those who were against it, did not speak. When the president asked those to rise, who had voted in the last school election, nearly everyone stood up."[82]

Although members of the local Equal Suffrage Club soldiered on, the National American Equal Suffrage Association in 1915, under the leadership of the Reverend Anna Howard Shaw, seemed bankrupt of organizational leadership. Shaw, who was born and raised in Michigan and who was held in especially deep affection among Michigan women, was an extremely gifted speaker. Her passion for the suffrage cause and her oratorical skills had served the national suffrage organization well. But, in 1915, a change was needed.[83] Carrie Chapman Catt, who had coordinated the New York referendum campaign, was recognized for her extraordinary organization skills, and with the continued defeat of state referenda, attention shifted toward the need for a federal amendment and the growing demand for new organizational strategies. In December 1915, Catt was elected president of the National American Equal Suffrage Association.

It is within this context that in late September 1915, Michigan suffragists from Kent and Ottawa counties met in Grand Rapids and "for the first time in the history of the state the counties were organized, altho [sic] city political equality clubs have existed for several years."[84] These women pledged support to a federal constitutional amendment and elected Mrs. C.B. Hamilton of Grand Rapids as chairman of the

---

[81] *HDS*, September 28, 1914, 2-4.
[82] *HDS*, November 18, 1914, 1, 8.
[83] In 1914 the suffrage issue was voted on in seven states. It passed in only two. In November 1915, major referenda votes took place in New York, New Jersey, Massachusetts, and Pennsylvania. It failed to pass in all four states. Coupled with the rise in membership and energy of Alice Paul's Congressional Union party and the growing commitment to passage of a federal constitutional amendment, a change was clearly needed. Flexner, *Century of Struggle*, 268-71.
[84] *HDS*, October 1, 1915, 2.

Fifth Congressional District. Ottawa County officers were assigned, and Mrs. R.N. De Merrell of Holland was made treasurer.[85]

On October 29, 1915, a headline in the local Holland newspaper read, "Local Suffrage Society Formed." The Reverend Caroline Bartlett Crane, a well-known suffrage leader within the state,[86] addressed the women of the Woman's Literary Club. In her introduction of Crane, Mrs. C.H. McBride, president of the club, indicated that this was the fourth time a suffrage speaker had lectured in Holland.

At the end of her speech, Crane was very direct about the reason she was there. She said:

> I have been asked to do some legislative work here today, and have with me a form of by-laws for such an organization. The business to be done by the new organization first is to elect a delegate to attend the convention to be held at Saginaw on the 11th to 13th of November, then to sign these resolutions I have for our state representatives, and then to subscribe for the 'Weekly Woman's Journal,' a suffrage paper, and the 'Michigan Suffragist.'"[87]

With De Merrell making the motion, the ladies agreed. They also approved the following slate of officers for the new local organization:

> President: Miss Katherine Post[88]
> Vice presidents: Mrs. Charles McBride and Mrs. W.A. Van Syckle
> Secretary: to be appointed by the president
> Treasurer: to be postponed since momentarily "they had no funds to treasure"

[85] Ottawa County officers included: chairman, Mrs. C. De Vos, Coopersville; vice chairman, Miss Margaret J. Bilz, Spring Lake; secretary, Mrs. C.E. Shupe, Grand Haven; and treasurer, Mrs. R.N. De Merrell, Holland. Ibid.

[86] The Rev. Caroline Bartlett Crane (1858-1935), one of the first wave of college-educated women, was a Unitarian minister in Kalamazoo and became known for her pioneering work in the area of public health. It could not have escaped the attention of the state suffrage association to use a woman of such reputation to enlist the support of the women in Holland to reorganize. Http://www.25.uua.org/uuhs/duub/articles/carolinebartlettcrane/html.

[87] *HDS*, October 29, 1915, 1, 3.

[88] Katherine Post (1887-1966) was the daughter of Kate Garrod Post (Mrs. J.C. Post), who was president of the earlier Equal Suffrage Club. Katherine was also the granddaughter of Anna Coatsworth Post, founder of the Bay View Reading Club and charter member of the Woman's Literary Club. Following her graduation from the University of Michigan in 1909, Katherine taught high school history in Houghton, Michigan, for

It was to the position of treasurer that Frances Beardslee was later elected.

In 1916, under the leadership of Katherine Post, membership in the Equal Suffrage Club increased. Monthly meetings were held in members' homes, and study papers were routinely presented and discussed. Although these papers focused primarily on the suffrage issue, other issues relating to women, such as prohibition and child labor, were also discussed. Reports from representatives attending county and state meetings were given.[89] Campaign literature received from the state and national suffrage organizations was discussed, and strategies for distributing this literature were identified.[90]

Presentations and discussions beyond Equal Suffrage Club meetings continued to be made. It was reported that at the WCTU meeting September 23, 1916:

> Mrs. DeMerell [sic] was in charge of the program and the subject, "The Value of Woman's Suffrage to Prohibition," was very clearly outlined. Miss Katherine Post in an excellent paper showed the meaning of equal suffrage and the moral and physical benefits experienced by the states adopting it. Mrs. Whitman, in an inspiring talk showed how votes for women would encourage national prohibition.

---

two years and in one other unidentified school system. She returned to Holland and in the fall of 1913 began teaching history at Holland High School, where she continued to teach through the 1918 academic year. It was during this time that she assumed leadership of the Equal Suffrage Club. Bentley Historical Library, University of Michigan, Necrology file for Katherine Cecelia Post.

[89] On November 25, 1916, it was reported, "The Women's Suffrage Club will meet Monday, November 27th at 3:30 P.M. at the home of Mrs. J.W. Beardslee, 26 East 12th Street. Mrs. Champion will give a talk on the Prohibition Campaign. A report of the State convention will be given; all members being urged to be present." *HDS*, November 25, 1916.

[90] On April 18, 1916, the *Holland Daily Sentinel* reported that the monthly meeting would be held at home of Mrs. A.H. Landwehr. "The chief feature of the evening was a paper on child labor, read by Mrs. Nystrom, showing the horror of child labor and its detriments to the nation. The paper excited much discussion among the members present. Mrs. Nystrom has been appointed as chairman of a committee for the purpose of getting good literature on suffrage and other subjects of interest to women, and also giving non members of the club a chance to read this literature. The Equal Suffrage club has been growing very fast since it was first organized last fall." "Eight Join Equal Suffrage Society," *HDS*, April 18, 1916.

An opportunity was given for questions and discussion, many ladies freely taking part....The article of Miss Post will be published in full in Monday's issue.[91]

Although President Wilson issued a proclamation of neutrality in August 1914, war broke out in Europe. As the war expanded, Americans were drawn increasingly into the conflict, and on May 7, 1915, the British passenger ship *Lusitania* was sunk without warning. One hundred fourteen Americans were on board. Following Wilson's reelection in November 1916 and presentation of his peace plan before Congress in January 1917, the United States entered World War I on the Allied side by declaring war on Germany on April 6 and on Austria-Hungary on December 7, 1917.

On Saturday, January 20, 1917, the Holland Equal Suffrage Club invited the public to hear Mrs. O.H. Clark from Kalamazoo, president of the Michigan Equal Suffrage Association, speak in the afternoon at the Woman's Literary Club. In her presentation, Clark underscored the progress made in advancing the suffrage cause, and in particular she described the presence and attention of President and Mrs. Wilson, who had attended the National American Suffrage Convention the previous summer. Such mention clearly seemed to indicate that the president was "warming up" to the suffrage cause. At the end of the program, it was reported that "a good many members were added to the society."[92]

The following evening, Clark was invited to address the young women of Hope College. As reported in the *Holland Daily Sentinel*, "she was introduced by Miss Katherine Post, who has done so much for suffrage in Holland."[93] Following her presentation on women's entry into higher education, the college women voted to establish a suffrage society of their own. Named the Susan B. Anthony Chapter of the Collegiate Suffrage League at Hope College, the following officers were elected: Olive Bertsch, president; Anna Whelan, secretary; Elsie Gowdy, chairman of the executive committee; and Katherine Post, adviser.[94] Under the benevolent care of the local Equal Suffrage Club, the collegiate group planned their work and joined club members in studying the issues.[95]

[91] "The Meaning of Suffrage," Catherine [sic] Post, *HDS*, September 25, 1916.
[92] "State Suffrage Head in Local Address," *HDS*, Jan 22, 1917.
[93] "Olive Bertsch Head of College Suffrage," *HDS*, January 23, 1917.
[94] Ibid.
[95] For their March 1917 meeting, it was reported that they met at the home of Mr. and Mrs. M.A. Sooy; Miss Johann Potts acting as hostess. "Miss Post,

As membership grew, the voice of the Equal Suffrage Club grew sharper. In March 1917, weekly advertisements began to appear in the *Holland Daily Sentinel*. Identified only as "Contributed by the Holland Woman's Suffrage Association," the paid ads were usually two columns wide and a full page in length. The content of the ads included cartoons, pictures, and carefully chosen articles by suffrage leaders.[96] To underscore their argument that women do not lose their household cooking skills when they become suffragists, one week a number of recipes were also included under the sub-headline, "Good Cooks Want Good Votes."[97]

---

[96] the president of the Holland Women's Suffrage club, was present to tell the girls of the work their society is doing and gave many valuable practical suggestions. Miss Post also handed out several papers giving reasons why women should vote, and answering the arguments of anti-suffragists." "Hope Suffragists Hear Arguments," *HDS*, March 23, 1917, 2.

For the Equal Suffrage Club meeting in April, 1917, it was reported:

The program was in charge of the Hope College girls. Their president Miss Olive Bertsch, told of their organization and plans for work. Miss Anna Whelan discussed women and their part in war. Miss Elsie Gowdy talked on the moral effects of woman suffrage. Miss Grace Yoemans spoke of the betterment of conditions in Kansas after women voted. Miss Schurman read an interesting article on the Woman's Work in the World. This program was listened to with great appreciation on the part of the members.

During refreshments an informal discussion followed regarding plans for the school election in July and the duty of every woman to exercise whatever right of voting she may have. The belief that suffrage is coming in France, England and Russia because of the womans [sic] part in the war was expressed and the hope that the U.S. would join her allies in this movement and not unite with Germany, Austria, and Turkey who oppose suffrage.

"Entire Suffrage Club to Act in July Vote," *HDS*, April 17, 1917, 1.

On March 6, 1917, Jane Addams penned an article titled "Is It Public-spirited?" which was accompanied by a sizeable picture of Miss Addams. An accompanying article titled "Not Originally Intended," was written by Madeline McDowell Breckinridge. *HDS*, March 6, 1917.

Again March 13, 1917, a two-column ad ran the full length of the page and was titled, "Protect Your Home With Two Votes Instead of One," *HDS*, March 13, 1917.

And again March 23, 1917, a two-column ad was run, "The Home and the Vote—A New Kind of Woman's Page; Showing That Woman Must Meddle With Politics Because Politics Has Already Meddled With Her," *HDS*, March 23, 1917.

[97] "Protect Your Home with Two Votes Instead of One," *HDS*, March 13, 1917, 4.

For Michigan suffragists, the goal of obtaining the presidential vote was fulfilled in April 1917, when the state legislature passed by a vote of 64 to 30[98] and Governor Charles Flowers (1845-1921) signed into law a limited suffrage measure.[99] The action allowed Michigan women to vote in the 1920 presidential election. However gratifying this was to the women of Michigan, full suffrage could only be obtained by amending the federal constitution through a popular vote, followed by ratification by a majority of the states. As events unfolded, such a referendum vote was scheduled to take place on November 5, 1918.

Following the U.S. declaration of war against Germany April 7, 1917, Holland's citizens became enveloped in a whirlwind of patriotic activities. Patriotic mass meetings were held, strategies for military preparedness were discussed, resolutions of patriotic support and readiness to serve the nation were written and sent to the leaders of the country.[100] For the women of the community, supporting the war effort included volunteering to aid the Red Cross. To this end, the expressed commitment of the DAR, the WCTU, and the Women's Literary Club was supplemented by a pledge of support from the Holland Equal Suffrage Club, when club members voted to cooperate with the DAR in supporting this work.[101]

Having arrived at the end of their fiscal year, members of the Equal Suffrage Club met at the home of Mrs. J.P. Oggel in May 1917,

[98] "Suffrage Bill Now Awaits Signature," *HDS*, April 19, 1917.

[99] According to the *Michigan Suffragist*, "The United States Constitution in Section 2, Article 1, provides that the electors for President and Vice-President "shall be appointed in such manner as the legislature may direct."...[sic] The State constitution says who shall be electors on other questions and specifically mentions male electors a number of times. Therefore, in order that women may vote for all officers mentioned in the constitution, and for all questions other than school and those involving direct expenditure of money, the constitution must be amended by vote of the electors at popular election, and the word male be stricken out of the paragraph defining electors." For this explanation of why the state legislature was limited to grant presidential suffrage only, see the *Michigan Suffragist*, no date, 2, as photocopied for inclusion in "How the Suffragists Changed Michigan," an educational resource packet, 1989, made available from the Michigan Women's Historical Center and Hall of Fame, Lansing, Mich.

[100] See *HDS*, April 17, 1917, 1-2; "Hope Holds Patriotic Mass Meet," *HDS*, April 11, 1917, 1; "W.L.C. Offers Clubhouse for War Work," *HDS*, April 11, 1917, 1; "Mrs. J.C. Post to Teach School Girls Knitting Saturdays: Put Aside Fancy Work and Make Bandages Is Call of D.A.R." *HDS*, April 13, 1917, 2.

[101] This list should not be understood to be inclusive. "Entire Suffrage Club to Act in July Vote," *HDS*, April 17, 1917, 1.

listened to annual reports, and elected officers for the following year. These officers were identified as Katherine Post, president; Mrs. P.W. Whitman, vice-president, Mrs. W.A. VanSyckle, secretary, Miss Anna Dehn, corresponding secretary; Mrs. J.W. Beardslee, treasurer, and Miss Laverne Jones, reporter.[102]

With new officers elected for the coming year, the next monthly meeting took place in June, when "over thirty" club members "rode out" to enjoy a picnic at the Pine Creek Bay home of Mr. and Mrs. A.H. Landwehr. According to the *Holland Daily Sentinel*, the speaker for the afternoon was Mrs. Williams from Grand Rapids, who was chairman of the Fifth Congressional District.[103] In her presentation Williams stressed the need for a federal amendment, the challenges that needed to be addressed by Michigan suffragists, and "especially she emphasized the needs of organization in Ottawa County, this county being one of the very few in the state still unorganized." She added:

> The members of the Holland organization have been cooperating in the various lines of activity here but there seemed one useful line in which no work had been done, namely the canning of fruits and vegetables in quantities to conserve the food supply.[104]

This project was one of many suffrage projects relating to the war effort, and immediately Post appointed a committee composed of VanSyckle, Eidson, and Jones to arrange for a canning demonstration in an effort to meet this need.[105]

If Frances Beardslee were present at this meeting, which in all probability she was, it would have been her last meeting. On Monday, June 4, 1917, delegates to the General Synod of the Reformed Church in America, meeting in Asbury Park, New Jersey, elected John W. Beardslee, Jr., to the position of professor of Hellenistic Greek and New Testament exegesis in the New Brunswick Theological Seminary

---

[102] "Miss Post Re-elected Suffrage Club Head," *HDS*, May 8, 1917, 1.

[103] Based on the Michigan "Suffrage Honor Roll" list, Mrs. Williams was probably Helen A. Williams from Grand Rapids. This list was put together by the Michigan Women's Studies Association as part of the celebration of the 75th anniversary of the 19th Amendment. Rachel Brett Harley and Betty MacDowell, *Michigan Women: Firsts and Founders*, vol. 2. Michigan Women's Studies Association, Inc. 1995.

[104] "Suffrage Club Will Make Demonstration," *HDS*, June 11, 1917.

[105] Also at this meeting a committee to interest women in the coming school election was appointed. This committee included Mrs. Olive, Miss Post, and Mrs. Shaw. Ibid.

in New Brunswick, New Jersey. Given her husband's acceptance of the position, the family, which now included two young sons plus John W. Beardslee, Sr., would be leaving Holland and moving to the East Coast. They were expected to move into their new home in early July.

It must have been extremely difficult for Frances Beardslee to leave her friends in Holland. It must have been especially difficult to leave the work of the Equal Suffrage Club. The suffrage issue in Michigan continued to gain strength. As the November 1918, election drew closer, those most vocal in their opposition to suffrage argued that women didn't really want the franchise.[106] In response to this, Michigan suffragists circulated and published petitions. Four hundred eight women from Ottawa County signed a petition that was published in the October 31, 1918 issue of the *Holland City News*. It stated:

> To the Voters Ottawa County
> We, the undersigned Women of voting age petition
> you to vote in favor of Woman Suffrage.
> November 5th, 1918.

Although Frances Beardslee's name did not appear on this petition, another petition containing 182,000 signatures[107] was published

---

[106] As noted by Ruth E. Hoogland, who writes:

> Organized opposition, on the other hand, was not as strong or as vocal as in the last election. The National Association Opposed to Woman Suffrage did place large advertisements in the Michigan papers that would print them, but otherwise the state anti-suffragists were too hurt by prohibition to stage an effective campaign. Their case against equal franchise, as it appeared in the Herald's November 3 edition, consisted of four major points, none of which was convincing: 1) The majority of women do not want the vote, 2) Soldiers cannot vote on it, 3) Suffragists have tried to ally war work with suffrage work, but it isn't connected, 4) Pro-German Socialist vote in New York City brought victory to New York suffragists.

Grand Rapids Herald, November 3, 1918, 4, as quoted in Ruth E. Hoogland, "Petticoats, Politics, and Public Opinion: A study of the Woman Suffrage Movement in Michigan, With Emphasis on Grand Rapids From 1910-1920," a paper written for History 400, Calvin College, December 31, 1975, and found in the Grand Rapids Public Library, collection 127, box 1, folder 1.

See also Flexner, *Century of Struggle*, 294-305.

[107] In the *Holland Sentinel* that number was reported to be 198, 215, "with additions still being made each day." "Nearly 200,000 Michigan Women Sign Petitions," *Holland Sentinel* (*HS*), November 4, 1918.

over the course of three days prior to the November 5 election with a portion of the names appearing in each of the three Grand Rapids newspapers.[108] That petition read:

> We, the undersigned women, petition you to vote
> "YES" for Woman Suffrage on November 5th.
> – 14,000 women in the City of Grand Rapids, 182,000 in the State of Michigan have signed this petition
> – Women are sharing equally with you the burdens of this country.
> – We are willing to work beside you – fight beside you – die beside you – LET US VOTE BESIDE YOU.

The name of "Mrs. F.E. Beardslee"[109] did appear on this petition.

It seems unfair to end this chronology without bringing the story of the suffrage movement in Holland, Michigan, to some kind of conclusion. Having learned from the election in 1912, suffragists were appointed by Mrs. Huntley Russell, organizer for the Fifth Congressional District, to provide "challengers" at each of the voting places. In Holland, Mrs. R. N. De Merrell and Mrs. W.J. Gohlke were given this responsibility.[110]

The outlook in Holland for passing the woman's franchise looked encouraging.[111] The day before the election it was reported, "Those who

---

[108] The first installment of names appeared Friday, November 1, 1918, in the *Grand Rapids News*. The second set of names appeared in the Saturday, November 2, 1918, edition of the *Grand Rapids Press*, and the third group of names appeared in the Sunday edition of the *Grand Rapids Herald*.

[109] Frances Eunice Davis Beardslee was Frances Beardslee's full name.

[110] "Challengers Are Picked for Election; Chairman Names a Number of Women for Ottawa County," *HS*, November 4, 1918.

[111] It is not the intention of the author to overlook the role of area churches in making their voices known on the issue of suffrage. However, it is beyond the scope of this study to identify and discuss the position of the Reformed Church in America. Reference may be made to Matthew Baasten's student paper, "An Examination of the Reformed Church's View on Woman Suffrage," which was written for Donald Bruggink's church history course at Western Theological Seminary, May 17, 1974, W88-0758, JAH. This paper evaluates the number of articles on suffrage, on prohibition, and on the war that appear between the years 1909 and 1920 in the *Leader*, a weekly publication of the Reformed Church in America that was published in Grand Rapids, Michigan.

An editorial appearing in the August 14, 1918, issue of the *Leader* suggests that the editor of the magazine took a very tepid view of the suffrage issue by recognizing changes in public opinion and the evolving

follow the signs believe that equal suffrage will carry Ottawa County this time, and indications throughout the state are of the same character. A radical change in sentiment in regard to this is noticeable among the voters of both parties."[112] Coupled with ideal weather conditions,[113] a record number of male voters cast their ballots in the City of Holland on November 5. Of the 2,769 ballots counted, 1,111 votes were cast in favor of woman's suffrage, and 1,658 votes were cast against granting the franchise to women,[114] thus defeating the measure by 553 votes or a margin of more than two to one. The following day, in a headline that read: "Dutch Still Are Against Woman Vote," the *Holland Sentinel* reported:

> There was thus not a single ward in the city that went in favor of suffrage—which would almost lead to the conclusion that the majority of the city don't want the women to vote!"
>
> However, if the returns up to two o'clock this afternoon are not overturned by later reports the state as a whole went in favor of suffrage, and the women of Holland and Ottawa county will profit by the vote in the other counties. Holland women will yet be able to vote in spite of their husbands who did their best to keep the ballot out of their hands.[115]

---

position of President Wilson. *Leader*, August 14, 1918, 4.

Unlike the Reformed Church in America, the referenda votes in 1912 and 1913 caused a sharp and public discussion of the suffrage issue among a group of Christian Reformed Church ministers in the Grand Rapids area. A larger body of materials surrounds this discussion. See Nicholas Huizenga, "Christian Reformed Church versus Feminism 1912-1913," Eastern Historical Committee, March 1984, Hekman Library, Calvin College, Grand Rapids, Michigan.

[112] "Electorate of Old Ottawa Ready to Vote," *HS*, November 4, 1918.
[113] "Republican Landslide in Holland," *HS*, November 6, 1918, 1.
[114] *HS*, November 6, 1918, 1.
[115] "Dutch Still Are Against Woman Vote," *HS*, November 6, 1918, 1.

It is interesting that the author of this newspaper article chose to note that it was "the Dutch element" that expressly failed to support woman's suffrage:

> The Dutch still have it in for Woman Suffrage. This is shown quite conclusively by the fact that the larger the Dutch element in the population in Ottawa county and Western Michigan, the larger the vote against suffrage. Holland voted against suffrage by considerably more than two to one, the exact figures being 1,315 [sic] against the issue and only 552 [sic] in favor of it. The north half of the county which also has a considerable Dutch population, also went on record

Passage of the suffrage amendment in Michigan gave Michigan women universal suffrage in 1918. Because not all women in all states had been granted this privilege, the Nineteenth Amendment was passed by Congress June 5, 1919. It was ratified by the State of Michigan June 10, 1919, and on August 26, 1919, the 19th Amendment to the U. S. Constitution became law.[116]

The Leading Ladies of Holland

When Frances Beardslee arrived in Holland in August, 1912, she was twenty-five years of age,[117] recently married, and altogether new to the community. As has been noted, her non-Dutch background made her an outsider.[118] But over the course of the next five years, she would meet impressive women who, like Frances, sought to grow personally and to bring about changes that would make the community safer, healthier, better educated, and more inclusive of women. A large number of church-minded and civic-minded women committed themselves to one or more of these endeavors, each of whom deserves a page of her own in any history of the women of Holland. Among this

---

against suffrage but not as strongly as this section. Apparently the American communities in that section helped to return a larger vote for suffrage than was the case here. To clinch the argument that it was the Dutch who did it, the vote in Allegan county is cited. There the Holland element is comparatively small and is confined to the northern fringe of the county. The vote in Allegan county went in favor of suffrage according to the returns so far available.

[116] In 1995 the Michigan Women's Studies Association published *Michigan Women: Firsts and Founders Volume II*, which was published in celebration of the 75th Anniversary of the ratification of the 19th Amendment. This compilation of names serves as a beginning point only and reflects the absence of records collected thus far for the Holland Equal Suffrage Club. The names, as they appear on this list, which denote involvement in Holland (as opposed to others in Ottawa County) include: Gerrit J. Diekema, Mrs. R.N. Demerell [sic], Elsie Gowdy, Grace Inman, Mrs. A.H. Landwehr, Mrs. Charles H. McBridge [sic], Mrs. Nystrom, Katherine Post, Mrs. J.C. Post, Mr. G.W. Rogers, Anna Whelan.

[117] Frances Beardslee was born on October 17, 1887 and died on June 28, 1975.

[118] John W. Beardslee III, the eldest of Frances and John Beardslee's sons, remembers his mother telling him that, when interacting with her Holland friends, she would often hear "Dutchisms" and observe the ladies laughing. When she inquired what the "Dutchism" meant, she was told, "You can't translate that into English."

large number of women, in the course of my research, a core group of eight leaders emerged.

This core group of women touched Frances's life most significantly and served as models for her. So brief a list can in no way be understood to be exhaustive or even inclusive of Holland's most outstanding ladies. It is only to say that these eight women affected Frances Beardlee's life significantly for one or another reason.[119] The eight women include Kate Garrod Post (Mrs. John C.), Lillie Bright Oggel (Mrs. John P.), Katherine C. Post, Iantha Aldrich DeMerrell (Mrs. Richard N.), Louise Landwehr (Mrs. A.H.), Christine Van Raalte Gilmore (Mrs. William B.), Anna E. Wheeler (Mrs. Charles C.), and Martha Diekema Kollen (Mrs. George E.).

All eight of the women in this core group were members of Hope Church. Of the eight, five were members both of the Ladies' Aid Society and the Ladies' Missionary Society. This suggests that the Christian faith and the church formed a major piece of their lives.

Six organizations have been identified in which Frances Beardslee was involved during her Holland years. Of the eight women mentioned above, only two women shared membership with Frances in all six organizations. These women were Kate Post and Lillie Oggel. Both women shared with Frances the experience of church life, civic life, and social life.

Kate Garrod Post represented both the inside and the outside of community life. Her marriage to a member of one of the community's founding families and her commitment to church life placed her at the heart of community life. Yet, her non-Dutch parentage and DAR involvement underscored her pride in who she was apart from Holland. She came to epitomize Dutch hospitality. Kate Post must have seemed brave to the newly arrived Frances, when Kate's name became known as president of the first Equal Suffrage Club. Not many others would have dared to advocate for woman's suffrage at that time, when the perception of women as "unwomanly" and unpatriotic was associated with suffragists and when so many women and men in the Holland community stood opposed to the suffrage cause. In this way, Kate Post put herself on the line for other women.

At the time of Frances's arrival, Kate Post had suffered the grief of her husband's tragic death at his own hand in 1903, and in 1909 the

---

[119] There is no order of importance in how the names are listed. Since it is not the purpose of this essay to research the lives of these individual women, comments about their lives will be limited to their relationships to Frances Beardslee as framed within the context of this essay.

public embarrassment of her son Richard's mysterious disappearance under shameful circumstances. Through it all Kate Post stood tall.[120] With the help of her friends, especially women friends, she moved beyond these tragedies to discover new and different ways to serve the community, especially the women, and in so doing she served as a model for Frances Beardslee, who would suffer her own family tragedies over the course of her life.

Katherine C. Post, Kate's daughter, was sixteen when her father died. Perhaps because of her brother Richard's disappearance and the aftermath of that family tragedy, Katherine went to work as a history teacher in Houghton, Michigan—rather distant from Holland in those days. But she returned in 1914 to teach at Holland High School, and her return must have been welcomed by her mother. Katherine Post was a contemporary of Frances Beardslee. Katherine was her own person and was remembered as brilliant and "a liberated woman before her time."[121] According to a teaching colleague, "She was sure of herself, but she had a right to be because she looked at things squarely....She was an independent thinker. I admired her, but I stood off and looked on. She was very independent."[122] Over the course of Frances Beardslee's life, there were a number of people who might have thought the same thing about her.

Frances and Katherine Post became lifelong friends. Although Frances's time was limited by caring for two young children, Frances and Katherine together worked on behalf of woman's suffrage. In the paper that was presented and published in September 1916, Katherine Post's rationale for supporting suffrage shines as a remarkable piece of

---

[120] According to the local newspaper:

> Mrs. J.C. Post and other members of the family of the missing Richard H. Post have determined to make good all losses in the forgery cases. Announcement of this intention was made today and appears in The Press on another page. When these matters are all straightened up, the affairs of the fugitive real estate man will be put into the bankruptcy courts for adjudication.

> "Amazing Deals of the Young Post," unknown newspaper, August 31, 1909, as found in T88-0160, JAH.

[121] These were the words used by Helena Winter as reported to the author by Fritzi Sennett. Telephone conversation notes taken June 15, 2001.

[122] Quoted from an interview with Lillian VanDyke, January 7, 2001. VanDyke taught English at Holland High School for many years, retiring in 1962. She taught with Katherine C. Post and remembered her well.

scholarship. For Frances, a commitment to excellence in scholarship always made a difference.[123]

As members of the Equal Suffrage Club especially, Frances Beardslee came to admire Iantha Aldrich DeMerrell and to appreciate Louise Landwehr. Iantha DeMerrell was a strong leader, and it was she who served as the first president of the Woman's Literary Club. But in September 1915, Iantha attended a suffrage meeting in Grand Rapids, at which time women in the Fifth Congressional District organized themselves to advocate for a federal amendment, and she agreed to serve as treasurer of the organization—the only woman from Holland so to serve at that time. And when the women of the Woman's Literary Club met October 29, 1915, to hear the Reverend Caroline Bartlett Crane request the organization of Holland's own Equal Suffrage Club, it was Iantha who moved the question to a vote. Iantha DeMerrell had her finger on the pulse of the times and pressed for change on behalf of women.

Louise Landwehr was also a strong voice in support of woman's suffrage and helped facilitate meetings of the Holland Equal Suffrage Club. Although few details of her life are known, Louise Landwehr, whose husband was one of the founders of the Holland Furnace Co., hosted many meetings of the club.

As the daughter of Albertus and Christina Van Raalte, Christine Van Raalte Gilmore held an honored position within the community. Married to the Reverend William B. Gilmore (who was a member of Hope's first graduating class), and a charter member of Hope Church, Christine Gilmore used her position, her Christian conviction, and her amazing personal gifts to organize and inspire other women in the cause of missions. She was passionate in her commitment to organize church mission societies and the Holland Classical Union. She moved the women who lived in the Midwest to become engaged with church women in the East as part of a national church network of women committed to the work and service of missions.[124] Christine Van Raalte

---

[123] In 1937 Frances Beardslee was appointed by the General Synod to the Hope College Board of Trustees. She was the first woman so to serve. She remained a board member for thirteen years.

[124] There are numerous tributes to Christine Van Raalte Gilmore for her years of service on behalf of missions. See "A Tribute to Mrs. C.V.R. Gilmore," *Golden Years in Miniature: A History of the Women's Board of Domestic Missions of the Reformed Church in America from the Time of Its Organization in 1882 as the Women's Executive Committee of the Board of Domestic Missions to Its Present Golden Anniversary Year*, 1932, for one such tribute.

Gilmore's leadership had a strong effect on Frances, and she learned much from their interactions that would serve her well through all of her years of service on the Woman's Board of Foreign Missions.[125]

Anna Wheeler was sixty-six years of age when Frances arrived. Anna herself was at one time an outsider to the Holland community, and she shared with Frances the bond of having lived in Connecticut. Anna and her husband arrived in Holland as pioneers in 1894, and over the years they became known for their hospitality. Anna was a charter member of the Woman's Literary Club, the Century Club, and the DAR, the only woman to hold this distinction. Anna had also been friends with Sarah Beardslee, Frances's mother-in-law, and it would not be difficult to imagine that Anna Wheeler represented both experience and wisdom in Frances's eyes.

Of all the leading ladies mentioned above, Martha Diekema Kollen's name is perhaps the most recognized among visitors to Holland. Kollen Park in Holland was given to the citizens of Holland by Martha in 1921 in memory of her husband, reflecting her early interest in conservation and beautification. For twelve years she served as president of the Woman's Literary Club. In July 1917, Martha Kollen began serving as a member of the Holland Board of Education, the first woman to hold this honor.[126] As the daughter of a former U.S. Congressman, Martha was extremely well traveled, and she spoke often to community groups about her travels. Mary Alcott Diekema, Martha's mother, was among the early women graduates of Hope College and taught Martha the art of entertaining.

Martha Kollen was twenty years older than Frances Beardslee. It is not known if Martha was active in the Equal Suffrage Club, but she did add her name to the petition requesting the franchise that was circulated and published locally.

These women and many others served as leaders in the Holland community.[127] In so many ways they shine as examples of "new women."

---

[125] From 1932-1942 Frances Beardslee served as chairman of the Missionary Candidate Committee of the Woman's Board of Foreign Missions. In this capacity she reviewed applications, interviewed candidates, and made recommendations for all those who sought to become missionaries under appointment of the Woman's Board of Foreign Missions. For a history of this position, see Kansfield, *Letters to Hazel*, 128-29. For many years Frances also served as treasurer of the WBFM.

[126] File "Teachers Directories 1910-1923," T88-0298, JAH.

[127] You are encouraged to read Helena V. Winter's paper, "Our Petticoated Pioneers 1850-1930," March 17, 1992, H96-1268, JAH.

When Frances Beardslee departed Holland in 1917, she went to her new responsibilities with significant strengths that were not obvious when she arrived in Holland—strengths that would not have been hers if she had failed to make these friends, or with them to find her way in the community.

PART 2

Tools for Understanding Historiography

History is the story of what has happened. Taken literally, historiography is writing about history, writing about the story of what happened. While all who write histories could be called historiographers—as Russell Gasero points out in his chapter, Edward Corwin was referred to in this way—historiography most often refers to the study of how history has been studied and preserved. It is, most often, an academic exercise, and could be considered a sort of navel gazing, except that the way in which we choose to tell our stories and the details we choose to emphasize say quite a bit about us. Anyone wishing to test this premise need only thumb through a copy of *Centennial Discourses of the Reformed Church in America*[1]—a collection of essays first presented as speeches in the United States' centennial year of 1876—and *Piety and Patriotism*[2]—a collection of essays on the very same topics prepared as a volume of the Historical Series in the U.S. bicentennial year.

[1] (New York: Board of Publication of the Reformed Church in America, 1877).
[2] James W. VanHoeven, ed. (Grand Rapids: Eerdmans, 1976).

As church history professor at Western, general editor of the Historical Series, and an early advocate of the modern Archives of the Reformed Church in America, Donald Bruggink has left a bigger imprint on the historiography of the denomination than anyone in the last century, certainly, possibly a larger influence than any other single person. As such, it seems appropriate to examine some modern Reformed Church historiography. Russell Gasero examines the development of the Archives, and how we have decided to save what we save. Laurie Baron, without whom much of this Historical Series would be an unreadable dream, tells us about working on these books. Don should be especially pleased that their contributions, both containing primary source material, not only tell our story but lay the groundwork for generations of historians we have not yet met.

CHAPTER 4

The Story of the Archives of the Reformed Church in America

Russell L. Gasero

Introduction

"Ziggy" is a popular cartoon strip which often provides needed insights into contemporary issues. In one strip from the 1970s, Ziggy stands on a hilltop while watching a beautiful sunset. Suddenly, across the sky there flashes a message, "Due to lack of interest, tomorrow has been canceled." The Reformed Church in America can be compared to that fellow standing on a hilltop because there is often a danger that the message may flash across, "Due to lack of interest, yesterday has been forgotten."

We have focused much energy and talent on the examination of our identity, the understanding of our structures, and the refinement of our processes for staffing the church, starting new congregations, and revitalizing old congregations. Often lost in all those efforts are the labors of those who preceded us and brought us to this point. We must be sure that we neither forget nor ignore our heritage. The documentary resources that serve as our institutional memory have had a very precarious life over the last three and three-quarter centuries, and the last few decades have witnessed years of growth and continued progress toward making the archives[1] a valuable resource for the Reformed Church in America.

Our heritage defines us as a people of God, provides guidance for growth into the future, and serves as our common memory along the course of our corporate journey. Our documentary heritage is the physical record of that journey.

Donald Bruggink has dedicated his life and ministry to helping the Reformed Church understand itself and its growth over time. He has brought that historical perspective into active work on contemporary problems facing the church in theology, liturgy, architecture, and a variety of social issues. My hope is that this brief offering helps honor that service by offering some sense of what archives are, how they can be used, where they are stored, and how the denominational archives came to be gathered in one location.

Archives—What Are They?

Everyone is familiar with saving the records that are considered vitally important for our well-being and our well-functioning. Hospital records, financial records, canceled checks, tax returns and receipts, savings account books, letters from relatives and friends all come to mind when we think about important records that have meaning for our lives. Where would we be if we didn't keep a record of checks written? How would our health be jeopardized if we didn't keep immunization records and other medical records? What would the Internal Revenue Service say if we couldn't produce a record that substantiates our deduction?

Such records comprise our personal and family archives and are vital for avoiding financial, legal, and personal difficulties. In addition, we all have collections of letters and papers that we rarely read, yet we hold onto them in fond remembrance of our past. Letters from parents, children, and friends all make up our documentary memory about earlier years in our lives and the written memories of loved ones. These are our archives.

The Church's Memory

The church also has a need to preserve a documentary memory. The life of the church as a whole is far more complex than the life and

[1] A note on capitalization: the lower-cased "archives" is used to distinguish the collection of materials from the "Archives," which is the formal office responsible for managing the Reformed Church in America's archival collection.

memory of a single individual. Financial dealings, legal considerations, and friendly correspondence all take place on a far grander scale than our daily, personal doings. Financial memory loss and legal errors can cost huge sums of money and will affect far more than one individual. The mass of information created on a daily basis by a denomination of 931 congregations and over 270,000 total members,[2] with missionaries serving on nearly every continent and with three colleges and two seminaries, must be managed very carefully. Paper is generated on a large scale every day and most of it is useful only for a short time and may then be discarded. *Records are created to help us keep track of our financial obligations and commitments. In a rapidly changing financial scene these records are short lived. Other records provide evidence of the church's decision-making and theological positions.* Records such as the minutes of the General Synod help define us as part of the people of God.

The Archives of the Reformed Church in America is the "storehouse" for this information. Its job is to determine which records are valuable for the future and which records can be disposed of in the present. The Archives also provides a vast informational database, which serves to define our identity over time as a people working for the kingdom.

It also includes records that have administrative, legal, financial, and historical value for the future. They are not simple housekeeping records, which indicate how many pencils the Finance Office ordered in 1978, for example, nor are they collections of old bulletin covers from an assortment of congregations which no longer want to store such paper in their own building. These records provide our denominational memory, which stretches back far beyond the lives of the present membership. As documentary evidence, they provide a profile of the faithfulness of the Reformed Church in America as God's people. As memory, they challenge us to grow into the future on the basis of our foundation established in the past. As unbiased witnesses, they indicate the bad times as well as the good times, periods of faithfulness as well as times of trouble and dissent.

The Office of Historical Services

The Office of Historical Services is responsible for the collection, care, and use of the Archives of the Reformed Church in America. This responsibility involves determining which records are of permanent value and which have no long-term usefulness; placing these records in

---

[2] *Acts and Proceedings of the General Synod of the Reformed Church in America*, 2008, 417.

appropriate relationship to each other so that retrieval can be quick and efficient; and helping researchers, scholars, students, and other users find and use the materials of which they have need.[3] In addition to its archival tasks, the office also managed the Historical Society of the Reformed Church in America and its publication programs active in the 1980s and 1990s, which included *Historical Highlights*, the *Dutch American Genealogist*, and Historical Society *Occasional Papers*. The Archives' budget is supported by the General Synod Council. The storage facilities and office space are rented from New Brunswick Theological Seminary, with offsite storage areas at Iron Mountain and in Cambridge, Ontario, Canada. In a sense, a better name for the Office of Historical Services would be the "Office of Chronicle Collection, Tradition Maintenance, and the Preservation of the Acts of the Disciples." It is so much more than just a mountain of paper.

What is in the Archives?

The Archives of the Reformed Church in America is the main repository for all denominational records from the level of the congregation through the General Synod. The current holdings include records from more than three hundred active and disbanded congregations, forty-five classes, all the regional synods, and the General Synod and its agencies such as the Board of Publication, the General Program Council, the Board of Domestic Missions, and other agencies and boards established during the last three and three-quarter centuries.[4] Mission records include documentation relating to China, Borneo, Japan, Mexico, the Middle East, India, and North America. Scholars from around the world use these records regularly for their research. Yet, it is important to realize that the Archives exists primarily to serve the needs of the denomination.

---

[3] Technically, these functions are known as appraisal, arrangement and description, and reference. For an introduction to archival theory and methods consult Greg Hunter, *Developing and Maintaining Practical Archives: A How-To-Do-It Manual*, 2nd ed. (New York: Neal-Schuman Publishers, Inc., 2003).

[4] For an introductory understanding of the RCA's structure and mission efforts, see Marvin Hoff, *Structures for Mission*, Historical Series of the Reformed Church in America, no. 9 (Grand Rapids: Eerdmans, 1985); to explore the entire history of the Reformed Church in one volume see Donald J. Bruggink and Kim N. Baker, *By Grace Alone: Stories of the Reformed Church in America*, Historical Series of the Reformed Church in America, no. 44 (Grand Rapids: Eerdmans, 2004).

Neither the operation nor the collection came into existence rapidly. The basis for the establishment of the Archives is built upon two factors: the Reformed Church has a long tradition of concern for keeping adequate and informative records, and the major emphasis of historical efforts in the Reformed Church has always centered upon the use of history for the future well-functioning and growth of the life and mission of the church.

However, it can be questioned whether the concern for history and the use of history ever went beyond slogan-quoting and back-patting in an antiquarian manner. From time to time, individuals with a keen historical sense and an interest in the preservation of important documentation have come to the forefront. Fortunately, they were able to accomplish great works with little assistance and even less financial support.

History of the Archival Effort

A concern for the preservation of the important documents in the Reformed Church was clearly indicated in the earliest formation of a church organization in America. The rules of order for the coetus provided for the maintenance and preservation of a record book. The early church was under the supervision of the Classis of Amsterdam in the Netherlands. When American independence was achieved, the church also became independent from the Classis of Amsterdam and established its own synod and local classes.[5]

From the start, a concern for record keeping and orderly processes was evident. In 1785, the "General Synod decreed that a book be purchased to record letters addressed to and sent from the body. The book was to be in the care of" the treasurer.[6] A few years later, in 1792, the synod desired to collect the records of its predecessor bodies, the coetus and the conferentie, and requested all classes to search out and gather the old records and also to present an "accurate and definite

---

[5] This history is well told by Gerald De Jong, *The Dutch Reformed Church in the American Colonies* (Grand Rapids: Eerdmans, 1968). While De Jong and others use the term, "General Synod," Edward Tanjore Corwin, in *A Manual of the Reformed Church in America* (New York: Board of Publication of the Reformed Church in America, 1902), 134, points out that there was no General Synod until the first particular synods were formed in 1800. Prior to that, the synod that was convened annually was known as the "Provisional Synod," although the term, "General Synod," was also used as early as 1794.

[6] *Acts and Proceedings*, 1785, 135.

account of the time of the formation of the congregations, and of the persons by whom it was effected, with an accompanying historical narrative of the most noteworthy events which have occurred from time to time."[7]

This could well be marked as the start of the denominational archives—if indeed records had been gathered and deposited. Instead, nothing happened. During the years which followed, inquiry was made from time to time concerning the location of the General Synod records and the means of their preservation and protection. While the importance of preserving adequate documentation about the church's programs and activity was never questioned, no extensive effort was made to insure the archives' proper housing and collection. The synod's notion of record keeping was focused primarily on current records. In 1800, the synod established a rule relating to the safekeeping of valuable and historical records. The minister of the congregation where the next annual meeting was to be held was responsible for preparing a copy of the minutes for the presidents of the individual classes. The stated clerk of the synod was responsible for storing and providing these records to the synod from year to year.[8]

Writing the Denomination's History

A new interest in the history of the church was sparked in the mid-nineteenth century. The General Synod of 1841 asked the Reverend Thomas De Witt to prepare a history of the Reformed Dutch church, which would include an account of its roots in the Netherlands. After some preliminary research and an inquiry as to the location of its earliest records, De Witt sadly reminded the synod of its action of 1792 and indicated that many records had already been lost. Despite this resolution, nothing seemed to have been brought into the archives. The only items that had been gathered were a succession of General Synod minutes.

De Witt chastised the synod by noting that it "is deeply to be regretted that it was not at the time diligently and faithfully attended to, as then many documents would have been recovered and preserved, and much traditional information, well authenticated, might have been gathered which are now lost."[9] His warning apparently came too late, because many valuable and irreplaceable documents had been given

[7] *Acts and Proceedings*, 1792, 241.
[8] *Acts and Proceedings*, 1800, 311-12.
[9] *Acts and Proceedings*, 1843, 272.

into the hands of individual ministers and subsequently were either lost or destroyed. With the hope of receiving the material he needed to write the history of the church, he wrote to many ministers and lay people, asking them to examine whatever consistory minutes or other church records they might have in their possession. He hoped that such a survey would help gather the needed records together and ease his task in preparing a comprehensive history. His goal was to gather the records and incorporate them into the denomination's archives.

De Witt lamented that the survey was unsuccessful and reported that "in order to procure the materials which may yet by diligent investigation be obtained, it is necessary for the individual engaged in preparing this historical work to possess leisure and means to visit personally different parts of the church, and personally to make thorough research."[10]

This failure to gather the records of the previous century sparked a new interest in historical matters in the denomination, which paralleled other interests in historical matters of the time. The records, housed previously in a large trunk, were transferred to a book case, funds for which were appropriated by the 1841 General Synod.[11] These records were then stored in the new consistory building of the church on Fulton Street (later the home of the Fulton Street Prayer Meeting). The building was fireproof and several documents, manuscripts, minutes, and synod papers were stored here.[12]

Apparently, the storage area was adequate, because the synod congratulated Thomas Strong, the stated clerk, on his "well-known taste and love of order, in the erection of fixtures which do credit to the Synod, and deserve their thanks."[13] That was in 1845, four years after the funds had been approved to buy a storage case.

This situation seems to have been adequate, because there is no mention of the archives for the next fifteen years. In 1860, the storeroom of John I. Brower, the treasurer of the Board of Direction of the corporate church, caught fire and burned, resulting in the loss of important papers. It was supposed that "no inconvenience will arise therefrom, as most of them were very old, and possess no pecuniary value."[14] Business books and receipts seem to have been lost. Most of the information had already been published in the annual minutes

[10] Ibid.
[11] *Acts and Proceedings*, 1841, 535.
[12] *Acts and Proceedings*, 1845, 518.
[13] Ibid., 487.
[14] *Acts and Proceedings*, 1860, 486.

of the General Synod. However, once again, interest was aroused in archival preservation and this resulted in the appointment of a committee to look into the situation. Its charge was to "suggest a plan for the collection and preservation of documents relating to the past history of the church."[15]

Permanent Archival Storage Area

The committee's work resulted in a new, permanent home for the denomination's archives. The records were transferred to the Gardner A. Sage Library on the campus of the New Brunswick Theological Seminary in 1876. Gardner A. Sage, "with wise and generous forethought, provided in the plan of the Hall that bears his name, a room perfectly secure, and ample for all the Synod's wants, which he has fitted up with shelves and other appurtenances, for the proper arrangement and deposit of the Synod's archives."[16]

As the records were being transferred to the library, their earlier lack of care and damage from so much transferring from place to place became apparent. The stated clerk reported that some volumes of the minutes were missing, many old papers had no dates, and many seemed to be missing. He reported to the synod that

> the archives were in a deplorable condition, perfectly confused, permeated with the dust of years and only partially preserved. This is not owing to the carelessness of former Stated Clerks, evidences of whose system and care in arranging papers are manifest, but to the fact that the Archives have never been deposited in a safe place, and that they have been mixed up with other less valuable papers whose fate they have shared.[17]

The committee responsible for the records' care made an effort to arrange them and then extended an offer to other church assemblies and congregations to deposit their records in this vault for safekeeping. This offer was regularly repeated at the synod meetings, and slowly records began to be deposited in the new storage room.

---

[15] *Acts and Proceedings*, 1866, 112.
[16] *Acts and Proceedings*, 1876, 568-69. For those visiting the Sage Library, this "double fireproof" storage room is now the handicapped access bathroom on the first floor—perhaps the safest bathroom in the region.
[17] *Acts and Proceedings*, 1876, 568-69.

Gathering the Colonial Correspondence

During this period of the development of a suitable storage facility, a similar effort was underway with regard to the collection of colonial documents relating to the church. The 1840s, which saw the initial interest in a denominational history, also generated interest in the collection of historical manuscripts. De Witt had notified the synod of the research of J. Romeyn Brodhead, which uncovered many valuable documents relating to the church in the Archives of the Netherlands. De Witt was given permission to have translations made for these at the expense of the synod.[18] This was not done, but Brodhead did secure transcripts and a loan of the original American letters for four years.[19]

These documents remained with Brodhead and De Witt for nearly thirty years. In 1871, they were turned over to the stated clerk and then deposited in the Archives four years later. De Witt translated letters from time to time and published them in the denominational newspaper, the *Christian Intelligencer*. These were documents that Brodhead used in the production of his historical works on New York State.

After the move to New Brunswick, attention was focused on the research in the Netherlands. De Witt passed from the scene, and his role was taken over by the Reverend Edward Tanjore Corwin, who became known as the historiographer of the Reformed Church in America. It was reported that there was still a considerable number of documents in the Netherlands that related to the colonial Reformed church. Corwin began the negotiations for this material in 1887. He had previously prepared a calendar of the documents in the denomination's archives and was quite familiar with the full scope of the holdings.

Through the end of the nineteenth century, Corwin continued gathering records in the Netherlands, arranging for the translation of those records, and gathering the records of the congregations and other church judicatories. Finally, the denomination had a history written, a complete list of its ministers and the churches they served, all established congregations and the ministers who served them, and a series of historical essays relating to missions, education, the colonial church, and other topics specific to the Reformed Church in America.[20]

---

[18] *Acts and Proceedings*, 1841, 42.
[19] *Acts and Proceedings*, 1842, 42.
[20] Corwin's work was significant, as evidenced by his compilation of synodical material in the *Digest and Index of Synodical Legislation* and his series, the *Manual of the Reformed Church in America*, which continues today as the *Historical Directory*.

As Corwin gathered the records and donated published volumes, they were piled in the storage room in Sage Library. Again, there was no individual available to see to the arrangement and preservation of this material. From time to time the stated clerk attempted to organize it according to the assembly or agency which created it.

Committee on History and Research

Time again passed and little mention was made of the denominational archives. A Committee on History and Research was appointed by the Synod in 1928 to serve as the custodian of the accumulated materials. Once again, a group saw to the proper arrangement and description of the archives and provided files and shelves for their general storage and maintenance. This committee used volunteers to perform the work and obtained assistance from the seminary library staff as their time permitted. Finally, John Walter Beardslee, III, professor of church history at New Brunswick Theological Seminary, was appointed to the position of archivist for the denomination (on a volunteer basis) and two part-time, retired individuals were employed to answer genealogical inquiries and undertake some routine archival work. The part-time workers were unable to meet the needs of an expanding collection and a church that was becoming increasingly aware of its heritage.

In 1978, the Commission on History, the successor to the Committee on Research and History, recommended the establishment of a full-time archival program with the appointment of a professional archivist. General Synod approved that recommendation, and I was appointed as the first full-time archivist for the denomination during its 350th anniversary year.[21] The commission developed the theological and operational rationale for the denomination's archival work, which has served as a firm foundation upon which to build.

The Sacred Trust of Remembering

Careful record keeping is one of the most important aspects of a successful ministry; church records are remembering instruments. Record keeping and record preservation fit naturally in the historical context of the Old Testament and God's command to Moses to preserve God's words for God's people. In fact, records management in the congregation is a ministry and a sacred trust that is essential for its well-functioning and continued growth. When the Commission on

---

[21] *Acts and Proceedings*, 1978, 201.

History prepared a proposal to establish the Archives of the Reformed Church in America, it presented several theological assumptions for archival preservation.

The proposal for the Archives was prepared for the commission by the Reverend Dr. Norman J. Kansfield, at the time librarian at Western Theological Seminary. It acknowledged that God controls history and by grace is directing the experiences of God's people through that control. There is a movement toward an end. That end is the full establishment of God's kingdom. The records which were to be preserved in the Archives document the unfolding of God's plan for God's creation as witnessed by our respective traditions. These primary documents of our individual heritages were to be preserved because they witnessed to God's revelation to God's people. The collection in the Archives should, the proposal insisted, document the faithfulness of a particular people's response to that revelation. The careful preservation of those records witnesses to and allows us to understand that faithfulness.

According to the commission's proposal, the essential purpose of the Archives is based on the understanding that God's self-revelation occurs within the history of God's people, and, by that presence, God has ordered and sanctified that history. History has a purpose and we recognize God's salvation history. How, the commission asked, can the presence of God be recognized in history unless we carefully preserve those records which document the course of our journey as a called people? [22]

With this focus, archives continue to serve a prophetic function. They are the records of a journey that offer a "road map" of our spiritual course. Careful selection of documents requires the archivist to be ever mindful that we are documenting the true path, and those times when we have strayed from what we perceived to be the true path.

Recognizing that God reveals God's self within history and controls and orders history and the experiences of God's people, it follows that God interacts with God's people within the events of human experience. For example, when we examine the personal records of a significant religious leader, we are able to discern the growth and development of a distinct religious personality. Archives provide assistance in understanding the way in which a person came to know God and how the religious tradition formed the world and life view of the individual.

---

[22] RCA Archives, Commission on History papers, Spring 1977.

Those records we collect also serve to demonstrate the faith development of a religious institution. Appraisal standards for religious archives have to take into account the evidential value created records offer for this aspect of institutional faithfulness. Within the Judeo-Christian tradition, leaders certainly saw the necessity of preserving certain records, which later became a sacred canon. This is true of virtually all religious movements. But, as we move closer to the present, we find that often the need to preserve records is expressed less and less. Archives stand in the line of men and women who first saw the need to preserve the traditions of the faith.

Archivist's Reflection on Don Bruggink

Here let me take an opportunity to reflect upon thirty years as archivist for the Reformed Church in America. I first met Don Bruggink at the Commission on History meeting in Princeton, New Jersey, in October 1978. He greeted me with the words, "We have a lot riding on you!" He has been a staunch supporter of our archival efforts as the responsibilities grew and as I began typesetting and formatting the volumes of the Historical Series in 1984 and took responsibility for compiling the data and producing the *Historical Directory of the Reformed Church in America* in 1992. I had the great opportunity to work closely with Don on the Historical Series publications and in the work of the commission. While not a formal student in a classroom setting, I have learned much from him about how faith, life, and theology intersect.

Within the Reformed Church, it is acknowledged that the life of our denomination is the profile of God's interaction with a specific people within a specific temporal context. The common tradition of the Reformed Church is one of the most significant factors providing us with a sense of cohesiveness as a distinct body within the larger church. The preserved record reflects our distinct witness and reaction to the revelation and leading of God. And the past is used in a very real manner. Today's programs are built upon the foundations of our common past; new programs must demonstrate continuity with old ones. The past is held up as a challenge to the present for greater effort in the future.

I learned from Don that the work of the Archives is truly stewardship. Stewardship relates to the management of affairs, generally of property or money, for the best interest of the work of the group. Most individuals have the notion that stewardship relates to how much money an individual donates to a given charity or worthwhile benevolent operation. But it does go beyond that.

Stewardship relates to the management of one's own being in terms of time, talent, and lifestyle. The Archives is the steward of the Reformed Church's heritage.

Conclusion

Over the course of three and three-quarter centuries, many opportunities were presented to the church to develop an adequate program for the preservation of its historical documentation. Time and again, individuals came to the fore prepared to grapple with the needs of the denomination concerning its history. Without those individuals, many essential materials would have been lost. Yet, with just a moderate amount of willingness on the part of the entire church, so much more could have been saved.

With the events leading up to the celebration of the 350th anniversary of the Reformed Church in America in 1978, the Commission on History recognized its opportunity to present a financially balanced, theologically sound, and administratively necessary archival and records management program.

Today, the Archives is recognized as the essential memory of the church, and it provides a firm foundation in the past for developing future programs. Hence, the outlook of the denomination's historical work is always future oriented, with a popular slogan of "looking back to see ahead."

It has been indicated that the record-preserving practices of the denomination have always had periods of quiet and periods of intense interest and activity. We are now in a period of activity. In 1980, the Commission on History established the Reformed Church Historical Society, and it has been pursuing an active publication schedule with the Historical Series, which has been under the general editorship of Don Bruggink since 1968. The Archives has established an initial records management consciousness among denominational staff and church leadership and records are accessioned with increasing consistency.

The records in the custody of the Archives date from the beginning of the seventeenth century to the present. These documents represent a fine research collection that regularly attracts scholars and genealogists. De Witt, Corwin, Brodhead, and others who saw the needs of a historically literate church would be pleased that the documentary heritage is now well cared for in safe, secure facilities. That documentary heritage lives so that the past can inform the present as it moves into the future.

CHAPTER 5

Bottoms Up—A Copy Editor's Perspective On the Historical Series of the Reformed Church in America

Laurie Z. Baron

A book editor!...I shall pray for her conversion to a more virtuous profession.

—Bishop Blackie Ryan, in Happy Are Those Who Mourn, *by Andrew Greeley*

Recently, I made the acquaintance of Andrew Greeley's famous puzzle-solving (and book-writing) bishop in the Blackie Ryan mystery series, and I liked him very much. So I was dismayed to discover his dim view of my occupation—dismayed, but not terribly surprised. No doubt many authors of books share his skepticism—probably every author would join in his prayer on at least some days. And if book editors in general fall under suspicion, then copy editors in particular can feel like the enemy. Just when an author thinks the work is finally done, the words settled on the page to the satisfaction of colleagues and readers and family members and even the publisher—in steps the copy editor to muck around in them. There are days when even I wonder if the work of copy editing is anything more than an outdated if not diabolical exercise in indulging the gleeful gotchas of the inveterate stickler at the expense of the long-suffering author who has to put up with her.

Nevertheless, the authors who have created the books in the Historical Series of the Reformed Church in America have been putting up with me mucking around in their words for what is fast approaching twenty years. Missionaries, denominational executives, scholars, pastors, and historians by trade and by love have been turning out with amazing dedication the stories of this relatively small body of Christians and their adventures and misadventures trying to be the church in the world. As copy editor for the series, I've had a ringside seat to this panoply of remembering, ever since the phone rang one day in 1989 or thereabouts, while I was engrossed in raising young children while patching together writing and editing work.

"Are you as good as Marsha Hoffman?" said the voice on the phone, which identified itself as Dr. Donald Bruggink. The question jolted me back to my first job at the *Church Herald* magazine, where Marsha Hoffman had been one of my predecessors in the position of copy editor. She had set the gold standard there, and I, too, came to regard her work with great respect. Now it looked as though I would have the opportunity to follow her again, this time into the Historical Series, if I could match her skill.

When I bravely asserted that, yes, I thought I was as good as Marsha, that clinched the interview. Soon I received my first manuscript to work on and, since it apparently passed muster, they've been coming ever since. Other jobs have come and gone, the small children have become grown women, but the volumes of the historical series just keep rolling off the presses—sixty of them now, and the pace has quickened. It is rare now for us to be working on only one book at a time; rather, there always seem to be two or three in various stages of preparation.

This accomplishment is, in itself, a remarkable thing—roughly sixty volumes in forty years published by a major Christian publishing house in order to record and pass along to the future the life and times of one small denomination. In recent years, several chroniclers from the Christian Reformed branch of the family have joined the series,[1]

---

[1] Robert P. Swierenga has been especially prolific, writing and editing, alone and in various partnerships, volumes including *Family Quarrels in the Dutch Reformed Churches of the 19th Century* (with Elton J. Bruins), Historical Series of the Reformed Church in America (HS) no. 32, 1999; *Dutch Chicago: A History of Hollanders in the Windy City*, HS no. 42, 2002; *Iowa Letters: Dutch Immigrants on the American Frontier* (with John Stellingwerff), HS no. 47, 2005; and *Old Wing Mission: Cultural Interchange as Chronicled by George and Arvilla Smith in Their Work with Chief Wakazoo's Ottawa Band on the West Michigan* (with William Van Appledorn), HS no. 58, 2008. Other CRC contributions include Harry Boonstra, *Our School*, HS no. 39, 2001; Janet

thus broadening the scope of the story and enhancing its value. The accomplishment is made all the more remarkable by the fact that the books are solicited, written, reviewed, selected, and prepared for publication almost entirely by people who will receive little or no pay for their efforts.

People who know of my association with this immense project assume that, as the one person who can be counted on to have read every word of nearly every volume going more than halfway back in the list, I should by now be an expert on Reformed Church history. But that's not the way the process works—at least, not for me. Instead, I have found that, if copy editing sometimes seems to be a dubious way to make a living, it is without doubt an odd way to read a book, although one that offers its own rewards and even, perhaps, a few insights that might otherwise be missed. I pass a few of these along for whatever interest they might hold for those who don't have the advantage of this odd occupation.

When I read for my own education or enjoyment, I look for what the words can deliver to me—an experience or emotion, insight, new information, vivid images, stories, and characters. While I'm sometimes pulled out of that larger experience by especially good (or bad) writing, that's usually a distraction from the main event. However, when I pull my editing cap over my ears and get to work, the writing *is* the main event. The copy editor's job is to try to enhance the larger worth of the book by concentrating on the individual words, marks, and spaces that form the sentences that build the meaning, paragraph by paragraph and chapter by chapter. While it is inevitable that this level of attention to detail will make close attention to the events and concepts in the book difficult, that's not a bad thing. In fact, it's a necessary thing if I am to see what is actually on the page, rather than what I might assume to be there from the larger sweep of thought.

This bottoms-up view is standard for the copy editor, who ordinarily receives a manuscript after the major revisions have been completed. In this last, most detailed, editing, anything is fair game for the blue pencil (which has, by the way, all but disappeared in the

---

Sheeres, *Son of Secession: Douwe J. Vander Werp*, HS no. 52, 2006; James A. De Jong, *Henry J. Kuiper: Shaping the Christian Reformed Church, 1907-1962*, HS no. 55, 2007; and a joint project among four social scientists (two RCA, two CRC), Corwin Schmidt, Donald Luidens, James Penning, and Roger Nemeth, *Divided by a Common Heritage: The Christian Reformed Church and the Reformed Church in America at the Beginning of the New Millennium*, HS no. 54, 2006 (all the above volumes published in Grand Rapids by Eerdmans).

wake of onscreen editing), as long as the change can be justified on some grounds beyond personal taste and does not alter the sense of the material. There is reward in this close attention to the page—reward that strikes me as akin to gardening, cleaning the "weeds" out, trying to hear the author's voice and let it shine out from the page as vividly as possible, so that the manuscript begins to resemble a freshly tended flower bed. It may be riotous or formal, but it blooms brightly, cleared of all that doesn't belong, bounded gracefully by its markers, conveying its designer's intent, and, at its best, full of happy surprises.

Sadly, this process is not as rewarding for authors. While the editor sees a project, a page of type itching to be polished into splendor (or at least serviceable prose), the writer sees lifeblood spilled. Most copy editors are writers too and understand the pain; nevertheless, when armed with the license to improve, we tend to regard the pain as beside the point, just part of the process.

Let me emphasize that the writers I've worked with have been overwhelmingly amenable to editing suggestions and most willing to answer questions and provide clarifications. Their graciousness, however, can't mask entirely the difficulty of this process.

A natural tension exists between the copy editor and the author, especially when one works so independently of the other. It doesn't take an overly suspicious nature to begin to see the copy editor as some variety of cave creature, darkly busy who knows where by who knows what authority making mischief for an author with arbitrary glee. Although my work for the Historical Series has come to include much more direct contact with authors as e-mail has made that practical, it is still Donald Bruggink, as the general editor, who is the author's primary contact in the publication process. Sometimes Don has found himself in the middle: puzzled or stricken or irate author on one side; copy editor stubbornly quoting style guide chapter and verse on the other.

In order to understand the nature of these distress calls, it will help to take a brief side trip into the matter of style. As used in the world of publishing, the word *style* has a technical meaning as well as the commonly understood one of an author's tone or particular bent or facility with the language. As opposed to this general usage, technical style refers to the way a publisher answers the thousands of questions that arise when converting thoughts to print: Which punctuation practices will we follow? How will we treat names of things and people? What to do about numbers, mathematics, abbreviations, footnotes, indexes, etc.? How to deal with the interruption of graphs, charts, and pictures with captions?

The core value that underlies establishing a style is consistency. At some point since the invention of the printing press, people began to suspect that written materials would be easier to understand if they spelled words alike, agreed about what punctuation to use where, and decided together which words were important enough to rate capital letters. From such a reasonable idea grew a whole subspecialty of the language arts, practiced zealously by copy editors on behalf of their publishers and backed by one or another of the style "bibles." In many years of copy editing, I have had at my side always the venerable *Chicago Manual of Style*, which, the preface tells me, began in the 1890s as a "single sheet of typographic fundamentals drawn up by a University of Chicago Press proofreader."[2] It now numbers 956 pages and is revised about every ten years. It turns out that trying to nail down every question of style is a little like trying to be good. The issues involved, once one begins tackling them seriously, approach the infinite.

Concerns related to grammar, syntax, punctuation, and style occupy a good deal of my working day. I used to think that few people who weren't copy editors or English teachers cared about these minute aspects of the written word. But the happy eagerness with which otherwise kind folk catch my spelling errors and ask unsolvable grammatical questions suggests that all of us who have learned to write in the English language are to some degree fascinated and flummoxed by its formulas, its seemingly endless flexibility within them, and its maddening intricacies.

It was a surprise and a delight when, a few years ago, *Eats, Shoots, and Leaves*, by British author Lynne Truss, appeared on the bestseller lists.[3] Who could have imagined that a book about *punctuation*—no matter how humorously presented—would tempt the pocketbooks of thousands of American readers? Her rallying cry, "Sticklers, unite!" must bring out the eighth-grader in each of us, the one determined, once and for all, to put the commas in all of the right places and none of the wrong ones, to make one last sally on the mysteries of semicolons before launching into high school (where, we were told, sloppy punctuation would not be tolerated).

Which is to say, simply, that all of us care about our words. We discover just how much we care when someone offers to improve them for us.

---

[2] Fifteenth ed., (Chicago: Univ. of Chicago, 2003), xiii.
[3] (New York: Gotham, 2003).

It still amazes me that the more "substantive" changes I suggest—different wording or moving sentences around, for example—are rarely challenged or even remarked upon by authors. (It is also true that the high level of writerly competence among the series' authors has made heavy rewrites a rarity.) Rather, if a question comes back to me, it's likely to be over a matter of style.

The pattern was set early, when the author of one of the first books I worked on was out-and-out angry over a word from which I consistently removed the opening capital letter. Fortunately copy editors, if they're lucky, have general editors to watch their backs. I got to hear the report second-hand from Don, the long-suffering arbiter of editorial policy—it fell to him to soothe the author's ruffled feathers, after confirming that we were following both the *Chicago Manual* and Eerdman's style guide. This incident would become typical in two ways that stand out for me. The first has to do with the feelings of authors and the second the actions of the general editor.

Perhaps the conventions of style inflict pangs on writers because they so often challenge our assumptions subtly without offering much in the way of explanation. For example, the way we respond to a word changes depending on whether it begins with a capital letter or a small one. Take one of the most hotly contested letters in my personal vocational history: the "c" that begins the word *church*; should it be big or little, and when and why? What does "the Church's foundation" say to you? If you saw instead, "the church's foundation," does it say something different? Does the first example bring to mind something theological—even divine—while the second evokes the basement? If so, the value you place on the word *church* changes with the size of its opening letter. That is true for many people, despite the tendency for words in American English to be democratized along with the rest of society. Our assumptions can lag behind accepted practice. And there's no particularly compelling reason for demoting so many nouns to "common" status; it's just the way things are.

Similar discomfort attends the removal of all but the first occurrence of "the Reverend" or other titles and honorary adjectives that appear in front of names. We want the things and people we value to appear on the page—and respectfully. To treat words without special distinction can feel a bit less than respectful, especially if it comes as a surprise. When the comfortable authority of "the Reverend Tobias Smith" on page one becomes the unadorned "Smith" by page two, it can threaten our sense of decorum. It can even reveal, perhaps, hierarchical impulses with which religious people can hardly help but live, but of which they are not always aware.

It's in this area of assumptions that questions most often arise from authors, and that brings me to the actions of the general editor. I know of a number of times (and there may be more than I know) when an author has raised a question or objection with Don about how his or her book has been edited. In every instance in which I've been involved, if I can show that our practice conforms to our style guidelines or the principles of good writing, Don has supported my change. That may seem like a small thing, but it feels large.

Because the series is church-centered and includes among its authors few "professional" writers, it might be reasonable to expect that publishing standards would sometimes be overshadowed by churchly conventions and relationships. But Don has never given me any reason to doubt that our work objective is always simply to produce the best books we can. Never has he said that I should concern myself with something "more important" than our editorial standards, never has he pushed me to skimp on care for the sake of speed, and never has he treated me as anything less than an independent expert in this exacting and increasingly archaic craft.

As a matter of fact, easily the most pleasant aspect of copy editing the Historical Series has been working in collaboration with Don and with Russell Gasero, who has served as the typesetter and layout designer during all of my tenure and more. The three of us have never worked out of the same office; instead, we have been operating as a long-distance work team for far longer than it has been business fashion. Given the infrequency of our face-to-face meetings and the complete absence of team-building exercises, flow charts, and psychological profiling, it's amazing that we've continued to work together peacefully and productively for so many years. Perhaps absence really does make the heart grow fonder.

But I have another theory. I believe that, in an increasingly impatient and pragmatic world, I had the good fortune to be invited into a project that is at its heart a labor of love, headed up by an editor who is also a lover of craft.

Don's expertise in church architecture is well known, but you don't have to have too many conversations with him to understand that his love of beauty extends far beyond his area of specialization to encompass all forms of artistry. His eyes light up recalling a masterfully performed ballet, an extraordinary evening at the symphony, a well-designed liturgy, even an elegant gesture of kindness. He is a pursuer as well as an appreciator of artistry. And the pursuit of artistry demands the exercise of craft.

It seems clear to me that it is not only important to the historian in Don to preserve the history of this denomination, it is also important to the artist in him that the form this history takes have the integrity—dare I say even the beauty?—of a well-crafted whole. Perhaps it is for this reason that on his watch even the humble craft of copy editing has been treated with the utmost urgency and respect.

Of course, all bets are off when editors put on their author hats. The level of energy, anxiety, investment, and e-mail activity among the editorial team rose to new heights when Don and then Reformed Church staff member Kim Nathan Baker took on the task of writing a popular history of the Reformed Church together. The plan was that Don would write the main text, Kim would contribute interesting sidebars, and the book would have brief chapters, lots of pictures, and be as approachable and inviting as a periodical. I would polish the pieces as they were produced. Not only was this two-author, multilevel approach to history ambitious, it resulted in months of editing flurry, as chapters and sidebars circulated among the three of us. Gone was the calm, urbane general editor; in his place was the harried author seeking to be understood—the exasperated author trying to keep too many balls in the air without full control over the outcome. For a few months, the series came to feel like a full-time job as e-mail communication flew.

While it's fun to be in on the process earlier than a finished final draft, it also offers more opportunity for frustration. "I don't think the reader will understand this theological term," I e-mailed Don at one point, with the innocence of the amateur. "Can you offer a word of explanation?" To the theologian my request sounded ridiculous, and I received a rather testy reply to the effect that if he had to explain the term it would take more pages than had been allotted for the whole chapter, and if readers didn't understand, they'd just have to remain ignorant. Climbing on my populist high horse, I responded pretty testily myself that readers might be ignorant but they weren't stupid and a few more words might just tell them enough to understand the paragraph. Into which dialogue Kim, the hitherto silent partner on the subject, rode to our rescue with his spare e-message: "My, how you two do go on!" Indeed. The message made me laugh, breaking the intensity of the exchange. How it was resolved I no longer remember, but the book came together eventually, text, sidebars, timeline, and all. Now, under the title, *By Grace Alone: Stories of the Reformed Church in America*,[4] it occupies a slim and surprisingly docile space on my shelf, given the hubbub surrounding its creation.

[4] HS no. 44 (Grand Rapids: Eerdmans, 2004).

I have confessed that I am not and will never be an expert in Reformed Church history. But slowly, over the years of the series, almost without my knowledge, something has been going on. Having spent so many hours with this chorus of voices, the voices have taken root in me. I may have forgotten the facts they recounted, but the vision of the missionaries, the passion and dedication of the preachers, the strength of mind of the institution builders, the endurance and faith of the pioneers, the diligence of those who told their tales—all these have sung their songs in my inward ear and still hum occasionally along my breastbone. They make me proud of my heritage, biological and spiritual.

When I watch a movie or read a novel that portrays missionaries as naïve religionists, trampling over cultures in their quest for souls, I remember the generations of the Reformed Church's faithful, loving, complicated servants of the gospel. Whether they served in China, the Arabian Gulf, India, or elsewhere,[5] these teachers, pastors, doctors, nurses, and farmers struggled among themselves and with denominational structures at home to find the best way to help the church grow from its native soil, wherever that might be. Their accounts have ruined me for the other, more sensational, stories.

When I hear cynicism expressed about ecumenical efforts or the rules of church government, my mind turns to Arie R. Brouwer's *Ecumenical Testimony*[6] or Allan J. Janssen's *Constitutional Theology*,[7] and I remember the passion with which these books were written. I want to put them into the critic's hands and say, "Read this. Understand why some people think this stuff is really important—then let's talk about how to do it better."

When I remember the unimaginable hardships endured by nineteenth-century Dutch settlers in Iowa,[8] or the complicated story of white-native relations as they played out in Michigan[9] and throughout

---

[5] Cf. Gerald F. De Jong, *The Reformed Church in China 1842-1951*, HS no. 22 (Grand Rapids: Eerdmans, 1992); Lewis R. Scudder III, *The Arabian Mission's Story: In Search of Abraham's Other Son*, HS no. 30 (Grand Rapids: Eerdmans, 1998); Eugene P. Heideman, *From Mission to Church: The Reformed Church in America Mission to India*, HS no. 38 (Grand Rapids: Eerdmans, 2001).

[6] No. 21 (Grand Rapids: Eerdmans, 1991).

[7] No. 33 (Grand Rapids: Eerdmans, 2000).

[8] Johan Stellingwerff, ed. Robert P. Swierenga, trans. Water Lagerwey, *Iowa Letters, Dutch Immigrants on the American Frontier*, HS no. 47 (Grand Rapids: Eerdmans, 2004).

[9] Swierenga, *Old Wing Mission*, HS no. 58 (Grand Rapids: Eerdmans, 2008).

the Reformed Church,[10] I am struck again by the faith of my ancestors, and also by their frequent blindness—and I am glad that their faith is part of my heritage, too, and I wonder if we really see any clearer today.

If I could've left *Family Quarrels in the Dutch Reformed Churches of the 19th Century*, by Elton J. Bruins and Robert P. Swierenga,[11] unfinished, I gladly would have, because it cut entirely too close to home, telling the story of how a church—my family's congregation for four generations—held the seeds of a conflict that split the Dutch immigrants into Reformed and Christian Reformed and generated bitterness that is still all too alive in the two communities. I felt it alive in me as my stomach churned, chapter by chapter.

And when I am tempted to take for granted women professionals, politicians, and ministers, I remember that their strength is built on the equally great strength of women like Sarah Doremus and a group of her friends,[12] who knew all about living in a "separate sphere" in a man's world. Without waiting for permission, they reached out to women who lived in much harsher, but still kindred, separate spheres in the places where Reformed missionaries were serving. In the process they created a powerful organization for mission. Their story is a revelation because so few stories of Reformed women have yet been told—and the new chapter of women's acceptance into the offices of the church that has just begun, in historical terms, has many more stories to reveal.

It could be that historical terms—learning to see the world in the terms history demands—is what this all adds up to. In my odd, upside-down reading of these books, checking endless footnotes, paying more attention to the commas than the sweep of history, history has nevertheless been sweeping over me. Because of that, I think I am a bit less quick to judgment, less apt to accept simplistic approaches to people or situations or to jump on the latest bandwagon, maybe a bit more tolerant of our slips and slides together as we try to figure out how to be church now. If these are the gifts that the study of history gives, then I am grateful to have received them, even by the back door and without going in pursuit of them. I would be happy for more of the people with whom I share pews to receive these gifts too.

---

[10] LeRoy Koopman, *Taking the Jesus Road, The Ministry of the Reformed Church in America among Native Americans*, HS no. 50 (Grand Rapids: Eerdmans, 2005).

[11] No. 32 (Grand Rapids: Eerdmans, 1999).

[12] Mary L. Kansfield, *Letters to Hazel: Ministry within the Woman's Board of Foreign Missions of the Reformed Church in America*, HS no. 46 (Grand Rapids: Eerdmans, 2004).

In the last few years, Don has taken to closing many e-mails to Russ and me simply, "Cheers." It's a perfect word for him to choose; it conveys him directly to the page—cheerful, confident, sometimes wry, taking life with lightness whenever possible. And it is, of course, a toast, an offering of celebration.

So, begging his forbearance, I'd like to conclude by appropriating his word and offering this toast:

To the deep river of faith that flowed and flows through the people who call themselves Reformed, to their many lives that have brought us to our lives, their faith that nourishes our faith;

To everyone who has had a hand in telling their stories—authors, historians of the commission, supporters, publishers, printers, and readers;

To Russell Gasero, archivist, the most patient of layout designers, and grand coworker; and especially

To Donald Bruggink, whose vision and energy instituted and sustains this remarkable body of work, and who has always made the copy editor's craft feel an honest and worthwhile part of it—

Cheers!

PART 3

Tools for Understanding Theological Education

Donald Bruggink belongs to a pretty exclusive club in the Reformed Church in America: the professorate. He continues to hold the office of General Synod professor of theology, since 1999 in emeritus status.[1] Fewer than one hundred women and men have been such teachers in the Reformed Church since John Henry Livingston was first elected into service two and a quarter centuries ago.[2] Since this denomination is one of the last to continue to maintain the office, that club is now globally exclusive.

As one of these teachers of the church, theological education and how it is practiced have loomed large among Bruggink's many interests. The essays in this section, all by scholars who have held that same office, address just that. First, Norman Kansfield examines the history of the theological professorate, reaching all the way back to its biblical

---

[1] The assertion that he remains a member of the professorate is made because he has not been transferred back to the care of a classis.
[2] Extrapolated from the list in Russell Gasero, *Historical Directory of the Reformed Church in America*, Historical Series of the Reformed Church in America, no. 37 (Grand Rapids: Eerdmans, 2001), 691-92.

roots. John Coakley reviews John Henry Livingston's contributions as the first RCA professor of theology and how he laid the groundwork for others who would follow. Finally, Dennis Voskuil looks at how regional differences and other tendencies toward individualism have been sources of tension—some of it creative—in how candidates for ministry have been prepared.

As the denomination grapples with the question of how to make the best use of this rare gift, these essays are particularly timely. It should please our honoree that he has inspired such contributions to the current debate.

CHAPTER 6

Teacher of the Church: The Office of Professor of Theology in the Reformed Church in America

Norman J. Kansfield

Introduction

The Reformed Church in America is perhaps the only Protestant denomination to continue to recognize the church office of professor of theology, or, as it has recently been titled, "General Synod professor of theology." The Reformed Church is involved currently in a quiet conversation concerning the future of that office. A judicial case, brought to the General Synod in 2005, made it clear that little was known about the office within the church, and much of what was known was problematic to the church. The president of the synod of 2007 was authorized to reconstitute a "General Synod Professors Task Force," first established in 2005. The task force was given this agenda:

1. To clarify the processes of accountability, appeal, and pastoral care for General Synod professors of theology currently outlined in the *Book of Church Order*, including any needed revisions to the *Book of Church Order*.
2. To coordinate the development of relevant policies and practices

within the seminaries and/or commissions or agencies of the church that do not require changes to the *Book of Church Order*, but that relate to the role of General Synod professors within the seminaries and within the life of the church, and further,
3. To review the nature of the office of General Synod professor,
4. To review criteria for eligibility to that office;
5. To clarify the responsibility of the office of General Synod professor of theology to the General Synod;
6. To examine the means by which the General Synod professors could be established as an ongoing body within the order of the church.[1]

While the question of the retention of the office is not raised in the six charges to the task force, that possibility is already reported to be part of the conversation. This essay is intended to make a contribution to that conversation. The author confesses to holding strong feelings about the continued usefulness of the office within the church. So, the reader should not be surprised to discover this essay advocating strongly for the continuance of the office.[2] The task force is expected to make its first report to the General Synod of 2009.

For more than forty years, the Reverend Dr. Donald J. Bruggink has fulfilled his ministry within the Reformed Church as one of its General Synod professors of theology. On Tuesday morning, June 14, 1966, he was elected to the office of professor of theology by a vote of 235 to 4.[3] This was, of course, not the first time, nor would it be the last time that the General Synod of the Reformed Church in America would elect someone to this office. As one reads the record of the actions of the synod of 1966,[4] one could conclude that the process of electing a professor of theology was recognized as an act of great significance. The synod seemed to be making its way along well-worn steps, but not with the assurance that comes with frequent repetition. The process must have felt similar to baking a cake using an old family recipe. The steps were not familiar enough to proceed without the yellowed recipe card, but neither were they strange, nor totally unfamiliar.

The process of Bruggink's election was put into motion when the Board of Trustees of Western Theological Seminary nominated him to

---

[1] *Acts and Proceedings of the Reformed Church in America*, 2007, 301; 2008, 111.
[2] The irony of the fact that the author is the only person ever to have been deposed from the office ought not to be overlooked.
[3] The synod was meeting at Hope College, Holland, Michigan, in its 160th regular session.
[4] *Acts and Proceedings*, 1966, 47-50.

the office. Western Seminary's president, the Reverend Dr. Herman J. Ridder, then placed the nomination before the synod June 13, 1966. A time for discussion and voting was set for the next morning. Election was by ballot. The Reverend Gordon L. Van Ostenburg, president of the synod, declared that Bruggink had been elected. A motion was passed for the General Synod to issue a call to Bruggink "to serve as Professor of Historical Theology and Church History [in] the [James] A.H. Cornell Chair of Historical Theology" in the synod's Western Theological Seminary. The Reverend Dr. Bruggink was presented to the synod and, when invited, addressed the body.[5]

The very formal character of these proceedings, even in those much more formal times, would have suggested to the delegates that this action was no usual action. They may not have grasped the full meaning of what they did. Some delegates may not even have understood what a professor of theology was, or what such a person did on their behalf. But there could have been no misunderstanding the fact that what the General Synod was doing that Tuesday morning was very important business indeed—different from the routine business expected of any General Synod.

During the one hundred eighty-two years between the election of the first professor of theology by the synod of 1784—the Reverend Dr. John Henry Livingston (1746-1825)—and Bruggink's election, only seventy-seven other men had been elected and installed into the office. During those years perhaps as many as twenty-five others had been elected but had declined to serve. (The election of the first woman would wait another thirty-two years, until the election of the Reverend Dr. Carol Bechtel in 1998.) This process provided the entire denomination, represented by delegates to the General Synod, an opportunity to add to the number of those it believed to be called by God to educate the next generation of pastors and teachers, to defend the faith against any challenge, and to carry out the theological research that would keep vibrant the denomination's understanding of its theology. The same process enrolled Bruggink in an ecclesiastical body—the professorate—even though the denomination had stopped formal use of the term three years earlier.[6]

But, in 1966, when the Reformed Church in America used this process to elect Donald J. Bruggink to the office of professor of theology,

---

[5] Ibid., 49-50.
[6] The *Acts and Proceedings* for 1963 are the last to use "professorate" as the title for the report on and actions concerning theological education.

it did so all by itself. No other North American Protestant tradition retains within its church order an office like that of professor of theology. Other denominations have taken a different route. Most have established theological seminaries (as the Reformed Church had done) and then empowered either the superintending boards of those schools or the schools' administrations to elect (or simply hire) theologians to teach in the schools. The Reformed Church in America focused, instead, upon calling persons to serve within an office of the church: professor of theology—doctor or teacher of the whole church. The process for electing a professor—like that old family recipe card—clearly demonstrated that the office was very important to the denomination. The purpose for having such an office remained (and remains) much less clear. Even though the denomination has codified the script for election to the office, it has failed to define fully the purpose and the function of those elected to the office. It has never fully explained to itself, nor to the rest of Christianity, what a professor of theology is to do and to *be* for the denomination and/or the whole church.

Doctor Ecclesiae and the Medieval Establishment of a Definitive Theological Canon

As the office of professor of theology is unique to this denomination, so the doing of theology is unique to Christianity. Christian theology is very unlike the rabbinic conversation in Judaism. Judaism has never developed the practice of speaking about itself theologically. The oral rabbinic reflection on the biblical message was codified as the Midrash. The rabbinic discussion of legal implications[7] of the biblical record became the Mishna and the Tosephta. These began to be written down during the second century CE. Within this rabbinic literature, the conversation about God is sensual, experiential, and anecdotal—a combination of precedent and common sense—consistent with the wisdom literature of the Old Testament.[8] The power and character of this literature can be felt in this brief excerpt:

> The first human, Adam, was created alone, to teach us that whoever destroys a single life, the Bible considers it as if that

[7] Care must be taken to remember that "legal" in this context is derived from *mitnah/mitzvoth*—the doing of a "blessing" or good deed—not the keeping of a rule or binding injunction.
[8] Efforts to accommodate the Jewish religious tradition to the Greco-Roman thought of the first Christian centuries can be recognized in the works of Philo Judaeus of Alexandria (20 BCE- 40 CE) and Titus Favius Josephus (Yosef ben Matiyahu) (37 - ca. 100 CE).

person destroyed the whole world. And whoever saves a single life, the Bible considers it as if that one had saved an entire world. Furthermore, only one person, Adam, was created for the sake of peace among all persons, so that no one could say, "My father was greater than yours...." Also, each person [was created singly] to show the greatness of the Holy One, Blessed be *Adonai*, for if a person strikes many coins from one mold, all of the coins look alike, but the King of Kings, Blessed be Adonai, made each person in the image of Adam, and yet not one of them resembles another. Therefore every single person is obligated to say, "The world was created for my sake." *Mishna Sanhedrin* 4.5

Christian theology, from its start, sounded very different from this. Quite surprisingly, the earliest Christian theology appears to owe more to Greco-Roman religious traditions than to the rabbinic tradition. Greeks and Romans during the biblical era thought and spoke about God in a way very different from Judaism. The word "theology" itself was first used by Plato (ca. 428-ca.347 BCE) in his *Republic* (book 2, chapter 18), but the Greeks had been doing theology since the seventh century BCE. Their theology consisted of systematic and philosophical reflection upon the gods, on worship and other human interaction with the gods, as well as on the origin, meaning, and governance of the world around them. Proclus (411-485 CE) edited Plato's theology, and a brief quotation from that work will provide us with a sense of what Greek theology sounded like:

> If therefore any falsehood occurs in the oracles of the Gods, we must not say that a thing of this kind originates from the Gods, but from the recipients, or the instruments, or the places, or the times. For all these contribute to the participation of divine knowledge, and when they are appropriately co-adapted to the Gods, they receive a pure illumination of the truth which is established in them.[9]

The Roman Empire facilitated the spread of Greek theology into the mainstream of Western thought just as Christianity was receiving its characteristic shape.

In Paul's letters, we meet a way of talking and thinking about God that is surprisingly consistent with this Greco-Roman theology. The content of his theology would be radically different, but Paul employed

---

[9] Proclus, *Platonic Theology*, "The Divine Nature," 1.2.

all elements of the classical disciplines of grammar, rhetoric, and logic. Paul taught Christianity to think about its message analytically—to understand Jesus so carefully that the message of Jesus could continue to be presented compellingly to cultures quite different from that in which Jesus had carried out his ministry. In Paul's writings we have a sharp-edged, clear-thinking, nonromantic analysis of Jesus that is shaped by logic, and a persuasive, high-impact, moving presentation of Jesus that is shaped by rhetoric.[10] Nothing makes this more clear than Paul's use of "therefore." We need only recall how (and how often!) Paul used that word in his letter to the Romans, for example:

> 2.1: "Therefore you have no excuse, O mortal..."
> 5.1: "Therefore, since we are justified by faith..."
> 5.12: "Therefore as sin came into the world..."
> 8.1: "There is therefore now no condemnation..."
> 12.1: "I appeal to you therefore, brothers and sisters..."
> 15.7: "Welcome one another, therefore, as Christ has welcomed you..."

In each segment of the letter Paul carefully sets out his case. He then says, "If that is true, then this follows." "We understand this. *Therefore* this." Nothing in Judaism had ever sounded like that. But Greek theology sounded exactly like that.

Each of Paul's epistles demonstrates how much Paul was willing to be shaped by the methodology of Greco-Roman religion in the proclamation of the Christian gospel to a particular situation. Paul's theology enabled him to take his understanding of Jesus and to shape it in such a way that both Jewish and non-Jewish hearers would be moved to believe in Jesus. There is no doubt that Paul's purpose was mission. Long before Christian theology was in any way formalized, Paul made it clear that the purpose of Christian (or "sacred" or "systematic") theology is to reinterpret the life and mission of Jesus in such a way that Jesus' life and mission can transform persons in different situations or cultures and in succeeding generations.[11] Paul's theology is nothing less

---

[10] The gospel literature, written a generation after Paul, constitutes memories of the life and ministry of Jesus shaped for the purpose of serving as a "Jesus database" available to those who would continue to use Paul's theological analysis and representation of Jesus to others who were increasingly distant from him in time and space.

[11] Paul's willingness to employ the form of Greco-Roman religious thinking may provide another insight into the relationship between Peter and Paul. Peter remained the ordinary Jewish believer who was willing to venture out of the ordinary in order to embrace the conversion and baptism of non-

than mission. The Pauline literature and the gospels were combined to provide the church with the data necessary to shape the Christian "biblical canon." Paul and the gospel-writers showed the church the way by which this biblical canon can be expounded constantly in ways that convince and make sense to succeeding generations, as well as to people in distant places.

So, with Christian mission Christian theology was born. From the earliest times, in the simplest ways, Christian pastoral leaders were expected to teach all believers how to *do* theology in their own lives by taking the content of Jesus' life and using the methodology of Paul to provide insight for their daily decisions. We can watch theology progress in the early councils, as the apostolic fathers came to conclusions and made decisions about the "natures" of Christ. These monumental decisions made it clear that careful steps needed to be taken to educate leaders of the Christian community in the methods of developing, maintaining, and teaching theology. The church began to identify some leaders expressly to think about and teach theology. As early as the third century, an office for teaching theology was established within the ecclesiastical structure.[12] These theological teachers were slowly gathered into faculties within cathedral schools. Over time, the teachers formed themselves into guilds. These guilds of *magistri*—masters—of theology became the predominating influence in the granting of additional *licentiae docendi*—licenses to teach. By the eleventh century, both ecclesiastical oversight and the power to license teachers of theology had been transferred from the diocese in which they were located to the direct oversight of the bishop of Rome.[13] In the twelfth century the titles *magister* and *doctor* were still imprecise designations for all those who held the *licentia docendi*, but by mid-fourteenth century these titles were well on their way to being recognized as academic degrees as well.[14]

Jews. But Peter's rationale continued to be structured on the basis of Jewish principles and religious material. Paul's rationale, while it employed the same Jewish religious material, was structured on Greco-Roman principles. His mission to the Gentiles was radically open to stating the gospel in emphatically non-Jewish ways, using non-Jewish principles.

[12] Robert W. Henderson, *The Teaching Office in the Reformed Tradition: A History of the Doctoral Ministry* (Philadelphia: Westminster, 1962), 16.
[13] Ibid., 18.
[14] Ibid. The place of theology as an academic discipline within broader education was secured at the same time as twelfth-century schools were transformed gradually into universities.

Throughout these twelve centuries, the place and character of theology as a scholarly discipline continued to be tenuous. Francis Schüssler-Fiorenza insists that theology, in any age, cannot claim great self-assurance:

> Theology is a fragile discipline in that it is both academic and related to faith. As an academic discipline, theology shares all the scholarly goals of other academic disciplines: it strives for historical exactitude, conceptual rigor, systematic consistency, and interpretive clarity. In relation to faith, theology shares the fragility of faith itself. It is much more a hope than a science.[15]

He then goes on to observe:

> In the twelfth century, the issue was not whether theology was a science, but rather whether faith is a knowledge. A common answer was that faith was more than an opinion but less than knowledge. Faith is neither a *scientia opinativa* nor a *scientia necessaria,* but *scientia probabilis.* Faith is, therefore, a form of knowledge that is a grounded opinion with probable certitude. In the twelfth century, *sacra doctrina* was not yet distinct from the interpretation of Scripture. "Yet the idea of a scientific theology, which apodictically derived its conclusions from evident principles, led to the notion of theology as an independent question, and consequently led to the question of its relationship to the other disciplines."[16]

The development of universities and the rise of scholastic philosophy made the thirteenth century a time of tremendous advance for theology. In fact, it was not until the thirteenth century that the term *theology* came into common usage for "Christian theology." Prior to this, the term continued to be used primarily to describe pagan discourse about God.[17] The thirteenth century saw that change:

> Christian discourse explicated God's "economy." It spoke of God's saving plan and action in Jesus Christ and in the Christian

---

[15] Schüssler Fiorenza, "Systematic Theology: Task and Methods," in Francis Schüssler Fiorenza and John P. Galvin, eds. *Systematic Theology,* vol. 1 (Minneapolis: Fortress, 1991), 18. I am deeply dependent upon this essay for much of my discussion of medieval theology.

[16] Schüssler Fiorenza, *Systematic Theology,* 20-21, translating and quoting Charles H. Lohr, "Theologie und/als Wissenschaft in frühen 13, Jahrhundert," *Internationale Katholische Zeitschrift* 10 (1981), 327.

[17] Schüssler-Fiorenza, *Systematic Theology,* 6.

community, [not about "God" in isolation]....As the medieval teaching evolved from a commentary on the Scriptures or from an exposition of questions appended to scriptural texts to a full-fledged systematic discussion of controversial issues, the term *theology* emerged as the umbrella expression for Christian doctrine. It was in the thirteenth century that the term *theology* came to have the comprehensive meaning it has for us today.[18]

Two areas within this "umbrella expression" are of particular importance to this study. Both of these areas of theological development find their fulfillment in the all-too-brief life and work of Thomas Aquinas (1225-1274). These areas are: (1) the primacy and authority of scripture in the doing of theology, and (2) the authority or *magisterium* of theologians to research, shape, and teach theology.

The first area is that of the primacy and authority of scripture.[19] For Aquinas, the following would have been definitive:

> Since Christian faith rests on the revelation given to the apostles and prophets, the canonical Scriptures have, for Thomas, a primal significance and authority. *Sacra doctrina* also uses the authority of the doctors of the church properly, but only with probable effect. *Sacra doctrina* relies on philosophers only as extrinsic and probable. It makes use of them only in those questions in which one can know the truth by natural reason.[20]

John F. Boyle, in his careful study, "St. Thomas Aquinas and Sacred Scripture," indicates that, for Aquinas, "the highest authority, which is intrinsic and proper to the science of sacred doctrine, is sacred Scripture. Of course there are other authorities, especially the fathers, but Thomas is careful to distinguish them from Scripture, which holds the highest authority."[21]

Establishing the priority of scripture for the doing of theology formed one major component of Aquinas's thinking regarding scripture. The other major component focused on the fashion in which scripture was to be interpreted. Nicholas A. Healy prepared the introduction for *Aquinas on Scripture: An Introduction to His Biblical*

---

[18] Ibid.
[19] Ibid., 24.
[20] Ibid., 24. Schüssler Fiorenza points out that Per Eric Persson corrects a typical reformation view of Thomas Aquinas and scripture. See *Sacra Doctrina: Reason and Revelation in Aquinas* (Philadelphia: Fortress, 1970).
[21] John F. Boyle, "St. Thomas and Sacred Scripture," *Pro Ecclesia* 4 (1995): 99.

Commentaries.²² This volume contains actual examples of Aquinas's exegesis and use of scripture. In introducing the volume, Healy makes clear that Aquinas saw the literal sense of scripture as "normative" and the "basis of all theological argumentation." "By insisting upon the priority and normativity of the historical and literal sense of scripture, Thomas could rule out...spiritual [neoplatonist] interpretations that conflicted with the plain sense of the text accepted by the tradition...."²³ Indeed, it was the literal sense of scripture which, alone, could become "the subject of preaching and teaching and the basis of the counter challenge to the new sects. For the friars, Scripture was about God's revelation of God in and through the history centered upon Jesus Christ."²⁴

Finally, for Aquinas, it has to be observed that the role of scripture is different in relationship to the different purposes of theological argumentation. W.G.B.M. Valkenberg, states:

> If the purpose is instruction in faith, authorities [sic] from Scripture are more important than *rationes*; if the purpose is the defence [sic] of faith by removing doubts and errors, *auctoritates* are the most important means as well, depending on the kind of authorities accepted by the opponents. But, if the purpose is a deeper understanding of matters of faith by students, *rationes* are more important than *auctoritates* since the purpose of such a *dispuatio magistralis* is that the hearers know why the sayings are true rather than knowing that they are true.²⁵

To sum up, Valkenberg quotes Aquinas: "Solely the authorities of holy Scripture may be used as proper and cogent arguments since our faith rests on the revelation to Prophets and Apostles, and on their canonical writings."²⁶

Once the authority and primacy of scripture were affirmed, thirteenth-century theologians could turn their attention to a second

---

[22] Ed. Thomas Weinardy, Daniel A. Keating, and John P. Yocum (New York: Continuum, 2005).

[23] Ibid., 8. Encouraged by the Neoplatonism of early commentators (such as Augustine and Jerome through Gregory and Bernard), *lectio divina* was, itself, "a form of prayer or, alternatively, a form of contemplation worth many prayers," 7.

[24] Ibid., 9.

[25] W.G.B.M. Valkenberg, *Words of the Living God: the Place and Function of Holy Scripture in the Theology of Thomas Aquinas* (Leuven: Peeters, 2000), 15, citing *Quodlibet* 9.3.4.

[26] Ibid, citing the *Summa Theologiae*, 1.1.8.ra 2.

pivotal problem that confronted them—the place of their ministry in the life of the church. What was the character of their *magisterium*, their own authority to research, shape, and teach theology and how did it relate to the ministry of priest, bishop, and pope?

"At the time of Aquinas, an understanding of magisterium prevailed that differs considerably from ours. Today it has become customary to refer to a magisterium, in a singular sense." This singular magisterium is vested in the episcopacy/papacy. "Thomas employed the plural term magisteria and distinguished between a pastoral magisterium and a teaching magisterium."[27]

Thomas Rausch helps us understand the shifts that had occurred previously:

> The Middle Ages saw the development of a challenge to the bishops' teaching authority, as well as the emergence of a new kind of council. From the work of the canonists and the growing prestige of the university *doctores*, a new kind of authority emerged, based not on pastoral role but on scholarship. The canonists of the eleventh and twelfth centuries developed a nuanced ecclesiology which held that the ultimate criteria for determining the validity of an ecclesiastical pronouncement or teaching were to be found, not in its source (whether pope or council) or juridical authority, but rather in the intrinsic truth of the decision and its reception by the Church.[28]

This shift provided the theological faculties of the universities with a dynamic new position from which to shape and teach theology. Their place within the life of the church was clearly recognized. They had a solid and reasonably secure platform from which to teach the conclusions of their theological studies. Avery Dulles has documented the fact that the doctrinal decrees of at least three ecumenical councils were submitted to faculties of theology for confirmation of their theological accuracy (the thirteenth, Lyon, France, 1245; the fourteenth, Lyon, France, 1274; and the fifteenth, Vienne, France in 1312).[29]

---

[27] Schüssler Fiorenza, *Systematic Theology*, 26. Yves Congar points out that the word *magisterium* took on its present meaning (i.e. solely as the teaching office of the pope and bishops) only under Pope Gregory XVI, about 1830. See Congar, "A Semantic History of the Term 'Magisterium'" in Charles E. Curran and Richard A. McCormick, eds., *Readings in Moral Theology, Number 3: The Magisterium and the Theologians* (New York: Paulist, 1982), 303.

[28] Thomas P. Rausch, *Towards a Truly Catholic Church: An Ecclesiology for the Third Millenium* (Collegeville, Minn.: Liturgical Press, 2005), 113.

[29] Avery Dulles, *A Church to Believe In* (New York: Crossroads, 1982), 109.

Within this context, Thomas Aquinas began to use the plural term *magisteria* and to distinguish between a pastoral magisterium and a teaching magisterium.[30] Schüssler-Fiorenza, citing Thomas's discussion at *Quodlibet* 3.4.1 ad 3 (Parma ed., 490-491), suggests that:

> Thomas distinguished between two functions, prelacy and magisterium, and two kinds of teaching, preaching and doctrinal competence. The function of prelacy (*praelatio*) belongs to the bishops, and their teaching involves preaching (*doctrina praedicationes*). Theologians have the function of magisterium, and their teaching involves Scholastic doctrine (*doctrina scholastica*). Whereas Thomas ascribes the title of magisterium primarily to the theologian in the forum of teaching magisterium, he ascribes to bishops a magisterium of prelacy and preaching. To quote Thomas' own terminology, bishops have a "pastoral magisterium" (*magisterium cathedrae pastoralis*), whereas the theologians have a "magisterial magisterium" (*magisterium cathedrae magistralis*).[31]

Aquinas was working with a vision that understood theologian and pastor as complementary offices: the pastor—ordained and responsible for the preaching, celebration of sacraments, teaching, and pastoral care that directly strengthened the spiritual life of Christians; and the professor—licensed and responsible for keeping the church's proclamation, or theology, fresh, vital, and truthful. The theologian's task, based in his (and we would now say her) scholarship, was to carry on creative research and writing in theology, in order continuously to provide those responsible for the pastoral care of God's people with a fresh, accurate, appropriate, and structured understanding of the meaning of Jesus—an understanding that would continue to make sense in the church's ever-changing context.

There is some evidence that this very creative structuring of the church's life functioned well for some time.[32] But there was high risk in this configuration of offices. Theologians could overstep their freedom and claim more for their theological conclusions than was justified. Popes and bishops—the ultimate pastors—could become

---

[30] W.A. Visser't Hooft, *Teachers and the Teaching Authorities: the* Magistri *and the* Magisterium (Geneva: WCC Publications, 2000), 14, 64-65. For a very helpful treatment of *magisterium*, see Richard R. Gaillardetz, *Teaching with Authority* (Princeton: Liturgical Press, 1997), chap. 6: "How the Church Teaches: the Ordinary Magisterium," 159-92.

[31] Schüssler-Fiorenza, *Systematic Theology*, 26.

[32] See Dulles, 109f.

fearful that the freedom of the theologians would lead to unreliable or unorthodox theological positions.[33] So, even before the thirteenth century ended, steps were taken to "control" the exploratory freedom of the theologians.

Boniface VIII (ca. 1235-1303) was the last pope to serve during the thirteenth century.[34] As he came to office in 1294, Boniface found himself and his office under assault from secular forces, old family enemies, and factions within the church. It ought not, then, to surprise us that a lot of his energy was expended in efforts to assure the spiritual and temporal supremacy of the papacy. These efforts culminated in the 1302 Papal Bull, *Unam Sanctam*, in which Boniface asserted that "it is absolutely necessary for the salvation of every human creature to be subject to the Roman Pontiff."[35]

Boniface VIII sought, in similar fashion, to develop a means by which the creative work of theologians could be directed perpetually toward Catholic orthodoxy. In 1298, he formalized the concept of *Doctor Ecclesiae* (Doctor or Teacher of the Church),[36] and he named four eminent "Fathers of the Church"—Ambrose (340[?]-397), Jerome (340[?]-420), Augustine of Hippo (354-430), and Gregory I (540-604)—as the Western church's first doctors of the church. Boniface went on to establish the means by which others could be approved for this office. To be chosen, individuals had to be: *eminens doctrina, insignis vitae sanctitas, Ecclesiae declaratio*—that is, they had to be eminent in teaching, they had to have lived a life of sanctity, and they had to have been formally declared "doctors" by the church (expressly by the pope or an ecumenical council). There were two other qualifications that

---

[33] In the church's recent history this fear can be seen in the May 24, 1990, Instruction entitled *Donum Veritatis: on the Ecclesial Vocation of the Theologian*, issued by the Congregation for the Doctrine of the Faith, Joseph Cardinal Ratzinger, prefect, and in the August 15, 1990, Apostolic Constitution entitled *Ex Corde Ecclesiae* promulgated by Pope John Paul II. Footnote 27 in *Donum Veritatis* goes to great lengths to deny that Thomas Aquinas ever envisioned more than one *magisterium*. The complete text of *Ex Corde Ecclesiae* is available online at http://www.vatican.va/holy_father/johnpaul_ii/apost_constitutions/documents/hf_jp-ii_apc_15081990_ex-corde-ecclesiae_en.html. The complete text of *Donum Veritatis* is available online at http://www.vatican.va/roman_curia/congregations/cfaith/documents/rc_ cfaith_doc_19900524_theologiag-vocation_en.html.

[34] He was pope from 1294-1303.

[35] *Unam Sanctam*, November 18, 1302, paragraph 4. The full text in translation is available on line at http://www.fordham.edu/halsall/source/b8-unam.html.

[36] *Sexto*, III, 22—"Gloriosus, de relique. Et vener. sanctorum."

doctors of the church had to meet: they had to be dead, and they had to have been canonized as saints. Their teachings were and are regarded as exemplary of the church's finest theology. They are, therefore, reliable guides in the work of shaping theology for the life and work of the church.[37]

Whether it was his intention or not, Boniface, in creating the office of doctor of the church, established a theological canon. The theological output of these persons became, by Boniface's action, an accepted body of theology against which all other theology could be measured. There was no claim that the theology of doctors of the church was free from error, nor that, taken together, it was exhaustive of all theological thought. What the works of the doctors had, however, was the papal seal of approval. That is all that was necessary for their work to become the standard against which all other theological work could be measured.

By the end of the thirteenth century, the following can be said about those who sought to teach theology:

1. Their task was recognized as different from the work of a parish priest or bishop.
2. They were not specially ordained to their work, but they were licensed for it, under the authority of the bishop of Rome.
3. They were recognized as having a specific magisterium or authority—the *magisterium cathedrae magistralis*—their scholarship was their authority to think through theological issues in the service of the work of parish priests as well as all who held the *magisterium cathedrae pastoralis*.

"Pastor and Teacher:" the Continental European Reformed Shaping of the Office of Professor of Theology

The first priority for the Reformers was to reshape ordinary church life so that it would actually work. They had to develop organizational structures hurriedly that would enable congregations to

---

[37] In addition to the four original doctors of the Western church, designated by Boniface VIII in 1298, the four doctors of the Eastern church—Athanasius (297-373), Basil the Great (309-379), Gregory of Nazianzen (330-390), and John Chrysostom (347-407)— and Thomas Aquinas (1225-1274) were added in 1568. One other doctor was added in the sixteenth century; four doctors were added in the eighteenth century; nine were added in the nineteenth century; and ten were added in the twentieth century, bringing the total to thirty-three. Among those named in the twentieth century were three women—Catherine of Siena (1347-1380), Theresa of Avila (1515-1582), and Thérèse of Lisieux (1873-1897).

be formed, ministers and church leaders to accept new ways of living, and ordinary church members to be educated for new duties. And they had to get things right from the start.[38] Toward these ends, John Calvin (1509-1564) sought to develop a church with a "teachable spirit." In *Institutes of the Christian Religion*, Calvin quietly makes this point:

> We see how God, who could in a moment perfect his own, nevertheless desires them to grow up into maturity solely under the education of the church. We see the way set for it: the preaching of the heavenly doctrine has been enjoined upon the pastors. We see that all are brought under the same regulation, that with a gentle and teachable spirit they may allow themselves to be governed by teachers appointed to this function.[39]

In similar spirit, Calvin asked his students, before studying the catechism, to pray, "I ask you, O my God, to create in me a true humility that will make me teachable and obedient, first of all to you, but also to those whom you have appointed to teach me."[40] Calvin spoke of his own conversion in precisely this way: "What happened first was that by an unexpected conversion [God] tamed to teachableness a mind too stubborn for its years."[41] Richard Osmer summarizes Calvin's quest this way:

> The piety of a teachable spirit as found in Calvin's thought is something quite different. A teachable spirit strives to be docile before God; but God in Calvin's view, has bound Christians to the ordinary means of grace found in the church's life. These represent objective checks on and helps in the Christian's struggle to hear God's Word and to obey God's will. Teachability before God thus leads to a teachable spirit in relation to the objective means of grace....Those objective means of grace that Calvin links explicitly to a teachable spirit are scripture and duly constituted leaders in the church.[42]

[38] John Calvin, *Institutes of the Christian Religion*, 4.3.10 (Philadelphia: Westminster, 1960), 1062.
[39] Calvin, *Institutes*, 4.1.5, 1017. See also 1.7.3, 77; 1.13.21, 145-46; 2.10.7, 434; 3.7.2., 691; 4.1.6, 1021; 4.3.1, 1054; 4.8.9, 1157; 4.14.10, 1285; 4.19.1, 1448, and 4.19.33, 1480.
[40] *Catechism*, 1545, quoted in Howard L. Rice and Lamar Williamson, eds. *A Book of Reformed Prayers* (Louisville: Westminster John Knox, 1998), 18.
[41] Quoted in T.H.L. Parker, *Calvin: An Introduction to His Thought* (Nashville: Westminster John Knox, 1995), 205.
[42] Osmer, Richard Robert, *A Teachable Spirit: Recovering the Teaching Office in the Church* (Louisville: Westminster John Knox, 1990), 55.

It was in the hope of that "teachable spirit" that Calvin structured the "office of teacher of theology" into the *Ecclesiastical Ordinances*, approved by the city of Geneva in 1541.[43] The sixth section of the document is headed, "There follows the second order which we have called the doctors." The section includes two paragraphs. The first states, "The special duty of doctors is to instruct in sound doctrine so that the purity of the gospel is not corrupted by ignorance or wrong opinion." The second paragraph suggests some of the tentativeness in Geneva in 1541. It says: "As thing [sic] stand at present, every agent assisting in the upholding of God's teaching is included so that the Church is not in difficulties from a lack of pastors and ministers. This is in common parlance the order of school teachers. The degree nearest the minister and closely joined to the government of the Church is the lecturer in theology."[44] Jeannine E. Olson appears to be correct when she suggests that "the second order of office....was less well defined than the others, as it was, in part, a project for the future."[45] Given the "unfinished" nature of Calvin's thinking about the office of teacher or professor, what things can be said with certainty about Calvin's view of the office? I believe that there are four concepts about which Calvin was clear:

First, Calvin did envision four offices within the church. In the introduction to the *Ecclesiastical Ordinances* of 1541, Calvin stated:

> First, there are four orders of offices instituted by Our Savior for the government of his Church: namely, the pastors, then the doctors, next the elders [nominated and appointed by the government] and fourthly the deacons. If we are to see the Church well-ordered and maintained we ought to observe this form of government.[46]

Second, Calvin understood the use of "pastors and teachers" in Ephesians 4.11 as two separate offices. He said:

---

[43] See G.R. Potter and M. Greengrass, *John Calvin, (Documents of Modern History)* (New York: St. Martins, 1983), 71-76, for the full text translated. This document is also available online at http://www.qub.ac.uk/iccj/sdixon/REFORMAT/GENEVA/ECCLEORD.HTM.

[44] Ibid., 72.

[45] Jeannine E. Olson, "Calvin and Social-Ethical Issues" in Donald K. McKim, *Cambridge Companion to John Calvin* (Cambridge: Cambridge Univ. Press, 2004), 157.

[46] Potter and Greengrass, *Calvin*, 71.

Those who preside over the government of the church in accordance with Christ's institution are called by Paul as follows: first apostles, then prophets, thirdly evangelists, fourthly pastors, and finally teachers. Of these only the last two have an ordinary office in the church; the Lord raised up the first three at the beginning of his Kingdom. And now and then revives them as the need of the times demands.[47]

Third, Calvin spared the professors any involvement in church administration or discipline. He was especially indebted to Martin Bucer (1491-1551) for his understanding of the importance of the office of professor of theology, as well as for his perception of how the office differed from that of minister of Word and sacrament.[48] With that perception clearly in mind, and perhaps remembering the differentiation between the *magisterium cathedrae pastoralis* and the *magisterium cathedrae magistralis*, Calvin determined, "Teachers are not put in charge of discipline, or administering the sacraments, or warnings or exhortations, but only of scriptural interpretation—to keep the doctrine whole and pure among believers."[49] In essence, Calvin created two pairs of offices: minister and professor, and elder and deacon. In each pair of offices, the first office participated in "discipline, administration of the sacraments,...warnings and exhortations." In each pair of offices, the second "are not put in charge of" such.[50]

Fourth, the work of the doctors or teachers is expressly to do and to teach theology. They are "to keep doctrine whole and pure among believers."[51] We return again to the *Ecclesiastical Ordinances*, where the simple notation is:

> The special duty of doctors is to instruct in sound doctrine so that the purity of the gospel is not corrupted by ignorance or wrong opinion. As thing [sic] stand at present, every agent assisting in the upholding of God's teaching is included so that the Church is not in difficulties from a lack of pastors and ministers. This is in common parlance the order of school teachers. The degree

---

[47] Calvin, *Institutes*, 4.3.4, 1056.
[48] See Paul Fries, "A New Office in the Reformed Church in America? Office and Ordination in the Reformed Tradition," *Acts and Proceedings*, 2005, 314-31, citing Willem van't Spijker, *The Ecclesiastical Offices in the Thought of Martin Bucer*, trans. John Vriend and Lyle D. Bierma, (Leiden: E.J. Brill, 1996), see esp. 420-23.
[49] Calvin, *Institutes*, 4.3.4, 1057.
[50] Ibid.
[51] Ibid.

nearest the minister and closely joined to the government of the Church is the lecturer in theology."[52]

Following Calvin, the Heidelberg Catechism, in 1563, linked the two offices of minister of Word and sacrament and professor of theology—or at least their distinct tasks—to the proper keeping of the Sabbath. In Question and Answer 103, the catechism asks and then answers:

> Question: What does God require in the fourth commandment?
> Answer: God desires, first, that the preaching office and the schools be maintained,
> And that I diligently participate in the congregation of God, to learn God's word, and to participate in the holy sacraments, to pray openly to God, and to offer Christian alms.
> Second, that I remain free from all evil works all the days of my life, and that I allow God to work in me through God's Holy Spirit, so that the Eternal Sabbath may already be part of my life now.

For those within the church to keep the fourth commandment, the church was going to have to safeguard two institutions—the ministerial preaching office and schools necessary to assure both the thoroughness of theological education for the preacher and the basics of learning for those who would listen. Anything less would profane the Sabbath. This theology was followed carefully by the Synod of Dort, 1618-1619, as it formalized a church order for the Reformed tradition in the Netherlands—a church order essentially developed by the synods of Wessel (1568), Embden (1570), Dort I (1576), and Middleburg (1581). In Article II, the Church Order of Dort defines the offices of the church in exactly the same fashion as these earlier synods:

> The Offices of the Church of Christ are fourfold, viz:
>
> 1. The Office of Ministers of the Word
> 2. The Office of Teachers of Theology
> 3. The Office of Elders
> 4. The Office of Deacons.

In Article XVIII, the Church Order goes on to specify:

> *The Office of Teachers or Professors of Theology* is to explain the holy

---

[52] Ibid., 72.

scriptures, and vindicate the pure doctrines of the Gospel against heresies.

The Church Order continues to make explicit the close relationship that the synod intended between any congregation and the process of theological education. In the very next section (XIX), the Church Order instructed: "The congregations shall endeavor to raise public funds for the support of *students of Theology*."

It was the context of ordinary life that gave rise to the Protestant version of the office of professor of theology during and immediately following the Reformation. From the late Middle Ages, the Reformation church inherited a general populace that was almost entirely illiterate. Very few church members could read and even fewer could write. The basic education of ordinary persons was therefore essential to a church that sought to be capable of constantly reforming itself according to the Word of God. Schoolmasters and schoolmistresses (!), tied to local congregations, would labor to raise the bar of general education. Professors of theology, who would labor "to teach and to defend"—"to explain the Holy Scriptures and to vindicate the pure doctrines of the Gospel against heresies"—would carry out their work in ways that, wherever the work was actually done, it would ultimately have the life of the local congregation as the intended sphere of its impact. This would explain the placement of the office between the office of the minister of the Word and that of the elder.

It would also seem that from the origin of the office within Protestantism, the leaders of the Reformation recognized that the enormous and pivotal character of the labor assigned to the office of professor of theology had to exempt the office from participation in the church's legislative process. So, from Calvin's time and at least into the late eighteenth century, professors of theology were "not put in charge of discipline, or administering the sacraments, or warnings or exhortations...."[53] The two-directional ministry of the office of professor was established to serve the educational needs of an ignorant church and to define the doctrine for the whole church, without any power to enforce conformity to that doctrine.

The Church Order of the Synod of Dort can be used as a summary of what we know about the office of professor of theology prior to the time of its importation into the American colonies. Four conclusions can be drawn: (1) The office was regarded as a necessary constituent element within Reformed ecclesiology. (2) The office, by its

---

[53] See p. 142, above.

placement between the office of minister of the Word and the office of elder, appears to have had congregational reference and relevance. (3) Professors were not "ministers of the Word," nor were they necessarily chosen from those who held that office (see Article III). (4) There was no order for the ordination of professors of theology. But then there was also no order for the ordination of elders or deacons. Only ministers of the Word—the officers with specifically sacramental ministry—were ordained.

One thing more needs to be said about Dort. Like Boniface VIII, the Synod of Dort established a theological canon, which the synod described as "Standards of Unity" ("Formulieren van Eenigheit"). The Belgic Confession and the Heidelberg Catechism were regarded as "accurately conceived modes of expressing divine truth intended to subserve 'Uniformity of Belief,' and to furnish means for the ready detection of error." In the nineteenth century, the Canons of Dort were, themselves, added to the Standards of Unity.[54] Corwin has observed, "Subscriptions have, therefore, been always required of Ministers and Professors to these Standards, and it is required that preaching shall be in harmony with the same."[55]

The Office Comes to America

In 1628, just nine years after the conclusion of the Synod of Dort, the first Dutch Reformed congregation in America was organized.[56] But, as Gregg Mast, in conversation more than a decade ago, carefully pointed out, to state that a church was organized is to misunderstand the event. What actually occurred April 7, 1628, when Dominie Johannes Michaelius stepped ashore on Manhattan Island, was that the first Dutch Reformed consistory in North America was completed. There had for some years been elders and deacons. There had even been two church officers designated as *krankenbezoekers* or *sieckentroosters*— "comforters or visitors of the sick"—Sebastiaan Jansz Krol and Jan Huyck. These gentlemen had begun leading Reformed worship services in 1626: "These, while awaiting a clergyman, read to

---

[54] Edward Tanjore Corwin, *A Digest of Constitutional and Synodical Legislation of the Reformed Church in America* (New York: Board of Publications of the Reformed Church in America, 1906), 688; citing *Post Acta*, Synod of Dort, 1619, Session 3, Section 6, 159; also Session 6.

[55] Ibid.

[56] This congregation, later known as the Church of St. Nicholas, was located within the Fort of New Amsterdam, at the tip of Manhattan Island, New York City.

the commonality there on Sundays texts of Scripture with the Creeds."[57] So, when Dominie Michaelius arrived in New Netherland, it was at last possible to convene a complete consistory and then to proceed properly to organize a congregation from among the two hundred seventy souls within New Amsterdam.[58] It was clear to all that this congregation was under the authority of the Classis of Amsterdam[59] and the Particular or Provincial Synod of North Holland. Exactly how the congregation was related to the classis or synod was never clarified.

Even though there was almost no new Dutch immigration after England's takeover of New Netherlands in 1664, many other congregations of the Dutch Reformed Church were organized within the American colonies. By 1700, their number had increased to thirty-one; by 1750, the number had skyrocketed to ninety-four. Even as the number of Reformed congregations in North America came to exceed the number of Reformed congregations within the city of Amsterdam, the question of their status was never clarified. It does not appear that any of these congregations was ever fully enrolled as a member of the Classis of Amsterdam. Nor is there any evidence, before 1737, that these congregations sought to create any kind of ecclesiastical structure among themselves. Such few Dutch pastors as there were for these congregations were appointed by or had their calls approved by the Classis of Amsterdam. But in what sense could it be said that they were members of the classis? Still, it is clear that Reformed congregations and their pastors understood clearly that they were related to each other in America by way of their relationship to the church in the Netherlands.

In 1737, an American ecclesiastical structure among the Dutch Reformed congregations did come into being. The structure was shaped by a document called *Fundamental Articles*,[60] and it included a general assembly of all congregations called the *coetus* (or "meeting, conversation, colloquium")[61] along with smaller gatherings of geographically related congregations called "circles" (Dutch, *kringen*). The *Fundamental Articles* stipulated that this new church structure

---

[57] Edward Tanjore Corwin, *A Manual of the Reformed Church in America* (New York: Board of Publication of the Reformed Church in America, 1902), 18.
[58] Ibid., 19.
[59] The offices of the East and West India Companies were located in Amsterdam. This is probably the reason that the North American "mission" "fell into the hands of the Amsterdam Classis," but "not without protests from other Classes which wished to have a share therein." Corwin, *Digest*, 33.
[60] Corwin, *Digest*, 147-49.
[61] This is, of course, one of the Latin words for "intercourse," sexual as well as social. Coetus is pronounced *seé-tus*.

was to remain "always in subordination to the Classis of Amsterdam, according to Articles 30 and 31 of the Church Order."[62] Please note the character of the names chosen for the organizational elements of this plan. The names suggest groups meant to be conversational and informal in nature, with neither authority nor power to act.

This structure held the American Dutch Reformed congregations together until about 1755. For three days, from May 27 through May 29 that year, twelve or thirteen of the Dutch Reformed pastors in America (representing about half of the total number of ministers, but only one-eighth of the congregations) met in New York City in *broederlijk conferentie*[63]—in "fraternal conference." In the course of that meeting, they committed themselves to two goals: (1) the establishment of a classis in America, in order to examine and ordain persons for the office of minister of the Word; and (2) the founding of an American educational institution, *Academij Seminarium*, as a means for educating persons for the pastorate.[64]

These gentlemen comprised one side of what was to become a horrendous argument that would rage within the Reformed Dutch Church until 1771 and that would affect church life for another couple of decades after that. This devastating controversy centered on the question of how best to organize the rapidly growing number of Dutch Reformed congregations in the American colonies. Were the congregations in America to continue to be the "diaspora" congregations of the Reformed Church in the Netherlands, or were they to begin to be reshaped into a structure that would ultimately become a Reformed Church in the American provinces? This question took the Dutch Reformed tradition into new, unexplored ecclesiastical territory, raising questions in no way envisioned by the Church Order of 1619.

The argument came to be called the coetus-conferentie controversy, and those gentlemen who met in May 1755, in spite of their calling themselves a "broederlijk conferentie," kept the 1737 name and continued to be known as the coetus. The coetus saw clearly the need for the quick and complete organization of American congregations into at least a classis, but probably also a synod.

Those who opposed the conclusions reached and the solutions proposed by the 1755 coetus came to be called the conferentie. This group also could count on the support of about half of the Dutch Reformed

---

[62] Corwin, *Digest*, 148.
[63] Conferentie is pronounced *con-fur-en'-see*.
[64] Manuscript minutes, Archives of New Brunswick Theological Seminary.

pastors and of about one-eighth of the congregations. Concerning the two issues identified above—the creation of an American classis with the right to ordain, and the establishment of an American means of teaching theology in preparation for ordination to the ministry of Word and sacrament—the conferentie adamantly opposed the first, and differed with the coetus regarding the second only in the location and structure of the means of educating pastors. The conferentie insisted that the American congregations should remain immediately under the authority of the Classis of Amsterdam. Regarding education for the pastorate, the conferentie agreed that it should be done in America, but it proceeded to obtain an act of the New York colonial legislature for the establishment of a professorship of theology, to be elected by the Synod of North Holland and located within the college established in 1754, now known as Columbia University.[65]

By 1771, most of the originative energy had gone out of the argument, and all of the patience of the mother church in the Netherlands had been used up. A way had to be found to end the controversy. The Classis of Amsterdam, which oversaw, as best it was able, the work of the Reformed congregations in America, sent back a "Plan of Union" with a young doctoral student who had just completed his degree in the Netherlands. That recently minted doctor of sacred theology, John Henry Livingston (1746-1825), was to spend the rest of his life working out the details of the plan that he brought back to America.

The genius of the Classis of Amsterdam's plan was to separate the teaching of theology from any American institution of college-level education. The Articles of Union, by which the coetus-conferentie controversy was finally brought to an end (a shaky end, but an end, nevertheless), put the matter this way:

> Concerning the Professorate (*Professoraat*), we will act according to the advice of the Reverend Classis of Amsterdam. We will provisionally choose one or two[66] Professors of Theology to teach Foundational, Constructive, and Exegetical theology,[67] and related disciplines in accord with the Dutch Reformed confessions, to which office we will choose, on favorable terms, such divines from the Netherlands as are of acknowledged learning, piety, and orthodoxy, and immutably attached to the

---

[65] Corwin, *Manual*, III (1879), 32-40.
[66] The Dutch reads "*een of 2*"
[67] The original reads "*Theologiam Didactio-Elenchicam, Exegeticam*, etc."

Netherlands Standards of Unity, said classis having promised to recommend suitable characters.[68]

Here we have, then, the first use of the collective noun: *professoraat* ("professorate"). Even when the American church opted to elect only one professor, that person was viewed as part of a collective—a collegial body that would always place the work of anyone who held the office within the context of "a company of professors" like Calvin's "company of pastors" in Geneva. It is exactly this collective noun—the professorate—and the 1784 election of two people to teach theology, that allows New Brunswick Theological Seminary to sustain its claim to be the earliest seminary in America.[69]

In the years immediately following 1771 and preceding 1784—years during which the American colonies prepared for and then fought a war for their independence—the character of the office of professor of theology was fine-tuned for uniquely American service. When the Classis of Amsterdam wrote to the Consistory of New York January 14, 1772, the classis said:

> Concerning the Professorate...meanwhile, it seems to us that possibly in the pressing necessity there is for a Professor of Theology, the brethren might find in their own body a suitable person, who although not born in the Netherlands, has studied and received his ordination there. However, far be it from us to limit the freedom of the Assembly in any degree; and we shall wait to hear what the General Meeting, when the Union has been formed, will represent to us.[70]

It is important to note three things the classis said. The first significant element is signaled by the words, "the brethren might find in

---

[68] Articles of Union, 1771, manuscript copy in the Archives of the Reformed Church in America. Other translations are available in the *Acts and Proceedings*, vol. 1 (1815), 57-74; in the *Digest of 1848*, 397-405; and in Edward Tanjore Corwin, ed., *Ecclesiastical Records of the State of New York (ERNY)*, vol. 6, 4210-18.

[69] On October 6, 1784, Hermanus Meyer was actually elected to serve as "Instructor of the Students in the inspired languages," at the same time that Livingston was elected to the office of professor of theology. Meyer continued in that office until his death in 1791. In 1786, the General Synod named him "Lector in Theology." While it would appear that the synod never elected him to the office of professor, he was clearly called to "complete" the earliest faculty.

[70] Corwin, *ERNY*, 4237.

their own body." This clause may be an exegesis of the second sentence of Article XXVIII of the Articles of Union—"We will *provisionally* choose one or two Professors of Theology..." (italics added). Choosing a professor from among the limited resources of the American church may have been envisioned only as a provisional expedient, until a professor from the Netherlands could be supplied.[71] This temporary expedient may have led in turn to the American election of professors from the company of pastors within the church. Second, the Classis of Amsterdam was certainly very well aware that it had just sent the very well educated and totally competent John Henry Livingston back to the American colonies. This paragraph of the classis's letter reads like a position description written for Livingston. Third, the classis was prepared to allow the American church's "General Meeting" a tremendous amount of autonomy.

As soon as the Articles of Union of 1771 promised the possibility of a fully constituted Dutch Reformed Church within the American colonies, the leaders of the American congregations began to spell out what it would mean to have the professorate fully functioning.

The office was understood as "fundamental to our Church Union,"[72] and as "an indispensable prerequisite for the well being of the church."[73] On the one hand, there was great concern for the establishment on American soil of a form of church government that was as "Dutch" as possible. This shows up even in the perception of the Synod of North Holland. From its July 28-August 6, 1772, meeting, it was reported:

> as we live so far removed from them, and possibly cannot be so well acquainted with the particular domestic circumstances of their churches as those who are there, their Rev. take the liberty to state that living under an English government, they are by their beloved rulers established in their "freedom" and in their "Ecclesiastical Acts," as a Netherland Church; and that they are surrounded also by a number of sects which have, all of them, a

---

[71] It may be in this same sense that the synod of 1789 responded to a request from the Classis of Hackensack to clarify what the synod of 1788 had meant when it "directed" the respective classes to "attend to this Article" (i.e. the professorate). The synod of 1789 explained that this "only meant an attending to this subject in its whole compass, in order that it may yet, with the blessing of the Lord, be brought to its desired completion." *Acts and Proceedings*, 1789, 197.

[72] Corwin, *ERNY*, 4270.

[73] Corwin, *ERNY*, 4274.

high regard for them from the fact that they bear the name of and are essentially one with the renowned Netherland Zion. From this it appears how necessary it is for them to prove in all things that they are indeed a Holland Church, and that they hold themselves, not only to the Doctrine, but also, as far as practicable, to the Form of Government established by the Synod of Dordrecht in 1618 and 1619; and that, therefore, it would be, not only for their respectable standing, but even for their safety, to have the name and the form of Government of the Churches in Holland....[74]

Twenty years later (1793), the professorate could, therefore, be described as "a subject which sustains so intimate a relation to our CONSTITUTION and the well-being of our Church" that the existence of the church could not be envisioned without the office.[75] As the church in the United States began to envision for itself an ecclesiastical existence beyond the consistorial/congregational stage, it was faced with the necessity of establishing all of the offices required for a truly national Reformed church in the Dutch tradition. The professorate was as necessary to its convening a synod or classis in the 1770s as the presence of a pastor was necessary in 1628 to convene a consistory.

There was also, throughout this period, a growing sense that these widely separated congregations were not going to be held together by the Church Order alone.[76] It was rather in the professorate that they cast their hope for unity. This was the sole office in the church that was answerable only to the General Synod. It was the only office that could be concerned for the welfare of the whole church at once. The professorate could, therefore, be responsible for the unity of the church by its teaching and defending a single theology, which was lived out within a single liturgy. Two centuries later, Craig Dykstra, vice president for religion at the Lilly Endowment, observed: "A school is the pivotal institution for insuring that a tradition's practices are passed on from one generation to the next, and that practices are reflected upon, argued about, and reformed, revised, and extended in new ways in new times."[77]

[74] Corwin, *ERNY*, 4251.
[75] Corwin, *ERNY*, 4368.
[76] See, for example, "Brotherly Correspondence" that was carried on by the Reformed Dutch Church with the Presbyterian Synod of New York and Philadelphia and the Associate Reformed Church, *Acts and Proceedings*, 1789, 190-191. See also the conversation regarding "Church Order" in the Synod of 1791, *Acts and Proceedings*, 1791, 217.
[77] *In Trust*, vol. 7, no.2 (New Year, 1996), 4.

In 1784, after the conclusion of the War of Independence, the Reformed Church was finally able to proceed with the plan for educating ministers in America. On the basis of the Articles of Union of 1771, the church elected two highly respected pastors to comprise its first theological faculty. Hermanus Meyer (1733-1791), pastor at Totowa and Pompton Plains, New Jersey, was called to serve as "Instructor of the Students in the inspired languages." John Henry Livingston (1746-1825), pastor in the Collegiate Church, New York City, was called to be professor of theology. Livingston's election transferred him from the office of minister of Word and sacrament to the office of professor. On May 17, 1785, during an "extra meeting" of the General Synod, "the Rev. Body have had the satisfaction of beholding the Rev. Professor J.H. Livingston publicly assume that office, with a learned and elegant dissertation in the Old Dutch Church in New York."[78] Three factors need to be observed about this occasion: (1) it occurred within the meeting of the General Synod; (2) it occurred within the "Old" or Garden Street Church building, built in 1693—an obvious attempt to relate the event to the earliest years of the Dutch church's presence in America; and (3) it occurred with a formal inaugural lecture, in Latin, entitled, *"De Veritate Religionis Christianae."*[79]

After the end of the war and the establishment of its professorate, the Reformed (Protestant) Dutch Church in North America, as the denomination had taken to calling itself, began the process of institutionalizing its new existence separate from the mother church in the Netherlands. It organized itself into a general convention or assembly and into classes in 1784.[80] The synod also commissioned Livingston to edit its first English hymn book and liturgy—*Psalms of David with Hymns and Spiritual Songs* (1789), as well as its first book of church order, the "Articles Explanatory of the Government and Discipline of the Reformed Dutch Church in the United States of America," (1792) (usually known simply as the "Explanatory Articles").

---

[78] *Acts and Proceedings*, 1785, 135.

[79] The complete Latin text was republished in the first edition of *Centennial Discourses* (New York: Board of Publication of the Reformed Church in America, 1877), 553-601. (In the second edition, the address was replaced by an index.) John Coakley has translated the *oratio inauguralis* in a close paraphrase. On the basis of that paraphrase a case can be made that Livingston saw the task of his office as that of providing the young American Reformed Church (and in some sense, the new nation itself) with a reliable understanding of helpful Christian theology, and so he attempts to sketch out the truth of Christianity as a whole.

[80] *Acts and Proceedings*, 1784, 128.

When the young denomination asked Livingston to prepare its first church order, Livingston was placed in the position of being able to shape the church's understanding of the office of professor of theology to the office that he held at that time. In that first church order, Livingston elaborated on the Church Order of Dort in this way:

> The distinction between the first and the second office in the church, that is, between the Ministers of the Word and Teachers of Theology, is founded in the nature of the respective offices. The former are those, who by preaching and ruling, instruct and govern the church; and are, as such denominated pastors or shepherds of the flock:[81] the latter are those who are set apart only to teach and defend the truths of the Gospel, and are, for that reason, excused from fulfilling the pastoral duties. This distinction was noted in the early ages of the Christian church. It was attended to at the Reformation, and was productive of important benefits, especially with respect to the education of candidates for the holy ministry. The Reformed Dutch Church preserves the same distinction and determines that the instructing and preparing youth for the service of the sanctuary not be left to every Minister, or any individual who may choose to assume that office.[82]

[81] This description appears to be so parallel to the Genevan *Ecclesiastical Ordinances* of 1541 that one might suspect Livingston had a copy of that work. It is important to note that the parity of all pastors was achieved within the Belgic Confession by the insistence that all ministers were "servants of Jesus Christ, the one Universal Bishop and only Head of the Church" (Article 31); whereas the "Explanatory Articles" defined the parity by observing: "All ministers of the gospel are equal in rank and authority; all are Bishops, or overseers in the Church..." (Article XVIII), following Calvin, 4.3.8., 1060-61.

[82] Article XIX, "Articles Explanatory of the Government and Discipline of the Reformed Dutch Church in the United States of America," *The Constitution of the Reformed Dutch Church in the United States of America* (New York: William Durell, 1793), 312. Livingston added a quotation from Theodor Beza's commentary on Ephesians, which has been translated:

> "*Pastors and Teachers*. I agree with Ambrose, who separated these two offices; since the argument that led Jerome and Augustine to combine them—that the conjunction is merely thrown in—is not very solid. I admit that the term Teacher is used broadly, as in I Corinthians 12, but nevertheless there appears to have been some distinction, because the placement in that compendium hardly seems to be of synonyms. Therefore the office of *Teacher* is to explain the Word of the Lord

All of that sounds very impressive and gives the sense that Livingston was making sure that he and his colleagues in the office played a significant role in the life of the young denomination. But Article XX, following the clear suggestion of Calvin, went on to say, "Professors of Theology, have, as such, no power, jurisdiction, or government whatever in the church...."[83] Article XXI detailed the method by which the General Synod alone was to elect professors of theology.[84] Article XXII established the "Formula of Subscription" to be signed by each professor before being installed into the office.

The "Explanatory Articles" required subscription to a "formula" (see Articles V, XI, and XXII) when people were licensed for and ordained to the office of minister of Word and sacrament or elected to and installed into the office of professor of theology. This requirement actually had its origin in the 1619 Church Order. No texts for these subscriptions were provided by Dort, but Article LIII of the Church Order did require, "The MINISTERS of the Word of God, as also the PROFESSORS of Theology, shall subscribe the confession of faith of the Reformed Church in the Netherlands...."[85] The texts of all three formulae for subscription in the "Explanatory Articles" consistently use the first person plural pronoun—"We the undersigned..."

With all of this detailed defining of the office of professor of theology, it is necessary to ask why one is not ordained to the office. There is no evidence that the Synod of Dort or any other synod ever gave consideration to this matter before the twentieth century. The

---

faithfully, and to rule the church as a School, that sound doctrine is taught, and true interpretations are held in the church, as Origen of Alexandria taught, as is explained by Nicephorus in his Ecclesiastical History, Book V, chapter 14.

And the office of *Pastors* (who are also called *Bishops*, as in I Pet. 3) extends more broadly, to devote himself wholly to the word and prayer, and to care in all ways for the Church entrusted to him; from which it is clear enough that these two offices should remain permanently in the Church of God." Beza, *On the Epistle to the Ephesians*, vi [i.e., iv]. 11. Quoted in Daniel Meeter, *Meeting Each Other in Doctrine, Liturgy, and Government*, Historical Series of the Reformed Church in America, no. 24 (Grand Rapids: Eerdmans, 1993), 107-108.

[83] *Constitution* (1793), 313.

[84] The "Explanatory Articles," at this point, provide the first version of that "old recipe card" to which allusion was made above.

[85] Subscription was also required of schoolmasters (Article LIV), although they were given the option of subscribing to the Heidelberg Catechism.

Belgic Confession, in Articles 30 and 31, indicates that those who serve as minister, elder, or deacon are to be elected by the congregation. The Church Order of Dort requires elders and deacons to be "confirmed" with "public prayers and engagements."[86] Only for ministers does Dort speak of ordination (Article IV). The "Explanatory Articles" requires only ministers and professors to subscribe to a formula.[87] Ministers, upon their ordination, and professors, upon their election and installation, were to be given "a diploma" or "certificate." In the case of professors, each was to be given "an instrument certifying the appointment, and specifying the duties of the office." This document was to be "signed in the presence of the Synod."[88]

All of these measures combined to define and place the professorate within the life of the church. The articles implied that each professor was a member of the General Synod, not of any classis. In speaking about "professorial certificates," for example, the "Explanatory Articles" observed: "All regulations....shall be formed by the General Synod alone; to which as well the Professors, as the Classes or Particular Synods shall submit, and always conform themselves."[89] However, the professors' relationship to the General Synod was nowhere stated explicitly until 1814. In 1809, when the General Synod asked Livingston to move from New York City to New Brunswick, New Jersey, Livingston simply packed up his earthly belongings and crossed the Hudson, without asking for a formal letter of dismissal from either the consistory of the Collegiate Church of the City of New York or the Classis of New York. Both assemblies were a bit peeved by this failure, which they regarded as a breach of good government (or, at least, good church etiquette). Livingston insisted that he had offended neither the church government nor church etiquette, since he was a member of and answerable to the General Synod alone. The General Synod, four years after the fact, concluded:

> WHEREAS, it is necessary that the ecclesiastical relation of the Professor of Theology should be clearly ascertained and settled....Therefore, *Resolved*, that by the Constitution of the Reformed Dutch Church, the Professor of Theology, as such, has no relation to, or connection with any particular Classis, and is amenable only to the General Synod, *whose officer he is....*[90]

[86] Articles XXII and XXIV. By the time of the "Explanatory Articles," ministers, elders, and deacons were all to be ordained. See Article XXVII.
[87] See Articles V, VI, XI, XII, XXII.
[88] See Corwin, *Digest*, xxiv.
[89] Article XXIII; *Acts and Proceedings*, 1792, 235-36; Corwin, *Digest*, xxvi.
[90] *Acts and Proceedings*, 1814, 30 (emphasis is mine).

With the institutionalizing of the General Synod, the institutionalizing of the professorate began as well. The ordinary agenda for meetings of the General Synod followed the formal structure that was apparently typical for meetings in the eighteenth century. Each major element within the agenda was called a *lemma*, from the Greek word for "premise, or principal element." We are still familiar with the word in the English "dilemma"—the predicament of being caught between two equally attractive options. The plural of the word is *lemmata*. So, the agenda was organized under several *lemmata* or "premises." Among these *lemmata* was a *lemma* entitled, "Professorate," by which the synod indicated its direct oversight of theological education within the denomination. As a result of this format, theological education was assured attention at each meeting of the General Synod. This format continued, with minor alterations to the name of the *lemma*, until 1963.

This institutionalizing continued in many more concrete ways. The need for students to have access to needed theological texts very early brought the matter of library resources to the attention of the synod. By 1794, as the church continued to attempt to find ways to raise money in support of the professors and their school, the synod named trustees to hold the cash, if ever any was raised. This first board of trustees was an amazing one. It included Dr. Peter Wilson (1746-1825), at the time professor of languages at Columbia College and founding principal of Erasmus Hall, Flatbush, Brooklyn; Senator John Vanderbilt of Brooklyn, who represented King's County in the New York State Assembly from 1784-1786, and had been in the state senate since 1786; Robert Benson (1739-1823), who in 1775 had been a member of the Committee of One Hundred (the body charged with governing the City and County of New York during the Revolution); he had been the clerk of the New York State Constitutional Convention in 1777 and since 1784 had served as clerk of the City and County of New York; and Richard Varrick (1753-1831), a leading Federalist who had served as attorney general of the State of New York, in the New York State Assembly from 1787 to 1788, and as mayor of the City of New York (1789-1801).[91]

Almost exactly coincident with the selection of trustees, a discussion was begun concerning the most advantageous location for the professorate, now increasingly being thought of as a fledgling institution. This conversation, which flourished in 1794, marked another piece of important evidence in New Brunswick Seminary's

---

[91] *Acts and Proceedings*, 1794, 263.

claim to primacy among seminaries. In 1794, the synod determined to move the seminary from New York City to Brooklyn—actually, to Flatbush.[92] In 1794, Brooklyn was not yet part of New York City. Indeed, Flatbush was not even part of Brooklyn. This location was well beyond the evils of city life. Livingston, along with Peter Wilson, had been instrumental earlier in establishing a secondary school, called Erasmus Hall, in Flatbush. Wilson (who was one of the first trustees) was the principal of the school. Livingston had a summer home in the neighborhood. So the seminary took up residence in Erasmus Hall (which building is still standing), and Livingston traveled back to New York City to preach on Sundays. The Collegiate Church, which had been paying all of Livingston's salary, now reduced its contribution to half, expecting the synod to pick up the other half. the synod did not.[93]

What can be said, then, about the office of professor of theology at the end of the eighteenth century?

1. The church had come to a rather consistent use of the collective noun, "professorate."
2. The office of professor of theology had a purpose or mission "to teach Foundational, Constructive, and Exegetical theology, and related disciplines in accord with the Dutch Reformed confessions."
3. The office was tied to the General Synod and answerable only to the synod. The membership of the General Synod is therefore made up of the professorate and the classes, just as the membership of a classis is made up of the "company of pastors" and the congregations.

---

[92] See *Acts and Proceedings*, 1793, 251-251; 1794, 449; 1796, 458.
[93] John Henry Livingston was almost certainly among the wealthiest people in the denomination at the time. He always lived in his own home and was cared for by his "man," an African American servant, but apparently not a slave. At the time of his death in 1825, he had no slaves. We have no data for earlier years. Also at his death, he bequeathed to each of his seven grandchildren—grandsons and granddaughters—no less than 2,005 acres of farm land. He left the residue of his estate to his son, Henry, with reference to property in the states of New York, New Jersey, and Connecticut. Livingston's wealth was broadly known and certainly figured into the church's early reluctance to support the seminary financially. Incidentally, he bequeathed the seminary "all my books which are in the Dutch language, together with all my dissertations and orations in the Latin language which are loose and unbounded." A copy of Livingston's will is in the author's possession.

4. The office was clearly set outside the sphere of church governance and was without any "power, jurisdiction, or government whatever...."
5. The office was a *sine qua non* of church structure above the congregational level.

Without Place or Power in the Nineteenth Century

In the language of the "Explanatory Articles": "Professors of Theology have, as such, no power, jurisdiction, or government whatever...." That very well describes the real position of the office at the beginning of the nineteenth century. Livingston had been begging the synod to get serious about its financial support of the office of professor of theology and of the seminary as an institution. In response to his first request, the synod determined to move the seminary to Brooklyn. In response to Livingston's next plea, the synod of 1797 responded by moving the seminary back to Manhattan and by appointing two other professors—the Reverend Dirck Romeyn (1744-1804), pastor in Schenectady, and the Reverend Solomon Froeligh (1750-1827), pastor in Hackensack and Schaalenburgh, as professors of theology. The logic of this move is not immediately clear.[94] But the action of the synod became catastrophic when, in 1822, Froeligh became one of the leaders of the secession called the True Reformed Church.[95]

Sensing that its professors deserved continuing care between its own meetings, the synod of 1807 established a Board of Superintendents consisting of three ministers from each of the two particular synods (New York and Albany) and three representatives from the Board of Trustees of Queens College (with which the professorate was soon to be covenanted).[96] This board was to "superintend the theological institution, assist the professor in arranging the course of instruction,

---

[94] It may be that the synod did not at this time envision the professorate ever functioning as a "faculty" or institution in one place. The synod's original appointment of professors had included one person in New Jersey and another in New York. By 1797, Hermanus Meyer had died (1791), and the Albany-Schenectady area had grown into a third area of denominational presence.

[95] The causes and history of the secession are detailed in *A History of the Classis of Paramus, R.C.A.* (New York: Board of Publications, 1902), 51-68.

[96] *Acts and Proceedings*, 1807, 367. The first superintendents were, from the Synod of New York: John Abeel (1769-1812), pastor, Collegiate Church, New York City; James VanCampen Romeyn (1765-1840), pastor, Second Church, Hackensack, New Jersey; and Jeremiah Romeyn (1768-1818), pastor in Harlem. From the Synod of Albany: Thomas Gibson Smith

[and] to attend the examinations of the students in theology previous to their licensure before classis...."[97] The covenant with the trustees of Queens College was fully actualized in 1809, and Livingston and his students were instructed to move from New York City to New Brunswick, New Jersey. Queen's College's new college hall (now known as Old Queens Hall) was only partially constructed, so seminary classes were first held in a building on the south side of Albany Street, just east of George Street. In 1811, classes, the library, and the chapel were all moved to the still only partially completed hall. For the next twenty years, the seminary, Queens College, and the preparatory school all carried on their activities within that one building. The seminary and the college continued to share the building until 1856.

Under the terms of the covenant, Livingston was named president of the college, but within a very short while there were no college students over whom to preside. It is quite clear that Livingston saw the absence of college students as an asset rather than a concern. The college remained without students for the rest of Livingston's life.[98]

In 1819, the General Synod elected the Reverend Thomas DeWitt (1791-1874; NBTS, 1812), pastor in Hopewell and New Hackensack, New York, as a professor of theology. After DeWitt had declined the call, the synod, clearly responding to something within DeWitt's reason for declining the call, voted the following action:

> Resolved, that the Professor now to be appointed, or any professor who may hereafter be appointed by the Synod, shall hold no Pastoral charge.[99]

John Ludlow (1793-1857; NBTS, 1817), pastor of the First Reformed Church in New Brunswick, New Jersey, was then elected and accepted the appointment.[100] The proscription of the synod of 1819 was incorporated into the Constitution of 1833.[101]

(1756-1837), pastor in Tarrytown, New York; Peter Labagh (1773-1858), pastor in Catskill and Oak Hill, New York; and John M. Bradford (1781-1827), pastor, First Church in Albany, New York. The superintendents from Queens College were Ira Condict (1764-1811), pastor, First Church, New Brunswick, New Jersey; John Schureman Vredenburgh (1776-1821), pastor, Raritan, New Jersey; and John Schureman (1778?-1818), pastor in Hillsborough, New Jersey.

[97] *Acts and Proceedings*, 1807, 366.
[98] Richard P. McCormick, *Rutgers: A Bicentennial History* (New Brunswick: Rutgers Univ. Press, 1966), 33-34.
[99] *Acts and Proceedings*, 1819, 39.
[100] *Acts and Proceedings*, 1819, 39; 1820, 15.
[101] Corwin, *Digest*, 556.

From the time that the faculty residential units in Old Queens Hall were completed (about 1813), two of the three faculty members lived in that building. Livingston lived on his farm, in his own elegant home, at the corner of Townsend Street and Livingston Avenue, about one mile southwest of the campus. In 1856, the Peter Hertzog Theological Hall was constructed, with a gift from Ann Hertzog, a member of the Third Reformed Church in Philadelphia, Pennsylvania. Hertzog Hall was built primarily as a residential facility for students but also included a refectory, a chapel, and a library. It had, however, neither classroom space nor residential space for faculty. In 1866, after a very creative interaction with the Rutgers College Board of Trustees, the General Synod ended up with sufficient cash to build three faculty homes. Two of these still remain: the President's House and #1 Seminary Place.[102] So, at the time it had been educating ministers for more than eighty years, New Brunswick Seminary was finally beginning to assemble a proper campus. But please take note. There was in this wonderful assemblage of structures no stated place to hold classes. The professors were expected to hold classes in their homes, usually in their studies. The current dining room in the President's House is the room originally designated as the professor's study. That room would have provided ample space for a group of ten to twelve students. Even this informal treatment of teaching space can be understood as one more fragment of evidence suggesting that the office of professor functioned much more powerfully than any sense of seminary as institution.

In 1866, seven of the eight men in the first class to graduate from Hope College, Holland, Michigan, requested the privilege of undertaking theological education "in the West." The General Synod of 1866 gave permission for theological classes to begin, and the General Synod of 1867 elected the Reverend Dr. Cornelius E. Crispell to the office of professor of theology "at Hope College," to "take charge of the class and give instruction in theology."[103] By this action, the synod now had members of the office of professor of theology in two institutions. The General Synod's 1867 action, authorizing and appointing a professor of theology "in the West," made it a simple matter for the synod of 1888 (when there were four professors in New Brunswick Seminary and two professors in Western Seminary) to envision the appointment of a professor of theology within the church's mission

---

[102] #3 Seminary Place—called Kooy House—was not constructed until 1882. While its exterior looks very similar to the other two remaining homes, the interior was of a totally different design.

[103] *Acts and Proceedings*, 1867, 273.

in Arcot, India. The mission was intent upon establishing a program of indigenous ministerial education. The Reverend Dr. William W. Scudder was a gifted and classically trained teacher around whom the life of such an institution could be shaped. Scudder was, therefore, elected to the office of professor of theology, to teach within the newly established Arcot Theological Seminary.[104] As a result of the presence of more than one seminary within the denomination, the "Form of Call for a Professor of Theology" was altered to add the words "a professor within their Theological Seminary at _____."[105]

The period between 1884 and 1888 also represents the beginning of the Board of Superintendents/Trustees' control of the awarding of the professorial certificates. In the "Plan of the Theological Seminary at New Brunswick," approved by the synod of 1888, it was stated:

> The Board shall, at its annual meeting, superintend an examination to be conducted by the Professors, of all the students connected with the School, on studies that have been pursued during the year. The members of the senior class, who pass their examinations satisfactorily, shall be recommended for Professorial certificates.[106]

While the text is unclear as to whether the board was recommending to the faculty, or the faculty was recommending to the board the awarding of professorial certificates, what is clear is that the board was in control of the process.

These dramatic steps in the transformation of the office of professor of theology were taken by the General Synod without any clear consideration of what the changes meant for the professorate. How could or would this newly extended body continue to function as a *professorate*—as a collective noun? It is just possible that the General Synod was sensitive to this matter. In 1886, it changed the name of its standing committee from the Committee on the Professorate to the Standing Committee on the Professorate and Theological Seminaries. This committee continued to report to the General Synod annually until 1963. Further, the synod of 1894 took an action that provides additional evidence of the church's awareness of and concern for the continuing welfare of the professorate as collective noun. The synod of 1894 voted to amend the constitution to enable the faculty of each

---

[104] *Acts and Proceedings*, 1888, 550, 552.
[105] Corwin, *Digest*, 551.
[106] *Acts and Proceedings*, 1888, 536; see also Corwin, *Digest*, 449.

seminary to have one delegate at the synod.[107] Unfortunately, the classes refused to approve the necessary amendment to the constitution, so the action was null.[108] On that symbolic note, the nineteenth century ended for the professorate.

How can the nineteenth-century professorate be summarized? Four conclusions appear to be justified:

1. The professors and the professorate appear to have functioned almost entirely or solely within the seminary(ies). The "Form of Call" was amended to specify within which seminary a professor was to teach. Professors did very little publishing "for the whole church." W.J.R. Taylor, writing in the *Centennial Discourses*, offered an emotional plea in this regard. He said:

> A theology that is so venerated and thoroughly scriptural should not be permitted to repose in the manuscripts of professors and students, illustrated only by oral instructions and supplemented by text books of authors in other lands and churches. May we not hope that, before this nineteenth century shall end, some gifted and learned professor or pastor may furnish the Reformed Church in America with a thorough exposition of her theology, based upon her three great symbols—the Belgic Confession, the Heidelbergh Catechism, and the Canons of Dordrecht? We ought to have such a work as Dr. Hodge has produced for the theology of which he is the most venerated living expositor, or something like those two noble volumes, the Christian Dogmatics of Dr. VanOosterzee of Utrecht.[109]

2. The professorate understood its role of "teaching and defending the truth of the Gospel" to be a warrant for maintaining a very conservative theology.[110]

3. After the death of Livingston in 1825, there was very little sense of *magisterium*, as "teacher of the whole church."

4. The origin and development of seminary boards, superintendents or trustees, led to a loss of clarity regarding the true position of the office of professor of theology in the church.

---

[107] *Acts and Proceedings*, 1894, 78.
[108] *Acts and Proceedings*, 1895, 131-32.
[109] W.J.R. Taylor, "The Peculiar History of the Reformed Church in America in Relation to Theological Education," *Centennial Discourses*, 199-200.
[110] See Norman J. Kansfield, "Philip Milledoler: Reluctant Inheritor," a lecture presented within the Standing Seminar in Reformed Church History, New Brunswick Theological Seminary, March 4, 1996.

Transformed in the Twentieth Century

Quite surprisingly, it is in the twentieth century that the office of professor of theology received the most attention (not all of it good, but still a lot of attention). The first significant change to be enacted occurred in 1907, when the General Synod voted:

> Resolved: that an amendment be made to the constitution in regard to the mode of election [of Professors of theology]: 1) that the Board of Superintendents of the seminary involved submit one candidate whom they have selected by a two-thirds vote—other nominations can also be made by Synod...[111]

This act, for the first time, passed the originative power in the selection of professors to the boards of the seminaries. An overture from the Particular Synod of New Brunswick to the General Synod of 1923 carried this matter through the next logical step. The General Synod was asked to instruct the seminary boards "to secure men as professors who are especially trained in their specific fields and that the Presidents of our seminaries [an office created by the General Synod of 1922] be given executive powers above that which they now possess." The concept, in its entirety, was adopted by the synod.[112]

In all of the years since 1809 (when the General Synod finally began to pay Livingston), the General Synod had been responsible for the salaries of its professors. In 1951, again upon the basis of an overture from the Particular Synod of New Jersey, the General Synod agreed to raise the salaries of professors to $5,000 per year. This, however, was agreed upon with the proviso that the additional "money be raised by the Boards of Superintendents/Trustees of the seminaries, and not by the Board of Direction (i.e., the "Board of Trustees") of the denomination."[113] This meant that the denomination was no longer directly responsible for the financial care of its professors or the professorate. This process was carried one step further when, in 1953, the Standing Committee on the Professorate and Seminaries recommended "that the salaries of professors in our seminaries be determined henceforth by the Boards of Trustees of the seminaries with the understanding that the responsibility for obtaining the funds rests with the Boards of Trustees."[114]

---

[111] *Acts and Proceedings*, 1907, 743-44.
[112] *Acts and Proceedings*, 1923, 166.
[113] *Acts and Proceedings*, 1951, 82-83.
[114] *Acts and Proceedings*, 1953, 65, 70.

From the creation of the seminary boards through the reassignment of responsibility for fund raising, a significant shift was occurring. This shift from direct synodical responsibility to board responsibility was mirrored in a drift from church and office to institution and function. The General Synod of 1955 continued the earlier pattern of synodical care, however, by establishing the seminaries' first sabbatical policy.[115]

The General Synod of 1958 was presented with two opportunities further to define the office of professor of theology. In the first case, the Reverend Dr. M. Stephen James, president and John S. Bussing Professor of Preaching and Pastoral Theology at New Brunswick Seminary, sought permission to retain his status as a professor of theology and, at the same time, to resign his responsibilities as professor of preaching and pastoral theology. His intention was to concentrate all of his energy on the "increasing responsibilities of the office of president." In the second case, the Board of Superintendents of New Brunswick requested that the General Synod elect Peter N. VandenBerge (whose name nowhere appears in the request), who was serving as librarian, to the office of professor of theology. The standing committee concluded:

> While we have no desire to minimize the importance of the office of Librarian in a Theological Seminary, we do raise a serious question as to whether some one destined to serve in that office is a Professor of Theology as our Constitution defines that ministry.[116]

Acting on the advice of its standing committee, the General Synod accepted the request of James to continue in the office of professor of theology while serving solely as president of New Brunswick. At the same time, the synod denied the request of the Board of Superintendents to elect VandenBerge to the office of professor of theology while he served principally as librarian.[117]

The decade of the 1960s represented something of a riptide for the professorate. The synod of 1960 authorized each seminary faculty to select two of their members to be delegates to the General Synod, thereby doubling the professorial representation and establishing the representation that continues to this day.[118] The same synod called together all of the professors of theology at both seminaries in what was

---

[115] *Acts and Proceedings*, 1955, 315.
[116] *Acts and Proceedings*, 1958, 61-64.
[117] *Acts and Proceedings*, 1958, 63.
[118] *Acts and Proceedings*, 1960, 57.

designated a "convocation." The results of the first of these convocations were reported to the synod of 1961. Additional convocations were reported in 1962, 1964, and 1966.[119] The professorate was thereafter not convened again until January, 1997.[120]

All of this positive attention to the professorate, which gave it an expanded definition and more precise function within the life and work of the church, must have sparked a kind of euphoria in those who held the office. But then the Reverend Dr. Henry Bast, president of the 1961 General Synod, exploded an incendiary when he recommended that the office of professor of theology be deleted from the life of the church. Bast said:

> We have excellent seminaries, well trained professors, devoted boards of trustees, and able dedicated students but we are operating these theological schools under a section of the Constitution that has not been changed since the 18th century.[121] I believe that it needs overhauling at some vital points. One concerns the office of Professor of Theology and my recommendation is that we drop the office....This means that Professors in the Seminary would be in office, ministers of the Word. College professors teaching courses relating to religion continue to hold the office of minister of the Word even when they are ordained and have Ph.D. degrees. If we adopt this recommendation this means that our Seminary professors would become members of Classes instead of members of the General Synod. This, I believe, would be an advantage.

President Bast went on to observe some of the reasons for his suggestion:

> The biblical evidence for the office is weak, if not non-existent, the historical evidence is not related to our present structure and function as a denomination in this country, for the fourth office in the Geneva Ordinances, the office of doctor, is only remotely related to our Professor of Theology in the Reformed Church in America. I have, however, one major reason for making the recommendation. I believe it will increase the efficiency of the operation of the seminaries. Our present practice gives almost immediate life tenure to a professor; in fact, in the present

---

[119] *Acts and Proceedings*, 1961, 69-70; 1962, 54-55; 1964, 54-55; 1966, 42.
[120] Log of January 11, 1997, meeting of the General Synod professors of theology.
[121] Obviously, Dr. Bast did not have the benefit of this present essay!

structure of the Constitution, once in office, it is intended that he should remain for the rest of his life....The elimination of this office would enable our boards of trustees to appoint men to teach in our Seminaries for three-year or four-year periods working up to eight or ten years before they were given indefinite or life tenure.[122]

With Bast's proposal, which in the end was defeated, a new confusion entered the church's conversation about the office of professor of theology. The confusion centered in the intertwining of ecclesiastical office or standing, on the one hand, and academic tenure and rank, on the other. This confusion was made official in 1963, when the synod, upon the recommendation of the Committee on the Revision of the Constitution, adopted the following text as an amendment to the Constitution:

The Office of Professor of Theology embraces the academic ranks of full professor and associate professor.

> The Office of Professor of Theology is to teach one or more branches of theology in a theological seminary; to administer the academic functions of the seminary, subject to the rules established by the General Synod and the Board of Superintendents or Trustees; and to exercise general supervision over the students.[123]

The Committee on the Revision of the Constitution, reviewing the recommendations of the Committee on the Professorate, concluded:

> a separate ordination to the office of Professor of Theology was unnecessary, since the gift of teaching is included among the gifts belonging to the office of the Minister of the Word. The Professor of Theology exercises that particular gift in an extraordinary manner, and while doing so is excused from the exercise of some of the other gifts belonging to the ministry of the Word. His office is therefore to be regarded as being part of, and subordinate to, his participation in the office of the Minister of the Word of God.[124]

---

[122] *Acts and Proceedings*, 1961, 268, 329, 331. This was not the only formal effort to eliminate the office. For example, the Classis of South Grand Rapids overtured the General Synod to amend the *Book of Church Order* to eliminate the office in 1992. *Acts and Proceedings*, 1992, 380-85.
[123] *Acts and Proceedings*, 1963, 134.
[124] Ibid.

While this perspective was expressed in a format whereby the synod never voted for or against the conclusions expressed by its committee, the perception of the office of professor of theology was subtly remodeled by the committee's comment, nonetheless. Therefore, in the early 1960s, the office of professor was intermingled inappropriately with concepts of academic rank and tenure, on the one hand, and was, on the basis of unsophisticated theology, allowed to be undifferentiated from the office of minister of Word and sacrament, on the other. The office's distinctive character was almost obliterated, or at least hidden from view by extraneous details gathered from the system of academic tenure, on the one side, and by issues relevant to the ministry, on the other.

Those who cherished the office looked with hope to a much anticipated report from the Commission on Theology. This report, "The Nature of Ministry," was presented to the 1968 General Synod. The report disappointed almost everyone. The commission was influenced powerfully by the "functional" view of ministry that was then popular in the church. The committee summarized its position by stating:

> The New Testament conception of ministry emphasizes function. Every variety of ministry is viewed as a service for Christ, rather than as a position of status, power, or privilege....We believe that the use of ecclesiastical office is still necessary in the church in our day....the offices must be viewed as ecclesiastical functions, performed within the structure of the church and under her direct supervision, and aimed at the equipment of the whole church for her ministry in the world. All ministries outside the structure of the church which are not functions of her judicatories, or which are not principally aimed at the equipment of the church for her mission, should not be considered as functions of an office, but as a part of the common ministry....The functional viewpoint means that commissioning to an office is related to a particular service, and that the office does not adhere to the person apart from that service....Commissioning to an office would not be "in general" or in the church at large, apart from a specific service, and only as long as that service is continued.[125]

The commission included only two sentences relating to the office of professor:

> The present office of professor of theology should be included within the office of minister of the Word as a special function

---

[125] *Acts and Proceedings*, 1968, 195-97.

of that office. This "fourth office" has never had a clear and unequivocal place in the Reformed tradition and in practical fact it has been an extension of the ministerial office.[126]

By means of this report, the Commission on Theology made official and permanent most of the confusions of the 1960s about the office of professor of theology.

But the entire denomination remained uncomfortable with the radical conclusions of the 1968 report. Within a very few years there were requests for a new study of offices within the church. The Theological Commission prepared another report and submitted it to the synod of 1980. This report's title, "The Nature of Ecclesiastical Office and Ministry," suggested clearly that this report drew very different conclusions from those drawn by the 1968 report. The 1980 report was, however, of very little direct help for the office of professor of theology, because the commission's report did not have a single thing to say about the office.

The General Synod of 1984 appointed "a committee of seven persons to undertake a comprehensive study of ecclesiastical office and ministry"—the third such study in less than twenty years. This committee, as if to make up for the Theological Commission's 1980 omission of the office of professor of theology, focused entirely upon the office of professor of theology. After delineating a rationale for retaining the office within the church, the committee sought to answer certain questions regarding the office. Its most striking conclusion was to state unequivocally that those elected to the office should be ordained to it. This conclusion led the committee to six further resolutions: (1) all professors of theology were to be voting members of the General Synod; (2) each faculty was to elect one professor to the General Synod Executive Committee; (3) all members of Reformed Church seminary faculties who had taught six or more years were to be nominated automatically to the office of professor of theology; (4) those who resigned from the office were to be dismissed to a classis; (5) the Commission on Worship was to prepare a liturgy for the ordination of professors; and (6) the Commission on Church Order was to propose appropriate revisions of the *Book of Church Order*.[127]

The synod of 1988 referred the recommendations back to the Committee on Ecclesiastical Office and Ministry and instructed the committee to consult with the Board of Theological Education, which,

---

[126] *Acts and Proceedings*, 1968, 198.
[127] *Acts and Proceedings*, 1988, 267.

at that time, was functioning as the Board of Trustees for Western and New Brunswick Seminaries, as well as for the Theological Education Agency. Apparently the Board of Theological Education was perturbed because the committee did not have among its membership anyone expressly representing its interests, nor had the committee consulted the board previously. The committee had also failed to include or to consult with the professors of theology.

In 1989, the committee reported again. This time it issued a new statement on the character of the office of professor of theology that affirmed clearly the continuation of the office, withdrew all of the other proposals of 1988, offered a series of clarifying amendments to the *Book of Church Order*, and, again, recommended that all professors be delegates to each synod. The synod approved all of these recommendations.[128] All of the changes in the *Book of Church Order* except the attendance of all professors at the General Synod were confirmed by the classes.[129] This is where the professorate found itself at the end of the twentieth century.

Hope for the Twenty-first Century

In 1932, Walter Lippman (1889-1974), American writer, journalist, and political analyst and commentator, was asked to present the commencement address for Columbia University. The year 1932 was the worst of the Great Depression. Unemployment had risen to 23.6 percent nationally. In Harlem, New York—Columbia University's neighborhood—unemployment stood at more than 50 percent. The Dow Jones Industrials had lost more than 80 percent of their value since October 1929. Ten thousand banks failed in 1932 alone (40 percent of all banks that had failed since 1929).[130] This was clearly a devastating context in which to be asked to give a university commencement address. But, when the moment arrived, Lippmann presented an important challenge to the young graduates. At the time of his address, three-quarters of a century ago, even Pulitzer Prize winners like Lippmann were not sensitive to the gender of language. In addition, Lippmann was addressing the graduates of an institution that in 1932 was still all male. Therefore, please forgive Mr. Lippmann for his exclusively male references and please do struggle to hear the message beneath the language. Lippmann began his address by saying:

> In addition to the anxieties he shares with all other men in days like these, there is a special uneasiness which perturbs the scholar.

---

[128] *Acts and Proceedings*, 1989, 209-217.
[129] *Acts and Proceedings*, 1990, 41.
[130] Hyperhistory.com, *Timelines of the Great Depression*, 1932.

> He feels that he ought to be doing something about the world's troubles, or at least to be saying something which will help others to do something about them....And yet, at the same time he hears a voice of another conscience, the conscience of the scholar, which tells him that as one whose business it is to examine the nature of things, to imagine how they work, and to test continually the proposals of his imagination, he must preserve a quiet indifference to the immediate and a serene attachment to the process of inquiry and understanding.[131]

He concluded the address by observing:

> The immediate has never been the realm of the scholar. His provinces are the past, from which he distills understanding, and the future, for which he prepares insight. The immediate is for his purpose a mere fragment of the past, to be observed and remembered rather than dealt with and managed.... Yet I doubt whether the student can do greater work for his nation in this grave moment of its history than to detach himself from its preoccupations....For this is not the last crisis in human affairs. The world will go on somehow, and more crises will follow. It will go on best, however, if among us there are men who have stood apart, who refused to be anxious or too much concerned, who were cool and inquiring, and had their eyes on a longer past and a longer future. By their example they can remind us that the passing moment is only a moment; by their loyalty they will have cherished those things which only the disinterested mind can use.[132]

Lippmann understood that a nation (or a denomination) benefits from having among its membership an order whose task it is to think about how and why things have come to be the way they are and where it appears they may be going. Thomas Aquinas recognized this fact, as did John Calvin, the Synod of Dort, and the Reformed Protestant Dutch Church in North America in the "Explanatory Articles." This is the purpose of the professor of theology. But all of them—Aquinas, Calvin, Dort, and our own denomination—failed to constitute the office

---

[131] Walter Lippmann, *The Scholar in a Troubled World* (New York: Press of the Woolly Whale, 1932), [1-2]. Pages are unnumbered. Numbers have been assigned, with page [1] being the recto following the title page. First published, *Atlantic Monthly* (August 1932), 148-52.
[132] Ibid., [29-30].

fully into the structure of the church. In Jeannine Olson's words, it was left to be "a project for the future."[133] The office of professor of theology was never completely defined as different from the office of minister of Word and sacrament. And, in Protestantism, the professorate was never fully constituted as an assembly of the church.

The failure of the church ever to structure completely the office of professor of theology and to provide it with an ecclesiastical home has led to a mindset of retreat. Present inclinations appear to want to collapse the office into some part of the existing church order, rather than to make concrete the vision sketched out by Aquinas, Calvin, Dort, and the Reformed Church in America throughout the history sketched above. On the basis of this history, four steps are here proposed properly to complete the vision:

1. The Commission on Theology should be charged with the task of determining anew what it is that the Reformed Church in America means when its speaks of "theology" and how it envisions the work of a "theologian." A specific definition of "professor of theology" should then be prepared. This definition should be built upon the definitions begun by Calvin, Dort, and the "Explanatory Articles." It should stand apart from the definition of minister of Word and sacrament. This definition should include, as the ordinary components of the professor's task, at least the following duties: (a) the teaching of theology to the next generation of pastoral leaders; (b) the advisement and critique of the mission and vision, the life and work of the denomination; and (c) the development of theology that is appropriate for the current and future needs of the church and society. Finally, the commission should determine whether "professor of theology" is a genuine office within the Reformed Church in America.
2. If the Commission on Theology determines and the General Synod concurs that the office of professor of theology is indeed a legitimate office within the denomination, the Commission on Worship should be instructed to prepare a service of ordination for those called to the office.
3. The Commission on Church Order should be charged with constituting the "professorate" as an assembly of the church, parallel to a classis and, like a classis, a member of and answerable to the General Synod. The membership of

---

[133] Olson, "Calvin," 157.

the professorate would include all professors of theology (as defined by the Commission on Theology). The professorate would have responsibility to superintend, care for, and discipline its members—the professors of theology.

4. The General Synod should develop some regular means for shaping an evolving agenda of the work it wants or needs the professorate to accomplish.

Above all, care must be taken to assure that the members of the professorate have time and opportunity to carry out the purely exploratory kinds of theological research that are not constrained by the needs or desires of the denomination's current program but that might contribute to the denomination's long-term vision and mission. Richard Osmer sees the church's present situation this way:

> Mainline Protestantism is at a crossroads. The path it chooses to travel today will be of great consequence well into the next century. Its continued diminishment cannot help but diminish the whole of...life. The challenges before it are great, to be sure. It must now come to grips with the fact that it is now one of many religious communities with influence and power....It must recognize its tendency to accommodate to the surrounding culture and confuse the Christian way of life with the American way of life.[134]

Osmer is convinced, as I am, that God has prepared a great open future for the church, and that theology that is clear and compelling will be at the center of the church's future successes. Nevertheless, Osmer warns:

> It will be unlikely, if not impossible, for any of these possibilities to come to pass without the emergence of a much stronger teaching office in the Protestant mainstream. Only as these churches come to grips with their need to determine their normative beliefs and practices, to reinterpret these beliefs and practices in shifting cultural and historical contexts, and to form institutions that give support to ongoing teaching at every level of church life will they develop the capacity to transform the problems that beset them today into new patterns of church life for tomorrow.[135]

The tradition of theology begun by St. Paul, in which the content and meaning of the life of Jesus are reinterpreted in ways that meet the

[134] Osmer, *Teachable*, 222.
[135] Ibid., 222-23.

changed demands of every new situation in need of the gospel's saving touch, waits to be fulfilled in the opportunity currently before the Reformed Church in America. May we bravely seize the moment and complete Calvin's "project for the future"—the professorate.

CHAPTER 7

John Henry Livingston as Professor of Theology

John W. Coakley

It was in 1812 that the General Synod of the Reformed Protestant Dutch Church, as the Reformed Church in America was then called, organized its seminary in New Brunswick, New Jersey, by adopting a document entitled, "Plan for the Theological School." This action established a board of superintendents that the synod itself would appoint. It also provided for the employment of professors, stated what would be expected from students, and set the rudiments of an academic calendar and a curriculum.[1] But traditionally, historians of the Reformed Church have dated the origin of New Brunswick Theological Seminary not to 1812 but rather twenty-eight years earlier. For it was in 1784 that the General Synod elected John Henry Livingston (1746-1825) to the office of professor of theology, for the theological education of candidates for the ministry in the church. For twenty-six years thereafter there was no school; Livingston served as professor on

---

[1] *Acts and Proceedings of the Reformed Church in America, 1771 to 1812*, 430-33; also in Edward Tanjore Corwin, *Digest of Synodical Legislation of the Reformed Church in America* (New York: Board of Publication of the Reformed Church in America, 1905), 440-42.

his own, teaching candidates for ministry in his own study in New York City, where he was also a minister in the Collegiate Church. Then, in 1810, he moved to New Brunswick, under an arrangement worked out by the synod, and began teaching students there, thus bringing the office of professor with him. So what happened in 1812 was that the synod, in effect anyway, organized the school around the pre-existing office of professor, which thus provides the historical continuity back to 1784.

The continuity is clear enough. But it is also true that a school and a professor are not quite the same thing. Here I will attempt to tell briefly the story of the first few decades of theological education in the Reformed Church not from the vantage point of the school, but from that of the professor, namely Livingston. My question here is not how the school came into being but how the professor fulfilled his role. The picture that emerges is of a leader who was highly respected for his leadership in the church, but not always for his teaching itself, learned and competent though that teaching certainly was.

The early history of the "professorate" in the Reformed Church, leading to Livingston's election as professor in 1784, is well known and I summarize it only briefly. The Classis of Amsterdam's reluctance to establish or recognize an institution to educate candidates for ministry on American soil had been a major issue in the mid-eighteenth-century struggle to form the church as an American body accountable to itself rather than to the mother church. The classis finally ceded this point in the Plan of Union that essentially formed the American church on its adoption by what was at first was called its General Body (later the General Synod) in 1771. The plan called for the choosing of "one or two Professors," from the Netherlands, "to teach Didactic, Polemic, Exegetic Theology &c., in accordance with the principles of the doctrine of our Dutch Reformed Churches," specifically not "in connection with any English Academy," but rather "in their own houses"[2]—presumably to preserve the church's purity of doctrine from such influences as an "English academy" [Princeton and Kings (Columbia) had been the main possibilities named] might exert. Two years later, on the appeal of the trustees of Queens College (later Rutgers) in New Brunswick, the General Body modified this part of the plan. The professorate would in fact be attached to what was in effect an "English academy," albeit its own, namely Queens College, and the synod wrote to the Classis of Amsterdam asking for recommendation of a Dutch candidate to

[2] *Acts and Proceedings*, 13-14.

become the first professor.³ The following year the classis replied, recommending not a Dutch candidate, but rather John Henry Livingston, on the unanimous recommendation of the faculty of his alma mater, the University of Utrecht. The faculty declared him to be "regarded above all others as best adapted for the Professorship in New York and New Jersey, on account of his qualifications for the office, his peculiar acquaintance with the languages, names and peculiar circumstances of the country, which in reference to the successful prosecution of the office, must all be taken into account. In these he must greatly excel any one who might be called from here, though superior in learning."⁴ The election was to have taken place in the meeting following, in October 1775. By then, however, the whole matter of the professorate was deferred "by reason of the pitiful condition of our land,"⁵ the Revolutionary War having begun. It was not until October of 1784 that Livingston was actually elected, by which time lack of funds made his removal to New Brunswick "impracticable."⁶

Though no doubt there would have been Dutch scholars "superior in learning" to Livingston, as the Utrecht faculty did not omit to mention in its recommendation, still Livingston's academic qualifications were excellent by any measure, and he was to be a productive theologian. In touch with the intellectual currents of his time, he gave expression both to Enlightenment ideas and to the emerging mission-consciousness of pietism. In his doctoral dissertation at Utrecht (1770) on the Sinaitic covenant, he was concerned to reconcile the conception of social contract as the foundation of government, such as he may have derived from John Locke, with the theocratic polity of Israel in the Old Testament, arguing that Israel's government was a special case for the purposes of historical preparation for the Incarnation, and that, even so, Israelite theocracy was not established without the consent of the governed.⁷ Then, in his inaugural oration as professor, given in May of 1785 and published that same year, he presented a lengthy rational defense of Orthodox Christian faith against deism. He set forth the familiar "supernatural rationalist" position of learned Protestant

---

3   Ibid., 39-40.
4   Edward Tanjore Corwin, ed., *Ecclesiastical Records of the State of New York*, vol. 6 (Albany: Lyons, 1905), 4279.
5   *Acts and Proceedings*, 61.
6   Ibid., 124.
7   John Henry Livingston, *De foederis sinaitici natura* (Utrecht: J. Broedelet., 1770), here esp. 12-13; John Coakley, "John Henry Livingston and the Liberty of the Conscience," *Reformed Review* 46, no. 2 (1992): 119-35.

divines of the time, recognizing natural revelation such as the Deists would have championed but denying its adequacy for salvation and rationally proving the trustworthiness of the Bible as witness to the supernatural revelation that yields the saving knowledge. Indeed, the lengthy address covers much of the ground that his lectures on didactic theology covered for his students at New Brunswick in the form that we have them, which dates from some thirty years later (see below).[8] Later, in 1799 and 1804, respectively, Livingston preached two influential sermons to the New York Missionary Society, asserting the inadequacy of a deistic understanding of religion to spread the gospel and exhorting churches to the evangelization of the world, on the grounds that the whole world was to hear the gospel before the beginning of the millennium, which he expected before the year 2000.[9]

For the twenty-six years subsequent to Livingston's inauguration, as is well known in all the histories of the Reformed Church, the synod failed to provide financial support for the professorate, and so from year to year Livingston continued, it seems, to fit his work with students around the edges of his pastoral work. In a brief experiment in 1796, at the encouragement of the synod, he relinquished half his salary in New York and took up residence in Flatbush, Brooklyn, to establish a "Divinity Hall" and be resident four days per week for his students. Once again, however, the synod provided no support, and, after a few months, he returned to Manhattan. In a dignified but exasperated letter that same year he declared, "The Professorate remains thus entirely forsaken, and no measures are pursued, or even proposed, to countenance and assist the institution."[10] After this, the synod informed Livingston that "it will be highly acceptable to them [the synod] if he can still continue to discharge the duties of the office under the discouragements that exist." At the same time, in a move that may have seemed to him to add insult to injury, the synod elected two other professors with the same authority as Livingston—Solomon Froeligh of Hackensack and Dirck Romeyn of Schenectady—in view of

---

[8] John Henry Livingston, *Oratio inauguralis de veritate religionis christianae* (New York: Samuel and Johannes Loudon, 1785).

[9] John Henry Livingston, "The Glory of the Redeemer. A Sermon, Preached before the N-Y Missionary Society in the Scots Presbyterian Church, 23rd of April, 1799," in *Two Sermons delivered before the New-York Missionary Society...* (New York: Isaac Collins, 1799). John Henry Livingston, *The Triumph of the Gospel. A Sermon delivered before the N-Y Missionary Society at their Annual Meeting, April 3, 1804* (New York: T. & J. Swords, 1804).

[10] *Acts and Proceedings*, 260-63, 465.

the "serious inconveniences" suffered by students, apparently because of the necessity of living in New York.[11]

Amid the "discouragement that existed," however, it appears that Livingston taught at least forty-six students over the twenty-six years prior to coming to New Brunswick, almost all of whom received from him the certificate that qualified them to be examined for ordination.[12]

Eventually, in 1810, came the move to New Brunswick. The reason for that move was that an opportunity had arisen for funding the professorate. In 1807, Queens College (now Rutgers) was in danger of closing its doors, and its trustees agreed to adjoin the college, in fact to subordinate it, to a theological school (seminary) if the General Synod would raise the money to support the theological professor and to help build and maintain a building that would be shared with the college, of which Livingston would also be the nominal president.

Livingston agreed to the plan only reluctantly; not only did he have misgivings about the prospects of a school located at a distance from the major concentrations of Dutch Reformed churches (which were to be found along the Hudson, on Long Island, and in the northern New Jersey river valleys), but he had no desire to leave New York, and he told his future biographer, Alexander Gunn, that he regarded the move as a "a species of martyrdom."[13] But he considered the prospective funding of the professorate—for which he had so long desired and advocated—to depend on his show of good faith by making the move. As he wrote to the consistory of the Collegiate Church, "It is suggested, and probably with great truth, that all further application for an increase of the funds, and even for obtaining a great part of what is already subscribed, depend upon the immediate removal of the professor to Brunswick."[14] All of this is consistent with his wish to see the professorate properly supported.

Livingston's credentials as an academic theologian, as I have said, were unimpeachable; Yet one senses that it was not so much his academic credentials as his stature and reputation as a churchman that made him the crucial figure in the success of the plan to establish the

---

[11] Ibid., 269-70.
[12] I have derived the figure from John Howard Raven, *Biographical Record, Theological Seminary, New Brunswick, 1784-1911* (New Brunswick: Laidlie Memorial Fund, 1912).
[13] Alexander Gunn, *Memoirs of the Rev. John H. Livingston* (New York: Rutgers Press, 1829), 382.
[14] Quoted in Gunn, *Memoirs*, 384.

church's seminary in New Brunswick. He had had a prominent role in the church's very formation in 1771, he had ministered for four decades in its leading congregation, had taken the lead in compiling its first hymnal, and had been the chief force in assembling and publishing its *Constitution*.[15] By 1810, at the age of sixty-four, he embodied the formative generation of the church's leadership, which by that time was becoming an honored memory.

This place in the church's esteem and memory accorded Livingston a kind of patriarchal status, to which he and others did not hesitate to call attention in the years at New Brunswick. Thus Livingston himself seems to have had a habit of addressing students and younger colleagues as "my son."[16] In the treatise he wrote for the General Synod on the question of "whether a man may marry his deceased wife's sister"—in which, incidentally, he defended some older mores against more recent ones—we find him casting himself as a fatherly St. Paul, observing that "those who have heretofore cordially united with me" are now dead, but "if, without presumption, the words of an aged Apostle might be adopted, I would humbly say: 'I have no greater joy than to hear that my children walk in the truth.'"[17] Gabriel Ludlow, of the seminary class of 1820, would later recall that "he wore the antiquated costume, of which an ample wig, of almost snowy whiteness, was a very conspicuous part. He carried a staff, but it did not seem necessary to his support, for his step was firm, steady, but was carried simply because such an appendage was suitable and becoming to one of his years and position."[18] Gunn, writing shortly after his death, found it irresistible to compare Livingston the departing New Yorker with Abraham who departed "at the seventy-fifth year of his age, from his country and kindred, and father's house, to go unto a

---

[15] On the hymnal, see James Brumm, *Singing the Lord's Song: A History of the English Language Hymnals of the Reformed Church in America*, Historical Society of the Reformed Church in America Occasional Papers, no. 2 (New Brunswick, 1990), 9-17; on his role in the *Constitution*, see *Acts and Proceedings*, 235-36, 245-46; Gunn, 311-20; Daniel Meeter, *Meeting Each Other in Doctrine, Liturgy and Government*, Historical Series of the Reformed Church in America, no. 24 (Grand Rapids: Eerdmans, 1993).

[16] Gunn, *Memoirs*, 382; Benjamin C. Taylor, "Recollections of Old Ministers, no. III: Rev. John H. Livingston, D.D.," *Christian Intelligencer* 43, no. 1 (February 29, 1872): 1.

[17] John Henry Livingston, *A Dissertation on the Marriage of a Man with His Sister in Law* (New-Brunswick: Deare and Myer, 1816), 7.

[18] Edward Tanjore Corwin, *A Manual of the Reformed Church in America* (New York: Board of Publication of the Reformed Church in America, 1902), 577.

land which God had promised to show him."[19] The seminary's Board of Superintendents made frequent respectful reference to his age, as in its report to the synod in 1817, which praises as a "venerable Father, who long since was designated by our mother church for the important trust" of the professorate.[20] And the otherwise puzzlingly unflattering portrait of the aged Livingston by an anonymous artist that is to be seen today in two versions in New Brunswick (presently in Kirkpatrick Chapel, Rutgers, and in the president's residence at New Brunswick Seminary) becomes explainable when we consider that Livingston's advanced age, and therefore his patriarchal status, is in fact what the artist wished to convey.

It would seem that Livingston's stature in the church—or perhaps indeed the leadership skills and personal qualities that underlay and justified that stature—paid off for the seminary. Though the financial situation of the first several years was indeed uncertain, and serious proposals were made to relocate him to New York or Schenectady where the support would be stronger,[21] still, it was finally Livingston himself who pulled the New Brunswick institution through. He solicited a gift of over $14,000 from his friend Elias van Bunschooten in 1814, and, in 1820, formulated a plan to raise $25,000 through subscriptions of $250 apiece from wealthy individuals. He became the first subscriber, for the doubled amount of $500, and enlisted energetic and influential lay helpers, with the result that in one year's time, the $25,000 was *over*subscribed. From then on the seminary could be said to be rooted securely in New Brunswick.[22]

---

[19] Gunn goes on to say, with characteristic expansiveness, that "this passage [i.e., a description of Abraham by "Dr. Hunter"] has not been quoted with a view to compare the subject of these memoirs to the venerable patriarch of old, or because it is supposed that the removal of the one, in its attending circumstances, bears much of a resemblance to that of the other; but simply for the purpose of observing that the *affecting impression*, which such a removal as it describes is represented to make upon the mind of a reflecting person, must be in a degree produced by every other that is so far similar as to combine the two circumstances of advanced age, and preeminent piety, or that takes place at a late period of life, from a desire to obey what is believed to be the divine will, and to promote the glory of God" (*Memoirs*, 380-81).

[20] Minutes of the Board of Superintendents, vol. 1, fol. 45-46, New Brunswick Seminary Archives, New Brunswick, New Jersey.

[21] Howard G. Hageman, *Two Centuries Plus: The Story of New Brunswick Seminary* (Grand Rapids: Eerdmans, 1984), 42-43; Gunn, *Memoirs*, 405-11.

[22] Hageman, *Two Centuries Plus*, 43-44.

If Livingston's stature in the church and, accordingly, his ability to attract funds were decisive in ensuring the future of the seminary, what can we say about his teaching? What do we know?

As for the content of the teaching: Livingston's teaching notes have been conserved in manuscript form in Sage Library at New Brunswick Seminary, in three volumes. Two of these are eclectic collections of bits and pieces of the lectures, or studies for lectures, in one case a single notebook and in the other case a bound collection of a variety of notebooks, which are not numbered consecutively. The fragments in these volumes are undated, and it may be that some of the material dates to his years in New York. In any event, the third of the manuscript volumes is clearly from the New Brunswick years. it comprises an apparently complete set of his lectures, in didactic theology, as given in 1815-16 (cf. Lecture 4 title), written on recto pages only in a hand that is not Livingston's—perhaps originally a set of notes taken by a student (of which Sage has several other examples)—but with numerous emendations in Livingston's hand and numerous additions on facing verso pages also in Livingston's hand. On a verso page a few leaves before the end, he notes his completion of the lectures for successive years: 1817, 1818, 1819, 1820, 1821, 1822, 1823, 1824. This would be, then, the copy that he himself used in his last years at New Brunswick.

This late version Livingston's lectures (which follows the outline that Ava Neal, an 1816 graduate of the seminary and sometime minister at Pompton Plains, New Jersey, published in 1832,[23] but with more detail at many points) consists of two parts. The first and briefer part, labeled "Introduction," distinguishes false from true religion, gives brief accounts of the false ones, including paganism (ancient and modern), Islam, Judaism, and Christian heresies, and then presents a taxonomy of the forms of "true" theology, including didactic, polemic, philological, prophetic, etc. The second part is labeled, "System of Didactic Theology." It begins, as Livingston did some thirty years earlier in his inaugural address, with a consideration of "natural religion." As in the earlier address, he accepts the principles but refutes the Deists' inference of their sufficiency. He then proceeds to a consideration of revealed religion, beginning with God-rejecting ontological arguments for the existence of God but accepting arguments which proceed from evidence of God's works. The lectures then proceed to a consideration

---

[23] Ava Neal, *Analysis of a System of Theology Composed Chiefly from Lectures Delivered by the Late John H. Livingston...* (New York: J.F.Sibell, 1832).

of the divine decrees, of the nature of humanity, of sin, and of redemption.

As for what these manuscripts reveal of Livingston's teaching, I am sure that a careful comparison both with the lectures of his own teacher, the Utrecht professor Gisbert Bonnet (which are conserved in manuscript in the library of the University of Groningen), and with such figures as his younger contemporaries, such as the Congregationalist Leonard Woods at Andover Seminary and the Old School Presbyterian Archibald Alexander at Princeton Seminary, would tell us much of interest. For example, one might address the question of what distinctive features of Dutch theological tradition, if any, Livingston may have mediated to the continuing life of the American churches that traced themselves to that tradition. But, as a matter of general impression, there is little of surprise in Livingston's lectures, and he sounds very similar to Alexander in essentials. I have in mind particularly his reliance on the "common sense" philosophy of the Scottish rationalists Reid and Beattie, in opposition to the skepticism of Hume and Berkeley, and his "rational supernaturalism"—the affirmation of rational religion, that is but necessarily augmented by revelation in the matter of sin and redemption—that he had articulated already in his inaugural address and that was, in any event, the common currency of learned Protestant divinity at the time.

If we turn from the content of Livingston's teaching and ask about its context at New Brunswick, we find in his last years some apparent tension with the Board of Superintendents. It is a tension which may suggest the other side of the coin of his "patriarchal" status, in the sense that he seems to have appeared to others and, perhaps, even to himself to be a force unto himself, who transcended the mere institutional responsibilities of a faculty member.

From the "Plan of the Theological School" of 1812, we know the subjects in the curriculum at that early moment in the school's life ("natural, didactic, polemic, and practical theology; biblical criticism; chronology and ecclesiastical history; ... church government and pastoral duties, and the Biblical languages")[24] but not the sequence in which they were taken or their scheduling in the daily life of the school.[25]

---

[24] *Acts and Proceedings*, 433.
[25] The omission of the sequence of courses in the curriculum is unfortunate, as it would afford comparison with the contemporary, and better known, curricula of Princeton and Andover. See Hageman, *Two Centuries Plus*, 37-38; Lefferts Loetscher, *Facing the Enlightenment and Pietism: Archibald Alexander and the Founding of Princeton Theological Seminary* (Westport, Conn.:

But, in the minutes for September 1821, by which time there was a second faculty chair (established in 1815),[26] there appears a statement of the "order of study at the theological college." It shows Livingston lecturing on didactic theology at noon on Mondays, Wednesdays, and Fridays to "the whole college," and the other professor, John Ludlow, teaching everything else—including Greek, Hebrew, Jewish Antiquities, Analysis of Sacred Scriptures, History of the New Testament Church, and Composition, in sessions distributed through the rest of the week.[27] That Livingston gave his lectures to "the whole college" is worth noting. The course of study was for three years, as it is now, and, as Livingston's notes at the end of his lecture manuscript make clear, he gave the whole course of lectures every year. This means that every student would hear the lectures three times. Furthermore, students were expected to transcribe these lectures word for word, as can be seen in the several student copies that are conserved in Gardner Sage Library. We can, perhaps, understand the pedagogy of the practice of sitting through the full set of lectures three times and making a meticulous verbatim record as like the pedagogy implied in the use of the catechism, which, once learned, provides the student a text always available for reference.

The minutes of the Board of Superintendents show that these practices did not sit well with everyone, as time went on. The minutes for June 1818 contain a report from a committee of three members, each of them at least thirty years Livingston's junior,[28] who had been appointed to "to inquire into the time and course of study, and the present state" of the school. The committee registered several concerns. In addition to noting that vacations were too long and that students were not paying enough attention to "the art of sermonizing," they criticized the emphasis on Livingston's "didactic theology" lectures in relation to the other subjects. "Your committee conceive that it would be advisable that the Professor of Didactic Theology go through the

---

Greenwood Press, 1983), 150-60; Glenn T. Miller, *Piety and Intellect: The Aims and Purposes of Ante-Bellum Theological Education* (Atlanta: Scholars Press, 1990), 47-121 (on Andover and Princeton, cf. the brief but, in context, illuminating comment on Livingston, 99).[26] Before Ludlow, who served from 1819 until 1822, this second professorial chair had been occupied by John Schureman from 1815 until his death in 1818; Ludlow was followed by John De Witt (d. 1831) in 1823. Hageman, *Two Centuries Plus*, 41-45.

[27] Minutes of the Board of Superintendents, vol 1, fol. 3-4.

[28] Cornelius Cuyler (b. 1783), Jacob Broadhead (b. 1782), Jacob Schoonmaker (b. 1777). Cuyler and Schoonmaker had each been his student; Brodhead had not. Corwin, *Manual*, 400, 340, 707.

whole of his course of lectures once in the first two years, and cause it to be carefully, yet rapidly reviewed by the students in the third year; this affording continually more time for attending to the other instructors." They also disapproved of the practice of verbal transcription: "Your committee believe that the students devote too much of their time to the transcribing of the lectures of the professor of Didactic Theology, and that they would be more benefited by taking notes and having recourse to thinking and reading of books."[29] After receiving the report, the board resolved "that this Board respectfully request the Rev. Dr. Livingston to publish his lectures, as a measure calculated to be of vast advantage to the students, to the institution, and to the church at large." Taken in isolation—which is how it appears in the board's report to the synod the following year[30]—the recommendation might well have seemed complimentary to the professor, in effect a statement of pride in his teaching. But, in the context of the board's minutes, it is evident that the *immediate* intended "advantage to the students" in the proposed publication was not so much to immortalize the lectures as to allow students to spend less time with them.

But Livingston did not give satisfaction in the matter of publishing his lectures. In reporting to the synod, the superintendents noted that they had "as yet received no answer to their request" that Livingston publish the lectures, nor did they receive one later. Later, in May of 1822, the superintendents passed a resolution that Livingston "be furnished with" a copy of a board decision from two years earlier, requiring an annual report from each professor on "the state of the school and an account of the conduct and attention of the students during the session of the school." Livingston replied with a general declaration that "the institution in all its branches has been cultivated with faithfulness and without interruptions [and] that the conduct of the students has been correct and exemplary and that they have attended to their studies with diligence and success"[31]—an evaluation that almost certainly did not satisfy the superintendents, whose minutes show that they were aware of a steady stream of student lapses and misbehavior.

The superintendents were not getting what they wanted from the professor. The impression that he could not be bothered with such trivialities was no doubt, in part, a function of his age and weariness. One also wonders whether, after a long career occupying the role of

---

[29] Minutes of the Board of Superintendants, vol. 1, fol. 61.
[30] *Acts and Proceedings*, 1819, 10.
[31] Minutes of the Board of Superintendents, vol. 1, fol. 120-21, 83-84.

professor as a solitary, he did not quite fit in with the collaborative approach that the hands-on superintendents were taking, nor quite acknowledge their authority. This seems understandable, even though their presence on the scene was a sign of the sort of commitment on the church's part to theological education that he had long desired to see.

The superintendents seem to have been impatient, if not unimpressed, with Livingston's teaching, and it would seem in general that his contemporaries, aware of his importance in the church's formative years, did not consider that his teaching per se would constitute his great legacy to the church, as indeed it has not. But it is worth remembering, by way of conclusion, that his students were not unappreciative of the substance of his teaching. Gabriel Ludlow wrote later that Livingston's "excellence as a theological teacher [lay]...in the comprehensive, clear, systematic view he gave of the whole and every part of that science [of theology]....And if to that you add that a full, clear precise definition was given to every doctrine and fact embraced in the system, and that the student was required to make himself at home upon all this, any thinking, unprejudiced man can appreciate the advantages attending such an effect."[32] In reading Livingston, for all the distance of many of his theological concerns from our own, I can understand Ludlow's appreciation.

---

[32] Quoted in Corwin, *Manual*, 578.

CHAPTER 8

When East Meets West: Theological Education and the Unity of the Reformed Church in America

Dennis Voskuil

In his "State of Religion" report to the General Synod in 1960, synod president Howard Hageman addressed a matter of "grave concern" to the Reformed Church in America: "our unity as a denomination." Aware of long-standing tensions between eastern and western sections of the church, Hageman offered a series of proposals to "bridge some of the gaps" in the denomination. The first of these proposals pertained to the two theological seminaries of the Reformed Church, New Brunswick Theological Seminary in New Jersey and Western Theological Seminary in Michigan.[1] Hageman recognized that unity in theological education was central to the unity of the denomination.

This essay will demonstrate that Hageman correctly identified theological education as a significant source of tension in the Reformed Church. In fact, from the colonial period to the present, disputes over theological education have both reflected and contributed to various sectional fractions in the denomination. Overall, efforts to consolidate

---

[1] *Acts and Proceedings of the General Synod of the Reformed Church in America*, 1960, 229-30.

theological education have failed. While a number of centripetal forces have been at work to unify theological training, the countervailing centrifugal forces have generally prevailed. In theological education, as in other matters, the Reformed Church in America has achieved a measure of unity, but it has been a unity marked by diversity.

The Colonial Church: Early Tensions

The Reformed Church in America traces its origin to April 1628, when the Reverend Johannes Michaelius organized a congregation in a mill on the southern tip of Manhattan Island, part of the Dutch outpost of New Amsterdam.[2] Before the arrival of Michaelius, the Dutch West India Company, responsible for the religious needs of the colony of New Netherland, had arranged for the services of lay leaders who were called *sieckentroosters* or *krankenbezoeckers*. Recipients of minimal theological training, these "comforters of the sick" were authorized to exercise limited pastoral functions. In addition to teaching the catechism, they were permitted to read scripture, prescribed prayers, and texts of sermons. Without special permission from ecclesiastical authorities in Amsterdam, they were not allowed to administer the sacraments or to perform marriages. In the Dutch Reformed Church, congregations were to be organized and led by theologically trained and ordained ministers of Word and sacrament.[3]

It is significant that New Netherland was settled immediately after the monumental Synod of Dort, which embraced a stringent form of Reformed orthodoxy that would shape theology in the Dutch Reformed Church for generations to come. While the early wave of Dutch immigrants settled in New Netherland primarily for financial rather than religious reasons,[4] they brought with them Dortian theology and ecclesiology.

---

[2] The most comprehensive history of the colonial period is Gerald F. DeJong, *The Dutch Reformed Church in the American Colonies* (Grand Rapids: Eerdmans, 1978). See also Arie R. Brouwer, *Reformed Church Roots* (New York: Reformed Church Press, 1977); and Donald J. Bruggink and Kim N. Baker, *By Grace Alone: Stories of the Reformed Church in America*, Historical Series of the Reformed Church in America, no. 44 (Grand Rapids: Eerdmans, 2004).

[3] For the role of the "comforters of the sick" in the colony see DeJong, *Dutch Reformed Church*, 11-20; and Brouwer, *Reformed Church Roots*, 28-30.

[4] See Russell Shorto, *The Island at the Center of the World: The Epic Story of Dutch Manhattan, the Forgotten Colony that Shaped America* (New York: Doubleday, 2004).

Following a bloodless coup in 1664, during which the English captured control of the colony, fault lines became evident in the Dutch church. Ecclesiastical tensions between the more cosmopolitan New York City congregations and those located in rural New Jersey and upstate New York increased. The arrival of the pastor Theodore Frelinghuysen and his relentless brand of Reformed piety during the early eighteenth century heightened these tensions.[5] What followed was the most devastating crisis in the history of the denomination: the coetus versus conferentie controversy. For eighteen years the small ethnic church was torn apart by these two intractable parties.

At the center of this unsightly row was the issue of ecclesiastical authority in the preparation and ordination of pastors for the church in North America. From the time the first colonial congregation had been organized by Michaelius, the American church had been a "mission church," generally under the authority of the Classis of Amsterdam. Pastors who were called to serve congregations in the colonies were expected to be trained and ordained in the Netherlands.

Given the distance between North America and Europe as well as the dangers inherent in sea travel, it is not surprising that the colonial congregations pressed the Classis of Amsterdam for permission to organize their own governing body even before the English captured New Amsterdam. Jealous of its power and concerned that an independent American church would sanction unqualified and heterodox pastors, the Classis of Amsterdam tenaciously resisted proposals which might lead to an independent classis.[6]

In 1737, the classis informed the increasingly impatient American congregations that they might organize as a *coetus*, an assembly of congregations that did not possess full classical authority, including the right to examine and ordain ministers. A familiar institution during the heyday of Dutch colonialism, coetus had already been established by Dutch Reformed churches in the East Indies, South Africa, Surinam, and, for a short while, Brazil. At a plenary meeting in New York City in 1738, an American coetus was established, and many of the participants expected that the action would lead ultimately to the formation of an independent colonial classis.[7]

---

[5] See DeJong, *Dutch Reformed Church*, 170-87. For a thorough treatment of the tensions in the colonial church and the role of Frelinghuysen, see Randall H. Balmer, *A Perfect Babel of Confusion: Dutch Religion and English Culture in the Middle Colonies* (New York: Oxford Univ. Press, 1989).
[6] DeJong, *Dutch Reformed Church*, 184-98.
[7] Ibid., 188-91.

While relative peace existed during the decade following the formation of the coetus, deep disagreements over the future of the church were never far from the surface. When the majority of the participants at a session in 1754 approved a restructuring proposal that virtually transformed the coetus into a classis, the church was fractured. Under the leadership of Johannes Ritzema and other pastors of the Collegiate Church in New York City, those congregations that opposed the decision of the coetus to create an essentially independent American church formed an alternative assembly known as the *conferentie* ("conference").[8]

The rancorous schism that followed devastated the Dutch Reformed Church. At a time when they should have been turning outward as the American colonies were moving toward nationhood, Reformed churches were consumed by bitter disputes. Congregations themselves were often fractured. In Hackensack, New Jersey, for instance, two ministers, two consistories, and two worshiping congregations could agree only to share the church building.[9]

To some degree, it was a sectional dispute. Those who supported the coetus and the movement toward independence were located in outlying regions to the west and north, such as New Jersey and upstate New York. Those who associated with the conferentie tended to be from more urban regions of New York. Those who joined the conferentie tended to be those who had opposed Frelinghuysen and the "new measures" that had stimulated an evangelical revival, the Great Awakening, throughout the colonies.[10]

The bitter dispute between the coetus and conferentie parties was finally resolved through the remarkable leadership of John Henry Livingston, the scion of a prominent Reformed family in New York who had enrolled at the University of Utrecht in preparation for a career in pastoral ministry. While in the Netherlands, Livingston gained the confidence of the leaders of the Classis of Amsterdam. He returned to America with a plan to unite the warring factions. This plan essentially proposed independence for the American church through the organization of general and regional bodies. The Articles of Union were approved at a meeting in New York City in October 1771 and ratified during the following year by the Classis of Amsterdam.[11] The agreement

[8] Ibid., 198-203.
[9] Ibid., 205.
[10] Ibid., 200-206.
[11] Ibid., 204-10; and Howard G. Hageman, *Two Centuries Plus: The Story of New Brunswick Seminary* (Grand Rapids: Eerdmans, 1984), 12-15.

paved the way for an independent American church that would train, examine, and ordain its candidates for the ministry.

Embedded in the dispute between the contending parties had been the issue of a theological school and professorate. On May 7, 1755, Johannes Ritzema, senior minister of New York's Collegiate Church and a representative on the board of governors of newly established King's College (later Columbia), proposed that the officially Anglican school establish a professor of divinity "according to the doctrines, disciplines and worship established by the National Synod of Dort." Apparently Ritzema had reason to believe that he would be chosen to hold such a chair. The proposal, however, failed to gain support, even from Ritzema's own consistory. Aside from financial obligations, the Dutch Reformed were concerned that their identity and independence would be co-opted by the Anglicans.[12]

Word of Ritzema's proposal quickly energized the coetus to renew a long-standing discussion about an American Reformed college. Theodore Frelinghuysen, the son of the lion of the Raritan Valley and a minister of the influential Albany church, called a special meeting of the coetus in New York May 30, 1755. The action taken at the meeting underscores the resolve of the coetus to establish its own center for theological training in America.

> We pastors and elders of the Reformed Church...in North America, being assembled in a coetus, and having established an alliance among ourselves, do resolve in these present critical times to strive with all our energy, and in the fear of God, to plant a university or seminary for young men destined to study in the learned languages and in the liberal arts, and who are introduced in the philosophical sciences; also that it may be a school of the prophets in which young Levites and Nazarites of God may be prepared to enter upon the sacred ministerial office in the church of God.

At this meeting the coetus also voted to assume all the powers of a classis, including ordination and examination of candidates for ministry.[13] The goal, of course, was an independent American church.

[12] David D. Demarest, "Historical Discourse," *Centennial of the Theological Seminary of the Reformed Church in America* (New York: Board of Publication of the Reformed Church in America, 1885), 67-69; Hageman, *Two Centuries Plus*, 8-9; DeJong, *Dutch Reformed Church*, 200-202; and Edward Tanjore Corwin, *A Manual of the Reformed Church in America* (New York: Board of Publication of the Reformed Church in America, 1902), 133-117.

[13] Corwin, *Manual*, 112-13; Hageman, *Two Centuries Plus*, 8-9; and DeJong, *Dutch Reformed Church*, 206-207.

Aware that the proposed college and seminary would be costly, Frelinghuysen was appointed to visit the Netherlands and seek funding. Because his own Albany congregation opposed the plans of the coetus, Frelinghuysen delayed his visit until 1759, by which time the divisiveness of the American church had become well known in the Netherlands. Frelinghuysen's efforts ended in utter failure.[14]

Plans to establish an American college continued to move forward despite the failure of Frelinghuysen and opposition from the church in the Netherlands. After a series of requests were denied, New Jersey Governor William Franklin approved a charter for Queens College November 10, 1766. The location for the school was debated by the supporters of the charter, but eventually New Brunswick was settled upon. The actual development of the college was delayed for a few years, in part because there was some sentiment that a chair in Reformed divinity should be created at newly established Princeton College. While the Classis of Amsterdam seemed to favor this association with Princeton, leaders of the American church were as unwilling to cooperate with the Presbyterians as they were with the Anglicans. Governor Franklin granted a second charter to Queens College in March 1770, this time addressing the issue of theological education. The trustees were to appoint a president who, as a member of the Dutch Reformed Church, would also serve as a professor of divinity.[15]

Classes began at Queens College in the fall of 1771, but without a Reformed president who was a professor of divinity. The plan of union that John Henry Livingston had brokered to end the bitter dispute between the coetus and conferentie included two articles on the subject of the theological professorate. Articles 28 and 29 stipulated that one or two professors teach theology "in accordance with the principles of the doctrine of our Dutch Reformed Churches," and that

> Such Professor or Professors shall have no connection with any English Academies, but shall deliver Lectures on Theology in their own houses, to such students only as can, by suitable testimonials, make it appear that they have carefully exercised themselves in the preparatory branches for two or three years, at a college or academy under the supervision of competent teachers in the languages, philosophy etc.[16]

---

[14] Hageman, *Two Centuries Plus*, 10; and DeJong, *Dutch Reformed Church*, 204.
[15] Hageman, *Two Centuries Plus*, 10-15. Governor Franklin was the illegitimate son of Benjamin Franklin.
[16] *Acts and Proceedings*, October, 1771, 13-14.

These articles had the effect of weakening Queens College, whose trustees expected that it would become a center for ministerial training. Reformed support for the school, especially from those of the coetus party, had been linked closely to its anticipated role in theological training. When the link between Queens and the professorate was severed by the plan of union, the appointment of a professor of theology was delayed while the American church and the Classis of Amsterdam engaged in a slow dance over who had the ultimate authority to nominate and appoint the American professorate.[17]

Finally, the "General Body" of the American church met in New York April 25, 1775, to receive the joint recommendation of the Classis of Amsterdam and the theological faculty of Utrecht for an American professor of theology. Not surprisingly, John Henry Livingston, by that time a minister in New York City, was the nominee. Action on the recommendation was put off until an October meeting, by which time the opinions of the congregations would have been solicited. By October, however, the war between the colonists and the British trumped the issue of theological education. A small delegation shelved the question of the professorship. "By reason of the pitiful condition of our land, the consideration of the subject of the Professorate is deferred."[18]

Following the war, which severely tested the fragile unity of the church, the General Body returned to the question of theological education. In 1784, John Henry Livingston was finally appointed as professor of sacred theology. In concert with Articles 28 and 29 of the Plan of Union, every student who sought to be ordained in the Reformed Church was required to study under Livingston and then to earn from him a certificate (later known as a "professorial certificate"), which then permitted the candidate to be examined for ordination. In 1810, Livingston left his New York Church and moved to New Brunswick, but the professorate remained separate from Queens College, later Rutgers. New Brunswick was the first free-standing seminary in America.[19]

In the end, the newly established church came together around its newly established theological seminary. While disagreements over location, finances, and appointments would crop up periodically, theological education was consolidated at New Brunswick.

Following years of fractious disputes between coetus and conferentie parties and further disagreement about the form of

---

[17] Hageman, *Two Centuries Plus*, 12-14.
[18] *Acts and Proceedings*, October, 1775, 61; Hageman, *Two Centuries Plus*, 14-15.
[19] Hageman, *Two Centuries Plus*, 13-21, 33-35.

theological training for the newly independent American church, unity in this area of the church's life was maintained—at least for a few decades.

Theological Education in the West

Unlike New Brunswick Theological Seminary, which originated as free-standing institution through the professorate, Western Theological Seminary began as a department of Hope College.[20] Even before commencement exercises took place in July 1866, seven of the eight initial graduates of the fledgling college had petitioned the General Synod to allow them to pursue theological education at their alma mater. Until that time, the majority of those men from the western region of the Reformed Church who sought to be ministers had completed undergraduate studies at Rutgers College before enrolling in the Theological Seminary of the Reformed Church in New Brunswick.[21] While granting the request of the seven to begin theological studies at Hope College that coming fall, the synod of 1866 was tentative and cautious. The synod referred the matter to the Board of Education and the Council of Hope College with the following instructions:

> That leave be granted to pursue their theological studies at Hope College, provided no measures shall be instituted by which additional expense shall be thrown upon Synod or Board of Education at this time; and provided further, the Synod reserves the right to withdraw this permission at any time it may deem expedient.[22]

The permission of the synod of 1866 was provisional indeed. Nine years later theological education in the West was suspended.

It would be a mistake to conclude that the Reformed Church in the East was opposed to theological education at Hope College. After all, just nine out of the 150 delegates for the 1866 synod were

---

[20] For a history of the theological training at Hope College, see Dennis N. Voskuil, "The Vexed Question: Hope College and Theological Education in the West," in Jacob E. Nyenhuis, ed., *A Goodly Heritage: Essays in Honor of the Reverend Dr. Elton J. Bruins at Eighty* (Grand Rapids: Eerdmans, 2007), 341-70.

[21] Wynand Wichers, *A Century of Hope, 1866-1966* (Grand Rapids: Eerdmans, 1968), 68-72; see also, Donald J. Bruggink, "Western Theological Seminary: The First Century," *Origins*, vol. XVX, 2001, 14-15.

[22] *Acts and Proceedings*, 1866, 96-97.

from Western classes (Holland, Illinois, and Wisconsin).[23] The eastern section of the Reformed Church supplied the majority of members and financial support until the early half of the twentieth century. Moreover, Hope College and its antecedent Pioneer School and Academy were built upon leadership and financial support which came from the East. The Dutch immigrants who made their way to the Midwest also had received considerable assistance from immigration societies established by members of the old Dutch Reformed Church. Two pastors, Thomas DeWitt of New York City and Isaac Wyckhoff of Albany, were especially helpful as the colony in Michigan was established under the leadership of Albertus C. Van Raalte. In fact, Van Raalte stayed with these pastors during his frequent forays in the East to raise financial support for Hope College from Reformed congregations and members.[24] It is fair to say that neither Van Raalte's colony nor its college would have survived without support from the Eastern church.

It must also be remembered that the notion of a theological school in the West was introduced years before the wave of Dutch Reformed immigrants began to swell communities in Michigan, Wisconsin, Illinois, and Iowa during the late 1840s. As early as 1836, the classis of Schoharie introduced a resolution at the synod that called for "a theological seminary, a college, and a preparatory school" in the Mississippi Valley.[25] During the ensuing years, the denomination's Board of Domestic Mission urged the denomination to establish schools to meet the needs of Christians who were moving west.[26] Yet, despite the early vision of institutions of learning in the West, and despite the support provided Dutch immigrant communities, the Eastern church consistently betrayed some ambivalence over the development of theological education in the West. The tensions and

---

[23] Ibid., 3-6.

[24] See Elton J. Bruins, "The Church at the West: A Brief Survey of the Origin and Development of the Dutch Reformed Church in the Middle West," *Reformed Review* 20 (December, 1966): 4-8; and Elton J. Bruins, "Early Hope History as Reflected in the Correspondence of Rev. Albertus C. Van Raalte to Rev. Philip Phelps Jr., 1857-75," a paper presented at the biennial conference of the Association for the Advancement of Dutch American Studies, Calvin College, Grand Rapids, Michigan, June 22, 2001.

[25] *Acts and Proceedings*, 1836, 493, 503-504.

[26] See *Acts and Proceedings*, 1843, 232-33; *Acts and Proceedings*, 1847, 191-92; and *Acts and Proceedings*, 1848, 309-11. See also Gerald F. De Jong, "Non-Immigrant Reformed Churches in the Middle West before the Civil War," a pamphlet published by the Particular Synod of Chicago (1978), for denominational efforts among nonimmigrants.

misunderstandings related to the Theological Department of Hope College must, in part, be interpreted in light of sectional differences.

And that brings us back to those seven pioneer graduates of Hope College who petitioned the synod of 1866 for permission to study theology at the college. Surely delegates at the synod, overwhelmingly from the Eastern churches, must have wondered why those young men were so intent upon staying in the Midwest. The theological seminary in New Brunswick offered outstanding orthodox Reformed training in a congenial, supportive environment. Looking back, William Moerdyk, one of the pioneers who petitioned the synod, admitted that the education the seven could have received at New Brunswick was "infinitely superior" to that which they received in Holland. The Theological Department at Hope "labored under great disadvantages." Not only was the small faculty overloaded, but the facilities were woefully inadequate: "We had no laboratories, no library to speak of." Still, Moerdyk insisted that the pioneer students did not second-guess their decisions. They did not despise Rutgers College or New Brunswick Theological Seminary but wanted their own institutions. "They loved the Reformed Church and her Eastern institutions full well, but they loved their own people, their fathers, the people's future and the future of the Reformed Church in the West, more."[27]

It must have been very difficult for the Eastern section of the church to comprehend fully how deeply devoted the immigrant churches were to their own institutions of higher education, especially theological education. Van Raalte and most of the other leaders of the immigrant churches had come to the United States, in part, to escape a state church in the Netherlands that they perceived to be compromised ecclesiastically and doctrinally. Convinced that the Herformde Kerk, the state church, had given way to a broad form of rationalism and relativism, Van Raalte and others had joined the *Afscheiding*, the Seccession of 1834, which had been led by Henrik De Cock. Many, like Van Raalte, had suffered some form of persecution.[28] Most of the leaders of the migration to America were secessionists who brought

---

[27] William Moerdyk, "The Establishment of Theological Instruction at Holland," in *Quarter-Centennial of the Western Theological Seminary, 1884-1909* (Holland, Michigan, 1909), 17-18.

[28] See Robert P. Swierenga and Elton J. Bruins, *Family Quarrels in the Dutch Reformed Churches in the Nineteenth Century* (Grand Rapids: Eerdmans, 1999), esp. 5-35. For a comprehensive treatment of the Secession of 1834, see Gerrit J. tenZythoff, *Sources of Secession: The Netherlands Hervormde Kerk on the Eve of the Dutch Immigration to the Midwest* (Grand Rapids: Eerdmans, 1987).

with them deep piety and devotion to orthodox Reformed theology. They also brought an abiding commitment to rigorous theological training, particularly for the pastors of their congregations.

It is not possible to read accounts of the Dutch colony in Michigan without noting the relentless yearning for a school of theology. In many respects, the succession of schools that were established in Holland, including Hope College, were viewed by the colonists as preparatory schools for theological education. William Moerdyk argued that the people of the colony desired above all "a school to prepare and qualify young men for the work of teaching and for preaching of the Word." Moerdyk maintained that all of the schools that were established in Holland were "the natural outcome of the purposes and prayers and efforts and sacrifices" of the early settlers who prized an educated ministry. "The goal of all instruction was theological instruction."[29]

Denominational tensions over theological education were exacerbated considerably following the decision of the 1877 synod to suspend the Theological Department at Hope College. While the department had not prospered, it had produced twenty-nine graduates from 1869 to 1877, most of whom had accepted calls to serve Dutch-speaking congregations in the Midwest. As promised, "Hope Seminary," as it was known, had trained "Western men for the Western work in Western schools."[30]

The issue that triggered the suspension was not directly related to the size or effectiveness of the Theological Department but to the overall financial condition of the college. Financially strapped since its inception, the college, through its president and council, had consistently solicited support from the denomination. While the 1877 report of the council expressed the usual concerns about finances and made the usual pleas for funds, there is no evidence that the council anticipated the drastic decision the synod was about to take.[31] It is important to note, however, that a longstanding disagreement regarding the Theological Department's rather ambiguous relationship

---

[29] Moerdyk, "The Establishment of Theological Education in Holland," 14-15.

[30] See Gerhard De Jonge, "In How Far Does the Western Theological Seminary Supply the Needs of the Western Field?" *Quarter-Centennial of the Western Theological Seminary* (Holland, Michigan, 1909), 53, also 54-60. De Jonge is reminding his audience of the plan of James Romeyn, of the denomination's domestic missions committee, to establish schools in the West.

[31] *Acts and Proceedings*, June 1877, 702.

to the council and to the theological professorate had been aired through correspondence to the synod by the college's president, Phillip Phelps, and professor Charles Crispell.[32] At any rate, the synod formed an ad hoc committee to address issues associated with Hope College. This committee, which was chaired by Hope professor John W. Beardslee, proposed a series of resolutions related to governance, salaries, endowments, and presidential prerogatives. It also proposed the resolution which "passed like an electric shock" through the West:[33] "Resolved, that in view of the present embarrassed condition of the finances of the college, the Council be directed for the present to suspend the Theological Department."[34]

Before voting on the resolution, the synod spent a full day and a half debating the pertinent issues. Phelps and Crispell were provided ample opportunities to speak. A substitute motion to delay the decision until the will of the church in the West could be heard was defeated. The motion to suspend passed by a vote of eighty-three to thirty-six. Because just seventeen delegates at the 1877 synod represented classes from the West, the vast majority of the "aye" votes were cast by the delegates from the Eastern classes.[35]

The decision to suspend theological education at Hope College elicited heated response across the denomination, especially in the West. The issue was debated thoroughly on the pages of *De Hope*, the Dutch language newspaper in Holland, Michigan. The most articulate defense of the decision came from Charles Van der Veen, one of four Western delegates who voted with the majority. In a three-part series published during the late summer of 1877, Van der Veen sought to dampen local outrage by arguing that there had been little displeasure in the West with the training of pastors at New Brunswick, and that a strong Hope College was more essential to the needs of the West than theological training. Van der Veen also indicated that "internal squabbles" between President Phelps and the Theological Department influenced the decision of the synod. The quarrels which had ensued

---

[32] The correspondence from Phelps and Crispell is noted in *Acts and Proceedings*, June 1877, 706.
[33] Henry E. Dosker, "Western Seminary Since 1884," in Corwin, *Manual*, 203.
[34] *Acts and Proceedings*, June 1877, 707.
[35] Ibid., 598-601, 708-709. One of the four delegates representing Western classes was Hope professor John W. Beardslee, who chaired the ad hoc committee that brought the resolution to suspend. The three others, Henry Viterwijk, Christian Van der Veen, and Jacob Van der Meulen, all pastors of churches in Michigan, were, like Beardslee, graduates of Rutgers College and New Brunswick Theological Seminary.

at Hope had become "a public scandal" that "grieved and discouraged her best friends, and much sympathy for her was cut off by it." In the end, Van der Veen expressed concern for the unity of the Reformed Church. Theological education at Hope College had "contributed to a seeming chasm between the East and the West." He suggested that if even a large denomination such as the Presbyterian Church "suffers in the cultivation of differences promoted by various theological schools," surely the Reformed Church would be affected negatively by the existence of two theological schools. "A small body, as ours is, languishes soon under that feeling of alienation." Van der Veen insisted that a focus upon "unity of understanding, of purpose, of endeavors" would be "guaranteed by the education of all ministers in one school and under one influence."[36]

Those in the West who opposed the decision to suspend theological education at Hope College sought to isolate the "real" reasons behind the action. Writing in *De Hope*, Dirk Broek would not accept the presenting reason: the financial condition of the college. Broek calculated that the Theological Department "hardly cost the church anything" and that the decision to suspend would worsen rather than improve the financial condition. Broek was certainly aware that sectional differences may have contributed to the decision to suspend. "There are perhaps some in the East who have been jealous of the establishment and growing of Hope College; they preferred to see everything united in New Brunswick." But Broek reminded his readers that most of the thirty-six delegates who voted against suspension came from the East and that the motion to delay the vote until the Western churches could be surveyed came from elder Samuel B. Schieffelin, who had always been a friend of Hope College. Broek, like others who decried the suspension, argued that the decision would be detrimental to the health of the denomination. Without a steady supply of Western-trained ministers the growth of the church in the Midwest would be stunted. The long-term well-being of the Reformed Church was dependent upon a theological school in the West.[37]

As Nicholas Steffens reflected back upon the "storm" that swept across the church in the West following the decision of 1877, he suggested that while the suspension was "occasioned by a lack of

---

[36] Christian Van der Veen, "Light on a Badly Misunderstood Matter," part 1, *De Hope II*, no. 49 (August 29), and part 2 *De Hope II*, no. 50 (September 5, 1877).

[37] Dirk Broek, "Something about the Cessation of the Theological Department at Hope College" *De Hope II*, no. 45 (August 1, 1877).

funds" at Hope College, the real cause was deep-seated opposition to a Western center for theological training. Some opponents claimed that the "unity" of the education of the ministry "would be broken," others that the seminary in New Brunswick would "suffer materially," and still others that the Reformed Church was "too small to allow herself the luxury of two theological schools." A graduate of New Brunswick who in 1877 was serving the Silver Creek Church in Illinois, Steffens confessed that he personally approved of the suspension. It was not until a year later when he was called to Michigan that he truly understood its negative impact. He soon realized that the General Synod's decision was "fraught with danger, and in the end detrimental to the development" of the church in the West.[38]

Henry Dosker later observed that while the ministers in the West were not in agreement over the suspension, the congregations "were very nearly unanimous" in their disapproval and disappointment. "It increased the unrest and suspicion that existed in certain quarters, and it stands closely related to the disturbing events of the seven years which followed."[39]

The "disturbing events" were associated with the controversy that exploded across the Western church over membership in the Masonic Lodge. Despite a series of overtures from the classes in the West, the synod refused to issue a blanket condemnation of lodge membership, leaving such decisions up to local consistories. Because the Afscheiding churches in the Netherlands had consistently condemned membership in secret societies, the Christian Reformed Church, a seceder group that broke with the Reformed Church in 1857, began to draw away a significant number of disenchanted members of the Reformed Church in America—especially in the West. Around 10 percent of the membership of the Reformed Church joined the Christian Reformed Church during the late 1870s and early 1880s. At a time when theological leadership was most needed in the West, theological training had been suspended.[40] Not surprisingly, disagreements over lodge membership

---

[38] Nicholas M. Steffens, "The Story of the First Twenty-Five Years of Restored Theological Instruction," in *Quarter-Centennial of the Western Theological Seminary* (Holland, Michigan, 1909), 40-42.

[39] Dosker, "Western Seminary Since 1884," 203.

[40] See Robert P. Swierenga and Elton J. Bruins, *Family Quarrels in the Dutch Reformed Churches in the Nineteenth Century: the Pillar Church Sesquicentennial Lectures*, Historical Series of the Reformed Church in America, no. 32 (Grand Rapids: Eerdmans, 1999), 108-35; and Elton J. Bruins, "The Masonic Controversy in Holland, Michigan, 1879-1882," in *Perspectives on*

strained relationships between East and West throughout the period of suspension.

There was little movement toward restoration of theology in the West until 1882, when an ad hoc committee of the synod was appointed to report on "the advisability of establishing a department of theological instruction at the west at an early day." In its report during the following year, the committee noted concerns that theological candidates in the West were attending seminaries of other denominations and could be lost to the Reformed Church. Moreover it noted that the Western church was "passing through a most perilous crisis," and that restoration of theology was a matter "of life and death." Acting upon the committee's recommendation, the synod voted to resume theological education in Holland in the autumn of 1884, with the provision that congregations making up the Synod of Chicago fully endow "the Professorship of Didactic and Polemic Theology."[41] By December of 1884, the endowment was met in full and theological studies had resumed at Hope College.[42] During the following year the Theological Department was established as a separate entity, with its own board of superintendents and a professorate under the auspices of the General Synod. Soon this institution became known as the Western Theological Seminary of the Reformed Church in America. Theological instruction was restored in the West.[43] The "darkest" period in "all the history of the Western Church" had ended.[44]

The restoration of theological education in the West did not end the infighting over that which gave rise to the suspension. Charles Van der Veen wrote a caustic article for the *Christian Intelligencer* that reveals the depth of the sectional tensions in the church in 1884. "It seems that we are once more to try the policy of giving the Western brethren what they want, partly as a salve for their injured feeling, and partly in the hope of thus preventing possible fresh disasters." Concerned that the real needs of Hope College would be overlooked, Van der

---

the *Christian Reformed Church, Studies in its History, Theology and Ecumenicity*, Peter De Klerk and Richard R. De Ridder, eds. (Grand Rapids: Baker Books, 1983), 53-72.

[41] *Acts and Proceedings*, 1883, 319-21.
[42] Wynand Wichers, *A Century of Hope, 1866-1966* (Grand Rapids: Eerdmans, 1968), 111-12; *Acts and Proceedings*, 1885, 741-42. Anticipating that the endowment would be met, the synod of 1884 appointed Nicholas Steffens to the chair. See *Acts and Proceedings*, 1884, 534-35. The 1884 synod convened in Grand Rapids, the first synod to meet in the West.
[43] *Acts and Proceedings*, 1885, 745-46, 750.
[44] See De Jonge, *Quarter Centennial*, 63, for "darkest" quotation.

Veen complained that "by the needless raising of the distracting issue of theology" new obstacles would be placed before the college. He expressed dismay at the indifference of the church to Hope College and "at the exaggerated notions of the value of a theological department." Van der Veen predicted that a theological department "could only be what it was in the past: The foe of education; the parasite of that institution; the egg from which secession will ultimately be hatched." At the end of the article, Van der Veen decried the senseless bifurcation of theological education. "There is no more need of two theological seminaries in our small church than there is of two Boards of Missions or two Boards of Education. We have had all these things in pairs—Eastern and Western."[45]

While few observers would have put the issue as sharply as Van der Veen, it is true that the restoration of theological education in the West reinforced denominational sectionalism. The decision to support two centers may have insured that both institutions would suffer periodically in terms of enrollment and financial support. And the decision certainly did not dampen long-standing tensions. At the turn of the twentieth century, Henry Dosker noted that the future of the Western Theological Seminary was still "far from secure," in part because leaders of the denomination were working "to undermine the foundations of the institution, or, at least to limit its growth and prosperity." Dosker elaborated:

> A short-sighted party, in the East, deemed the Eastern Seminary all-sufficient for the needs of the church, practically following the lines of the old "Conferentie" party on many points. At the West there was a reactionary party which perpetuated the traditions of the men who, since 1866, had opposed the establishment of theological instruction at the West.[46]

In his sober assessment of the future of the Western Seminary, Dosker referenced a convulsive period in the history of the Reformed church: the coetus conferentie schism. The more things change...

Theological Education and the Unity of the Reformed Church in America: The Last Century

It is perhaps ironic that the restoration of theology in the West occurred during the centennial year of the establishment of theological

---

[45] Christian Van der Veen, "On Hope College and the Restoration of Theology," *Christian Intelligencer* 55 (March 26, 1884).

[46] Dosker, "Western Seminary Since 1884," 205.

education in the East. Speaking at a gala celebration at New Brunswick in 1884, Cornelius Crispell, a graduate of New Brunswick who had gone on to serve as the first professor of theology in the Theological Department at Hope College, took pains to allay any concerns of his alma mater that the Western church did not hold the institution in the highest regard.

> The desire for Theological Instruction in the West did not originate in any real or supposed infirmities of the Mother Seminary here. It was not a want nor a doubt of orthodoxy, nor a felt lack of efficiency in instruction *here*, that gave rise to the longings for training the men of the West into a living ministry *there*.[47]

For his part, Charles Scott, a professor at Hope College and a former teacher in its Theological Department, brought news from Michigan that on the very day in which the centennial celebration had commenced, theological instruction had resumed in Michigan. "When another hundred year is passed, a sister seminary will take her place by the side of this in the glorious history of our Church."[48]

These expressions of centennial good will accurately reflect their constituents' genuine esteem for the "mother seminary," but belie the tensions that existed in the church over the re-establishment of theological education in the West. During the next century and a quarter, the Reformed Church continued to struggle to overcome sectional differences across the denomination in the important arena of theological training. Despite persistent efforts, theological education was never fully consolidated. In the end, the Reformed Church sought to honor both unity and diversity.

During the twentieth century, the church periodically explored the possibility of consolidating the theological schools. For instance, a committee that had been established to consider the conditions of seminaries reported in 1923 that both seminaries were experiencing the hardships of low enrollments and insufficient financial support. The situation was especially difficult for New Brunswick, which appeared to have "lost its former vital contact" with congregations. The committee noted that an "alarmingly small" number of ministerial

---

[47] Cornelius E. Crispell, "Historical Sketch of Theological Instruction in the West," in *Centennial of the Theological Seminary of the Reformed Church in America* (New York: Board of Publication of the Reformed Church in America, 1885), 171.

[48] Charles Scott, "Address," in *Centennial of the Theological Seminary*, 250.

students were coming out of Reformed homes in the East, and that not a few of this small number were attending the seminaries of other denominations.[49]

Fully cognizant of the many challenges faced by those who provided theological education for the Reformed Church, the committee considered four options that had found "public expression" in the church.

> 1. The elimination of either the Western Theological Seminary or New Brunswick Seminary.
> 2. The combining of these two institutions at some central point.
> 3. The dividing of the courses in such a way that the first half shall be given in one Seminary and the last half in the other.
> 4. The seeking of an arrangement on the part of our New Brunswick Seminary with a Seminary outside of the Reformed Church, the Western Seminary continuing as it is.[50]

With respect to the first option, the committee acknowledged that the Reformed Church was "numerically small" and that "the burden of supporting two seminaries and holding them up to the high standard of efficiency" of some of our sister denominations "was almost beyond the strength" of the church. Such a proposition would cut "the Gordian Knot" and provide for a larger faculty and concentrate financial resources. In the end, of course, the committee found that closing either seminary, or consolidating them, was fiercely resisted by both sections of the denomination. The thirteen resolutions that were actually put forth, therefore, were remedial and hardly bold or far-reaching.[51]

During the depth of the Great Depression, a time of severe financial pressures for both seminaries, there was another impulse toward consolidation. While the overtures from the classes of Paramus and Ulster to bring the seminaries together were not acted upon by the synod of 1936, a discussion to that end had found expression in the denominational paper.[52]

In 1948, the synod's Standing Committee on Education noted in its report that "the possible merger" of the New Brunswick and Western Seminaries had been discussed and that a "thorough study" had been made by a proper committee, which concluded that "union of the seminaries would result in losses...which would outweigh possible

---

[49] *Acts and Proceedings*, 1923, 94-96.
[50] Ibid., 96-97.
[51] Ibid., 97-101.
[52] *Acts and Proceedings*, 1936, 15, 255, 316.

financial and other gains." The committee suggested that the seminaries seek "closer cooperation and synchronization of curriculum" as well as "a possible exchange of professors and extension services." The report concluded that the seminaries "preserve their identity" and that the "best purposes of the Church" could best be served at that time "by dropping the discussion of the issue."[53]

In his report to the synod in 1960, synod president Howard Hageman spoke with eloquence about his desire to see various constituencies of the Reformed Church brought together to meet the needs of the denomination in a changing culture. Two of his four specific suggestions regarding denominational unity had to do with theological education. First, noting that nothing was more essential to the unity of the denomination than the professorate, Hageman recommended that professors, members of the General Synod by their office, meet as a committee the day preceding the meeting of the synod. Second, Hageman recommended that a single board of theological education be created to facilitate decisions regarding faculty and curriculum. Admitting that he had once considered steps to unify Western and New Brunswick, Hageman noted that the Reformed Church had long before decided that "we need both seminaries." Therefore, he was "not disposed to raise that question again."[54] In acting upon Hageman's recommendations, the synod of 1960 moved toward cooperation rather than unification of theological education.

During the following June, the faculties of the two seminaries did begin to meet per Hageman's recommendation. The reports of those convocations tended to support his suggestion that these meetings would promote better understanding and lead to cooperation. The 1961 report of the Standing Committee on Professorate and Theological Seminaries noted that the convocation was "one of the finest things to have occurred in the life of the two seminaries" in many years. "Real unity of mind and purpose" was evident as the faculties worked on synchronizing their curricula in a way that would accommodate students who wished to train at both seminaries. Plans were also made for an annual lectureship to be shared by the institutions. Following another meeting in 1962, it was reported to the synod that the convocation had produced "the finest spirit of fraternity and cooperation" as the faculties "opened their hearts to each other and dealt constructively with their common interests and problems."[55]

[53] *Acts and Proceedings*, 1948, 87-90.
[54] *Acts and Proceedings*, 1960, 229-30.
[55] *Acts and Proceedings*, 1961, 67-70; and *Acts and Proceedings*, 1962, 54.

Hageman's second proposal was that a single board of theological education would govern both seminaries on behalf of the General Synod. Considering the history of resistance to loss of local control of ministerial training, it is remarkable that a succession of synods moved quickly to establish such a board by 1967. Already in 1963, the synod established the Permanent Committee on Theological Education to oversee the work of the boards of New Brunswick and Western seminaries. At the same time the Permanent Committee on the Professorate was dissolved.[56] In 1967, the Permanent Committee on Theological Education recommended that it be dissolved along with the boards of trustees of the two seminaries and that in their place a single Board of Theological Education be established. The actual recommendation, which came through the General Synod Executive Committee, proposed that the General Synod "set up a single Board of Superintendents for the present two seminaries for the purpose of establishing a single theological seminary for the Reformed Church in America." On the floor of synod this recommendation passed, but not without an important change in wording. The phrase, "single theological seminary," was deleted and replaced by the phrase, "unified program of theological education." It was obvious that the synod was not yet prepared to consolidate the seminaries. Still, a motion from the floor was adopted that directed the newly consolidated board to study and act upon "a site or sites of the B.D. program and/or centers of continuing theological education."[57]

If the synod of 1967 did not approve full consolidation of the seminaries, its decision to move to a single board of governance with the mandate to move toward the unification of theological education is truly remarkable. After so many years of resistance, why was there such strong movement in this direction?

In part, the willingness to consider consolidation was made possible by the fact that New Brunswick Theological Seminary had reached a crossroads in its long and illustrious history. Faced with financial shortfalls, declining enrollments, and deteriorating facilities, New Brunswick's Board of Trustees at its 1964 fall meeting considered a recommendation to sell all of its property to Rutgers University and relocate to a less populated location. While it held that recommendation for additional study, the board authorized its officers "to explore the possibility of merger with Western Theological Seminary." During

---

[56] *Acts and Proceedings*, 1963, 55-56; and *Acts and Proceedings*, 1964, 46, 51.
[57] *Acts and Proceedings*, 1967, 50-51, 55, 146-47, 166-68.

the following January, officers of the New Brunswick board met with officers of the Western board. The New Brunswick board subsequently recommended that the Permanent Committee on Theological Education study the advisability of merging the two seminaries. At the 1965 synod, this committee reported that while there were "a number of factors which indicate that a single seminary would be advantageous," it was the judgment of the committee that continuation of the two seminaries was in the best interest of the denomination "under present conditions." The seminaries were encouraged to seek opportunities for "more effective unification and coordination of theological education."[58]

In the fall of 1965, at a faculty colloquy, Western's president, Herman Ridder, read a letter from the Board of Trustees of New Brunswick and its president, Wallace Jamison, which suggested that it was in the best interests of the church to have one seminary. This letter stimulated a series of discussions and negotiations that involved both seminaries, the General Synod Executive Committee, the General Synod Council, and the Committee on Theological Education.[59] Still, in the spring of 1966, the New Brunswick board voted to raze venerable Suydam and Hertzog Halls and replace them with a new all-purpose building.[60] During a period of great uncertainty about the future shape of theological education for the Reformed Church, New Brunswick made the decision to retrench. In the same manner during the following year, just before the seminary boards were formally consolidated, Western's board went on record disapproving the proposed union of the two seminaries.[61] Both institutions, it appeared, were fearful of being completely swept away in a swirl of consolidation and unification.

Still, the momentum for change was great. Under the direction of the newly consolidated Board of Theological Education, the seminaries developed a bold and innovative curriculum that would unify the two seminaries while providing adaptable and relevant training for pastors

---

[58] *Acts and Proceedings*, 1965, 31, 46-47; see also Hageman, *Two Centuries Plus*, 176-82, and Norman J. Kansfield, "President Ridder's Role in Theological Education," in George Brown, Jr., ed., *Herman J. Ridder: Contextual Preacher and President*, Historical Series of the Reformed Church in America, no. 59 (Grand Rapids: Eerdmans, 2008), 38.

[59] Donald J. Bruggink, "Beginning the Second Century," *Reformed Review*, 44 (Spring, 1991): 187.

[60] Hageman, *Two Centuries Plus*, 178.

[61] *Acts and Proceedings*, 1967, 44.

in a fast-changing culture. Originally called the "Two-Level, Two-Site Design" it came to be known as the "Bi-Level Multi-site Program." This four-year program required that students spend the first two years of their seminary training in the urban environment of New Brunswick, New Jersey, and the final two in the more suburban and rural culture of West Michigan.[62] It was the board's intention that the traditional three-year programs be phased out and that all candidates for ministry move through this new curriculum. When candidates for the new program arrived at New Brunswick in 1969, both seminaries were in the process of phasing out their three-year Bachelor of Divinity programs.[63]

Meanwhile, the board moved closer to full unification of the seminaries when Herman Ridder, the president of Western, was appointed to be president of both seminaries in 1969. At the same time, local deans were established at the two sites, Norman Thomas at New Brunswick and Elton Einengenburg at Western. Further consolidation of administrative responsibilities took place during the next two years as a business manager and a student recruiter were hired to serve both institutions. A common catalog was even published to promote the Bi-Level Multi-Site Program.[64] With self-reported "high enthusiasm and harmony" and with none of the expected "marks of sectionalism and provincial loyalty," the members of the board were putting into place a unified program of theological education for the Reformed Church.[65]

While fully aware of the history of sectional tensions, the board hoped that new unified programs would be "the vital bridge to understanding" between East and West.

> That it contains risks and is partially a dream, we admit. But with the opportunity we have to "dare" to more adequately meet the needs of the church and through it the needs of this revolutionary world, we cannot but seize the opportunity, and to do so with dispatch.[66]

---

[62] *Acts and Proceedings*, 1969, 36-39. The best studies of the Bi-Level Multi-Site Program are Hageman, *Two Centuries Plus*, 176-90; Bruggink, "Beginning the Second Century," 187-92, and Kansfield in Brown, *Herman J. Ridder*, 21-52. Many of the concepts of the Bi-Level Multi-Site Program were developed by Ridder soon after he became the president of Western Theological Seminary. See Herman J. Ridder, *A Proposal For Theological Education* (Holland, Michigan: Western Theological Seminary, 1967), included as Appendix B in Brown, *Herman J. Ridder*, 421-38.

[63] *Acts and Proceedings*, 1970, 27-28.

[64] Ibid., 27-31, and Kansfield in Brown, *Herman J. Ridder*, 40-41.

[65] *Acts and Proceedings*, 1969, 39.

[66] Ibid., 1969, 43.

There was pushback from the churches, however. The 1970 synod received a flurry of overtures asking it to reconsider the four-year multi-site program. These overtures were defeated, and the intrepid Board of Theological Education moved forward. The 1971 report of the board noted encouraging signs in the enrollment for the Bi-Level Multi-Site Program. Given a choice, most incoming students opted for the new curriculum rather than the old. Overall enrollments at the seminaries swelled. At New Brunswick, student housing was insufficient to meet the demand. This positive news from the board was tempered by the fact that both sites had sizeable operating deficits.[67]

The unified program took a significant blow in May of 1971 when Ridder accepted a call to serve the Central Reformed Church in Grand Rapids. An effective and popular leader, Ridder had been identified closely with the development and implementation of the Bi-Level Multi-Site Program. He resigned the presidency, at least in part, because he believed the program would have a better opportunity under the leadership of someone less closely tied to it. The board appointed Lester Kuyper as an interim president. A professor of Old Testament at Western who was nearing retirement, Kuyper had gained trust across the denomination during his long tenure.[68] Although he was loved and respected, Kuyper did not provide the same sort of visionary and forceful leadership that Ridder had.

The board's report to the synod in 1972 reflected the sober reality that the unified program of theological education was struggling. Not only were both seminaries facing increased costs and mounting deficits, they were also experiencing decreasing enrollments in the Bi-Level Multi-Site program. The old three-year curriculum was becoming the more popular option for entering students. One of the significant drawbacks to the two-site curriculum was the requirement of a mid-program move. Those who were married with children found it particularly difficult to relocate.[69]

The search for a permanent president of the unified program was also proving to be difficult and contentious. Seeing the value of aligning theological education with the overall program of the denomination, the presidential screening committee recommended that Arie Brouwer, the executive secretary of the General Program Council, also be

---

[67] *Acts and Proceedings*, 1970, 85-87; and *Acts and Proceedings*, 1971, 27-30.
[68] *Acts and Proceedings*, 1971, 32-33; see also Bruggink, "Beginning the Second Century," 188-89.
[69] *Acts and Proceedings*, 1972, 25-27.

appointed to serve as the president of both seminaries. When the board named Brouwer as its candidate, there was considerable resistance to this consolidation of power, and Brouwer graciously declined the invitation.[70]

The Synod's Review Committee on Theological Education also took note of the growing resistance to the unified program within the faculties, administration, and the board. The Bi-Level Multi-Site Program was creative and innovative, and it was obvious that "such radical departures from the status quo" had caused tensions. While not wishing to make a final judgment about administrative structure, the curriculum, or sites, the committee suggested that "flexibility and courage" were essential if the progress made to that point was to be "consolidated and furthered."[71]

The "thorny problem"[72] of the permanent site (or sites) for theological education was answered in 1973 when the synod received the long-awaited report of a special committee, which had been given the task of recommending locations for the denominational offices as well as for theological education. Those who held out hope that theological education would be located on a single site were disappointed. The committee recommended that the two existing locations be retained as the primary sites of the denomination's higher theological education. Among the factors that led to this recommendation were historical and geographical ties, the need for varied experience, institutional allegiance and support, and the retention of Reformed Church students who would likely enroll at other seminaries. The committee concluded with this telling observation: "A strength of the RCA is its unity within its diversity. To eliminate one of the Seminaries would be to weaken that strength."[73]

The vision of unified theological education faded quickly and quietly. In its 1973 report to the synod, the board announced that Howard G. Hageman and I. John Hesselink had been appointed to serve as presidents of New Brunswick and Western respectively. The two seminaries were fully reconstituted as separate institutions in terms of administration, faculty, fundraising, recruitment, and curricula.[74] The Bi-Level Multi-Site would die on the vine when the last two participants

---

[70] Ibid., 25-27; see also Bruggink, "Beginning the Second Century," 189-90.
[71] *Acts and Proceedings*, 1972, 30-31.
[72] Ibid., 26.
[73] *Acts and Proceedings*, 1973, 185-90, especially 188.
[74] Ibid., 28-31.

graduated in 1977.⁷⁵ The "Brave New Experiment"⁷⁶ had ended. The unified Board of Theological Education alone would survive the re-regionalization of theological education in the Reformed Church, at least for a few years. To meet the distinctive needs of the seminaries, the board was divided into subcommittees that were devoted to New Brunswick and Western, even as the members also met in plenary sessions. Over time this arrangement proved to be unwieldy and costly. Concluding that "real trustee loyalty and ownership" resided in a particular institution, the board was restructured dramatically in 1992, and the seminaries were governed again by their own boards of trustees. By the following year, the Board of Theological Education, the principal unifying force in theological training, was dissolved.⁷⁷

The return to normalcy for the theological seminaries did not bring an end to tensions over theological education. In his report in 1983, synod president James I. Cook, a professor at Western Seminary, took note of the growing number of Reformed churches that had been planted along the West Coast of the United States and the concomitant need for a regional seminary to train pastors for these congregations. Reformed Church candidates for ministry were enrolling in increasing numbers at Fuller Theological Seminary and, according to the standards of the church, these candidates would need to be vetted and approved by the theological professorate of the denomination before being approved for ordination. Cook proposed that an ad hoc committee be constituted with instructions to bring a recommendation regarding theological education on the West Coast to the following synod.⁷⁸ Many observers expected that the Committee to Investigate the Inauguration of Theological Education in the Far West would recommend that Fuller be embraced as a third training center for the denomination. The actual recommendation was more far-reaching. The committee proposed that the denomination create a third agent of theological education, the Theological Education Agency, which would be located on the Fuller campus and through its certification committee would guide all Reformed Church students enrolled at seminaries other than New

---

75   For a roster of the nineteen graduates of the Bi-Level Multi-Site Program and the years of their graduation, see Kansfield in Brown, *Herman J. Ridder*, 48.
76   The chapter in Hageman, *Two Centuries Plus*, that dealt with the Bi-Level Multi-Site Program was titled, "Brave New Experiment." See 183-90.
77   *Acts and Proceedings*, 1992, 293-95 and *Acts and Proceedings*, 1993, 297.
78   *Acts and Proceedings*, 1983, 32-33.

Brunswick or Western. Upon approval of the General Synod in 1984, such an agency was established.[79]

With the establishment of the Theological Education Agency, theological training both reflected and contributed to growing regionalization and congregationalism in the Reformed Church. An increasing number of prospective pastors sought their theological training at non-Reformed seminaries. In part this was due to convenience and cost, but it was also evident that some students enrolled at non-Reformed Church seminaries for other reasons as well. While students under the auspices of the Theological Education Agency were required to take courses in Reformed Church standards, polity, missions, and history, some were not immersed in the central values and core ethos of the denomination. As the Reformed Church faced controversial issues at the close of the twentieth century, agreement and reconciliation were difficult to achieve, in part because of disparate theological training.[80]

When the Board of Theological Education was restructured in 1992, the Reformed Church was left with three distinct and separate agencies of theological training, each of which reported directly to the General Synod. In part because the church no longer had a single coherent forum to adjudicate divergent voices in theological education, the 1994 synod established the Task Force on Standards for the Preparation for the Professional Ministry in the Reformed Church in America.[81] Despite its ungainly title, the task force was able to develop sets of principles to guide the process of ministerial preparation and establish standards to ensure the quality of the education which ministers of Word and sacrament would receive. To consolidate the implementation of theological education more effectively, the task force proposed that the Theological Education Agency be dissolved and replaced by the Ministerial Formation Coordinating Agency. In addition to assuming the responsibilities for certifying those students who chose to attend non-Reformed Church seminaries, the new agency

---

[79] *Acts and Proceedings*, 1984, 213-18.

[80] As one privileged to teach courses in Reformed Church history and missions to Reformed Church students who do not attend New Brunswick and Western, I am aware that their motivations are varied. It is important to note that the Reformed Church in America has always welcomed ministers of Word and sacrament who have attended non-RCA seminaries. See, for instance, the list of ministers and the theological schools at which they received their training compiled by Edwin Tanjore Corwin in *Manual*, 1044-82.

[81] *Acts and Proceedings*, 1994, 278.

would also provide a forum for the many stakeholders of theological training in the denomination.[82]

In 1998 the synod approved the far-reaching recommendations of the task force, including the establishment of the Ministerial Formation Coordinating Agency. Those who expected that this new agency would unify theological education were disappointed. Due to travel costs and the fact that the board of the Ministerial Formation Coordinating Agency did not possess the power to effect change, eventually it ceased to meet as originally constituted. While the agency continued to guide the work of students attending non-Reformed Church seminaries and those who were pursuing an alternate route to ordination, it had failed to coordinate theological education across the denomination.[83]

Early in the twenty-first century the unity of theological education was further fractured when the General Synod approved the establishment of a new ministry designation of "commissioned pastor." While there had long been a desire in the church to enhance and facilitate the ministerial gifts and leadership skills of the laity, Carol Mutch, the 2001 General Synod president, challenged delegates that year to find ways for lay leaders to be identified, acknowledged, encouraged, trained, and called to answer God's call.[84] Mutch's concerns for lay leaders coincided with a confluence of interest groups that were determined to move the church to invest gifted lay leaders with certain measures of pastoral authority: those representing small congregations unable to support trained ministers of Word and sacrament, ethnic congregations who were finding it difficult to call theologically prepared pastors, and new church plants who were seeking pastors who had training and aptitude to organize new congregations. Those who attended the Lay Pastoral Ministry Summit in Chicago during October 2001 were convinced that all of these ministry needs could be met by establishing within the structure of the Reformed church a ministry designation of "commissioned pastor." A recommendation to this effect was approved by the 2002 General Synod.[85]

---

[82] *Acts and Proceedings*, 1996, 322-46.

[83] *Acts and Proceedings*, 1997, 330-52, and *Acts and Proceedings*, 1998, 358-69. As a member of the task force and, as president of Western Theological Seminary, an ex-officio member of the Board of Ministerial Formation Agency, I was disappointed that the agency did not become a more effective voice for the standardization of theological education.

[84] *Acts and Proceedings*, 2001, 29-39.

[85] *Acts and Proceedings*, 2002, 291-98.

While the commissioned pastor was ordained to the office of elder and was commissioned through the authority of a classis to serve a specific congregation, the essential functions of the ministry designation were those of minister of Word and sacrament—preaching, administering the sacraments, serving as presiding officer of consistory, elder and deacon meetings, performing marriages, etc.[86] Initially there were few guidelines for the training of commissioned pastors, and such training was generally arranged by local classes and regional synods. While suggested standards for training did emerge at the denominational level, the seminaries and Ministerial Formation Coordinating Agency were little involved in that process and the standards were interpreted uniquely in different parts of the church. Overall, the commissioned pastor program, to this point, has contributed to even greater regionalization of theological education.

Conclusion

Because the Reformed Church has placed a high value on a well trained pastorate, theological education has had a central role in the life of the denomination. From colonial times to our own there has been a persistent tension between unity and diversity of theological education. Most often this tension has been evident along sectional lines—East and West. It has also been felt in differences over theology and polity. Because the landscape is ever shifting, it is difficult to draw hard and fast conclusions about the future of theological education in the Reformed Church in America. Considering the history of our denomination, however, it is most likely that the tension will remain and that there will continue to be "unity within its diversity."

---

[86] Ibid.

PART 4

Tools for Understanding God and God's Church

Like every professor of theology in the Reformed Church, Donald Bruggink was first a minister of Word and sacrament. Before he taught pastors and teachers he was one, at the Fordham Manor Reformed Church in the Bronx, New York. It was in that challenging, changing context that he first began helping parishioners grapple with the nature of God and relate the nature of God's church to the world. These are roles that he has never abandoned, continuing his ecclesiastical work as an active member of the Third Reformed Church in Holland, Michigan, and as a member of various commissions of the General Synod.[1]

---

[1] It is quite probable that, given his membership on the commissions on History and Christian Worship (two terms each), and his permanent assignment to the Commission on History as a consultant since 1978, Donald Bruggink has attended more commission meetings than anyone in the history of the denomination, or at least more than anyone who was not staff to the General Synod. See Elton J. Bruins, "Donald J. Bruggink's Contribution to Reformed Church in America Historiography," *Reformed Review*, 52/3 (Spring 1999), and Norman J. Kansfield, "The Committed Self: The Public Career of Donald J. Bruggink," *Reformed Review*, vol. 52, no. 3 (Spring, 1999).

The essays in this final section all examine God's church and, through them, seek to understand the nature of God or how others have understood it. First we have Jeffrey Tyler's theological reflections on how human diversity is meant to be played out in the kingdom of God from a Reformed perspective; considering Bruggink's fondness for cities and their diversity, this is especially appropriate. Allan Janssen looks at Reformed understandings of the ministry of the state and how the church is called to speak publicly. This editor looks at another public face of the church—its worship—and how Reformed understandings of aesthetic in worship (a favorite theme of Bruggink's) have changed over time. Finally, John Hesselink examines an important aspect of the Calvinian understanding of God, the nature of the atonement; this harks back to Bruggink's first teaching assignment at Western—theology—and creates a symmetry to these essays which the editor hopes he will appreciate: the first and last essays have been written by those who have known him longest among these authors.

CHAPTER 9

Human Diversity and Christianity Imagined: Past, Present, Eternal

J. Jeffery Tyler

Imagine the celestial human race, a sea of faces stretching out toward the horizon of eternity.[1] When we survey humanity in heaven, what do we see? Perhaps we envision a gathering of familiars up close—

---

[1] This essay is dedicated to the Reverend Dr. Donald J. Bruggink, James A.H. Cornell Professor, Emeritus, of Historical Theology. Bruggink taught generations of students at Western Theological Seminary not only the history of the Reformed tradition, but also the narratives and theologies of western and eastern Christianity as a whole. His legendary and ongoing travel seminars to Greece, Italy, Northern Europe, and Turkey have further highlighted the global history and impact of the Christian faith. Moreover, as founding and general editor of the Historical Series of the Reformed Church in America Bruggink has consistently supported the publication of a significant number of volumes on the contributions of the RCA to world missions (see series list, pp. 334-338). Likewise, Bruggink's career as a scholar of architecture, including his seminal *Christ and Architecture: Building Presbyterian/Reformed Churches* (Grand Rapids: Eerdmans, 1965), coauthored with Carl H. Droppers, is also international in perspective. Indeed, at the writing of this essay, Bruggink is organizing the American Institute of Architects Conference in Rome, which will meet in October of 2008.

family, friends, and acquaintances—with an endless backdrop of others all equally radiant, happy, and identical. In similarity and sameness this human ocean seems to clone our own racial, ethnic, and national profile—one species no longer divided and wounded by diversity of pigment and culture; one species created in our own image. In the great by and by, everyone will look like me and mine. Or will they?

Let us consider a second possibility. A new heaven and a new earth sparkle with the redeemed, a human race recast in the original mold of Adam and further transformed in the likeness of Christ. The superior race God first intended now inhabits the heavenly Jerusalem. The apostle Paul describes a people becoming one in this life and seamless in the life to come: there is neither Jew nor Greek, slave nor free, male nor female (Gal. 3:28), neither circumcised nor uncircumcised, Scythian nor barbarian; rather, "Christ is all and in all" (Col. 3:11).[2] In eternity humanity will be free of racism and ethnocentrism, slavery and oppression, misogyny and ageism. In short, heaven will be a grand melting pot, in which a formerly warped and corrupted species is cleansed of its racial and multicultural impurities in order to produce a homogenous, identical species, a humanity reflecting Christ with complete symmetry and uniformity. All things Greek and Jewish, Ethiopian and Syrian, Roman and Persian, Chinese and Japanese, Korean and Vietnamese, Indonesian and Maori, Russian and German, French and English, Kenyan and Nigerian, Mexican and Peruvian—all human culture and ethnicity—will burn away in the forges of the grand by and by. Likewise, the shape and texture of gender will vanish. Is this view a biblical vision of the renewed people of God?

Perhaps our longing for the end of wars and rumors of war amplifies our desire for an eternal people safely monolithic, monochrome, and regimented. Oneness in Christ ensures that all are welcome, equal, and find dwelling together in peace: "So then you are no longer strangers and aliens, but you are citizens with the saints and also members of the household of God..." (Eph. 2:19). Yet even in this celestial household do not individual believers retain something of their temporal character and distinct identity? And if individuals are so present, what of each people, tribe, and nation? Lack of oppression, hierarchy, and patriarchy need not lead to bland uniformity. Indeed, a third heavenly vista can be found in scripture, a vision of humanity created and recreated in diverse and multicultural splendor. In this vision the first peoples of the earth

---

[2] Unless otherwise indicated all biblical quotations cite the New Revised Standard Version.

multiply, cover the earth, and develop distinctive families, cultures, and nationalities. The Creator observes the nations unfold, express, and create in the very image of their Maker. Likewise eternity will not lead to the obliteration of difference, but to the full healing and flowering of a human diversity formerly obscured in the millennia of alienation, bigotry, and violence.

If this vision has historical and biblical integrity, then it is necessary to affirm that true Christianity is first and foremost a multicultural religion—yesterday, today, and tomorrow. Living out the petition, "Thy will be done, on earth as it is in heaven," means that every believer must seek to embrace the diversity of humanity—local, national, and global—as part and parcel of the true body of Christ now and forever more. But what evidence actually exists for these various models of a monolithic or a complex eternal family?

Christianity as a Historical Faith

The Christian faith is historical through and through. History is an essential characteristic of Christianity. We might even fashion a "historical creed" as follows: God created heaven and earth, time and history; God is at work in this history and one day will bring this age to a close; most decisively God has entered the very stream of time in a particular place and in the "fullness of time" in Jesus the Christ (Gal. 4:4). Remembering the deeds and work of God in scripture is the weighty responsibility of the faithful. The Old Testament echoes with the command to remember the Passover, to recount the covenant with Yahweh generation after generation. The people of God are called to recall this history and live out of its lessons. Indeed, after the death of Joshua, the Israelite tribes are beset by disunity, idolatry, and war. Recurring suffering and violence can be traced back to a staggering ignorance of their heritage and their God: "...that whole generation was gathered to their ancestors; and another generation grew up after them, who did know the Lord or the work that he had done for Israel" (Judg. 2:10). To obey the covenant is to remember in word and deed the mighty works of Yahweh, to ground faith in reality and history.

Moreover, a good deal of the Old Testament narrative is devoted to the exceptionalism of the people of God—the Hebrews, Israelites, and Jews. They are called to nurture their own distinctive identity among the restive and ravenous kingdoms of the Near East. Though a small people, they are the chosen of Yahweh. Their relationship to the nations of the earth is both hostile and hospitable; biblical voices demanding ethnic and racial purity among the Israelites (e.g., Deut. 20: 16-18) contrast sharply with those proclaiming Yahweh as benevolent and welcoming Lord to all the nations of the earth (e.g. Isa. 25:6-9).

Christianity in turn emerges in the land of the chosen, a region at the crossroads of international trade and the ancient empires of Europe and Asia, Mesopotamia and Africa. Here the Jewish peoples of Jesus' day wrestled with the pervasive influence of Greek culture, the brutality of Roman occupation, and diversity among the very people of God. Indeed, there were many cultures among the Jews and their related kin—Judean, Galilean, Idumean, and Samaritan—and numerous hotly divided sects—Pharisees and Sadducees, Essenes and Zealots, among others. Diaspora Jews, scattered across the Roman Empire and east into Persia, brought their acculturated Judaisms to Jerusalem, Passover, and Pentecost. Jesus of Nazareth was born into a fractious, divided land, a multicultural world within and surrounding the Jewish homeland. His message would be devoted initially to the Jews (Mark 7: 24-30) and eventually to the nations of the earth (Matt. 28:19-20). The trajectory of the Christian faith would be global.

Indeed, within twenty years of its inception, Christianity began to jettison its exclusive Jewish ethnicity and identity, beginning with the elimination of circumcision as a rite of conversion and a necessary sign of devotion (Acts 15). The great Jewish apostles Peter and Paul—a Palestinian and a Diaspora Jew respectively—set their sights on the Gentiles across the Roman Empire. The faith moved ever outward from Palestine, promoting diverse church communities and proclaiming a kingdom of God free of borders geographic, political, and cultural. After the apostolic generation, Greeks, Romans, and North Africans developed the seminal theological ideas of the faith, while Syrians and Egyptians turned to desert and wilderness to deepen and toughen the spiritual disciplines. Missionaries traveled to India, China, and among the so-called barbarian peoples of northern Europe. Armenians and Ethiopians, the Irish and the Slavs, were among the first converts on the fringe of the Roman Empire, and many in those cultures remain Christian to this day. The first centuries of the faith were profoundly multicultural within and outside of the Roman Empire. As Christianity spread across the globe, each culture this faith encountered, infiltrated, and sometimes saturated in turn gave shape to the faith. Each culture emphasized and highlighted particular religious expressions and behaviors while repressing and concealing others. We know Christianity today not only through scripture, but also through the diverse cultures and peoples who embraced, preserved, expressed, and confessed the faith. For nearly two thousand years, the very survival and transmission of Christianity has been thoroughly multicultural.[3]

Among all the peoples and periods of history, the ancient Jewish and Greco-Roman cultures, in which Christianity emerged, still provide the first and essential matrix of meaning. It is impossible to understand the Bible or the intentions of the first believers without a rudimentary grasp of their world, its customs and ideas. Even as these cultures shaped the original worldview of the faithful, they did not restrict the global and multicultural flexibility of Christianity. Subsequent believers have not been required to imitate or recreate the exact cultural practices and societies of the ancient world. There is no religious mandate to make a pilgrimage to Jerusalem or Rome, to return to the geographical beginnings of the faith. Christianity continues to unfold, to take root and become incarnate in new places and cultures. It belongs to all the peoples of the world in real space and time.[4]

---

[3] There is no religion without culture. We are both political *and* cultural creatures. I favor the following definition of culture: "Culture is the fabric of our lives: the languages, expressions, customs, rituals, habits, and performances that shape and define how we live and make sense of the world." Much like the Christian Savior, Christianity is incarnate in specific places and among specific peoples.

[4] It may seem that history, though an intriguing characteristic of Christianity, is not truly essential to the faith. Early Christian authors would claim otherwise. For example, Irenaeus of Lyons (d.c. 200), in his voluminous *Against Heresies*, defends the historic and apostolic faith against those associated with gnosticism. Irenaeus rooted the faith in locales steeped in apostolic history and pointed to the universal similarity of Christianity across diverse places in the Roman Empire (the original meaning of "catholic"). Irenaeus formulated this position in response to certain "teachers" who espoused a secret Christianity, based on esoteric mythology and personal revelatory dreams; "Against Heresies," in *Early Christian Fathers*, ed. C. Richardson (New York: Macmillan, 1970), 358-72. In fact, gnostic tendencies have endured and have experienced a resurgence in recent years; see, for example, Timothy Freke and Peter Gandy, *Jesus and the Lost Goddess: The Secret Teachings of the Original Christians* (New York: Three Rivers, 2002), wherein the historical nature of Christianity is denied in favor of a mythological and symbolic message of the faith. The popularity of Dan Brown's *The Da Vinci Code* (New York: Anchor, 2006) attests to both the ignorance of history among the general populace and the faithful as well as the promotion of a version of Christianity and western Christianity that is largely ahistorical; see J. Jeffery Tyler "*The Da Vinci Code*, Jesus, and History: Imagining Christianity Past and Present," *Reformed Review* 59 (2006): 261-82.

Within this global vista of Christianity, can we not also say that God has some special plans and preferences for certain nations? From "a city on a hill," to manifest destiny, to "God bless America"—is not the United States of America God's ultimate cultural creation and chief global concern? Are not the founding fathers truly the reappearance of Old Testament patriarchs and early Christian apostles? Does not human history and Christian religion culminate in the American Dream? Do not the peoples of the earth await with deep yearning God's gracious gifts of democracy and capitalism through the USA? The sweep of Christian history attests to this pervasive and dangerous form of idolatry—the equation of God and gospel with a single people and culture. And this idolatrous tendency is not unique to the United States.

It is precisely Christian diversity through history that counters the pervasive and stubborn resilience of cultural and political idolatry. Princes, politicians, and presidents have gladly donned the Christian mantle and baptized their campaigns and wars with bodacious proclamations of divine favoritism. Since the cessation of Roman persecution in the fourth century, ardent believers have fallen prey to this pervasive temptation. Cultures, kingdoms, and nation states have been enthroned as the true and final incarnation of the Christian faith from the Roman Empire to the *Holy* Roman Empire, from Byzantium to Czarist Russia, Reformation Germany to Habsburg Spain, Victorian England, and even on to Nazi Germany. Missionaries have circled the globe, all too often bringing cultural imperialism in the guise of the gospel. Yet once and future kingdoms of quintessential Christianity have not endured; they come and go as will one day happen to the USA. Ultimately no one culture, nation, or ethnicity, including ancient Jewish and Greco-Roman, can rightfully claim to be the full and final embodiment of Christianity.[5]

[5] After Jesus and Paul, no Christian thinker has had more impact on Christianity than Augustine of Hippo (d. 430). In his magnum opus, *The City of God*, Augustine addressed contemporaries who were horrified by the declining fortunes of the Roman Empire. While pagan Rome had endured for centuries and come to dominate the Mediterranean and much of Europe, the empire was in rapid decline in Augustine's day and precisely at the moment it had become most Christian. Did this turn of events not establish the fallacy of Christianity and the virility of the pagan gods? Why did the Christian God abandon the faithful and their empire? Empires and kingdoms rise and fall in the vicissitudes of human history, Augustine asserted; this is the nature of earthly kingdoms and their lust for self-aggrandizement and temporal glory. The future of Christianity

In fact, at this very moment a profound religious sea change is underway in the global configuration of Christianity. The dominance of western forms of Christianity—Mediterranean, European, and North American, ascendant for two thousand years—is coming to a dramatic end. The future of global Christianity belongs to the southern hemisphere—to Africa and Latin America preeminently. By the end of the twenty-first century, Christians from North America and Europe will likely find themselves on the religious, political, and cultural margins of the faith as Christianity finally goes global. Meanwhile, western Christendom is fading away even as the chords of "God Bless America" affirm a cultural idolatry that may well outlive genuine and widespread Christian faith in the USA.[6]

In short, Christianity belongs to all who believe, regardless of race and ethnicity. Each people incarnate the presence of Jesus the Christ anew through the church in particular times and places. Yet Christianity is the exclusive property of no single culture, civilization, or nationality. Human diversity is part and parcel of Christianity—past, present, and future.

Still, one vital and telling issue remains. Is human diversity within Christianity and beyond the original intent of the Creator, or is it merely one more legacy of the Fall—one more example of human brokenness? Are Christians expected to make the best of diversity as the wretched and lamentable condition of a broken, divided, violent humanity? If so, then perhaps racially segregated churches best reflect the future, each reminding us that someday our differences will be dissolved in a grand refashioning of the original unalloyed and unmixed race God intended. Those who celebrate diversity and multiculturalism foolishly cherish a world bathed in alienation, genocide, and blood. No wonder attempts to be multicultural so often ring hollow and awkward in our churches and on our college campuses.

Mono-Christianity—A Biblical Model

A common objection to multiculturalism goes something like this: we should not seek diversity for its own sake. There is nothing

---

lies elsewhere—with the church and the eternal city of God. So Jesus of Nazareth confirmed : "My kingdom is not from this world" (John 18:36).

[6] See Philip Jenkins, *The Next Christendom: The Coming of Global Christianity* (Oxford: Oxford Univ. Press, 2002). For extensive demographic evidence of the global shift of Christianity over the past century, see the *World Christian Encyclopedia: A Comparative Survey of Churches and Religions in the Modern World*, ed. D.B. Barrett (Oxford: Oxford Univ. Press, 2001).

intrinsically good or necessary about this view. In fact, a kaleidoscopic humanity is lamentable at best. Granted, reconciliation among races and nations is necessary to promote tolerance and cooperation, to avoid violence and war. But utopian melodies from "It's a Small World After All" to "We are the World" obscure the underlying tragedy of our differences.

In the popular political parlance: multiculturalism in and of itself is "politically correct" and in reality much worse than a mere catch-phrase. Yes, yes, racism and bigotry should not be tolerated. Every human being deserves civil and full human rights. But is human diversity truly essential to genuine Christianity or does it fundamentally pervert the faith? We have already seen that the history of Christianity is profoundly diverse. The future of the faith is global in scope. But is this historical development at its best the result of the neutral evolution of religion and at its worst another kind of human alienation and violence? And if so, should not Christians of varied races and cultures endure their differences until God can sort out the human wheat and chaff in heaven and restore the true and pure human *race*? Perhaps multicultural Christianity is the legacy of ethnic and genetic perversion, of human sinfulness now etched in blood and prejudice across the global canvas. Beneath and amidst the layers and mixtures of bastard peoples lies the original master race awaiting its heavenly epiphany. Meanwhile, some nations, races, and ethnicities prosper on the earth; their closer approximation to the once and future human race are confirmed by the shine of their pale, Aryan skin, the sophistication of their western civilization, and the visage of their anglicized Jesus.

This version of reality—heavenly and earthly—relies on a network of biblical passages that make clear that a divided and varied humanity are among the plagues of human sin—alienation and violence, earthquake and flood, famine and drought, diversity and multiculturalism. The breakdown of pristine humanity begins with the Fall in Genesis 3, occurs yet again among the sons of Noah (Gen. 9: 20-27), and escalates due to divine punishment at the Tower of Babel (Gen. 11: 1-9). In the aftermath of human scattering, God creates a new and set apart people; Abraham receives his divine call and covenant, the people of Israel are mandated to cleanse Canaan of its godless peoples and settle their long-awaited promised land. The failure of the twelve tribes to annihilate Canaanite diversity sews the seed of eventual destruction and exile. The northern tribes of Israel are lost to the nations. The Jews learn to guard their ethnic and religious purity in Babylon and Persia. They return to Palestine to wall off Jerusalem from the world and to hear the anguished cries of Ezra, who rends his garments and tears out his hair over Jews yoked to the pagan peoples of Canaan (Ezra 9:2-5): "We have broken faith with our God and have married foreign women from the peoples of the land, but even now there is hope for Israel in spite of this. Therefore, let us make a covenant with our God to put away these wives and their children, according to the counsel of my lord..." (Ezra 10: 2-3).

In the shadow of the Old Testament, the New resonates with the creation of the church, a new community and people extending to the ends of the earth and yet intended for oneness of purpose, calling, and human identity. Paul's vision of an elect race—neither male nor female, Jew nor Greek, slave nor free—mandates a single people made equal in Christ and points toward a heavenly human symmetry untrammeled by the anguished divisions of a fallen world. As history unfolds, the faithful must choose a single cultural manifestation of Christianity enforced upon all by the western Christian powers, or the church must be divided and safely segregated in cultural cul-de-sacs until the plague of diversity can be washed away, leaving one people thoroughly homogenized and baptized in unity and uniformity. Given this future, should the gospel be saddled and shackled with visions of liberation for the urchin races and cultures of the earth, when such multicultural utopianism defies and mocks the Creator's eternal designs?

But what if this vision of a monolithic humanity and Christianity is not the last word from scripture? Imagine for a moment a vastly different biblical narrative, which foreshadows the multicultural history of Christianity and envisions the unfolding of human diversity as divinely ordained and empowered for this world and the one to come.

Multicultural Christianity—A Biblical Model

Let us ponder a different reading of the Bible, which reopens the puzzling issue of multiculturalism. In this approach human diversity originates not in the Fall but earlier, in the very fabric of a creation deemed "good" through and through. What if the Creator designed a plan and formed a world to house a robust, varied, and diverse humanity? Indeed, according to Genesis 1, the cosmos in its very inception is kaleidoscopic. The Creator shapes and enlivens a universe with a range of heavenly bodies above and a dazzling array of plant and animal life below.

At the outset humanity appears gendered and generational—male and female, adult and child. In plurality humans reflect the image of

God (Gen. 1:27). The genealogies of Adam, Eve, and Seth confirm the remarkable proliferation of the human family, a multiplication marred by the hostility of Cain and his descendants and the intercourse of heavenly creatures with the daughters of earth (Gen. 6:1-7). The flood insures a rebirth of the species; Noah and his progeny again people a diverse planet. Moreover, the Table of Nations—not the Tower of Babel—provides the interpretive key. Genesis 10 describes the restoration and multiplication of the human race, a National Geographic map of the ancient world that celebrates the diversity of peoples in their families, languages, lands, and nations (Gen. 10: 5, 32). In the mirror of the Table of Nations the earlier divine command, "Be fruitful and multiply and fill the earth and subdue it" (Genesis 1: 28; 9:7), suggests not only numerical expansion, but also a dazzling proliferation of peoples, cultures, and languages that confirm and conform to the fertile imagination of the Creator.[7] Indeed, the development of linguistic diversity in Genesis 10 actually precedes the more particularized confusion of tongues at Babel (Gen. 11). There is no mention of the Fall, flood, or human sin in the Table of Nations. Apart from the sequence of presentation, no one people or culture receives divine preference; there is no mention of Israel. Rather, this is a second creation, focused not on the general creation of life or one distinct family as in Genesis 2-4, but on the plurality of nations and peoples.[8]

With the Table of Nations as backdrop, the Tower of Babel appears as an expression of cultural imperialism and ancient ethnocentrism.

[7] Deuteronomy 32:8 echoes Genesis 10: "When the Most High apportioned the nations, when he divided humankind, he fixed the boundaries of the peoples...." Georg Bertram underscores the neutrality of this passage: "From the first patriarchs there does not descend a single humanity, but a group of nations divided according to clans and differing in language, custom and situation. The attempt to resist this in Gn. 11 has its origin in human pride. God intervenes to re-establish the order imposed by Him. Similarly, in Dt. 32:8 the division of the world into nations is a divine order and not a punishment for human sin..." "ἔθνος" in *Theological Dictionary of the New Testament*, vol. II, ed. G. Kittel (Grand Rapids: Eerdmans, 1964), 367.

[8] The tendency of a reader to fixate on Genesis 3 and 4 obscures this approach to the early chapters of Genesis. While Genesis 1 is cosmic in scope and abstract in its description of humanity, the second through fourth chapters of Genesis focus on a single human family and turn quickly to the Fall. Although hostility toward earthly creatures (woman vs. the serpent), pain in childbirth and subjection to the male (the fate of woman), and alienation from labor and agriculture (fate of the male) are listed as the consequences of human sin, no mention is made of human diversity as a legacy of the Fall (Gen. 3:14-19).

One city and tower, one nation, name, and language promise to redound to the glory of a monolithic humanity wedged against human diversity and seeking equality with the Creator (Gen. 11: 2-5). The people of Babel are compelled to scatter, become many, and fill the earth (Gen. 11: 6-9). The divine plan mandates human complexity, not willful, boastful uniformity.

But what of Israel, God's chosen people, set apart from the heathen nations of the earth to be the one holy and faithful race? Although much of the Old Testament focuses on the internal religion and politics of the Israelites and Jews, a wider perspective is also apparent. For example, Abram is not only the founding patriarch of the Israelites, but also a promised blessing to all peoples: in Abram "... all the families of the earth shall be blessed" (Gen. 12:3). As the freshly named Abraham he will be "the ancestor of a multitude of nations" (Gen. 17: 4). Indeed, the kingdom of Israel is intended to shine as a beacon to the peoples of the earth; the Temple of Jerusalem will be a gathering place of worship for all nations (see, for example, Isa. 25: 6-9; 45:22-23; 56: 6-8). Furthermore, the book of Jonah offers a censure of religious and ethnic prejudice as well as a reminder that all people belong to God, even the foreign and pagan Ninevites and their home, that great city of 120,000 people "and also much cattle" (Jon. 4:11, RSV). Even more intimately, Rahab and Ruth, the Canaanite survivor and the Moabite widow, are foreigners welcomed into the household of the faithful and the line of kings (Josh. 6: 25: Ruth 1:15-17; 4: 10-12; Matt. 1:5-6). In sum, is not Israel God's rejoinder to Babel, a single people and culture devoted exclusively and humbly to the redemptive power of Yahweh and created as a witness to the nations? For sin and brokenness infect all of life, warping even the cornucopia of nations and their cultures and bringing strife to the four corners of the earth.

Given this Old Testament framework, which confirms the goodness of human diversity and seeks the restoration of the nations, the unfolding of a multicultural Christianity is natural and essential. The kingdom of God proclaimed by Jesus of Nazareth is not ultimately confined to any one people, place, or culture. The so-called Great Commission of Jesus reaches far beyond Israel: "Go therefore and make disciples of all nations..." (Matt. 28: 19). Meanwhile, at the very geographical center of Jewish devotion, Jesus chastises moneylenders and overturns their tables in the Temple compound; he does so not only in response to the mixing of mammon and worship, but also in obedience to the vision of Isaiah. Jesus declares, "Is it not written, 'My house shall be called a house of prayer for *all the nations*?'" (Mark: 11:

17; cf. Isa. 56:7). The Messiah anticipates the arrival of the nations and makes Mt. Zion ready for their homecoming.

The New Testament vision of Christianity is global in scope. The faith will not be confined to Israel or to Palestine. The first apostolic sermons at Pentecost undo the curse of Babel; one message is heard in many tongues (Acts 2). Diaspora Jews visiting Jerusalem and hearing Peter's proclamation in their own languages remind us that even the Jewish people scattered throughout the ancient world are already diverse and multicultural. The voice of the Holy Spirit does not resort to one dialect but adapts to the cultures and tongues of the many. Subsequently at the gathering of apostles known as the Jerusalem Council, the multicultural future of Christianity is sealed (Acts 15). Gentile converts must not become Jews first in circumcision and culture in order to become Christians. Indeed, the very future of Christianity resides among the nations of the earth.

Given the teaching of Jesus and the apostles, it might be worthwhile to raise some new questions about the perspective of the apostle Paul in particular. When Paul asserts, "There is no longer Jew or Greek, there is no longer slave or free, there is no longer male or female; for all of you are one in Christ Jesus" (Gal. 3:28), does the apostle truly envision a monolithic and racially identical humanity? Does he imply that the diversity of his day will vanish as the new Christian master race emerges? This seems highly unlikely. The simple route to a single humanity is a return to Jewish faith and culture, to demand that all Christians become Jews. Paul rejects this solution, even as he links Gentile Christians to the promise given to Abraham: "...if you belong to Christ, then you are Abraham's offspring, heirs according to the promise" (Gal. 3:29). The distinction between Jew and Greek refers primarily to the division between the Greeks, representing the peoples of the earth, and the Jews, God's chosen people. According to Paul, God's "chosen" are not only the Jews but all those who receive the gospel, regardless of national and cultural identity. The elimination of diversity among the nations is not Paul's focus in Galatians. In fact, he ministers across the varied peoples of the Roman Empire without demanding that they be identical in culture. Paul's call to oneness in Christ suggests unity and equality in the Christian community, but not racial uniformity or cultural amalgamation. There is no melting pot in Pauline Christianity. Indeed, his epistles display remarkable cultural dexterity as he deals with the complex and subtle needs of his many congregations and their distinct environments; he is "all things to all people" (1 Cor. 9:22).

Most telling in the New Testament are the grand visions of John's Apocalypse—the Book of Revelation. We are often reminded at funerals of that future day when life will be made whole, when God will wipe away every tear, vanquish death, and dwell among the faithful forever (Rev. 21: 4). The grieving long for their own consolation as well as for the peace of deceased loved ones. Yet, most of the visions in Revelation are vast in scope, reaching out to the whole people of God. In fact, the words of comfort cited above echo the prophet Isaiah and his proclamation of hope to the world: "... he will destroy on this mountain the shroud that is cast over all peoples, the sheet that is spread over all nations. He will swallow up death forever. Then the Lord will wipe away the tears from all faces..." (Isa. 25:7-8). When the veil is torn away, death vanquished, and the faithful consoled, who stands in the eternal presence of God?

The Revelation of John envisions a new heaven, a new earth, and a new humanity, restored to its vital and original diversity. In eternity there is not one nation but many, as there were once nations upon the earth. In heaven the peoples of the earth gather—one and multiple—to worship: "Lord, who will not fear and glorify your name? For you alone are holy. All nations will come and worship you..." (Rev. 15: 4). Most profoundly, in heaven there will be a celebration and restoration of the earth's many human families. Revelation 21 portrays the heavenly city, crowded around a grand procession—a parade of the earth's peoples each bringing forth the gifts and achievements of their own traditions and cultures:

> ...the city has no need of sun or moon to shine on it, for the glory of God is its light, and its lamp is the Lamb. The nations will walk by its light, and the kings of the earth will bring their glory into it. Its gates shall never be shut by day and there will be no night there. People will bring into it the glory and honor of the nations.... (Rev. 21:23-26)

The heavenly Jerusalem will be illumined both by divine radiance *and* by light reflected from "the glory and honor of the nations," resplendent for all eternity throughout the city.[9] Diversity and cultural achievement

---

[9] The Greek words *doxa* and *timē*, glory and honor, have a rich ancestry, referring both to God and to humanity, to personal achievement and inner worth as well as material possessions and earthly treasure. Humanity shares in glory and honor by bearing the image of God. Glory and honor are also the dazzling artifacts and accomplishments of the nations offered

will give heaven some of its dramatic and dazzling human texture.[10]

There is more than glory and honor for the nations of the earth. The last book of the Bible weaves together images of primordial and cultural splendor. The final dwelling place of humanity includes both the fertility of Eden's paradise—the river and tree of life—and the splendor of civilization and culture transformed—a city—*the* heavenly Jerusalem. Here the natural beauty of creation's first day mingles with a sterling symbol of human achievement—a gleaming city.[11] And here—in the garden and in the city—there is healing for the nations, a leafy balm offered to all the peoples of our world who have suffered unspeakable tragedy, brutality, and death, whose divinely sparked creativity and legacy have been eviscerated by natural disaster, war, and genocide. They will take their rightful places among the nations of the Creator and unveil all that was lost, pillaged, and torn asunder in the maelstrom of history.[12] In the heavenly city our attention is drawn to a river and a

---

in tribute to the Creator, the final glorious act of eschatological salvation. This glorious display at the culmination of salvation echoes the searing displays of glory in the New Testament, including the angelic choir at the birth of Christ (Luke 2:9), the transfiguration of Christ with Moses and Elijah (Luke 9:29-31), and the blinding appearance of Christ to Saul en route to Damascus (Acts 22:11); "δόξα," by G. Kittel, *Theological Dictionary of the New Testament*, vol. II, 236-50; "τιμή," by J. Schneider, in *Theological Dictionary of the New Testament*, vol. VIII, 170-73; "δόξα" and "τιμή," by S. Aalen, in *New International Dictionary of New Testament Theology*, vol. 2, ed. C. Brown (Grand Rapids: Zondervan, 1967), 44-51.

[10] C.S. Lewis speaks eloquently of the eternal destination and ultimate transformation of human beings, but one wonders if he underestimates what might remain of humanity as a whole, the nations and their achievements as well as the glory of individual human beings: "There are no *ordinary* people. You have never talked to a mere mortal. Nations, cultures, arts, civilisations—these are mortal, and their life is to ours as the life of a gnat. But it is immortals whom we joke with, work with, marry, snub, and exploit—immortal horrors or everlasting splendours (C.S. Lewis, *The Weight of Glory and Other Addresses* [New York: Macmillan, 1949, 18-19]).

[11] It is crucial to note that cities in the Roman world were by their very nature cosmopolitan—a mixing of peoples and races—from Jerusalem to Alexandria to Rome. An eternal Jerusalem would also be diverse.

[12] George Caird writes, "Nothing from the old order which has value in the sight of God is debarred from entry into the new....The treasure that men find laid up in heaven turns out to be the treasures and wealth of the nations, the best they have known and loved on earth redeemed of all imperfections and transfigured by the radiance of God"; *The Revelation of St. John the Divine* (New York: Harper & Row, 1966), 279-80; cited in Steven Bouma-Prediger, *For the Beauty of the Earth: A Christian Vision for Creation Care* (Grand Rapids: Baker, 2001), 115.

tree where the creator and redeemer God nurtures and restores the one and the many:

> Then the angel showed me the river of the water of life, bright as crystal, flowing from the throne of God and of the Lamb through the middle of the street of the city. On either side of the river, is the tree of life with its twelve kinds of fruit, producing fruit each month; and the leaves of the tree are for the healing of the nations. (Rev. 22:1-22)

The very end of scripture imagines the renewal of humanity in its manifold glory and diversity, a multiplicity intended by the creator at the very beginning of scripture in Genesis.[13] There is no hint here of the restoration of a master race or a single homogenized people. The families and nations of the earth are the human jewels of this heavenly place, reflecting in their own gifts and expressions the light of God. This Creator envisioned their glory, witnessed their mutual hatred and alienation, and now gives them their original and intended magnificence in a new heaven and a new earth. At long last, the creation birthed in perfection at the beginning of scripture is made full and mature in the unfolding and healing of the nations.

This narrative of multicultural Christianity—past, present, and heavenly—does justice to the biblical story, echoes the history of Christianity, and confirms that efforts to embrace and celebrate the entire human family are consonant with the very good news of the divine kingdom. Diversity and multiculturalism matter on earth as in heaven. They are part of the Creator's original design for humanity—for this world and the world to come. When one nation or culture is enthroned as *the* incarnation of Christianity, then the Tower of Babel rears its ugly head once more. When churches remain segregated in worship and congregational life, then truly the body of Christ is torn asunder, alienated and weakened by addiction to cultural blindness and blandness, racial bigotry, and ethnic prejudice. Let us instead be devoted to the Creator's original intention, to the fullness of all things and the fullness of humanity.

---

[13] Michael Wilcock describes this scene eloquently: "Two elements have been added to the pristine simplicity of the Genesis picture by the experience of human history. Instead of a garden only, there is now the developed structure of a garden city: Eve, 'the mother of all living' (Genesis 3:20), has in the plan of God become the ancestress of a great society of nations"; Wilcock, *I Saw Heaven Opened: The Message of Revelation*, The Bible Speaks Today (London: Inter-Varsity, 1975), 212.

To look in the faces of those whose skin pigment, and language, and culture differ from our own is to savor the imagination of the Creator and the tenacity of a diverse creation.[14] To segregate, belittle, and discriminate against those different from ourselves is to insult and deny the Creator who seeks the full and myriad expression of our robust humanity. To embrace a diverse and multicultural Christianity is to anticipate the life to come. When we can imagine that plain of eternity and see the Creator's glory shine in the many splendid and diverse faces of the human family, then we will embrace the God of all life and the myriad peoples we were always meant to be.

---

[14] What will we see truly? Will skin color or distinctive facial characteristics still mark human diversity? Or will the nations and peoples of the earth, though still distinct, be transformed in ways we can scarcely imagine and still retain their distinctiveness? Will the transformation of the nations rival that of individuals (1 Cor. 13:12)?

CHAPTER 10

The Ministry of the State: A Reformed Approach to Public Theology

Allan J. Janssen

The front page of the April 24, 2008, *New York Times* reported from Russia that under the presidency of Vladimir Putin, the Russian Orthodox Church has become the de facto official religion in that country.[1] Protestant worship has been discouraged and proselytizing has been banned. To American readers this sounds antediluvian. This arrangement violates the freedom of the individual, the plurality of religious traditions, and above all the separation of church and state enshrined as it is in our constitution. Understood from the perspective of the history of the church, however, Putin's attitude, while diverging from that of the Christian West, is hardly unique.

---

[1] This essay is a version of a lecture to students of New Brunswick Theological Seminary's International Summer School of Theology held in Doorn, the Netherlands, in July 2008. The topic of that summer school was "Public Theology in a European Context." It was Donald J. Bruggink who first introduced me to the possibilities of international study when my wife and I took part in one of his summer seminars, the one patterned on the "grand tour" of Europe. Indeed, it was through Dr. Bruggink that I made my first, glancing, brush with the *Gereformeerden* in the Netherlands.

I place beside that development the 36th article of the Belgic (or *Netherlandish*) Confession. I quote it in its entirety:

> We believe that
> because of the depravity of the human race,
> our good God has ordained kings, princes, and civil officers.
> God wants the world to be governed by laws and policies
> so that human lawlessness may be restrained
> and that everything may be conducted in good order
> among human beings.
>
> For that purpose God has placed the sword
> in the hands of the government,
> to punish evil people
> and protect the good.
>
> And the government's task is not limited
> to caring for and watching over the public domain
> but extends also to upholding the sacred ministry,
> with a view to removing and destroying
> all idolatry and false worship of the Antichrist;
> to promoting the kingdom of Jesus Christ;
> and to furthering the preaching of the gospel everywhere;
> to the end that God may be honored and served by everyone,
> as required by God's Word.
>
> Moreover everyone,
> regardless of status, condition, or rank,
> must be subject to the government,
> and pay taxes,
> and hold its representatives in honor and respect,
> and obey them in all things that are not in conflict
> with God's Word,
> praying for them
> that the Lord may be willing to lead them
> in all their ways
> and that we may live a peaceful and quiet life
> in all piety and decency.
>
> And on this matter we denounce the Anabaptists, the anarchists,
> and, in general, all those who want
> to reject the authorities and civil officers
> and to subvert justice

by introducing common ownership of goods
and corrupting the moral order
that God has established among human beings.

The Belgic is, of course, one of the fundamental confessions of the Reformed church, still at the confessional heart of the Protestant Church of the Netherlands, the South African Reformed churches, and the Reformed Church in America. Yet it sounds a world as distant from ourselves as does the Russian arrangement. In this essay, I intend to explore that oddity as we reflect (1) on public theology and (2) on A.A. van Ruler's contribution to the discussion. For this article, in all its strangeness, offers a window to how the Reformed understand "public theology." It also brings to the surface the complexities, difficulties, and perhaps the unsolved contradictions of that approach. I will make the discussion not easier, but more difficult.

This will be largely, I argue, because this confession dates from the sixteenth century (1561) and so emerges from a worldview alien to our own. In this article, we find ourselves in a strange land with few landmarks to fix our place. We know we "aren't in Kansas any longer" when, in the first clauses, we meet kings and princes, ordained by God (!) and not chosen by a sovereign people. But we lose our bearings almost completely when we hear that a government's task goes beyond the maintenance of public order (a hoary responsibility for governments of all stripes) and extends to "upholding the sacred ministry with a view to removing and destroying all idolatry and false worship of the Antichrist...." And if that weren't enough to throw us off, the confession goes on to state that the government's task includes "promoting the kingdom of Jesus Christ and to furthering the preaching of the gospel everywhere." If that doesn't sound like government meddling to American ears, I don't know what does!

But it isn't just our ears that can't quite make sense of this. This part of the confession was contested by a number of Reformed people from within the Dutch context early in the twentieth century. I'm thinking primarily of those we call the *Gereformeerde*, specifically followers of the outsized figure of Abraham Kuyper.

Kuyper was the leader of a group of Reformed Christians in the late nineteenth century who left the public (Reformed) church, calling themselves the "sorrowing ones." (Their movement was called the *Dolientie*, "the sorrowing.") They would form part of the major secondary branch of the Reformed, the Reformed Churches in the Netherlands. The argument over Article 36 was long and complex—and took up an enormous amount of paper—and I have neither the time nor the expertise to follow that trail here. It is sufficient to note that for the *Gereformeerden*, the gospel's impact on politics and culture remained crucial, but it was to happen not as the state lived out its responsibility to God, but as the citizen *and* the legislator lived out his or her life before God. Citizens could gather in Christian organizations, including political parties, and so influence the government. Kuyper and his followers were far more modern and even realistic as they maintained that it was not the government's task to support the ministry, nor to promote the gospel. The upshot was a rewriting of the confession so that the offending bit, where the government's task is not limited to maintaining public order but goes on to "upholding sacred ministry," is now replaced as follows:

> And being called in this manner
> to contribute to the advancement of a society
> that is pleasing to God,
> the civil rulers have the task,
> subject to God's law,
> of removing every obstacle
> to the preaching of the gospel
> and to every aspect of divine worship.
>
> They should do this
> while completely refraining from every tendency
> toward exercising absolute authority,
> and while functioning in the sphere entrusted to them
> with the means belonging to them.
>
> They should do it in order that
> the Word of God may have free course;
> the kingdom of Jesus Christ may make progress;
> and every anti-Christian power may be resisted.[2]

This change took place in 1910. I wager that it finds resonance with early twenty-first century folk. It should; we're two hundred years and a major cultural shift from the original confession. We don't live in a world where the government promotes one version of religion over another, and for good reason. We've lived through wars of religion and don't want to return to the day when the sword determines the religion of a people.

[2] *Ecumenical Creeds and Reformed Confessions* (Grand Rapids: CRC Publications, 1988), 117.

But before we get there too quickly, we need to see where we have come, for only by so doing might we see that we haven't really progressed as far as we might claim.

Charles Taylor, a Canadian Roman Catholic philosopher, offers a glimpse into the world from whence we have come in his monumental, complex, and brilliant book, *A Secular Age*.[3] In it he argues that our modern, disenchanted, individualistic world was not always so. In fact, our ancestors lived in a world where, as persons, they were, he says, "porous" to another world, that of spirits.[4] Furthermore, life in this world was lived socially. The social collectivity lived as an organism and the ruler could, without metaphorical reserve, be called the "head" of that body.[5] Since this collectivity lived within a larger world of "principalities and powers" (to use a Pauline phrase) it was crucial to "get it right." How things "are" was not a matter of personal opinion; it was a matter crucial to the survival of the people (and subsequently the individual person). Heresy and unbelief, then, were not simply a threat because they might attract naïve souls and so lead them to perdition; their presence threatened the very existence of the society itself. Consequently, the ruler responsible for the well-being of the ruled was charged with warding off this threat, as real to our ancestors as the threat of terrorism (or disease or economic collapse) is to our societies (and indeed to us viscerally).[6]

This, then, is the world into which the Belgic Confession was born. We are not yet even to the precursors of Enlightenment thought and the notion of what Taylor calls the "buffered" individual.[7] This was not the age of tolerance. Wrong religion had profound and disastrous consequences. We were not dealing with matters of individual opinion. And religion had to do with far more than the destiny of individual souls. It had to do with the survival of societies and peoples.

---

[3] The Belknap Press of Harvard University Press: Cambridge, 2007.
[4] Taylor, *A Secular Age*, 42.
[5] At the time of the Dutch war for "independence" against Spain, even a popular William of Orange was thought to be out of bounds when he took leave from the Spanish crown. "In the opinion of many sixteenth century people authority was holy and given by God. Subjects had as their first duty to honor the right of the prince." A. Th. Van Deursen, *De last van veel geluk: De gescheidenis van Nederland, 1555-1702* (Amsterdam: Uitgeverij Bert Bakker, 2004), 106.
[6] Seen from this perspective, Calvin's role in the infamous affair with Servetus can be understood as something more than an academic argument about the Trinitarian nature of God.
[7] Taylor in fact argues that the Reformation was central to the process of development that led to our secular age.

A mid-twentieth century commentator on the Belgic Confession, A.D.R. Polman, himself *Gereformeerden*, discerns four foundational principles behind Article 36's claims of governmental responsibility. These emerge, he claims, from basic Reformed commitments.

First, "every creature must honor God. This includes the government, which is established by God."[8] One notices here that a government is not the product of a social contract (real or presumed). Sovereignty does not devolve to the populace but remains with God, who establishes whatever government, and in whatever form, is in existence. Not only is the government established by God, but it is required to "honor God." As God's creature and along with all other creatures, its task is to subject itself to God as God is worthy of tribute.

Second, "In its governance, every authority is bound to God's Word and in particular to God's law."[9] Because it is *God's* law, one ignores it at peril. This would include particularly governments, since their very *raison d'être* is the establishment, execution, and adjudication of law. A law not in conformity to God's law would be, if not absurd, disastrous. Note that this is *every* authority. One might suppose, as one will as we enter the modern world, that a government will be officially "neutral." The government does not officially "worship" God. Nonetheless, it is not free to ignore what God has in fact both set down and revealed as law.

Third, "The distinction and the independence of the church and the government must always be maintained."[10] Thus the Reformed would introduce the notion of the vocation of the government in God's economy. The church would not become the state nor the state the church. The Reformed did not intend that the church dictate the laws of the state, nor that the state regulate the religion. This is not England, where the king is the head of the church. Neither is this Rome, where the church calls the shots for the government. Instead, the church and the government each have their particular vocation. In fact, each is to remain within the boundaries of its own vocational duties.

This would not always be easy. One can see this worked out architecturally on the Dam Square in Amsterdam. At the center stands what is now called the "palace." It was built as the new town hall for a city flexing its new economic muscle. As one looks across the square toward the palace, to the right, stands the Nieuwekerk,

---

[8] A.D.R. Polman, *Onze nederlansche geloofsbeliljdenis* vol. 4 (Franeker: T. Wever, n.d.), 267.
[9] Polman, *Onze nederlansche*, 267.
[10] Ibid., 270.

an impressive edifice that also declared the importance of the city. The short street between the two is called "Moses and Aaron Street." Moses—the legislators or the government, and Aaron—representative of the cult, religion. If you spend a little time inside the palace you will see a number of very large paintings where Moses stands as the central figure. In this way, the town councilors were saying very clearly, "We're on the Moses side of matters. And we all know who was most important in the biblical story." Furthermore, the fact that the Nieuwekerk does not have a steeple rising above the palace, and the church itself is tucked to the side, is itself a statement of relative importance.

On the other hand, one can see the relation between church and state worked out in the seating patterns in the churches. You can still find the old pews set aside for the magistrates. They were given seats of honor in the church. But those seats most definitely sat *beneath* the Word. The preachers spoke God's Word, and both church and state lived under the obligation of that Word.

This leads to Polman's fourth principle. "Scripture demands a continual cooperation" between church and state.[11] The two are not in competition, but both stand under God's Word. And it is God who has a way in which God desires God's people to live. Each has its own task. The church does not establish laws about murder, say, or child abuse. The church does not regulate traffic and the building of sewers. The church does not set up a tax code. Nor does the church punish wrongdoers. That doesn't mean that such matters do not have a moral dimension that comes under God's guidance and are not addressed by scripture at some level. But the church isn't in the business of making, assessing, or executing laws. Nonetheless, God's Word must be spoken, and the church *is* in that business. Each works with the other under divine dispensation.

In these principles one can see several Reformed themes emerge clearly. First, the principles operate out of an understanding that the Bible speaks God's intentions. This is particularly true of the Old Testament. There the Reformed saw the pattern of God's way with the world on clear display. Israel, after all, began its political life at Sinai. God's law embraced the entire life of a people. This way was not abrogated, but fulfilled, in the newer testament.

Second, scripture witnessed God's sovereignty in all of life. There is no neutral area. Citing John Calvin, Polman claims that "civil authority serves not only that humans may live, eat, drink and be

---

[11] Ibid., 271.

sustained...but also that no idolatry, no desecration of God's name, no blasphemy against his truth...should arise and grow among the populace."[12] Civil government does include how we eat and drink, and it does that under God's sovereignty. Likewise, what humans worship, that to which humans give their final commitment, that as well stands under God's sovereign rule.

Third, Christ is Lord of all of life. Theologically, God's rule finds its core in the ascension of Jesus. If the risen Jesus is Lord, then the claims of the book of Revelation hold. He is "king of kings and lord of lords, and he shall reign forever." That lordship allows no other lordship alongside, for any other lordship would be in enmity. Or to shift from the Johannine to the Pauline, this is from the famous Christ hymn in Colossians: "[The Messiah] is the image of the invisible God, the firstborn of all creation; for in him all things in heaven and on earth were created, things visible and invisible, *whether thrones or dominions or rulers or powers*—all things have been created through him and for him" (Col. 1:15,16, emphasis added).

There is an intolerance here. And with that we turn to the thought of A.A. van Ruler. Indeed Van Ruler claimed that Yahweh is an intolerant god; this god is not patient of other gods.[13] Van Ruler delighted in saying the outrageous, in part to draw attention, but more to draw his hearer beyond the taken for granted. In this case, though, it leads us to discuss what is perhaps more difficult yet, his notion of *theocracy*. Theocracy stood at the center of his understanding of God's way with the world. Nonetheless, the word jars us. Theocracy evokes images of a Taliban-style government, standing athwart the freedom of the individual, a throw-back to the pre-Enlightenment world described by Taylor. Theocracy is the rigid world of Calvin's Geneva or the fevered dreams of the American religious right.

But before one writes off Van Ruler as a benighted representative of the past, we do well to be drawn into the theological reasons he can speak of theocracy. Contemporary Dutch theologian H.W. de Knijff claims that for Van Ruler the notion of theocracy is quite simple: "...it is simply identical with the fact that through God's revelation God makes himself present in the world."[14] It is *how* God is present that so interests

---

[12] Ibid., 273.
[13] "De verhouding russen kerk en staat," in *Theologish Werk* VI (Nijkerk: Callenbach, 1973), 129.
[14] "A.A. van Ruler anno 1995," in *De waarheid is theocratish: bijdragen tot de waardering van de theologische nalatenshcap van Arnold Albert van Ruler*, Girrit Klein and Dick Steenks, ed. (Baarn: G.F. Callenbach, 1995), 20.

Van Ruler. He envisions theocracy from three perspectives. First, one can conceive theocracy as "giving political form to life and thought in the ordering of the world by the church so that life comes to be seen as an ellipse with two foci—church and state—or—Lord's Supper and civil law."[15] The goal to which God works is the kingdom of God, and God uses *both* the church and the state to accomplish that end. Here one finds the distinction Polman described above. It is described as an ellipse with two foci. This describes a duality, a certain "twoness" that is, Van Ruler says, both original and underivable. Neither the church nor the government has the last word. It is God's way with the world. And it can't be "solved" by finding a common denominator.[16]

Second, one understands theocracy from out of a theology of the Word that engages all of life and does so as event.[17] This is God who takes history seriously. Church and state exist together within history. Indeed, one of Van Ruler's most important essays is his inaugural lecture at the University of Utrecht, "The kingdom of God and history."[18] Reality is one, for Van Ruler. One cannot separate the reality one meets in history from another reality. To do so would be gnostic, in his opinion. The upshot is that God is not only at work in history, but in all of history. There is no separate domain that belongs to God while other domains can be seen as neutral.

Third, and perhaps most importantly for Van Ruler, theocracy can be understood as

> ...an all-embracing notion of life and thereby think of an entirely peculiar *Seinsverstandnis* [understanding of existence] and penetrate to the last and deepest roots of existence, so far that no concept remains that is not touched by biblical doctrine. Moses and Aristotle do battle in our European consciousness.[19]

Israel's God intends a way of life in history that includes not only the cult, but politics, family, society, art, science, indeed the entire of life. In fact, the cult exists as God's means of salvation of the world. But it is the salvation *of* the world and not *from* the world.

This will set some of our notions on their heads. Van Ruler will argue, for example, that the Reformation understanding of the biblical

---

[15] *Religie en Politiek* (Nijkerk:Callenbach, 1945), 153.
[16] *Verhouding*, 127.
[17] *Religie*, 153.
[18] "Het koninkrijk Gods en de geschiedenis," in *Verwachting en Voltooing* (Nijkerk: G.F. Callenbach, 1978), 29-38.
[19] *Religie*, 153.

God's way with the world sees the state in a more direct service to God than the church.[20] As Van Ruler has said famously and severally, God's intention is not "to make humans Christian, but Christians human."[21] The state is engaged in sanctification. All of existence is to be set under the "holy order of God's law."[22] The church does not order common life. The church does not set tax law, for example. Nor does the church enforce traffic laws or the regulative apparatus of the modern bureaucratic state. The church is not here for that purpose.

And as tasks of the state, these actions are not neutral. They reflect a religious way of being in two ways. The first is how God is seen as involved with the world. Is it to be a pagan understanding, by which God is already present *in* the world, in the blood, or within reality itself? Or does God come *to* history? That is, is this something, as Van Ruler says, that we do not complete, but that is *given*?[23] God's creation is not to be seen vertically, as though nature is to become supernature, through a process of elevation. For Van Ruler, that's a Roman Catholic understanding. Rather, the goal is "that we live ordinary life on earth in God's presence according to his will."[24] The state and its authorities do not exhaust our earthly, everyday existence. But they play an enormous role as God's service in that reality.

The second way the state's actions are not neutral is much more prosaic. The state simply cannot escape questions of religious value. Take for example, marriage laws, Sabbath regulations, public vows, abortion, or homosexuality. The state must rule in one way or another. How it rules betrays the god it honors.

An illustration from another discipline, anthropology, gives us insight as to how this works. Clifford Geertz, in his *Interpretation of Culture*, reports how cultures are themselves thick admixtures of religion and ethos:

> In recent anthropological discussion, the moral (and aesthetic) aspects of a give culture, and evaluative elements, have commonly

---

[20] *Verhouding*, 135.
[21] Among other places in "Christ Taking Form in the World," in *Calvinist Trinitarianism and Theocentric Politics: Essays Toward a Public Theology*, trans. John Bolt (Lewiston: Edwin Mellen, 1989), 132.
[22] *Religie*, 163. One notices a contrast with Karl Barth, who attempted to work out justice from the concept of justification. Barth was working Christocentrically, while Van Ruler took a more pneumatological approach. See Barth, *Community, State and Church* (Garden City: Doubleday, 1960).
[23] *Religie*, 155.
[24] *Verhouding*, 136.

been summed up in the term "ethos," while the cognitive, existential aspects have been designated by the term "world view." A people's ethos is the tone, character, and quality of their life, its moral and aesthetic style and mood; it is the underlying attitude toward themselves and their world that life reflects. Their world view is their picture of the way things in sheer actuality are, their concept of nature, of self, of society. It contains their most comprehensive ideas of order. Religious belief and ritual confront and mutually confirm one another; the ethos is made intellectually reasonable by being shown to represent a way of life implied by the actual state of affairs which the world view describes, and a world view is made emotionally acceptable by being presented as an image of the actual state of affairs of which such a way of life is an authentic expression.[25]

A state cannot be neutral because the culture cannot be neutral.

So, which God is to be acknowledged and honored? Is it to be the God of Israel? Or some other god? The gods are not tolerant. Even the gods who are "tolerant" reject the god who isn't tolerant. This is because we are in the realm of truth, and truth is not tolerant of falsehood.

Where does this leave us? For Van Ruler it is not with the modern, neutral state. That is an impossibility. Instead, the state lives as a servant of God. It is the "state with a Bible."[26] In fact, Van Ruler goes so far as to say that is not a matter of the state and the church, but the state and the Bible. It is not that the church calls the shots, but that the government rules in agreement with God's commands and promises.[27] Revelation is not the private reserve of the church. Governors and legislators, judges and bureaucrats read and hear scripture's story with its call to kingdom life. They can know that society has been set on a course that is being shaped by God's future kingdom impinging on the present.

In this way the state is in fact engaged in the destruction of all idolatry and the removal of false worship of the Antichrist. This sounds odd because, I think, it brings to mind images of government agents descending like avenging angels to smash statues dedicated to

---

[25] (New York: Basic Books, 1973), 126-27.
[26] Here Van Ruler stands in the direct tradition of Ph. J. Hoedemaker, nineteenth-century Dutch theologian, often considered the father of confessional theology. He broke with A. Kuyper largely over the interpretation of Article 36. A "state with a Bible" is his phrase. See *Een staat met den Bijbel* ('s-Gravenhage: Bloomendaal, 1941).
[27] *Religie*, 291.

gods—modern-day iconoclasts. Or if our understanding of idolatry is more sophisticated (remembering Calvin's remark that our minds are idol-making factories), we might picture the government as enforcing worship of the Christian god. And we're back in the wars of religion. But before we dismiss Van Ruler out of hand, we do well to pay attention to what we do in fact expect of government. To take but one example, we expect of our government that it work toward the goal of eliminating racism, or at least the expressions of prejudice that have blotted our history. Everyone agrees that this is a worthy goal. But of course, everyone did not; otherwise why have we been so troubled? In any case, we are talking about values here, and behind values are the gods that beckon in one way or another. Or the demons. It cannot be otherwise. So the state is engaged in a battle with the gods, whether it knows it or not. It follows the commands and promises of some god. And, Van Ruler would argue, it *must* do so. This is not in the sense that it follows a moral injunction, but because a state *in fact* does so. Otherwise it wouldn't be a state. Even if it withdraws to a stance of refereeing the playing field so that all the players have an equal chance, even then it has committed itself to values, and so to a god.

Van Ruler can put this in two ways. On the one hand, he takes on humanism as a modern approach. But this is not neutral, he says, because it too works from a set of presuppositions, even if those are only that everything is subject to doubt.[28] But this lands us in the second way Van Ruler has of putting it: we are in the place of nihilism,[29] which, he and others argued, was exactly where Europe was in the middle of the last century. He could put the matter in another way: "The neutrality of the state is a denial of the confession that Christ is the king of kings."[30] The state that does not listen to the Bible will have ceded its responsibility not only to God (in its vocation as minister) but, we might add, to the population. For if committed to a false god, the result will be chaos and death. To put it in contemporary terms, it will leave society subject to the "isms" that plague it: racism, sexism, ageism, classism—you can add to the list. Furthermore, it will leave us subject to the will of the strongest, so that we find ourselves in the battle of civilizations. It will turn out that Callicles—and Nietzsche—were right.[31]

---

[28] *Verhouding*, 134.
[29] *eligie*, 239.
[30] *Religie*, 246.
[31] Callicles is an interlocutor of Socrates in Plato's long and varied dialogue, *Gorgias*. Callicles argues that the powerful determine what is good. See Edith Hamilton and Huntington Cairns, eds., *The Complete Dialogues of*

So what's the church's role? Does the church recede from the stage? Hardly. The church's task is to function as the bearer of the gospel and it exists as a *gestalt* of the kingdom.[32] Its proclamation is public; that is, it does not preach only to those in its pews. God's Word is, as we have seen, to be heard by all. And the church is the bearer of that Word. So that it reminds the government of what that Word says, and does so on all sorts of matters. It may, as it has, remind the government that reliance on nuclear weapons is an expression of idolatry. The church has a prophetic task.

But it does more. It prays for those in power. This is no mere formality. Engaged in an encounter with the living God whose Son is in fact the king of kings, the church prays for the well-being of the government that it may fulfill its task of liberating society of all idolatry. In so doing it supports the government and may in fact do so even as it will sound critical of certain policies of the government, and even of its current expression.

And there is more yet. The government cannot be about its task so long as it is subject to false gods. The church brings the message that liberates, that frees not only individual persons, but institutions from the tyranny of demons. The state needs to be "exorcised" before it can be about its task. This happens as the church's message of salvation reaches those who are in positions of authority. We can imagine this as we think of believers who are, say, legislators. As persons they can see God's kingdom reality shining through from the future into the present. They are themselves not subject to the kind of fear that propels us to rely on military strength to protect ourselves. But there is something more afoot. It isn't just individual persons who are liberated, but the institution of the state itself. For it too is created reality. And God's action in Christ through the Spirit is to bring all creation into the kingdom of God's loving rule or, as Van Ruler would put it, the great round dance of delight.

If the church has a certain task in relation to the government, what is the government's task in relation to the church? Van Ruler would agree with Article 36 that the government "upholds the sacred ministry." That doesn't mean "state church," or not necessarily. Nor

---

Plato (Princeton Univ. Press, 1961), 265 ff. In the Stephanus numbering, Callicles's argument with Socrates begins at 482. Remarkably, Plato does not have Socrates prevail.

[32] See my *Kingdom, Office and Church: A Study of A.A. van Ruler's Doctrine of Ecclesiastical Office*, Historical Series of the Reformed Church in America, no. 53 (Grand Rapids: Eerdmans, 2006), chap. 3.

need it mean direct support of the church by the state, a violation of the value so dear to us Americans, the separation of church and state. It does mean that the government creates an open space where the church can live and function, free of interference of ideology/idolatry. It does mean that the state does not use the church as a handmaid to its own power, and that the church's role is to bless what the state does, a very real danger even in so-called free societies. The state "upholds sacred ministry" because God not only established the state, but the state needs the salvation proclaimed by the church. And the society does as well. The good order of the society, and so the well-being of its citizens is at stake.

We detect here, I think, something of the premodern understanding that Taylor described. And we see the reason why Van Ruler dissented from Kuyper and the alteration of the Belgic Confession. Society and its government is not based on a social contract, real or implied. We are not collectivities of individuals, but communities of people, and *as institutions* objects of God's saving action. The church bears the message that is salvation not only to persons but to society and to government as well. Just so the government carries out its responsibility to its citizens as it protects that space where the church can be about its God-given task.

I began my discussion of Van Ruler with the notion of an intolerant God. God is who God is and is not patient of another god. The God of Israel, Yahweh, is not tolerant of those who hurt and destroy God's creation, that which God has called forth in love, and that includes in the first instance the "least of these." That said, Van Ruler will also argue that genuine tolerance is possible *only* with the God Christians worship. The other possibility is nihilism, a chaos in which intolerance reigns supreme, and which if might does not make right, it does win the day. This is not the tolerance of a sort of general humanism.

What might he mean? It has to do, I think, with the nature of God. This is the God who in Jesus Christ justifies sinners. That is, this God welcomes the stranger, the outsider, the very one who has disqualified him or herself from communion with God and with fellow humans. This God does not require uniformity but delights in plurality, difference. This God intends a rule that is love in justice, so that there is room for each and for all in this kingdom.

The way of this God is the way of the cross. Followers of this God will move aside to give place to the other, even to their own hurt. They will not defend themselves and their rights, but because their place is secure they will give way to the other. Followers of the Lord Jesus will live a way of peace.

Such a way may appear to fail, to give way to the forces of destruction. But we can live the kingdom only in torso, only in the *gestalt* given to us in the presence, only, as Van Ruler might say, in the kingdom of Christ, itself a *gestalt* of the kingdom of God. We live toward the eschaton, where all shall stand in delight in before God. Still, the eschaton takes root in the present, and we live with one another, state and church, with the tolerance of the God who stands against all that threatens to hurt and destroy. This is truth. It is truth as *troth*, truth as faithfulness, the faithfulness of God.

Does this resolve our problems with Article 36? Of course not. Instead, it allows us to see the complexity of the issues before us. And if we are serious about "public theology," it is not simply about bringing our theology out into the public. It is about a *God* who is public, and hence a theology that talks about this God must, in the nature of the case, be public indeed. And this, so I hope to have made clear, is fundamentally a Reformed theology.

CHAPTER 11

Not Only for Necessity: The Problem of Aesthetics in Reformed Worship

James Hart Brumm

On the television program "Saturday Night Live," in the 1980s, there was a sketch about a game show called "Common Knowledge." The premise was that the then-U.N. Ambassador from the United States, Jeanne Kirkpatrick, was on this quiz show pitting her knowledge against a couple of high school students. She loses, because the program is geared toward common knowledge, what "everybody knows" to be true, rather than knowledge of actual facts.

We begin this study with what "everybody knows" to be true about the Reformed tradition: that there was no place for beauty or art in Zwingli's or Calvin's theology, and certainly not in their worship. The common knowledge position is that classic Reformed worship was entirely cerebral, entirely read and spoken, with no place for symbol or imagination. Therefore, worship in Presbyterian and Reformed churches in our day and age is either irrelevant to contemporary society or must abandon the Reformed tradition—and, indeed, many of them have—in order to adapt to said society.

Even when we acknowledge that what everybody knows, or thinks they know, is not necessarily true, we are left with the question of how we moved from the austerity of sixteenth-century Zurich and Geneva to the banners, instruments, colors, and drama that can be part of a modern Reformed liturgy. To answer that question, we shall expand the parameters of our conversation a tiny bit, for this is not an issue only of art, but of a Reformed worship aesthetic. It is about art, but it is about more than art. As William Dyrness points out: "Reformation teaching and practice constitutes a—sometimes systematic, sometimes impulsive—dismantling of an old way of thinking about God's presence in the world, and an equally intentional construction of a new way of imagining God and the world."[1] Art in worship is part of a larger issue for the Reformers, who have no trouble with beauty, symbol, and structure, as long as beauty, symbol, and structure do not get in the way.

Zwingli and Calvin

The first thing "everybody knows" that we need to examine is that the fountainheads of the Reformed tradition—Huldrych Zwingli and John Calvin—had no interest in art and no room for art and beauty in their theology or their worship. This is a misunderstanding of the situation. As a youth, Zwingli showed signs of becoming an excellent musician; already before the age of twelve, he was noticed by Heinrich Bullinger: "he had a good voice and enjoyed music."[2] By 1496-97, his talent had attracted the attentions of the Dominican monks at Berne, who wanted him to enter their monastery for a probationary year in order to pursue his musical studies more exclusively and to sing in the chapel choir. His parents opposed this, because they didn't want him making such a major life decision at such an early age based on nothing but an interest in music.[3] He maintained a musical interest throughout his life, and this person who is remembered as being opposed to hymnody even wrote a hymn of his own:

> A Christian Song,
> Written by Huldrych Zwingli as he was Attacked by the Plague
>
> 1. At the Beginning of the Illness.
>
> Help, Lord God, help
> in this distress!

---

[1] *Reformed Theology and Visual Culture: the Protestant Imagination from Calvin to Edwards* (Cambridge: Cambridge Univ. Press, 2004), 91.
[2] Quoted in Charles Garside, Jr., *Zwingli and the Arts* (New Haven: Yale Univ. Press, 1966), 8.
[3] Garside, *Zwingli*, 9.

I think that Death
   is at the door.
Come, Christ, before!
   For thou hast conquered Death.

To thee I call:
   be it thy will,
pluck out the dart
   that wounds my heart.
Allow me not
   one hour of peace, to pause for breath.

And if thou yet
   wouldst have me dead,
amidst my early days,
   yet may I still thee praise.
Thy will be done!
   Naught can me stun.
Thy tool to make
   I am, or break!

For takest Thou
   my spirit now,
from earth away,
   thou dost so, lest it go astray
and others' state
   and pious lives contaminate.

2. In the Midst of the Illness

Comfort, Lord God, comfort!
   The illness grows;
I am in throes
   of agony and fear.
Therefore draw near
   to me, in grace and mercy.

Thou dost redeem
   him who can trust,
as all men must,
   all his hopes place
in thine own grace,

and for thee all else set aside.

Relief has come;
　my tongue is dumb,
I cannot speak one word.
　　My thoughts are dark and blurred.
Therefore 'tis right
　that thou the fight
shouldst carry on
　for me, thy son.

I am too weak,
　dangers to seek;
nor can I fight
　the devil's taunts and evil might;
yet will my soul
　be thine for aye, complete and whole.

3. In Convalescence

Healed, Lord God, healed!
　I do believe
the plague dost leave
　my body now.
And lettest thou
　the sinner's scourge depart from me,

then shall my mouth
　through all my days
show forth thy praise
　and wisdom more
than e'er before,
　whatever dangers may beset me.

And though I must
　become as dust
and suffer death, I know,
　perhaps with greater woe,
than did befall
　and me appall,
as I did lie
　to death so nigh,

yet will I still
> my part fulfill
in this our world,
> and all things bear, for Heaven's reward,
with help from thee,
> who art alone to life the key.[4]

Calvin's appreciation of the arts is written right into his theology in many places. Far from thinking that arts were a problem, he wrote this in his commentary on Genesis 4:20-22: "The invention of arts, and other things which serve to the common use and convenience of life, is a gift of God by no means to be despised and a faculty worthy of commendation."[5] He went on to say that music "can be adapted to the offices of religion, and made profitable to men."[6]

> I am not gripped by the superstition of thinking absolutely no images permissible. But because sculpture and painting are gifts of God, I seek a pure and legitimate use of each, lest those things which the Lord has conferred upon us for his glory and our good be not only polluted by perverse misuse but also turned to our destruction….Therefore it remains that only those things are to be sculptured or painted which the eyes are capable of seeing…. Within this class are some histories and events, some are images and forms of bodies without any depicting of past events. The former have some use in teaching or admonition…"[7]

But it wasn't just the utility of teaching or praise that mattered to Calvin in all of this:

> [God] meant not only to provide for necessity, but also for delight and good cheer. Thus the purpose of clothing, apart from necessity, was comeliness and decency. In grasses, trees, and fruits, apart from their various uses, there is beauty of appearance and pleasantness of odor (cf. Gen. 2:9). For if this were not true, the prophet would not have reckoned them among the benefits

---

[4] As it appears in Oskar Farner, trans. D.G. Sear, *Zwingli the Reformer: His Life and Work* (New York: Philosophical Library, 1952), 35-37.

[5] John Calvin, trans. John King, *Commentaries on the First Book of Moses Called Genesis*, vol. 1 (Grand Rapids: Baker, 1979), 217.

[6] Calvin, *Commentaries on Genesis*, 218.

[7] John Calvin, trans. Ford Lewis Battles, *Institutes of the Christian Religion* (Philadelphia: Westminster, 1960), 1.11.12, 112.

of God, "that wine gladdens the heart of man, that oil makes his face shine" (Ps. 104:15). Scripture would not have reminded us repeatedly, in commending his kindness, that he gave all such things to men. And the natural qualities themselves of things demonstrate sufficiently to what end and extent we may enjoy them. Has the Lord clothed the flowers with the great beauty that greets our eyes, the sweetness of smell that is wafted upon our nostrils, and yet will it be unlawful for our eyes to be affected by that beauty, or our sense of smell by the sweetness of that odor? What? Did he not so distinguish colors as to make some more lovely than others? What? Did he not endow gold and silver, ivory and marble, with a loveliness that renders them more precious than other metals or stones? Did he not, in short, render many things attractive to us, apart from their necessary use?[8]

For Calvin, beauty is something created by God, which, therefore, must be good. Likewise, God has given people the capacity to create art and music and dance, and therefore art and music and dance must be good. Last, but not least, there is the aspect of delight; we delight in beauty, God delights in beauty, and God delights in our delighting. As Dyrness points out, "The theme of beauty and splendor of creation play a major role in Calvin's theology as a whole."[9]

Art and aesthetics were important to Calvin, and, for him, had a place in the worshiping life of congregations. He knew that "the psalms can stimulate us to raise our hearts to God and arouse us to an ardor in evoking with praises the glories of his holy name."[10] In his own church in Geneva, St. Peter's Cathedral, Calvin never removed the ornate seats in the choir—which would be used as consistory pews instead—the stained glass representations of apostles in the chancel, or the organ, nor did he remove the organ or the elaborate decoration from the cathedral's Mary Chapel; they are all still visible to this day. And, in what is certainly his best known example of welcoming the nonverbal, the symbolic, the aesthetic into worship, Calvin argued for weekly celebration of the Lord's Supper: "it was ordained to be frequently used among all Christians in order that they might frequently return in memory to Christ's Passion, by such remembrance to sustain and strengthen their faith."[11]

Calvin had a deep appreciation for beauty and art, but he also recognized the potential for abuse. His primary concern was that the

---

[8] Calvin, *Institutes*, 3.10.2, 720-21.
[9] Dyrness, *Reformed Theology*, 72.
[10] John Calvin, *Works* (Brunswick: C.A. Schwetschke, 1863), X:1, 12.
[11] Calvin, *Institutes*, 4.17.44, 1422.

art would attract attention to itself and the artist rather than drawing attention to God.[12] Music was useful to worship "if only it be free from vicious attractions, and from the foolish delight, by which it seduces men from better employments, and occupies them in vanity."[13] This is why he limited music in worship to the unaccompanied unison singing of psalms.[14] Even the bread and cup of Communion were not to be enjoyed for their own sakes; even though the elements became the body and blood of Christ for partaking believers through a mystery of the Holy Spirit, they did not remain body and blood, nor were we to adore them as Christ in his place.[15] Art, for Calvin, was primarily a problem when it detracted from God.

Zwingli was dealing with a special set of issues in Zurich. In Zurich, the musical program especially had grown more and more complex in the years leading up to Zwingli's arrival. Felix Hemmerlein, cantor of the Great Minster, created progressively larger and more complex choral programs, driven in part by competition with the other large congregation in the city, at Fraumünster. This continued after Hemmerlein, and the various orders of monks and nuns in the city became known for their choral showiness. By the late fifteenth century, an "organ race" had begun to see which instrument would be best.[16] The teacher Oswald Myconius commented on the nature of all of this shortly after leaving the city in 1520:

> One can occasionally hear nothing but a single sound which is drawn out through the modulations of a hundred kinds without words, such as would be thought ridiculous even in an amorous air. All this provides no advantages, in that neither singers nor listeners can understand what is sung because the musical racket drowns out everything, and the words are made incomprehensible.[17]

---

[12] Davis A. Young, *John Calvin and the Natural World* (Lanham: Univ. Press of America, 2007), 10.
[13] Calvin, *Commentaries*, 218.
[14] For a deeper examination of this, see James Hart Brumm, *Singing the Lord's Song: a History of the English Language Hymnals of the Reformed Church in America* (New Brunswick: Historical Society of the Reformed Church in America, 1990).
[15] Calvin, *Institutes*, 4.17.35, 1411.
[16] Garside, *Zwingli*, 17-20.
[17] "Guter Rath an die Priester der Schweiz, welche die Zürcher verlästern, ihr Lästern einzstullen" (1524), translated and quoted by Garside, *Zwingli*, 20-21.

Also influencing Zwingli were Erasmus and the iconoclasts who were active in Zurich even before he arrived. Erasmus, with his strong philosophical divide between flesh and spirit, maintained that God was spirit and so could not be pacified by corporeal things.[18] The iconoclasts pointed to the art and music of the two great churches and blamed them—because of the money they cost—for taking food out of the mouths of the poor of the city.[19] Suddenly, the overly ornate religious aesthetics were a social justice issue in Zurich.

Zwingli's evolving worship theology, much more so than Calvin's, called the entire concept of liturgy into question. He maintained that Christ called primarily for silent, private worship, and, while he allowed for the idea that the formal gathered worship needed to be observed and maintained as a witness to the world, he came to the conclusion that the more elaborate the liturgy, the more it directly defied the command of Christ.[20]

Zwingli's circumstances led to a much more stringent response than Calvin would have, with a rejection of art and music—primarily choral music—in worship[21] and a downplaying of the sacraments (a logical response to his Erasmian leanings). Both Swiss reformers had read their Plato, who wrote of music's power to end-run reason, appealing directly to people's emotions.[22] But Calvin's secondary influence in this regard was Augustine,[23] leading him to believe that the risk of emotional manipulation was counterbalanced by the surpassing delight of praising God. While there is no explicit evidence of it, one can easily infer that this attitude toward music transferred over into his approach to various worship aesthetics, including liturgy, art, architecture, and even the sacraments. In the end, for Huldrych Zwingli, there was no need for the symbolic: true belief was itself symbolized by the hearing of the Word.[24] For John Calvin, images can be useful, but only when joined to the proclaimed Word.[25] In any case, what the progenitors of the Reformed tradition sought was a new paradigm for

---

[18] Garside, *Zwingli*, 37.
[19] Lee Palmer Wandel, *Voracious Idols and Violent Hands: Iconoclasm in Reformation Zurich, Strasbourg, and Basel* (New York: Cambridge Univ. Press, 1995), 190.
[20] Garside, *Zwingli*, 40-42.
[21] Ibid., 44.
[22] Charles Garside, Jr., *The Origins of Calvin's Theology of Music: 1536-1543* (Philadelphia: American Philosophical Society, 1979), 22-23.
[23] Garside, *Origins*, 26.
[24] Garside, *Zwingli*, 147.
[25] Dyrness, *Reformed Theology*, 71.

aesthetics and how they were used, "a new way of imagining God and the world."[26]

The Reformation's Spread and Aftermath

This paradigm shift would manifest itself in a number of ways in Reformed communities across Europe and, eventually, in North America. What is just as important to note is that the shifts would continue to happen. Another thing that "everybody knows" about the Reformed position on aesthetics in worship proves difficult: there is not, nor has there ever been, any one Reformed position on art or aesthetics in worship.

It has already been mentioned that there were iconoclasts in Zurich even when Zwingli arrived there, before anyone in Geneva had heard of John Calvin. There have been iconoclasts as long as there has been art in worship, because, as long as there has been art in worship of any sort, there have been disagreements about how big or small a role it should play.[27] Indeed, there have been iconoclasts ever since the days of the prophet Amos, and probably before:

> Take away from me the noise of your songs; I will not listen to the melody of your harps. But let justice roll down like waters, and righteousness like an ever-flowing stream.[28]

The sixteenth-century Reformers did not create iconoclasm. They did, however, unleash quite a bit of it. In many places across the continent, in Lutheran as well as Reformed communities, iconoclasts took the work of the reformers, and their attempts to reshape the aesthetics of worship, as a mandate for wholesale removal of images and desecration of art, often driven primarily by secular forces in the community. In fact, Calvin and Zwingli, as well as Luther, were most often at work attempting to interpret the iconoclastic impulses toward something less destructive, to get these people to modify their agendas, to put a stop to the iconoclasm entirely, especially where it moved toward violence and riots.[29]

Zurich, as we have already mentioned, had a social justice agenda to its iconoclasm, delineating a Christian economic worldview, arguing that money should be spent on people before paraments, on food before

---

[26] Ibid., 91.
[27] Garside, *Zwingli*, 1-2.
[28] Amos 5:23-24, New Revised Standard Version.
[29] Wandel, *Voracious Idols*, 8.

sculpture. And, because the iconoclasts were active in Zurich before Zwingli, they most certainly had an effect on his thought.[30] Iconoclasts in Strasbourg destroyed not only statuary, windows, and paintings, but altars as well, drawing a direct connection to another part of the aesthetic—the liturgy—where the laity saw themselves as having been shut out. In Basel, the most profound incidents of iconoclasm took place February 9, 1529, in a set of riots that caught the attention of many across the Reformed world; participants sought to point up the fundamental division between lay and clergy and the separation of the laity from a life of piety that only the clergy seemed able to enjoy.[31]

Destruction of art was frowned on by the leaders of the Reformation, however, and the congregations of the Reformed tradition continued to seek ways to reconcile the needs of their communities to Zwinglian and Calvinist theology in this matter. In England, Thomas Cranmer grudgingly admitted that the bodily nature of Christ and the saints allowed images of them:

> I will not utterly deny but they may be had. Still for charity sakes they should be kept out of the church. For the goodness that may come from them is not comparable to the evil of idolatry. Why not lift your eyes and your hands to heaven where God is?[32]

Religious plays died out in England by the 1560s, but it seems to have been more an economic than a religious consideration that killed them. As religious plays and the accompanying celebrations grew more and more expensive, other priorities, such as care of the poor, simply made them impractical. In addition, moral problems and civic unrest around the plays and festivals led many communities to abandon them. While Elizabethan divines began to watch secular plays more closely, because of the clear appeal to the eye, their chief concern seems to have been to interpret the Sabbath and the seventh commandment more strictly: anything that promoted libidinous feelings or kept one from church was likely to be forbidden.[33] Religious plays would not have carried such

---

[30] "Before iconoclasm, Zwingli would not have known the 'beauty' of a whitewashed wall in a church: no Christian church presented such an 'image' to the eyes of its congregation....these white walls did not represent a transcendent aesthetic, but a realignment of the relation between the world of the flesh and the world of the spirit, a realignment that rejected the asceticism of the traditional religious as false and accepted the world of the laity as itself religious," Wandel, *Voracious Idols*, 194.

[31] Ibid., 190-91.

[32] Thomas Cranmer, *Catechism*, as quoted by Dyrness, *Reformed Theology*, 96-97.

[33] Dyrness, *Reformed Theology*, 119.

baggage with them. But, as religious drama faded, preaching became the primary performance venue in late sixteenth-century England, becoming more and more dramatic and employing more and more of the techniques of the theater.[34]

In Hungarian churches prior to the late seventeenth century, economic circumstances made it impossible to build new Reformed spaces and limited changes in formerly Roman Catholic spaces to whitewashing over frescoes and rearranging the furniture. In effect, the new aesthetic was superimposed upon the old. Pulpit and table hangings remained in use and continued to be created, with elaborate designs and religious symbols.[35] New wall paintings and wood carvings replaced the old frescoes they covered up.[36]

French and Dutch Calvinists, despite certain iconoclastic movements, continued to celebrate God in visual arts. Reformed consistories in France and the Netherlands allowed church-member artists to create work for Roman Catholic congregations that would not be allowed in Reformed churches.[37] In French sanctuaries, wall tablets with the Decalogue and sometimes the Lord's Prayer were a standard feature and might often include paintings of figures such as Moses, Joshua, and Aaron.[38] Bells were also a prominent part of these buildings,[39] as was elaborate art on the tokens that proved that one had attended a preparatory liturgy, and so admitted one to the Lord's Table.[40] In Dutch Reformed churches, painted altarpieces were replaced with boards on which the Decalogue and other scripture passages were written in decorative calligraphy. Paintings could be used in areas of the church outside of the sanctuary, and the sanctuary itself could have ornate choir screens, pulpits, and tombs. Any stained glass in the buildings that was not overtly Roman Catholic or liturgical

---

[34] Ibid., 120-21.
[35] George Starr, "Art and Architecture in the Hungarian Reformed Church," in Paul Corbin Finney, ed., *Seeing Beyond the Word: Visual Arts and the Calvinist Tradition* (Grand Rapids: Eerdmans, 1999), 303-304.
[36] Ibid., 306-09.
[37] Philip Benedict, "Calvinism as a Culture?" in Finney, *Seeing Beyond the Word*, 36.
[38] Raymond A. Mentzer, Jr., "The Reformed Churches of France and the Visual Arts," in Finney, *Seeing Beyond the Word*, 216-17.
[39] Mentzer, "Reformed Churches of France,"200. In Dutch church buildings, the bell towers, bells, and organs were often owned by the town, not the congregation.
[40] Ibid., 222-23.

was retained, and new commissions were made for stained glass with figurative scenes.[41]

Architecture began to shift as well. French Calvinists in the sixteenth and seventeenth centuries designed worship spaces to encourage hearing of the Word and participation by all in the liturgy; many of these sanctuaries were shaped as amphitheaters, with the table and pulpit central and pews arranged around the pulpit and table in concentric rings.[42] Netherlands congregations, including the Oude Kerk in Amsterdam, were arranged with provisions for the congregation to be seated at long tables in the sanctuary for celebrations of the Lord's Supper.[43]

The American Experience

When the Puritans moved to North America and settled in New England, they brought their literalism and their discomfort with metaphor or poetry in proclaiming the Word. They set up meeting houses in the center of their communities with clean, plain lines. Scripture itself was, for these Puritans, all the imaginative source they required.[44] But one of the leading first-generation New England Puritan divines, John Cotton, took a different approach to proclamation, allowing for mystery, poetry, and even the occasional play.[45] He enjoyed using imagery in his sermons such as streams, light, fountains, night giving way to morning; while explaining these abstractly, he would return continually to the image throughout the sermon.[46]

By the middle of the eighteenth century, when New England Puritanism was divided into deeply rationalist and more emotive pietist camps, Jonathan Edwards attempted to unify these streams. He sought to connect the believers' perception of beauty with the recognition of the activity of God in their lives. While Calvin allowed that painting and music were pleasurable but dangerous, Edwards moved beyond

---

[41] Ilja M. Veldman, "Protestantism and the Arts: Sixteenth and Seventeenth Century Netherlands," in Finney, *Seeing Beyond the Word*, 410-12.
[42] Mentzer, "Reformed Churches of France," 200-201, 212. In Geneva's Reformation Museum, there is a painting of the Huguenot Temple at Lyon that reflects this layout.
[43] Donald J. Bruggink, "A Brief History of Architecture of Reformed Churches in America," in James Hart Brumm, ed., *Liturgy among the Thorns: Essays on Worship in the Reformed Church in America*, Historical Series of the Reformed Church in America no. 57 (Grand Rapids: Eerdmans, 2008), 92-93.
[44] Dyrness, *Reformed Theology*, 165.
[45] Ibid., 180.
[46] Ibid., 178.

Calvin, insisting that the affections could work to draw people to God, since beauty pointed to God at work[47] (that last part being quite consistent with Calvin's thought). This comes on the heels of another shift in Reformed thought: the slowly growing acceptance of hymns in worship, following the theology of Isaac Watts, which, like Edwards, expanded upon that of John Calvin.[48]

The Great Awakenings brought a different shift in the aesthetic of Reformed worship—or, more precisely, exacerbated the earlier English trend toward preaching as performance. Preachers were touring from town to town, afternoon revivals were attracting large crowds, and this preaching emphasis, already strong in the Reformed tradition, became overwhelming. The primarily Zwinglian liturgy—a preaching service with an occasionally attached Eucharist—which was already prevalent among churches of the Reformed tradition in North America,[49] fed into this idea of the sermon as a main liturgical event. After the U.S. War for Independence, many New England Congregationalists—spiritual heirs of the Puritans—began to replace their meetinghouses with churches in the style of British architect Christopher Wren. This design oriented everything on an axis from main entrance to pulpit,[50] increasing the emphasis on the pulpit and de-emphasizing the table and font, matching the reduced emphasis on the sacraments.

By the late nineteenth century, similar changes had become prevalent in most American Protestant churches. They became auditorium-like spaces with a stage for a chancel and a choral gallery behind. While the furnishings had been focused toward the pulpit since Calvin's day, the emphasis on the pulpit was increased, and Communion tables and baptismal fonts became smaller and were often slid out of the way most of the time.[51] This auditorium type of arrangement has been carried over into the architecture favored by "contemporary worship" in the present day.

---

[47] Ibid., 274-79.
[48] Brumm, *Singing the Lord's Song*, 17-21. By exegeting the phrase "psalms, hymns, and spiritual songs" from Colossians 3:16 more broadly than Calvin did, Watts created an argument that opened the door for scripture-based hymns in worship that were not necessarily metrical scripture.
[49] Howard G. Hageman, *Pulpit and Table: Some Chapters in the History of Worship in Reformed Churches* (Richmond: John Knox, 1962), 33.
[50] Gretchen Townsend Bugglein, "Elegance and Sensibility in the Calvinist Tradition," in Finney, *Seeing Beyond the Word*, 437-38.
[51] Donald J. Bruggink, "Liturgy and Architecture" in Garrett C. Roorda, ed., *Companion to the Liturgy: a Guide to Worship in the Reformed Church in America* (New York: Half Moon Press, 1971), 61-62.

Nineteenth-century Romanticism produced, in some quarters, a reaction to Revivalism's de-emphasis on liturgy and art. The Oxford Movement, which began in the 1830s in England, led to split chancels with antiphonal choirs and Communion tables pushed against back walls to resemble high altars.[52] Antependia, sometimes in liturgical colors, became more prevalent, candlesticks and crosses began to adorn chancels, and ministers began to wear stoles, all of which seemed to wander into churches of the Reformed tradition without a lot of critical examination.[53] With this, two streams had formed: one leaning toward Oxford and another toward the revivalists.

This was reinforced by a Reformed liturgical theology that developed around concerns similar to the Oxford Movement and led by two scholars—Phillip Schaff and John Williamson Nevin—teaching at the German Reformed seminary in Mercersburg, Pennsylvania. Both of them saw the profound teaching power of mystery and poetry to convey the Word of God:

> Next to the Word of God, which stands in unapproachable majesty far above all human creeds and confessions, fathers and reformers, popes and councils, there are no religious books of greater practical importance than catechisms. Hymn books, and liturgies. They shape the moral and religious sentiments in early youth; they feed the devotions in old age; they are the faithful companions of the most solemn hours in the house of God, around the family altar and in the silent closet; they give utterance to the deepest emotions, the purest thoughts, the highest aspirations; they urge to duty and every good work; they comfort in affliction, and point to heaven at the approach of death.[54]

This position argues that Christians learn about God through nondidactic means, through the poetry, structure, and even mystery of liturgy, just as much as they do through teaching. It harks back to Calvin's thoughts about the Lord's Supper as a companion to the Word preached; it is a new argument for a Reformed aesthetic that is

---

[52] Bruggink, "Liturgy and Architecture," 62-63.
[53] Charles W. Krahe, Jr., "Liturgy and Ceremonial," in Roorda, *Companion to the Liturgy*, 53-56.
[54] John Williamson Nevin, "The New Liturgy," *Mercersburg Review*, vol. 10 (1858): 199.

not entirely stark and simple but that is Word-driven. For Nevin and Schaff, proclamation involves both speech and action.

> Some liturgical forms, in this view, have immense educational worth. It is of vast account to have the mind stored from the beginning with the wholesome words of sound doctrine and right religious feeling, even where the sense of them may not be at first properly perceived or duly laid to heart. Especially important is it, we may say, that such preoccupation of the mind should be secured in the way of forms which utter and act forth, not simply the knowledge of religion, but its actual power and life—the faith of the Church in this manner going before the faith of her infants and children, her novices and catechumens, and struggling to form itself in them as the hope of glory.
>
> "As an eagle stirreth up her nest, fluttereth over her young, spreadeth abroad her wings, taketh them, beareth them on her wings," so doth this holy mother of us all fulfil [sic] here her sublime office of winning the fledglings of baptismal grace to a true heavenward flight. There is no teaching in religion like this *in-forming* process, which puts into the soul, with divine authority, the outward word of religion, in order to make room for the coming of the same word in its inward power and glory. If it may be said with truth that the familiar songs and ballads of the nation are of more power for the character of it than its laws, there is still room to affirm of these established forms of Christian belief and worship, that they go far beyond all other modes of culture in determining what turns out to be at last the actual institution of nominally Christian men. Catechisms for the young, in this way, are of more account than systems of theology for the old. Hymns are perpetual sermons. Texts of Scripture stick in the mind like proverbs, enforce their own lessons, where all commentaries are dumb and forgotten. What a world of education is comprehended, in this way, in the articles of the Creed, and the petitions of the Lord's Prayer. Do *they* lose their force by repetition? Are *they* formal, because they are familiar? Would it be an improvement to have them continually in new paraphrases and versions, or to have them superseded altogether by free effusions extemporized for the same purpose and use? There is irony, as all can at once feel, in the very question. These simple formularies are powerful for the purposes of devotion and faith, just because they echo

> in the same words always, from childhood to old age, and from one century onward to another, which has been the worship of the one Catholic Church through all times. And why should we not learn from this the importance of uniform liturgical services generally, for the best kind of religious training, that namely which casts the mind, from the beginning, into the very mould of the "things which are most surely believed" among Christians, and stamps at the same time with their ineffaceable image and superscription? A good Liturgy is an organ of religious education, more efficient than a good Catechism or a good Confession of Faith. It reaches farther and works deeper. The Prayer Book of the Church of England has more to do with her theological spirit than the Thirty-Nine Articles. Every Church needs such help in her prophetical office, even if she might afford to undervalue it in her priestly office. Without it, her educational apparatus, at best, can never be more than half complete.[55]

Nevin and Schaff, in advocating their liturgical reforms, were not afraid to make their readers think in poetic terms and to insist that this, rather than dry rationalism, is the natural state of Christianity:

> A sacrament is the presence of the supernatural, in a mystery, under a natural and sensible form. Christianity in this way has its central significance for faith in the Lord's Supper, the sacrament of Christ's body and blood; and around this, accordingly, the worship of the church has revolved from the beginning.[56]

In the end, the Mercersburg theology had limited immediate influence, inside the German Reformed Church as well as outside. There were various small liturgical experiments that appeared in North America and Scotland during the final decades of the nineteenth century, and the changes in furnishings proved to be rather popular among certain congregations, as noted above.[57]

One of those experiments was the ongoing attempt at liturgical revision in the Reformed Church in America, which resulted in a liturgy that was proposed in 1873 but never adopted. Among the Mercersburg-type aesthetics included in this liturgy was a lectionary that included

---

[55] John Williamson Nevin, *The Liturgical Question with Reference to the Provisional Liturgy of the German Reformed Church: a Report by the "Liturgical Committee"* (Philadelphia: Lindsay & Blakiston, 1862), 11-13.

[56] Nevin, *Liturgical Question*, 24.

[57] Hageman, *Pulpit and Table*, 97-100.

a liturgical calendar: four weeks of before-Christmas and up to eight weeks of after-Christmas, along with a celebration of the circumcision of Jesus on January 1, and nine Sundays before Easter, Good Friday, five Sundays after Easter, Ascension Day, the Sunday before Pentecost, and twenty-eight Sundays after Pentecost.[58] The committee that created this proposal reported its reasoning to the General Synod of 1871, arguing that nonverbal items, such as the rhythm and flow of worship and the active participation of the people, are essentially Reformed:

> They deem it important, in view of the growing opinion in the minds of many Ministers and Elders, that the true idea of worship, requires a more full expression on the part of the people of their devotional feelings than is presently afforded them. Many consider it also desirable, that it be made more obvious not merely that the Gospel minister is not by virtue of his office a Priest, but that the people themselves are a royal Priesthood, with all the power and privilege of prayer.
>
> "It is also supposed that if the people take a more active part in the worship of the Sanctuary, a happy influence will be exerted, especially upon the young, by enlisting their personal influence in the services....
>
> Our historical position is without a doubt that of a *Reformed* Presbyterian and *Liturgical* Church! neither [sic] falling into the formality of Episcopacy nor into the baldness of Puritanism. So we have stood for two centuries, and so we stand today. *The Evangelical Presbyterian and Liturgical Church*....
>
> Your Committee, therefore, hope to be able to present it to the Churches [sic] in a form which will so commend it to the piety and wisdom of the Church, that its increasing use will place us before the world in our true historic position as a *spiritual Liturgical and Reformed Church*.[59]

Finally, the committee made arguments from Article 67 of the Articles of Dort for the need for nonverbal, poetic, liturgical proclamation of the Word:

---

[58] *The Liturgy of the Reformed Church in America as reported to the General Synod of 1873, by the Committee on Revision* (New York: Board of Publication of the Reformed Church in America, 1873), 7-8.

[59] *Acts and Proceedings of the General Synod of the Reformed Church in America*, 1871, 281-83.

> This article bears witness to the ancient usage of our Church. The evident design of that usage was to bring into devout remembrance, year after year, the vital facts of the Advent, Death, and Resurrection of Our Blessed Lord [sic], and of the Mission of the Holy Comforter. Thereto this Order of Scripture Lessons is adjusted, with the hope that if any, in the exercise of Christian liberty, shall use it, such use may be found to edification.[60]

But it would be the mid-twentieth century liturgical movement that would finally help basic Mercersburg principles come into the life of most North American Reformed congregations.[61]

The Modern (and Post-modern) Era

In 1902, French Calvin scholar Émile Doumergue gave a series of lectures in the Salle de la Réformation in Geneva—the former home of John Knox's church in exile and teaching center for Calvin's Genevan academy—entitled *L'art et le sentiment dans l'oeuvre de Calvin* ("Art and Emotion in the Works of Calvin"). He argued against the image of Calvinism as anti-art by employing what he called "the protestant method, which consists of putting listeners in the situation where they can decide for themselves against error and in favor of the truth."[62] Doumergue was joined by no less a Calvinist than Abraham Kuyper in arguing for a romantic idealist interpretation of artworks as manifestations of a "larger guiding spirit."[63] There was growing pressure for more symbolism, more aesthetic, in every aspect of Reformed worship. Howard Hageman saw it as an interest fueled by changing understandings of the psychology of worship (a term which no one would have considered seriously before the twentieth century):

> No impartial observer can deny that the fascination with the psychology of worship was historically a terrible revenge, especially in the Reformed churches, on a way of worship which had blithely ignored the congregation for centuries, leaving them to sit in motionless silence listening to one man do everything. Nor would anyone in his right mind want to surrender the real

---

[60] *Liturgy... 1873*, 6. Ironically, while this liturgy was never formally adopted, it was distributed to every congregation in the RCA.

[61] Christopher Dorn, "The Liturgy for the Lord's Day and the Lord's Supper: Critical Turning Points," in Brumm, *Liturgy among the Thorns*, 36 ff.

[62] Philip Benedict, "Calvinism as a Culture?" in Finney, *Seeing Beyond the Word*, 21.

[63] Ibid., 23.

gains which the psychology of worship won for us. But we can lament the fact that in so many instances the first impulse to alter the traditional way of worship in the Reformed churches came from a psychology that had little or no theological orientation.[64]

This may well be a more eloquent way of describing what Charles Krahe, Jr., observed about these unexamined shifts in how worship occurred:

> If Reformed worship were to have any outward beauty at all, it should be the "beauty of holiness" (Psalm 96:9) shining from the faces of the members of the assembly. If it were to have any form or comeliness, it should be no other than, "He has commanded in His Word" (H.S. 96). If it were to have any rubrics at all, it should find them in the admonition of Paul (I Cor. 14:50), "Let all things be done decently and in order."
>
> With the dissolution of older traditions here in America, however, we find many departures from these basic principles in conservative as well as liberal circles. Some have been attracted to the informality of neighboring groups and have substituted that for the simplicity of the old. They are not the same. Simple Calvinistic worship was filled with the kind of formality that surely is appropriate when people enter into the presence of their King.
>
> Others have borrowed from churches with another liturgical tradition, much ecclesiastical furniture, and millinery designed to improve upon the "barrenness" of the old Reformed service. In doing so, they often adopted things that are out of place in our circles completely and instituted ceremonies and practices which are meaningless and even a bit ridiculous.[65]

Even so, for all of this unintentional, unexamined drifting into new liturgical styles and aesthetics, Karl Barth gave a new perspective to how art and proclamation fit together in Reformed theology:

> ...the Christian worship in which our own exposition and application of Holy Scripture is most solemnly expressed usually takes place not freely or in a neutral place, but in a "church"

---

[64] Hageman, *Pulpit and Table*, 99.
[65] "Liturgy and Ceremonial," in Roorda, *Companion to the Liturgy*, 51-52. "H.C. 96" refers to question and answer number 96 in the Heidelberg Catechism.

which even by its architecture and furnishings more or less directly and faithfully reminds those who gather in it, including the one who speaks, of their "confessional position." Even if it is mainly a witness to the helplessness of the 19th century the "Church" confronts us with Church history. And what happens in it happens not only in the presence of God and His angels, not only in the presence of the departed spirits of the past, but also—with whatever freedom and responsibility—in the presence of the confession, by which in strength or weakness, in loyalty or apostasy, our "Church" is the particular "Church." In the same way our hymn-book which, good or bad, is always used in worship, confronts us with our Church history. Together with the text of the Bible our own exposition and application of the word of the Church's praise is a third trigonometrical point, and at varying distance behind it there always stands the Church's confession. Finally, even the order of worship can more or less definitely play the same role.[66]

There was also an ecumenical impetus, clear by the post-World War II era, toward revival in worship, and that was bringing pressure to bear on Reformed churches to re-examine their worship life. Already in 1927, at the first Faith and Order Conference in Lausanne, and again in 1937, at the second conference in Edinburgh, the subject of the vitality of sacramental life in all our congregations was receiving renewed scrutiny. When the Faith and Order Commission published *Ways of Worship* in 1951,[67] Gerardus van der Leeuw, former professor of the history of religion at the University of Groningen and later minister of education and cultural affairs in the Netherlands, prepared a paper for that volume discussing the challenge that renewal of sacramental life presented to the Reformed churches: they must unite Word and sacrament in worship, much as Calvin had conceived four centuries earlier. Further, the Reformed tradition had to move away from an almost exclusive focus on the death of Christ in celebrating the Supper in order to give greater attention to the celebration of resurrection in the same meal. Richard Paquier and *Eglise et Liturgie*, a group of Swiss

---

[66] Karl Barth, tran., G.T. Thomson and Harold Knight, *Church Dogmatics, vol. 1, The Doctrine of the Word of God, part 2* (Edinburgh: T & T Clark, 1956), 651.

[67] Pehr Edwall, Ereic Hayman, and William D. Maxwell, eds., *Ways of Worship: the Report of the Theological Commission on Faith and Order* (London: SCM Press).

Reformed pastors and laity, called for ecumenical renewal of the church and liturgical reform, following in the footsteps of Mercersburg, based on studies of the early church.[68]

In 1950, the General Synod of the Reformed Church in America appointed a standing Commission on the Revision of the Liturgy, whose work would be culminated in *Liturgy and Psalms* in 1968. The first major report of that commission, in 1955, produced powerful responses, but these had the laudable effect of producing some of the first denomination-wide discussions of how and why we worship. Because the commission was being influenced heavily by the ecumenical discussions, by Barth, and by Mercersburg, not all of the responses were immediately enthusiastic:

> ...let us not confuse our study of the Liturgy by raising the question of how Episcopalians or Baptists do it, but rather let us ask ourselves how the Church services in the Reformed Church became what they are today, what they were in the past and how we may improve them in the present. Since we still confess to believe in One Holy Catholic Church which has existed throughout all ages, we ought to inquire with great care concerning the structure of congregational worship in the past....
>
> No one, of course, desires to elevate the Reformers to a sort of Protestant sainthood, but we certainly cannot ignore them. I personally doubt that the Reformed Church in America suffers from an overdose of historical consciousness. It seems to me that we suffer far more from the ills of liberalism, congregationalism, fundamentalism, and individualism. If we are truly a Reformed Church, we ought to pay at least a little attention to what our forefathers tried to give us in their liturgies. The more we steep ourselves in a study of our historical origin, the more we shall become convinced that the Reformers came to their views by intently listening to the voice of Holy Writ.[69]

In an article entitled, "Shall We Approve the Revised Liturgy?"[70] Bert Van Soest, Morris Folkert, and Arthur Johnson advocate spending more time on revising the liturgy and call for more attention to the

---

[68] Dorn, "Liturgy for the Lord's Day," 37-39.
[69] James C. Eelman, "Our Liturgical Heritage: Some Comments on the Revised Liturgy," *Church Herald* 13, no. 8 (February 24, 1956): 8.
[70] *Church Herald* 13, no. 9 (March 2, 1956): 11, 20.

original sin of the worshipers and humanity's need for grace in several places in the book. By April, in the article "Straining Out a Gnat," Gordon Girod was presenting arguments for classes to reject the version:

> On the matter of practice, the Reformed Church now stands at a fork in the road. Either we will, or we will not be a more liturgical church. Let us face this fact honestly. Perhaps the majority of the Reformed Churches do favor a more liturgical mode of worship. That is what they will have in following the new liturgy. But those who favor the present simplicity and freedom of the present order of worship should also be advised of what the Revised Liturgy will mean for them.[71]

After the 1955 proposal was rejected, James C. Eelman discussed the need for the church to continue learning and discussing even as the commission continued its work: "A better understanding of what we believe and confess will greatly simplify the work of any committee on the Revision of our Liturgy."[72] The self-examination certainly continued.

> It is evident from the result of their work that the committee members kept the words of the famous Dutch liturgist Van de Leeuw in mind: "Liturgy is not something to be prepared and made by man, as a scientific textbook, or even as a novel or a poem is made. The Church is a living body and its liturgical forms are an expression of its life. Liturgical renewal is neither emendation nor creation, but an attempt to enter, or re-enter the liturgy which has been alive ever since the first liturgy of the Upper Room."[73]
>
> We (the commission) honestly believe that in every revision suggested we have been true to our heritage and anxious to make this Liturgy a living expression of the faith of our people. Only time and faithful use in the spirit of being true to our Reformed heritage while providing for our day and generation will ultimately determine the value of the committee's work. What is submitted are not *new* but *revised* forms which aim at giving

---

[71] Gordon Girod, "Straining Out a Gnat: More Thoughts on the Revised Liturgy," *Church Herald* 13, no. 6 (April 20, 1956): 22.
[72] "Where Do We Go From Here? Some Thoughts on Our Liturgical and Theological Needs," *Church Herald* 13, no. 37 (September 28, 1956): 13.
[73] Jan W. Falkenburg, "An Order of Service for Sunday Morning," *Church Herald* 14, no. 3 (January 18, 1957): 12.

the church a living, relevant, and usable Liturgy that will express the unity and faith of our people in being a confessing Church of Jesus Christ.[74]

The Constitution of the Reformed Church...requires that the Order of Worship used by each church shall be "in accordance with the Liturgy." We are given the freedom to add but not to subtract. This being the case, ought we not to be concerned about the orders listed in our new revision? Seven orders are given in all....even the simplest order given is more liturgical than what is commonly used in a large number of our churches. If we are to take our constitution seriously, which I feel we must or risk disintegration as a denomination, then these forms should give a minimum order which is common to all and allow further additions according to the discretions of each consistory.[75]

All of this is preparatory to noting the view of the sacraments that is taken in the proposed revised liturgy. I believe it is quite clearly that of *sacramental efficacy*, that sacraments *do* confer the grace which they signify. The theology of this liturgy is obviously that of the Belgic Confession, that the signs and the things signified are bound together....

Do we believe that the New Testament places the emphasis *upon the sacraments or upon confession* as the means of our reception into the body of Christ?[76]

The committee has greatly improved on the didactical form for baptism. But I am not clear as to the meaning in the Baptismal Prayer that God will "bless with Thy Word and Spirit the water of this sacrament." Certainly we do not believe in the efficacy of holy water. What do we want our people to understand by these words?

The baptism into membership in the Holy Catholic Church is a most worthy emphasis. It is true to our doctrines and is in accord with our ecumenical faith.[77]

The prayer asks God to "bless with his Word and Spirit the Water of this Sacrament"....In 1958 we were taught to ask to

---

[74] Gerritt T. Vander Lugt, "Liturgy Means the Work of the People," *Church Herald* 15, no. 46 (November 28, 1958): 12.

[75] Garrett A. Wilterdink, "Some Suggestions for Our Revised Liturgy," *Church Herald* 16, no. 16 (April 17, 1959): 5

[76] Garrett A. Wilterdink, "Some Comments on the Proposed Revised Liturgy," *Church Herald* 21, no. 7 (February 14, 1964): 23-24.

[77] LeRoy C. Brandt, "Some Comments on the Proposed Revised Liturgy," *Church Herald* 21, no. 9 (February 28, 1964): 22.

"bless this child"....I find the change inexplicable. Water is but the material element of the sacrament. The sacrament itself, which included the word as well as the material element, is the means of grace....

In both the 1958 and the 1963 revisions there is a permissive declaration that "this child is now received into the membership of the Holy Catholic Church." Not only is this contrary to reformed theology, which views the child as a member of the covenant community by birth, but to the liturgy itself, which asks the parents whether they acknowledge that their child is "numbered among his people."[78]

These concerns address repeatedly the issues of simplicity over against symbolism and meaning in structure, as if the two cannot coexist, and the issue of mystery, especially in the sacraments. Portions of the denomination were clearly uncomfortable with the idea that God might be working literally in these elements—despite the consistency with Calvin—in ways that we cannot entirely see but that are more than symbolic. This is an artistic, poetic aesthetic with which the Reformed Church was struggling.

The denomination struggled, but the revised liturgies were ultimately approved, and they were published in 1968. Increased interest in the sacraments resulted in the increased prominence of pulpit, font, and table in sanctuary architecture.[79] Fortunately, some discussions of worship and aesthetic continued. Arie Brouwer believed that the new liturgy should simply be a beginning:

> But perhaps more serious still is the sheer, utter, total foreignness of the content of our worship. The language is that of Zion, but we live in Babylon. The frame of reference is otherworldly, but we live in this world—and if we depended for our salvation on the way we worship, we should never see another.
>
> But our worship is after all primarily an activity of the Holy Spirit. It is he [sic] who moves us to offer ourselves to God. And therein lies our hope. The contemporary growing awareness of

---

[78] Raymond Van Heukelom, "Some Comments on the Proposed Revised Liturgy," *Church Herald* 21, no. 10 (March 6, 1964): 10.

[79] Bruggink, "A Brief History," 95-96. See also Donald J. Bruggink and Carl H. Droppers, *Christ and Architecture: Building Presbyterian/Reformed Churches* (Grand Rapids: Eerdmans, 1965) and Bruggink and Droppers, *When Faith Takes Form* (Grand Rapids: Eerdmans, 1971).

the Holy Spirit has also penetrated the movement for liturgical renewal. The consequence has been an increasing dissatisfaction with a strictly historical approach to liturgical revision. There is an increasing awareness that liturgical renewal will come only as we have faith in the liturgical creativity of the Holy Spirit.

This then must be the next step in our movement toward liturgical renewal. The Committee on Revision of the Liturgy has done yeoman's service. But let us not fail to hear the admonition it has continually held before the church: that liturgical renewal is a process.[80]

In other quarters, conversations grew up around what seemed to be primarily utilitarian ends. George Brown reported on one congregation's experience:

It all started with a classical youth workshop in the fall of 1969. The young people in the workshop were particularly interested in making worship more meaningful. Some expressed frustration with the lack of openness among adults in their churches and their unwillingness to explore new ways of worshipping. As the discussion continued, the Rev. Lynne Joosten, Secretary for Youth Life, suggested some ways to help make worship more meaningful.

The handful of young people from the Pottersville Reformed Church who attended the workshop were excited. On the way home they talked about what *they* could do. A direct outcome was the decision of the youth group to plan a special worship service to take place around Thanksgiving.

The members of the congregation who entered the church's "Community House" the Sunday evening before Thanksgiving found chairs gathered in a circle around a simple table, set with a cup and a loaf of bread. Light from a single fixture over the table created a mystical aura in the room. Readers presented Brian Frost's "Bread is Made for Laughter." The old, familiar Thanksgiving hymns seemed fresh and new when sung to guitar accompaniment. The prayers were the prayers of the people, with individuals sharing items of concern found in local newspapers and then praying silently for each concern.

---

[80] Arie R. Brouwer, "The Liturgy Is In," *Church Herald* 32, no. 46 (November 15, 1968): 8. Brouwer was then secretary for program for the Reformed Church in America.

> Because this service was different from the kind of worship services usually experienced by the congregation, the young people were apprehensive about the way the adults might respond. But the appreciative remarks by those attending soon dispelled this feeling. And the young people began to gain confidence in their ideas about worship.
>
> It might be said that the stage was set for education in worship.[81]

Brown begins by talking about the value of having more active participation in the liturgy, but ends up discussing liturgy as an educational tool. In a report on a survey taken by the Commission on Christian Worship in 1975, Arlen Salthouse mentioned choirs, guitars and other instruments in addition to organ and piano, banners and changing liturgical colors, liturgical drama, and even liturgical dance.[82] All of these added different arts and aesthetics to congregational worship but seemed also to be driven by the desire to allow a larger percentage of the congregation to participate. In another *Church Herald* article, just a few months later,[83] Richard Cole wrote about the value of drama in worship in terms of reclaiming its medieval teaching function and increasing participation in worship leadership. In his final book, *The Divine Formula*, Erik Routley described worship as a "team sport" requiring "crowd control," and advocates an exegesis of 1 Corinthians 14 to support his point:

> The ideal meeting, says Paul, is one to which every member has brought something—an experience, an explanation, a song, or whatever it is (oh, well, even a 'tongue', one hears him saying, leaning over backwards not to sound over-severe); and where when you have brought it...you don't insist on sharing it unless it really will be a help to the community.[84]

---

[81] George Brown, Jr., "Worship: the Work of the People," *Church Herald* 27, no. 30 (August 28, 1970): 19. Brown was pastor of the Pottersville church and a graduate student in religious education at Princeton Seminary at the time the article was written.

[82] Arlen R. Salthouse, "Worship in the RCA," *Church Herald* 33, no. 16 (August 6, 1976): 23.

[83] Richard Cole, "Why Drama in the Church?" *Church Herald* 22, no. 25 (December 10, 1976): 12-13.

[84] *The Divine Formula: a Book for Worshipers, Preachers, and Musicians, and All Who Celebrate the Mysteries* (Princeton: Prestige, 1986), 87. Notice how the very Reformed Routley is openly discussing the idea of worship as celebrating mysteries.

Routley moves on to another utilitarian reason for the building up of aesthetic, art as an attracting and binding social force.

> It is perfectly clear that the modern interest in liturgical forms on the part of the heirs of the puritan traditions is the product of modern social conditions. If a church is no longer a family, if people now always move from place to place (and ministers as well), if no church expects to bury the same people they once baptized, the 'family' image breaks down—and indeed where people try to preserve it it survives only in a rather oppressive kind of possessiveness—the lamentation that 'all our young people leave us', or the tiresome insistence that only people who have been in the same church for twenty years or so qualify for a call to eldership. What has happened is simply the removal of that assurance that you knew what people were bringing with them that supplied in the 'free' worship of other days what the removal of liturgy had taken away.[85]

This reasoning was later echoed by Leonard Sweet, as noted here by Paul Janssen:

> Whether you like him or not, one of the leading influences on the direction of worship in the Reformed Church in America is the Reverend Dr. Leonard Sweet....Sweet specifically calls the church to develop practices that have an epic shape about them. Commenting on the popularity of the television show "Who Wants to Be a Millionaire?" Sweet claims that it was successful because it "made the transition from rational to Experiential, from representative to Participative, from word-based to Image-based, from individual to Connected. In other words, it is EPIC programming. The recovery of Christianity in the next millennium is likely to be based on whether or not the church can carve (not cast) its ministries into more EPIC shape.[86]

The result of this ferment is that an entirely new view of the arts and aesthetics is growing up. It is witnessed by the creation, within the Christian Reformed Church in North America, of the magazine *Reformed Worship*, started by Emily Brink, and the Calvin Institute for Christian Worship, founded by John Witvliet.

[85] Routley, *Divine Formula*, 103.
[86] Paul Janssen, "Worship among the Thorns: Observations from the 2004 Survey on Worship," in Brumm, *Liturgy among the Thorns*, 192-93.

> "Full, conscious, and active" participation is growing in many Reformed congregations, not as the result of denominational directives, as in the Roman Catholic Church, but through the broader and deeper cultural influences and theological reflection at work in virtually all Christian communions, and especially from the "Praise & Worship" approach to worship leadership. In contrast to current Roman Catholic practice, however, too often in Reformed churches the musicians are front and center, and the danger of performing for the congregation rather than enabling them to sing is much greater.[87]

Again we have a utilitarian approach to aesthetic: arts, poetry, and architecture are all good for increasing participation. Taken by itself, this approach could almost be seen as an inappropriate reversal of Calvin's utility, for while it focuses attention upon the congregation instead of the artist, it is still not using art to focus our hearts upon God. Fortunately, this is not the entire theology for those who have thought it out.

> Kierkegaard supposedly claims that God is the audience (in worship), the worshipers are the actors, and the minister is the prompter....
>
> *Is* God properly relegated to the audience? Most definitely not. The Reformed tradition has long talked of worship as a meeting between God and the people of God. We may have been one-sided on the proclamation side, letting the minister act for both God and the people and limiting the congregation to the role of hearers of the Word. But we should not now go to the other extreme and consider God a guest in our midst. I am actually beginning to hear that language—talk of inviting God to come to *our* worship. The Call to Worship becomes our call to each other, at a human level, and the Invocation a request for God to join us.
>
> Who is host? We or God? Here the psalms help us remember that it is we who enter God's presence. We don't need to invite God; we need to know how to come before him. God calls us to worship. "Let us come before him" (Ps. 95), "come before him with joyful songs....Enter his gates with thanksgiving" (Ps. 100).

---

[87] Emily Brink and John Witvliet, "Music in Reformed Churches Worldwide," in Lukas Vischer, *Christian Worship in Reformed Churches Past and Present* (Grand Rapids: Eerdmans, 2003), 336.

God dwells with his people. We come in response to God's call to us. The simple children's song has it right: "Come into his presence singing Alleluia."

So let's not be so eager to relegate God to a passive role. We do need to become active in bringing our worship to the Lord. Worship leaders do need to learn more about their prompting role. But we've carried Kierkegaard's analogy too far if God becomes our audience. In Scripture, sermon, and sacrament, God is active.[88]

Conclusion: Toward a Theology of Aesthetics in Reformed Worship

> The alternative to the misuse of visible symbols is neither to reject them nor to consider them as ends in themselves, but to use them properly as a means to worship.[89]

It is tempting to stop right there, because that might be, if not a theology of aesthetics, a good guideline for the use of aesthetic elements—be they visual art, music, performance, or structure—in Reformed worship. What we have seen in our brief tour that what our common knowledge always told us was true was not entirely so: Calvin and Zwingli and the Reformed founders were not opposed to aesthetics as much as they were trying to improve the focus and use of aesthetics in worship. Neither is the movement of the last few decades—an increased use of various visual and performing arts and an increased emphasis on structure and symbol in addition to the proclamation of the Word in worship—a denial of Reformed roots. On the other hand, it may be worse than a considered denial, since much of this shift has happened without serious examination, and even more has happened for utilitarian reasons focused more on filling pews than on pointing hearts and minds to God.

But there is another piece to all of this that Calvin hints at but never entirely fleshes out; that is, art for the purpose of delighting in God's creation, because God delights in creation. Calvin himself said that beauty—and by extension structure—have a place that is "not only for necessity." As Gregg Mast insisted ten years ago:

> It was Calvin who tied the external to the internal through the work of the Spirit. It was he who reminded us that God

---

[88] Emily R. Brink, "Who's the Host?" in *Reformed Worship* 33 (Fall, 1994): 2.
[89] John W. deGruchy, *Liberating Art from Theology: A South African Contribution to the Ecumenical Debate* (Grand Rapids: Eerdmans, 1991), 101-102.

accommodated our flesh and blood through using holy symbols and holier actions. But it was also Calvin who described a God who "stooped" to our humanness, who condescended to our place in the universe. It seems to me, therefore, that if we are to move forward in our quest to worship God with our souls and minds and bodies—our whole being—there needs to be more affirmation of the first means of grace, the elegant book which contains the goodness and beauty of creation. If the beauty is to be a window into God's presence rather than a wall to block it, we need a new perspective.

This perspective will not only affirm that God is the source of the beauty and goodness of creation, but also that God can be seen and experienced in the good and the beautiful. Although such an experience can offer us a glimpse of the Creator (and at its most elegant moments, even invite us to come near), it remains the role of the Word to bring us into the saving knowledge of God's grace. This acknowledgment of the Word's critical role, however, should not cause us to ignore the elegant book before us.[90]

Mast calls for a balancing act, and so does deGruchy, and so does Calvin. It is arguable that, as long as we are not paying attention to the art at God's expense, or saying, "Look at what that artist did," in worship—any more than we would say, "Look at what that electrician did," as we enjoy the ambiance of our living room or, "Listen to what the second chair cellist did," when listening to a symphonic piece that is not a cello concerto—we can use all sorts of arts.

It is also helpful to remember the lesson of the Pottersville church youth, mentioned above. It is possible to create an aesthetic for worship that is appropriate to the proclamation of the Word and different from what the congregation normally does without making the liturgy more complicated. Simplicity and a rich, varied aesthetic are not antithetical to each other.

Finally, art can serve the proclamation of the Word and point to God while still being enjoyable. Calvin talked about music moving our hearts and minds; drama can do the same, helping us imagine the good news in new ways, as can visual arts. Simple changes of colors, simple movements from table to font to pulpit, careful juxtapositions of prayers and songs all can help us grow in our understanding of God

---

[90] Gregg Mast, "An Elegant Book," *Reformed Review* 52, no. 3 (Spring, 1999): 285-86.

and God's creation and our place in it.

The most important rule is to remember what we are here for, to remember that we are creatures of both mind and heart, of both Spirit and flesh. If the art and the symbol overwhelm the Word, then we are have lost our way. However, we are just as far from God's intention for us if we are completely didactic, completely rational, and have lost our awareness of the mystery of a God who chooses to work through water, bread, and cup that are not in themselves holy but through which holiness is conveyed to us. All of this will be easier for us if, in our diligence to think through what we are doing, we do not over-think. Let us not worry too much about having all the answers, but remember the words of Isaac Watts:

> Where reason fails with all her powers,
> there faith prevails, and love adores.[91]

This sort of an aesthetic is much more work than plain-old "common knowledge," but it should bring us—and God—much more delight.

---

[91] Isaac Watts, "We Give Immortal Praise," in Erik Routley, ed., *Rejoice in the Lord: A Hymn Companion to the Scriptures* (Grand Rapids: Eerdmans, 1985), Hymn 624.

CHAPTER 12

Calvin on the Atonement: A Reexamination

I. John Hesselink

Preface

I am delighted and honored by the invitation to contribute to this festschrift for my old friend, Donald Bruggink. I may well have known our honoree longer than any other contributor to this volume except Gene Heideman. I first met Don when he came to Central College in Pella, Iowa, in 1947. I was a sophomore at that time. We soon discovered that we had many common interests and were both involved in activities as diverse as forensics (debate), campus Christian organizations, and later the United World Federalists!

The editor of this volume informs me that before Don assumed the chair in church history at Western Seminary he taught systematic theology briefly and was greatly influenced by Paul Van Buren's Basel dissertation, *Christ in Our Place: The Substitutionary Character of Calvin's Doctrine of Reconciliation*.[1] Hence it was proposed to me that I write an essay on the atonement in Calvin's theology. This has been a special interest of mine ever since we studied this subject with the late Professor

---

[1] (Edinburgh: Oliver and Boyd, 1957.) Karl Barth was Van Buren's advisor.

Eugene Osterhaven,[2] but, in all my writings on Calvin's theology, I have never written on this subject before. Thus, this modest, maiden effort.

Introduction

Until fairly recently, studies of Calvin's Christology and, more particularly, his view of the atonement[3] have been few. Two studies of Calvin's Christology appeared in the 1930s, one by the French pastor, Max Dominice, *L'humanité de Jesus d'après Calvin* (1933), the other by the Dutch scholar E. Emmen, *De Christologie van Calvin* (1935), but neither treats the atonement. The same is true of two studies of Calvin's Christology in English that appeared in the same year (1966), viz., *Calvin's Catholic Christology* by E. David Willis,[4] and Marvin P. Hoogland's Th.D. dissertation at the Free University in Amsterdam, *Calvin's Perspective on the Exaltation of Christ in Comparison with the Post-Reformation Doctrine of the Two States*.

However, something of a breakthrough occurred in 1956 with the appearance of a slight work by the Dutch-American Presbyterian theologian John F. Jansen, *Calvin's Doctrine of the Work of Christ*.[5]

[2] One of the books we read in this connection was *Why the Cross?* by H.E. Guillabaud (London: Inter-Varsity, 1937/1950). It reflects Calvin's view, but there are no references to Calvin in this book.

[3] It is interesting that the word "atonement" is a special English term for which there is no precise equivalent in Dutch or German. The Dutch *verzoening* and the German, which is very similar, *Versöhnung*, are usually translated as "reconciliation." The editor's preface to the first part volume of *The Doctrine of Reconciliation* IV.1 of Karl Barth's *Church Dogmatics* notes that the German word *Versöhnung* includes the ideas of both "atonement" and "reconciliation," G.W. Bromily and T.F. Torrance (Edinburgh: T & T Clark, 1956/61), ix.

[4] The subtitle indicates the special focus of this influential study: *The Function of the So-Called Extra Calvinisticum in Calvin's Theology* (Amsterdam: E.J. Brill, 1966).

[5] (London: James Clarke, 1956). In the meantime, several important general studies of Calvin's life and theology appeared, but none of them do justice to Calvin's doctrine of the atonement. A. Mitchell Hunter, *The Teaching of Calvin* (London: James Clarke, rev. ed. 1952) doesn't discuss Calvin's Christology at all. Wilhelm Niesel, *The Theology of Calvin* (London: Lutterworth, 1956, original German 1938) only discusses the natures of Christ and completely omits any discussion of the work of Christ in chapters 15-17 of Book II of the *Institutes*. Francois Wendel (*Calvin. Origins and Development of His Religious Thought* [Harper & Row 1963; original French version 1950]) is a little better but concentrates on the relation of predestination to the death of Christ. A more recent work of a similar nature, *John Calvin's Ideas*, by Paul Helm (Oxford: Oxford Univ. Press, 2004) has only a brief section, largely critical of others, which deals with the atonement.

Jansen's study is largely limited to the so-called *triplex munus*, the threefold office of Christ. Finally, approximately half a century after the works by Jansen and Van Buren, we have two excellent studies of Calvin's Christology, one specifically about the atonement—*Calvin and the Atonement* by Robert A. Peterson, Jr.[6]—and the other a more comprehensive study, *Calvin's Christology*, by Stephen Edmondson.[7] These studies are supplemented by a very new book, *The Theology of John Calvin*,[8] by Charles Partee, emeritus professor of Pittsburgh Theological Seminary. Partee devotes more than fifty pages (in manuscript form) to the work of Christ. This is an exceptionally fine treatment that places Calvin's view of the work of Christ in the context of both the history of the doctrine and modern discussions of the atonement. In addition, there are essays in two recent works: Henri Blocher's chapter, "The Atonement in Calvin's Theology" in *The Glory of the Atonement*, edited by Charles E. Hill and Frank A. James III,[9] and two chapters in *A Theological Guide to Calvin's Institutes*, edited by David W. Hall and Peter Lillback.[10] The treatment of the *Institutes* 2.12-15 there is by Derek W.H. Thomas—"The Mediator of the Covenant"—and of Book 2, chapters 16 and 17, by Robert Peterson—"Calvin on Christ's Saving Work."

Of these recent studies, Blocher's essay is particularly valuable because he is of French origin (but now teaches systematic theology at Wheaton College as well as the Faculté Libre de Theologie Evangélique in France) and relies more heavily on Calvin's sermons than Van Buren, Peterson, Partee, and the contributors to the *Theological Guide to Calvin's*

---

[6] (Fearrn. Rosshire, England: Mentor, 1999.)
[7] (Cambridge, England: Cambridge Univ. Press, 2004). Edmondson is assistant professor of church history at Virginia Theological Seminary (Episcopalian).
[8] (Louisville: Westminster John Knox, 2008).
[9] (Downer's Grove: InterVarsity, 2004). This volume is a festschrift in honor of Roger Nicole.
[10] (Phillipsburg, N.J.: P & R Publishing, 2008). I should also point out that this by no means exhausts the number of good brief treatments of Calvin's view of the atonement. Two, in particular, merit mentioning: Robert S. Paul, *The Atonement and the Sacraments* (London: Hodder & Stoughton, 1961), chap. 3, "The Reformers and Their Followers"; and Timothy George, *Theology of the Reformers* (Nashville: Broadman, 1988), 219-33. Here George points out five differences between Calvin's approach to the atonement and Anselm's, with which it is often identified. There are also important studies of this theme in other languages, e.g., that by Olivier Fatio, the eminent Genevan professor: "La Conception du salut chez Calvin," in *Le Salut Chrétien Unité et diversité des conceptions à travers l'histoire*, ed. Jean-Louis Leuba (Académie internationale des sciences religieuses: Paris: Desclée, 1995).

Institutes. However, none of these authors makes use of Calvin's two catechisms, a lacuna I shall fill.

Even so, I face two different types of challenges in this essay. One is that this subject has been treated so well in the recent works just cited. Is there anything new I can add? Since this is not an area of expertise in my studies of Calvin, I feel a little like Dostoevsky who was in awe of the great nineteenth-century novelist Nikolai Gogol and remarked that he (Dostoevsky) had "crawled out from under Gogol's overcoat." Even so, my approach here differs from all my predecessors. Moreover, there is nothing wrong with standing on the shoulders of others as long as one isn't guilty of too much plagiarism.

The other challenge is that Calvin's view approximates the so-called penal substitution view, which Vincent Taylor, the British specialist in this area, once described as "a notion which modern Christianity has no option but to discard."[11] The objections to the penal substitution view on the part of many moderns are that it is sheerly objective, leaving out the subjective, experiential aspect of Christ's death; that it is individualistic, ignoring the ecclesial and social dimension of the atonement; that it is basically Anselmic (*Cur Deus Homo*) with its concomitant problems, above all the failure to ground the atonement in God's love; and that it thinks primarily in terms of propitiating God's wrath or satisfying his justice, with little or no attention paid to the key motif of sacrifice and the *christus victor* aspect of the atonement.[12]

Mention of this last dimension, *christus victor*, brings to mind the very influential book by Gustaf Aulén with that title.[13] The major contribution of this book was to recapture what he called the "classic" or patristic theory of the doctrine of the atonement as a cosmic drama, a battle between the forces of good and evil, and Christ's victory over the devil and the powers of darkness. Where Aulén was misleading

---

[11] *The Atonement in New Testament Teaching* (London: Epworth, 1940), 10. Taylor modified this judgment in his final study of the atonement, *The Cross of Christ* (London: Macmillan, 1956), 94. More about this anon.

[12] Then there are the more extreme reactions not simply to the penal substitution theory but more fundamentally to the violence imaged in the cross of Christ. This type of criticism comes from certain pacifist and feminist theologians. For an example of the former see J. Denny Weaver, *The Nonviolent Atonement* (Grand Rapids: Eerdmans, 2001). For the latter see Joanne Carlson Brown, "Divine Child Abuse" in *Daughters of Sarah*, vol. 18, no. 3 (1992).

[13] *Christus Victor: An Historical Study of the Three Main Types of the Idea of the Atonement* (London: SPCK, 1931; New York: Macmillan, 1969).

was to narrow the atonement theories to three—classic, penal, moral influence—and conclude that Luther's view was basically the classic and Calvin's the penal. This oversimplifies both Luther's and Calvin's views. Luther also holds to a penal view and there is in Calvin's theology a strong element of the *christus victor* position.[14] Frances M. Young also faults Aulén for an inadequate understanding of the church fathers, in particular

> Origen's understanding of sacrifice [which] shows that Aulén's distinction between sacrifice offered to God and ransom offered to the devil is not valid; both sacrifice and ransom were, for Origen, part of the cosmic drama of victory over the opposing evil powers, accomplished by God himself on behalf of the human race.[15]

Enough prolegemena. Now to Calvin himself.

Why the Cross?

This is, in effect, the question raised by Anselm in his classic work *Cur Deus Homo?* (Why did God become man?). The question is a perennial one, for one could speculate endlessly as to why this method of obtaining our salvation—admittedly a cruel and violent one—was the only one a sovereign, loving God could use.[16] Calvin refuses to speculate.

---

[14] For Luther, see Paul Althaus, *The Theology of Martin Luther* (Philadelphia: Fortress, 1966). "Luther does not hesitate to use the word "satisfaction" in speaking of Christ's conflict with the demonic powers and uses the same expression in describing the way in which Christ satisfied God's righteousness," 290, n. 42. Robert Paul also maintains that "the penal theory is strongly present in Luther's theology," although it is not "the most important motif," *The Atonement and the Sacraments* (London: Hodder and Stoughton, 1961), 94. For Calvin, see the Basel dissertation by Charles A.M. Hall, *With the Spirit's Sword. The Drama of Spiritual Warfare in the Theology of John Calvin* (Zurich: EVZ Verlog, 1968).

[15] *Sacrifice and the Death of Christ* (Philadelphia: Westminster, 1975), 89. Others point out that Aulén's critique of Anselm is not fair and that he "makes too sharp a contrast between the 'satisfaction' and the 'victory' motifs, as if they are mutually incompatible alternatives," John R. W. Stott, *The Cross of Christ* (Downer's Grove: InterVarsity, 1986), 229-30. Another objection to Aulén's almost exclusive emphasis on Christ the victor motif is that "this theory says nothing about the past." Past sins are not thereby atoned for. See Leon Morris, *The Cross of Jesus* (Grand Rapids: Eerdmans, 1988), 24-25.

[16] D.M. Baillie in his modern classic, *God Was in Christ: An Essay on Incarnation and Atonement* (New York: Scribner's, 1948), discusses some of the

He has no use for those who "with vague speculations captivate the frivolous and the seekers after novelty. One such speculation is that Christ would have become man even if no means of redeeming mankind had been needed" (*Inst.* II.12.3). Calvin eschews such speculations and simply assumes—on the basis of scripture—that, in fact, Christ did come to redeem us from sin.

In his Geneva Catechism (1545) the minister asks, "Was it then of importance that he [Christ] should assume our flesh?" The answer:

> Very much so; because it was necessary that the disobedience committed by man against God be expiated [redressed; French] also in human nature (Rom. 5:15). *In no other way* indeed could he be our mediator to effect reconciliation between God and man (1 Tim. 2:5; Heb. 4:14; 51).[17]

In the *Institutes*, Calvin makes essentially the same argument. The title of chapter 12 of Book II is simply, "Christ Had to Become Man in Order to Fulfill the Office of Mediator."[18] In the opening paragraph he proceeds to elaborate. Note that now he grounds the necessity of the incarnation in "the heavenly decree of God."

> Now it was of the greatest importance for us that he who was to be our Mediator be both true God and true man. If someone asks why this is necessary, there has been no simple (to use the common expression) or absolute necessity. Rather, it has stemmed from a heavenly decree, on which men's salvation depended. Our most merciful Father decreed what was best for us. Since our iniquities,

---

possibilities including the ancient question, "Would Christ have come if Adam had not sinned?" Baillie then adds, "Calvin deprecated the asking of curious questions as to whether God would have become man if there had been no Fall, on the characteristic ground that we know from Scripture that Christ actually did come to redeem us from sin, and that is enough," 158, Baillie in a note refers to the *Institutes* II.12.4-6.

[17] Question 51, emphasis mine. Translation of J.K.S. Reid in the *Library of Christian Classics*, vol. 22 (Philadelphia: Westminster, 1954), 97. Question 52 elaborates this point. Question: "You say, then, that Christ had to be made man in order, as in our own person, to fulfill the requirements of our salvation?" Answer: "That is what I think. For we must obtain in him whatever is lacking in ourselves; and *this can be done in no other way*" (emphasis mine).

[18] I am usually using the translation of Ford Lewis Battles in the *Library of Christian Classics* edition, vol. 22), ed. John T. McNeill (Philadelphia: Westminster, 1960). Henceforth, references to the *Institutes* will be in abbreviated form and cited in the text.

like a cloud cast between us and him, had completely estranged us from the Kingdom of Heaven [cf. Isa. 59:2], no man, unless he belonged to God, could serve as the intermediary to restore peace. But who might reach to him? Any one of Adam's children? No, like their father, all of them were terrified at the sight of God [Gen. 3:8]. One of the angels? They also had need of a head, through whose bond they might cleave firmly and undividedly to their God [cf. Eph. 1:22; Col. 2:10]. What then? The situation would surely have been hopeless had the very majesty of God not descended to us, since it was not in our power to ascend to him. Hence, it was necessary for the Son of God to become for us "Immanuel, that is, God with us" [Isa. 7:14; Matt. 1:23], and in such a way that his divinity and our human nature might by mutual connection grow together (*Institutes,* II.12.1).[19]

A little later the reformer gives an answer that is reminiscent of Athanasius in his classic study, *De Incarnatione.*[20] Another way of answering the question of why God became man is to say, "Who could have done this had not this self-same Son of God become the Son of man, and had not taken what is ours so as to impart what was his to us, and to make what was his by nature ours by grace" (*Institutes,* II.12.2).

The notion of the necessity of the atonement is brought out again in a sermon on Isaiah 53:12, "Because He was reckoned among

---

[19] Emil Brunner points out that the church fathers discussed the "necessity" of the atonement at great length. He concludes that "the idea of relative necessity which Calvin formulates (following earlier thinkers) (*Institutes,* II.12.1) is the right one; that is, from the point of view of the Christian knowledge of sin we cannot imagine any other possibility of atonement than that which has actually taken place in Christ," *The Mediato. A Study of the Central Doctrine of the Christian Faith* (London: Lutterworth, 1934/1949), 472, n. 1. Berkouwer refers to a "holy and divine necessity" in God becoming man in Christ. This "necessity" is "free from all arbitrariness because of the personal mercifulness and justice of God," G.C. Berkouwer, *The Work of Christ* (Grand Rapids: Eerdmans, 1965), 53.

[20] Derek W.H. Thomas points this out in his chapter, "The Mediator of the Covenant," based on *Institutes* II.12-15, and refers to specific passages in Athanasius's classic. Thomas also comments, "Calvin carefully nuances the doctrine of theosis here," in *A Theological Guide to Calvin's Institutes: Essays and Analysis,* ed. David W. Hall and Peter A. Lillback (Phillipsburg, N.J., 2008), 209 and note 19. On the question of Calvin and theosis—a topic of considerable current interest—see J. Todd Billings's Harvard dissertation, *Calvin. Participation and the Gift: The Activity of Believers in Union with Christ* (Oxford: Oxford Univ. Press, 2007), 55.

the sinners, and bore the iniquity of many... (Calvin's translation). Calvin comments, since "we were far too weak to stand before God laden with our sins, a way to clear us of them could not be found in all the world."

> So *it was necessary* that, to give us relief, our Lord Jesus should come forward *in our place* and be accused of all our offences; yes, even that they should be imputed to Him before God his Father and that He should be held responsible for paying for them[21] (emphasis mine).

Here we see several motifs that will crop up later—substitution, imputation, and payment—but it is interesting to see that in a sermon Calvin would also allude to the "necessity" of the atonement.

Thus, the answer to the question *cur Deus homo* is a multifaceted one. On the one hand, it is due to a divine decree. On the other hand, the decree is not arbitrary for it stems from the character of God and the plight of humanity. There is, therefore, a certain necessity underlying the atonement, but it is a relative necessity, not an absolute one. If it were the latter, it would infringe on the freedom of God. In a fine discussion of this issue, Henri Blocher maintains that, in some places, Calvin "mitigates the affirmation of necessity."[22] For example, in another sermon on Isaiah 53, Calvin suggests that God "was well able to save us without any means, but we always presuppose that life had to be gotten for us by Jesus Christ."[23] Also, "It is true that God was well able to rescue us from death by another means, but he did not want it...."[24]

Blocher concludes: "In view of the infinite distance between the creator and the creature, Calvin feels it would be unseemly audacity to speak of necessity for God."[25] Perhaps so, but for the most part Calvin

---

[21] Sermon VII in *Sermons on Isaiah's Prophecy of the Death and Passion of Christ*, trans. and ed. T.H.L. Parker (London: James Clarke, 1956), 140. Calvin also refers to the "necessity" in the first sermon in this series (on Isa. 52, 13-53), 35: "It was very necessary for Him [Christ] to receive all our faults and blemishes so that we might be purged and cleansed of them."

[22] "The Atonement in John Calvin's Theology," in *The Glory of the Atonement*, 300.

[23] Sermon on Isaiah 53:11. CO 35, 666.

[24] Sermon on Isaiah 53:10, cited by Blocher, 300. Parker translates the latter phrase quite differently: "It is true that God could draw us out of death by some other means, but He did not wish to, *nor was it proper*" (emphasis mine), *Sermons on Isaiah's Prophecy*, 115.

[25] Blocher, "The Atonement in John Calvin's Theology," 301.

seems quite comfortable with the notion of necessity, not imposed from without but ordained freely as the best, if not the only, way to redeem a fallen race.

The Love of God and the Wrath of God

Calvin is alleged to hold the theory of penal substitution "in its harshest form,"[26] but those who make such charges fail to take into account the rich variety of motifs in Calvin's understanding of the atonement and above all his emphasis on the love of God that initiates it. Those familiar with Calvin's theology invariably point to two key passages in the *Institutes* that indicate that Christ's redemptive work derives from God's love. The first is in II.6.3. However, he sets the stage for this in the previous section (II.12.2) by concluding that scripture teaches us "to perceive that apart from Christ, God is, so to speak, hostile to us...." Then Calvin spells out the tension between our sinfulness, which deserves judgment, and God's prevenient love.

> For God, who is the highest righteousness, cannot love the unrighteousness that he sees in us all. All of us, therefore, have in ourselves something deserving of God's hatred. With regard to our corrupt nature and the wicked life that follows it, all of us surely displease God, are guilty in his sight, and are born to the damnation of hell. But because the Lord wills not to lose what is his in us, out of his own kindness he still finds something to love. However much we may be sinners by our own fault, we nevertheless remain his creatures. However much we have brought death upon ourselves, yet he has created us into life. Thus he is moved by pure and freely given love of us to receive us into grace. Since there is a perpetual and irreconcilable disagreement between righteousness and unrighteousness, so long as we remain sinners he cannot receive us completely. Therefore, to take away all cause for enmity and to reconcile us utterly to himself, he wipes out all evil in us by the expiation set forth in the death of Christ; that we, who were previously unclean and impure, may show ourselves righteous and holy in his sight. Therefore, by his love God the Father goes before and anticipates our reconciliation in Christ. Indeed,

---

[26] So J.V.K. Brook, as cited in Paul, *The Atonement and the Sacraments*, 98. Paul does not deny that "the idea and images of penal theory are undeniably there," both in Luther and Calvin, but they must be seen in the context of other motifs in Calvin's doctrine of the atonement such as sacrifice and the obedience of Christ, 98, 105.

"because he first loved us" [1 John 4:19], he afterward reconciles us to himself (II 12.3).

In the next section, after citing passages such as Ephesians 1:4-5, John 3:16, and Romans 5:10, Calvin quotes a lovely passage from Augustine.

> "God's love," says [Augustine], "is incomprehensible and unchangeable. For it was not after we were reconciled to him through the blood of his Son that he began to love us. Rather, he has loved us before the world was created, that we also might be his sons along with his only-begotten Son—before we became anything at all. The fact that we were reconciled through Christ's death must not be understood as if his Son reconciled us to him that he might now begin to love those whom he had hated. Rather, we have already been reconciled to him who loves us, with whom we were enemies on account of sin. The apostle will testify whether I am speaking the truth: 'God shows his love for us in that while were yet sinners Christ died for us' [Rom. 5:8]. Therefore, he loved us even when we practiced enmity toward him and committed wickedness. Thus in a marvelous and divine way he loved us even when he hated us. For he hated us for what we were that he had not made; yet because our wickedness had not entirely consumed his handiwork, he knew how, at the same time, to hate in each on of us what we had made, and to love what he had made" (II.16.4).[27]

As we shall see later, the reformer also refers frequently to Christ's sacrificial death appeasing the wrath of God and satisfying God's justice, passages which taken out of context seem to confirm the concerns of those who reject the penal substitution theory. As Robert Paul points out, Calvin "can speak on one page of Christ expiating with his own blood the sins that make us hateful to God. Yet the whole point of his argument rests upon the fact that it was God the Father's mercy which alone made Christ's action possible."[28] Paul refers only to the passages from the *Institutes* cited above, but there are also some moving

---

[27] This is from Augustine's commentary on *John's Gospel* cx.6 (MPL 35, 1923f).

[28] *The Atonement and the Sacraments*, 105. Calvin also speaks of God's mercy as being that which prompts the sending of the Son for our salvation. "The mercy of God is the source from which redemption springs." For it is "from this mercy as from a fountain the prophet [i.e., the psalmist] derives redemption," Comm. Psalm 130:7. "Christ came forth to us from

lines in one of Calvin's sermons on Isaiah 53. There he refers to Romans 12:1 and then comments, "By this he [Paul] shows that in the sufferings of Jesus Christ we have a testimony of the infinite love of God. It is if He laid bare to us His heart and set before us His inmost feelings to testify to us how dear we are to Him and how precious our souls are to Him."[29]

This is spoken in reference to believers. But what about our state apart from Christ? There do we experience only God's wrath? Does God hate us because of our sin and rebellion and only come to love us after Christ has died on our behalf and assumed our guilt? What can we make of a statement like the following? "In some ineffable way God loved us and yet was angry toward us at the same time until he became reconciled to us in Christ" (*Institutes,* II.17.2).[30] A partial answer is found in Calvin's commentary on 2 Corinthians 5:19: "I admit," says Calvin, "that the love of God is prior in time and also in order as regards God (*quantum ad Deum*), but from our point of view, the beginning of love is placed in Christ's sacrifice. For when we think of God apart from a mediator, we can only conceive of God as being angry with us, but when a mediator is interposed between us, we know that he is pacified towards us.[31]

Randall Zachman's take on this is that "to say that the death of Christ satisfies the wrath of God does not mean that it changes God's will from wrath to mercy by paying satisfaction to the justice of God, but rather means that the wrath and curse of God have been transferred to the incarnate Son of God."[32] Paul Helm adds, in reference to the above passage from the *Institutes* (II.17.2), "There is, therefore, an

---

the fountain of God's free mercy," Comm. 2 Cor. 5:19. Robert Peterson treats this matter at greater length in the first chapter of his book, *Calvin and the Atonement*. It reads: "The Starting Point: The Free Love of God in Jesus Christ," 13. He quotes here from Calvin's commentary on John 3:16: "Christ shows the first cause and, as it were, the source of our salvation....For there is no calm haven where our minds can rest until we come to God's free love." Cf. Paul Van Buren, "The gift of the Mediator is the realization of God's eternal love and therefore the final revelation of God's eternal will." He then cites Calvin's commentary on 1 John 4:10, *Christ in Our Place*, 8.

[29] Sermon on Isaiah 53:7-8 in *Sermons on Isaiah's Prophecy of the Death and Passion of Christ*, 95.

[30] This assertion is based on Calvin's interpretation of 1 John 4:10, which refers to Christ being the "propitiation" or "expiation" for our sins.

[31] Cf. further Henri Blocher's discussion of this issue in *The Glory of the Atonement*, 295.

[32] *John Calvin as Teacher, Pastor, and Theologian* (Grand Rapids: Baker Academic, 2006), 256. Cf. *Institutes*, II.16.6

important change in the beliefs of people when they exercise faith in Christ. They change from regarding God as a judge to regarding him as a Saviour, even though (unbeknown to them) God eternally loves them in Christ."[33]

Zachman and Helm do not mention Calvin's commentary on Galatians 3:13, but this is a key text in regard to the question. The text reads, "Christ redeemed us from the curse of the law by becoming a curse for us." Calvin asks, "But how does it happen, someone may object, that a beloved Son is cursed by his Father?" Calvin gives two answers, the second one more important:

> Christ took our place and thus became a sinner [!] and subject to the curse, not in himself indeed, but in us; yet in such a way that it was necessary for him to act in our name. He could not be outside God's grace (*neque extra Dei gratiam*), and yet he endured his wrath. For how could he reconcile him to us if he regarded the Father as an enemy and was hated by him? Therefore, the will of the Father always reposed in him.[34]

Here it is not the love of God, but rather its parallel, the grace of God, which seems to be in tension with the wrath of God. However, Christ, who endured the curse in our place, did this within the framework of the will of God and the grace of God.

This is brought out even more forcibly in a sermon on Galatians 2:3-4. Here Calvin raises again the question as to how God could both hate us and love us before our reconciliation was effected by Jesus Christ. The answer is that God always "loved us despite the fact that in the person of Adam we were fallen away from God and utterly corrupted." At the same time, God "abhorred" in us our sinfulness that required "an atonement to be made in the blood of our Lord Jesus Christ, and by the sacrifice which he offered." Thus was "all hatred between God and us done away."[35]

---

[33] *John Calvin's Ideas* (Oxford: Oxford Univ. Press, 2004), 398. Francois Wendel made the same point much earlier: "The sacrifice of Christ modifies, at least from the human point of view, the attitude of God towards men. In reality that attitude is unchanged and immutable; it cannot therefore be influenced *a posteriori* by the work of Christ. That work is limited to the removal of the obstacle that prevents the divine love from making its way toward men," *Calvin*, 231.

[34] Translation by T.H.L. Parker in the Torrance edition (Grand Rapids: Eerdmans, 1965), 55.

[35] *Sermons on Galatians by John Calvin*, trans. Arthur Golding and slightly modernized (Audubon, N.J.: Old Paths Publications, 1995), 35.

In this context Calvin reminds us again that Christ's atoning sacrifice did not bring about a change in God's eternal purpose. For "we should not think that the coming of the Lord Jesus Christ to pacify God his Father was such that he persuaded him [God] to alter his purpose," as some people perversely imagine. Rather as the apostle Paul reminds us here (in Gal. 2:2-3), "the cause why Jesus Christ was delivered up for our sins was that God had so ordained it."[36]

I will conclude this section with a reminder of the point made at the outset, viz., that in our reconciliation the initiative remains with God, even when Calvin speaks of propitiation and satisfaction rendered to God through Christ's sacrificial death. And that initiative is prompted by God's love and mercy. In the words of Francois Wendel, it is God's "love for men which has removed the barrier constituted by sin and the divine wrath that was the consequence of it, by deciding to accept the satisfaction to be offered by Jesus Christ."[37]

The Atonement as Propitiation and Satisfaction

We have just seen a reference to "satisfaction" being offered to God by Christ. This language and that of propitiation and expiation are what turns off many moderns[38] and causes them to reject any notion of penal sacrifice. Four passages from different types of sources

---

[36] Ibid., 34. "The wellspring of our redemption and salvation consists in the ordinance and everlasting purpose of God the father," 38. Cf. 1 Pet. 1:19-20: "You were ransomed...with the precious blood of Christ, like that of a lamb without blemish or spot. He was destined before the foundation of the world but was made manifest at the end of the times for your sake." Calvin comments, "Doubtless before God created man he foresaw that he would not stand firm for long in his integrity. Hence, according to his wonderful wisdom and goodness, he ordained that Christ should be the redeemer who would deliver the last race of man from ruin. In this there shines forth more clearly the unspeakable goodness of God that he anticipated our disease by the remedy of his grace (*gratiae suae remedio*) and provided a restoration to life before the first man had fallen into death," trans. W.J. Johnston, Torrance edition.

[37] Calvin, 231. The references here and elsewhere in this discussion to God's wrath do not sit well with those who want to think of God only in terms of his love. However, it is a thoroughly biblical notion. Cf., for example, Rom. 1:18; 5:9; Col. 3:6, and 1 Thess. 5:9. In Eph. 2:3, we are told that we were by nature children of wrath." The wrath of God has past, present, and future dimensions.

[38] By "moderns," I am referring primarily to people of the last half of the twentieth century. In Thomas Hywell Hughes's book, *The Atonement: Modern Theories of the Atonement* (London: Allen & Unwin, 1949), which

will illustrate Calvin's understanding in this regard. From his first catechism (1538)

> For because God was provoked to wrath by man's disobedience, by Christ's own obedience he wiped out ours, showing himself obedient to his Father, even unto death. And by his death he offered himself as a *sacrifice* to his Father, in order that his justice might once for all be *appeased* for all time, in order that believers might be eternally sanctified, in order that the eternal *satisfaction* might be fulfilled. He poured out his sacred blood in *payment* for our redemption, in order that God's anger, kindled against us, might be extinguished, and our iniquity might be cleansed (emphasis mine).[39]

Here, in one of Calvin's earliest writings, we have his explanation of our redemption in a nutshell. There is no significant change in any of his later writings. All of these motifs—Christ's obedience, his death as a sacrifice, the appeasing[40] of God's justice, and the payment for our redemption—are all developed in the *Institutes* and the reformer's commentaries and sermons.

In the final edition of the *Institutes*, we read much the same:

> By his obedience Christ truly acquired and merited grace for us with his Father....I take it to be a commonplace that if Christ made satisfaction for our sins, if he paid the penalty owed by us, if he appeased God by his obedience—in short, if as a righteous man he suffered for unrighteous man—then he acquired salvation for us by his righteousness, which is tantamount to deserving it (II.17.3).[41]

---

obviously covers only the first half of the twentieth century, he lists eighty-three books on the atonement in his bibliography—most by British authors—and only a few of them are sympathetic to the penal substitution theory, viz., James Denny, J.K. Mozley, and P.T. Forsyth, although there are variations in each case. Moreover, none of them interact with Calvin seriously.

[39] Section 20.iv. Trans. Ford Lewis Battles, in *Calvin's First Catechism* by I. John Hesselink (Louisville: Westminster John Knox, 1997), 23. Lest one think that Calvin has thereby captured the whole of the meaning of the atonement, he immediately adds, "But there is nothing without mystery in that redemption."

[40] The Latin original is *placaretur*, the French (of the 1537 version), *pacifiee*. Hence one could translate this key word as "pacify."

[41] In this section and the preceding one Calvin cites a host of relevant scripture passages such as 1 John 2:2 and 4:10; Col. 1:19-20; 2 Cor. 5:19 and

The only motif missing in this passage is the significance of the blood of Christ, which speaks particularly to the sacrificial aspect of Christ's death on the cross. However, he treats this at some length in the next section. "But when we say that grace was imparted to us by the merit of Christ, we mean this: by his blood we were cleansed, and his death was an expiation for our sins. 'His blood cleanses us from all sin' [1 John 1:7]" (II.17.4).[42]

In his commentary on this text (1 John 1:7), Calvin relates the saving significance of the blood of Christ to our reconciliation and the satisfaction motif against the "sophists" who maintain, according to Calvin, that "pardon of sins is given us only in baptism" and that afterward "God is reconciled only by satisfactions. John assigns the whole and not simply the half to the blood of Christ."

> The sum of what we have said, then, is that believers are assured that they are accepted by God because he has been reconciled to them through the sacrifice of Christ's death. And sacrifice contains cleansing and satisfaction. Hence the power and effect of all these belong to Christ's blood alone."[43]

Despite the fact that the imagery of the blood of Christ is quite biblical, many moderns are revulsed by this notion, and even sympathetic Calvin interpreters do not pay much attention to this subject.[44] Calvin, on the other hand, is not reluctant to use this shorthand way of

---

21; Eph. 1:4-5 d& 6, 2:3 and 2:15-16. Cf. many other scripture references cited in II.17.5, which treats "Christ's death the price for our redemption."

[42] References to Christ's blood are numerous in the New Testament. Calvin refers here (in II.17.4) to some of them: Matt. 26:28; Luke 22:20; Heb. 9:12-13, 14, 22, 26, 28. After quoting these passages Calvin adds, "This readily shows that Christ's grace is too much weakened unless we grant to his sacrifice the power of expiating, appeasing, and making satisfaction (*vim expiandi, placandi, et satisfaciendi concedimus*)."

[43] Comm. 1 John 1:7.

[44] Paul Van Buren (*Christ in Our Place*), Stephen Edmondson (*Calvin's Christology*), and even Robert Peterson (*Calvin and the Atonement*) do not highlight this concept in their studies, although they quote passages in which the word appears. Peterson, however, does say in passing, "Calvin has much to say about the 'blood' of Christ," and points to Calvin's commentaries on Heb. 9:22; Col. 1:20, and 1 John 5:6 Particularly germane is the commentary on Rom. 3:25: "By mentioning blood alone Paul does not mean to exclude other parts of redemption, but rather to include the whole of it in a single word.... Thus, the whole of our expiation is denoted by taking a part for the whole."

referring to the sacrificial aspect of Christ's death even where the word does not appear in the text he is discussing, for example, in a sermon on Isaiah 53:4-6. The emphasis here is on the fact that although the death of Christ is a once-for-all event, it has continuing consequences for the life of believers. Hebrews 10 informs this rhetoric, where again the blood of Christ is prominent. At the same time, note how this passage alone—and there are many others—responds to two of the criticisms of the penal substitution theory, viz., that it is so objective it has neither any continuing significance nor evokes any subjective response.

> For God was not satisfied with sending his Son once for all, and exposing Him to death, and smiting him with His wrath though He loved Him as His only begotten Son (for although it seemed as if He wanted to overwhelm Him completely and He showed extreme severity against Him, yet He was always the well-beloved Son, as we have said, and it all took place that we might be absolved)—He was not, I say, satisfied with that, but daily sets before us this treasure that we may enjoy it. He declares to us that Jesus Christ, who once had His side pierced, today has His heart open, as it were, that we may have assurance of the love that He bears us; that, as He once had his arms fastened to the cross, now He has them wide open to draw us to Himself; and (since He desires all these things to turn to our profit) that as once He shed his Blood, so today He wishes us to be plunged within it (*soyons plongez*) So, when God invites us so sweetly, and Jesus Christ sets before us the fruit of His death and passion, showing us that His blood is always new (as the Apostle puts it in the Epistle to the Hebrews) and not a blood which dries up or fails, but consecrated by His heavenly power, is always new, let us know that its power is not diminished but retains always the full and complete force that it has had from the beginning.[45]

All of this is brought together in a comprehensive manner in a discussion of the benefits of the death of Christ in two questions and answers in the Geneva catechism. The minister asks, "Can we infer from this [the agony of Christ on the cross] what benefit (*fructum*) the faithful obtain from the death of Christ?" In this answer three benefits or fruit are listed. A fourth is added in the following answer:

---

[45] *Sermons on Isaiah's Prophecy of the Death and Passion of Christ* by John Calvin, 82. Something akin to the moral influence theory is found in the following sermon (on Isa. 53:7-8): "The grace that God shows us in our Lord Jesus Christ ought always to draw us to repentance," 96.

Certainly. For a beginning, we see it to be a sacrifice by which he expiates our sins in the sight of God, and so appeases the wrath of God and restores us to grace with him. Then, too, his blood is a laver in which our souls are purged of every stain. Lastly, the memory of our sins is erased, so that they never come before God; and thus the handwriting by which we were declared guilty is cancelled and abolished.[46]

The minister continues and asks further, "Does it not offer us any other advantage (Fr. *utilite*) besides?" The answer is tantamount to a fourth benefit of Christ's death: "Yes indeed,...if we are true members of Christ, our old nature is crucified, and the body of sin is destroyed, so that the lusts of perverse flesh no longer rule in us."[47]

In this neat summary, which, to my knowledge, is not referred to by any other Calvin scholar, we have most of the basic elements of Calvin's view of the atonement: sacrifice, expiation of sin, appeasing God's wrath, the cleansing power of Christ's blood, the forgiveness of sins, and the new life in Christ. What is missing here is the motif mentioned earlier, viz., the love of God as that which initiates our redemption, and also the importance of Christ's obedience in accomplishing our salvation. This has been alluded to in some of the quotations cited earlier.

Another dimension not mentioned thus far is the relation of the cross to the resurrection of Christ. For by Christ's "resurrection he swallowed up death, broke the fetters of the devil, and reduced all his power to nothing (1 Pet. 5:22)."[48] Space limitations prevent a full discussion of this theme.[49] One more passage must suffice: Although "the whole of redemption is contained in the cross and all its parts, the resurrection of Christ does not lead us away from the cross" but rather represents its consummation.[50] According to J. Pannier, the editor of a French edition of the *Institutes*, "The victorious note in Calvinist piety [derives] from its view of the resurrection.[51] This also is borne out in

---

[46] Question 71. *Calvin: Theological Treatises*, 100.
[47] Ibid., Question 72.
[48] Ibid., Question 73. "Our common nature with Christ is the pledge of our fellowship with the Son of God; and clothed with our flesh he vanished sin and death together that the victory and the triumph might be ours," *Inst.* II.3.2. Cf. II.12.2 and II.16.7.
[49] For a fuller discussion see Van Buren, *Christ in Our Place*, chapter 6, "Resurrection and Ascension," 81-89; and my book, *Calvin's First Catechism*, 125-28.
[50] Comm. Galatians 6:14.
[51] Cited in the *LCC* edition (McNeill-Battles) of the *Institutes* 520, n. 34.

Calvin's emphasis on the kingship of Christ, the subject of our next section.

The *Munus Triplex*

The doctrine of the three-fold office of Christ is one of the few doctrines that is uniquely Calvinian. A pioneering study of this subject is John F. Jansen's *Calvin's Doctrine of the Work of Christ*,[52] the focus being Christ's work as prophet, priest, and king. This is a fine study except for one weakness. Because Jansen cannot find any reference to the prophetic office of Christ in any of Calvin's exegetical writings, and the three offices only appears in the later editions of the *Institutes*, he concludes that there is a tension between Calvin the exegete and Calvin the dogmatician.[53] However, as Edmondson observes in his recent study of Calvin's Christology, among Calvin scholars "there is seldom any support" for Jansen's thesis.[54]

Calvin's doctrine of the threefold office has been treated at length in several Calvin studies,[55] so here I will only concentrate on the special redemptive significance of Christ's priestly office. It should be kept in mind, however, that Christ's priestly work is inseparable from that of king and prophet. But Christ's office as priest is the foundation for understanding his role as mediator. As "a pure and stainless Mediator," Christ's function is to reconcile us to God" (*Inst.* II.15.6). As Edmondson points out, Christ's substitutionary sacrifice must be understood within the broader priestly framework of his mediation."[56] Commenting on John 16:24, Calvin admonishes his readers, "We are

---

[52] (London: James Clarke, 1956). Cf. the more balanced study of Klauspeter Blaser, *Calvins Lehre von den drei Ämtern Christi* (*Theologische Studien*, vol. 105 [Zurich: EVZ Verlag, 1970]).

[53] Ibid., 59. The early church taught a twofold office of Christ (as king and priest) but "it was not developed into a full doctrine." Eusebius was the only church father to refer to a threefold office, but again it was only Calvin who developed it into a full-fledged doctrine, Otto Weber, *Foundations of Dogmatics*, vol. 2 (Grand Rapids: Eerdmans, 1983), 172.

[54] *Calvin's Christology*, 162. For specific examples of those who reject Jansen's thesis see Peterson, *Calvin and the Atonement*, 46-47. Edmondson also points out, "We should accept Calvin's categorization of Christ's prophetic office with these other two as a Messianic office, for through this office Christ, as Mediator, brings God's covenant to fruition," 164.

[55] The best treatment of this matter is by Edmondson, cited above. Cf. Otto Weber, *Foundations of Dogmatics*, 172-77; Robert Peterson, chap. 3; Derek Thomas, in *A Theological Guide to Calvin's Institutes*, 219-25.

[56] *Calvin's Christology*, 96, n. 15.

more than ungrateful if we do not keep our senses fixed on the true high priest who is exhibited to us as our propitiator through whom we may have free and ready access to the throne of God's glory.[57]

The presupposition of Christ's priesthood is the incarnation. The eternal Word had to become one with us, had to assume our flesh in order that he might accomplish our reconciliation. For "we are strangers to God and to his worship until a priest comes in between us and undertakes our cause." But Christ could not do this unless he was one with us. The special significance of this is that "the salvation of all of us is effected by and turns on the priesthood of Christ."[58]

Calvin, not surprisingly, finds the biblical basis for this office of Christ in Hebrews 7-10. The sum of the argument here, according to the reformer, is that "the priestly office belongs to Christ alone because by the sacrifice of his death he blotted out our own guilt and made satisfaction for our sins [Heb. 9:22]." Then Calvin cites Psalm 110:4 and Hebrews 5:6 and 7:15 (references to Melchizedek) and concludes:

> God undoubtedly willed in these words to ordain the principle point (*sancire... voluit caput illud*)[59] on which our whole salvation turns. For we or our prayers have no access to God unless Christ, as our high priest, having washed away our sins, sanctifies us and obtains for us that grace from which the uncleanness of our transgressions and vices debars us. Thus we see that we must begin with the death of Christ in order that the efficacy and benefit of his priesthood may reach us" (*Inst.* II.15.6).

As Calvin notes elsewhere, there are two aspects of Christ's priesthood, viz., Christ's sacrificial death and his continual intercession on our behalf (see Rom. 8:34). "They are the two parts of his priestly office, for when Christ is called priest (Heb. 7:17), the meaning is that once by his death he made expiation for our sins to reconcile us to God, and now, having entered the heavenly sanctuary, he appears in the presence of the Father for our sakes that we may be heard in his name."[60]

Thus Christ's priestly work has both objective and subjective effects. It is both the basis of our salvation and also the means of

---

[57] Comm. John 16:24, T. H.L. Parker translation.
[58] *Commentary* on Heb. 5:1, trans. W.B. Johnston.
[59] Here the Battles translation is not the best. Cf. Beveridge: "His purpose was to ratify that point...."
[60] *Commentary* on 1 Tim. 2:6, T.A. Smail translation.

our access to God in prayer. Not only that, it is also the basis for the priesthood of all believers.

> Now Christ plays the priestly role, not only to render the Father favorable and propitious toward us by an eternal law of reconciliation, but also to receive us as his companions in this great office [Rev. 1:6] (*nos asciscat in societatem tanti honoris*).[61]

This is the way Calvin ends his brief exposition of the priestly office of Christ (apart from a few supporting texts and a closing blast at the "papists" view of the mass) in the *Institutes*. As Van Buren observes, "The representative character of priesthood means that He [Christ] acts in our place in so close a union with us that we are all involved in his work."[62]

The opening lines of chapter sixteen are a fitting way of concluding this section: "What we have said thus far concerning Christ," Calvin begins, "must be referred to this one objective (*scopum*): condemned, dead, and lost in ourselves, we should seek righteousness, liberation, life, and salvation in him" (II.16.1).[63]

Calvin and Anselm

Those who are familiar with the history of the doctrine of the atonement will recognize that Calvin has moved far from Anselm's classic approach to the death of Christ, although there is some affinity with it, i.e., its objective nature. However, here there is already a significant difference. With Calvin there is a beautiful blend of the objective—how Christ's death affects God—and the subjective, the consequences of the atonement for us and our daily Christian living.[64]

Robert Peterson and Timothy George, among others, enumerate several other differences with Anselm. Above all, there is the context

---

[61] Again, the Battles translation is rather free. Cf. Beveridge: "admit us into this most honorable alliance." However, *societas* could best be translated as elsewhere when Calvin defines the church, viz., as a "society." On this subject see J.R. Crawford, "Calvin and the Priesthood of All Believers," *Scottish Journal of Theology* 21/2, June 1968, 145-56.

[62] *Christ in Our Place*, 67.

[63] Calvin then refers to Acts 4:12 and alludes to Matthew 1:21 and Luke 1:31, after which he adds, "We must note in these words what we have touched on elsewhere: the office of Redeemer was laid upon him [Jesus] that he might be our savior" (*Inst.* II.16.1).

[64] "Indeed, Calvin's approach to Christ's reconciling death is governed thoroughly by his attention to this subjective, rhetorical effectiveness of his language ...," Edmondson, *Calvin's Christology*, 107.

and the matter of imagery. Anselm's images in *Cur Deus Homo* are taken from the feudal world of that time. Although both Anselm and Calvin employ the notion of satisfaction,[65] with Anselm it is God's honor that must be satisfied; with Calvin, God's holiness and justice.

Second, "Calvin differs from Anselm in that he rejects the dilemma, 'either satisfaction on punishment,' and puts in its place the notion of satisfaction via punishment."[66] Third, in Anselm's theory the life of Christ had no salvific value, whereas Calvin stressed that "the whole course of Christ's obedience" (*Institutes*, II.16.5) was essential for our salvation. Fourth, in contrast to Anselm, although Calvin uses the legal language of penal satisfaction in his discussion of the atonement, the notions of sacrifice and the christus victor motif are also found in Calvin. Finally, as has been noted above, there is a subjective dimension in Calvin's understanding of the atonement, missing not only in Anselm but in some of the proponents of the penal substitution view. "An efficacy inheres in the death of Christ," according to Calvin, "which ought to be manifest in all Christians unless they intend to render his death useless and unfruitful" (*Institutes*, II.16.7).[67] In short, "The atonement issues an ethical call to us by which we enter into our Lord's work of salvation."[68]

Conclusion

The penal substitution motif is clearly prominent in Calvin's understanding of the atonement, but it is not the only one. Nor does it assume the prominence found in later scholastic theology. As noted above, some of the ways in which Calvin differed from Anselm are ways in which Calvin transcends the penal view of atonement. Robert

---

[65] In the revised version of his book *Calvin and the Atonement*, Peterson is remarkably candid in retracting much of a paragraph he wrote in the first edition (1983) of this book. On the matter of satisfaction he wrote earlier, "Calvin was not largely dependent upon Anselm in this" (i.e., the notion of satisfaction). Now (in 1999) he writes, "Upon further reflection, I now maintain that Calvin does build upon Anselm's idea of satisfaction, but moves beyond Anselm and develops his own view, which was to become standard in reformed Christianity," 131.

[66] Ibid., 134. To support this contention, Peterson cites the *Institutes* II.17.3, which I have quoted earlier.

[67] The latter points are found in Timothy George's *Theology of the Reformers* (Nashville: Broadman, 1988), 221-23.

[68] Robert Paul, *The Atonement and the Sacraments*, 108. Paul also points out several other features of Calvin's thought which modify "the harshest features of the penal theory," 106-107.

Peterson, in his comprehensive study of Calvin and the atonement, treats the subject in terms of six images employed in attempting to explain the atonement, viz., Christ the obedient second Adam, Christ the victor, Christ our legal substitute, Christ our sacrifice, Christ our merit, and Christ our example.[69]

T.H.L. Parker finds five images and motifs in Calvin's presentation of Christ's reconciling work: (1) sacrifice, (2) satisfaction, (3) obedience, (4) cleansing (expiation of sin), (5) victory.[70] Van Buren still maintains, however, that if there is one overarching theme in Calvin's discussion of the atonement it is that of Christ as our substitute.[71]

All of this points to the fact, recognized by many Calvin scholars, that Calvin does not have a theory or doctrine of the atonement. Instead we have a variety of biblical motifs, as Calvin understood them, which he did not try to systematize in a logical fashion. Even sympathetic interpreters like Robert Peterson and Henri Blocher concede there are "rough edges"[72] and in some places an "inner tension"[73] in his handling of this subject. This does not mean, however, that Calvin leaves us with an incoherent presentation of our reconciliation in Christ. According to Henri Blocher, Calvin "achieved a high degree of integration...with the various biblical languages of atonement."[74]

---

[69] These are the titles of his chapter headings. The first three chapters treat "The Starting Point: The Free Love of God in Jesus Christ," "The Prerequisite for Atonement: The Incarnation," and "Christ's Threefold Office of Prophet, Priest and King," *Calvin and the Atonement*. However, in a later essay, "Calvin on Christ's Saving Work" in *The Glory of the Atonement*, Peterson concedes that Blocher is correct in his criticism that he (Peterson) "failed to give pride of place to penal substitution," 245.

In the concluding chapter 4 of his book Peterson discusses the question much debated in Calvinistic circles, viz., the extent of the atonement. There are passages in Calvin that indicate both a universal atonement and a limited atonement, but the latter predominate. The definitive study of this subject is the dissertation by Jonathan Rainbow, *The Will of God and the Cross: An Historical and Theological study of John Calvin's Doctrine of Limited Atonement* (Allsion Park: Pickwick, 1990). Cf. the more recent treatment of Raymond A. Blacketer, "Definite Atonement in Historical Perspective" in *The Glory of the Atonement*, 304-23. Peterson—wisely, I think—concurs with Robert Letham's judgment: "My position is that Calvin was ambiguous or contradictory on the question but that he maintained the intrinsic efficacy of the atonement," *The Work of Christ* (Downer's Grove: InterVarsity, 1993), 266.

[70] *The Oracles of God* (London: Lutterworth, 1947), 87ff.
[71] *Christ in Our Place*, IX, 125.
[72] Peterson, *Calvin on the Atonement*, 87.
[73] Blocher, "The Atonement in John Calvin's Theology," 300.
[74] Ibid., 203. "It is not easy to harmonize all of Calvin's thoughts on the work

In fact, Stephen Edmondson maintains that "we best understand Calvin's Christological thinking if we pursue it under the rubric of Christ as Mediator, the rubric that Calvin himself repeatedly offers." Edmondson acknowledges that a characteristic of Calvin's Christology is its "eclecticism—that it embraces a variety of biblical themes and addresses a multitude of existential situations in the breadth of its exposition." But—and this is important—Calvin's eclecticism does not leave us with a doctrine that is scattered and unfocused."[75]

Perhaps the best way of concluding this essay is with two examples of Calvin's powerful rhetoric as he explicates the notion of the "happy exchange,"[76] for here he reaches eloquent heights that should resonate with any believer, whatever their theory of the atonement may be. Calvin alludes to this briefly in the context of his Christology. Part of this was quoted earlier, viz., that the God-man took "what was ours so as to impart what was his to us" (*Institutes*, II.12.2). A few lines later Calvin continues, repeating the above phrase,

> Ungrudgingly he took our nature upon himself to impart to us what was his, and to become both Son of God and Son of man in common with us. Hence that holy brotherhood (*sancta illa fraternitas*) which he commends with his own lips when he says, 'I am ascending to my Father and your Father, to my God your God' [John 20:17]. In this way we are assured of the inheritance of the heavenly kingdom; for the only Son of God, to whom it wholly belongs, has adopted us as his brothers. For if brothers, then fellow heirs with him' [Rom. 8:17].[77]

---

of Christ, partly because he holds to a substitutionary atonement that is nonetheless ineffectual until we are united with Christ," *Grace and Gratitude* (Minneapolis: Fortress, 1993), 56, n. 17.

[75] *Calvin's Christology*, 220.

[76] The expression is found first in Luther. For references see *LCC Institutes*, 1362, n. 8. Calvin calls it the "wonderful exchange" (*mirifica commutatio*) in the *Institutes* IV.17.2).

[77] This important passage is cited by Francois Wendel, Derek Thomas, Robert Paul, Ronald Wallace, and Stephen Edmonson. Edmondson sees here (and elsewhere) a confirmation of the theme of his study of Calvin's Christology: "It is this share of the divine life through our relationship with Christ our brother that I have labeled our covenant fellowship with God, realized through Christ's work as Mediator," *Calvin's Christology*, 231. Derek Thomas adds, "Calvin carefully nuances the doctrine of theosis here," "The Mediator of the Covenant," 209, n. 19. On this subject see further Todd Billings's Harvard dissertation, *Calvin, Participation and the Gift*, 51-61.

The reformer does not use the expression "happy" or "marvelous" exchange here. That occurs in his discussion of the Lord's Supper and this is where he soars to eloquent heights. Beyond the rhetoric, however, one should note that this "marvelous exchange" "could be taken as the regulative conception of Calvin's thoughts on the atonement."[78]

> This is the wonderful exchange which, out of his measureless benevolence, he has made with us; that, becoming Son of man with us, he has made us sons of God with him; that, by his descent to earth, he has prepared an ascent to heaven for us; that, by taking on our mortality, he has conferred his immortality upon us; that, accepting our weakness, he has strengthened us by his power; that, receiving our poverty unto himself, he has transferred his wealth to us; that, taking the weight of our iniquity upon himself (which oppressed us), he has clothed us with his righteousness[79] (*Inst.* IV.17.2).

Much the same sort of thing occurs in a sermon on Isaiah 53: 9-10: The phrase "marvelous exchange" does not occur here, but the language and the thought are similar.

> Consider Jesus Christ the only Son of God: He was imprisoned and we are released; He was condemned and we are acquitted; He was exposed to utter disgrace and we are set up in honour; He descended into the depths of hell and to us the kingdom of Heaven is opened.[80]

Both of these passages are summarized in a sense in Calvin's comments on a phrase in John 13:31: "And God is glorified in him (Christ)."

> For in the cross, as in a splendid theatre, the incomparable goodness of God is set before the whole world. The glory of God shines, indeed in all creatures on high and below, but never more

---

[78] Brian A. Gerrish, *Grace and Gratitude*, 56, n. 17.
[79] This, too, is one of the most admired passages in the Calvin corpus. Ronald Wallace comments, "Calvin dwells constantly, always in an arresting way, on the paradoxes involved in this exchange, whereby we find 'acquittal in Christ's condemnation and blessing in his curse,'" *Calvin, Geneva, and the Reformation* (Grand Rapids: Baker, 1988), 244.
[80] *Sermons on Isaiah's Prophecy*, 109. In an earlier sermon in this series (on Isa. 53:4-6) Calvin does refer to the fact that "our Lord Jesus Christ made such an exchange (*eschange*) for us," 69.

brightly than in the cross in which there was a wonderful exchange of things *(admirabilis rerum conversio)*—the condemnation of all men was manifested, sin blotted out, and salvation restored to men; in short, the whole world was renewed and all things restored to order.[81]

To comment on these passages is like gilding the lily, so I will simply conclude by claiming that the least one can say is that this is a remarkable view of the atonement and then go one step further and submit that this is a distinctive contribution to the doctrine of the atonement.

---

[81] Comm. John 13:31, T.H.L. Parker translation.

A New Hymn

James Hart Brumm
Kathleen Hart Brumm

The people of the Reformed Church in America have been singing people ever since the denomination's earliest days. Whether singing the psalms and canticles or singing scriptural hymns and songs with strong covenantal and social justice emphases, the people's song has always been part of this church's worship.

Donald Bruggink, as part of his general love of beauty and art, is known to be a lover of congregational song and a hearty singer in his own right. He is also a professor of theology—formally emeritus now—and was born 145 years after the election of the denomination's first professor of theology, John Henry Livingston.

So it seemed this volume was the appropriate place to include a new hymn and tune celebrating the theological professorate in this anniversary year. The text is presented in poetic form below and interlined with the tune after that. Since hymns and tunes are created to be interchangeable and often created separately, tunes are given names of their own. The name of this tune, also, seemed appropriate under the circumstances.

What does this Ebenezer mean,
   this rock which has a name?
Or stones piled in the Jordan's bed
   which look like much the same?
It means God brought us safely here,
   we followed and believed,
and someone gave her life to share
   the story you received.

Why do we eat a meal of lamb,
   strong herbs, and unraised bread?
And why would someone take the cross
   which should be mine instead?
Because Redemption passed this way,
   our lives have been restored
and someone gave his life to share
   the Good News of our Lord.

How is a nurturing presence in
   this water, bread, and wine?
And how are we all gathered as
   one flawed yet faithful line?
The Spirit, bold, mysterious,
   blows us where she has willed
and people give their lives to share
   the power with which we're filled.

Who are these, called by great I AM,
   who gives us each a role,
who helps us to map out the Way
   by which we are made whole?
These scholars call the church to learn,
   extend salvation's reach.
By grace, they give their lives to share
   what God gives them to teach.

A New Hymn 323

What does this Ebenezer mean
James Hart Brumm

BRUGGINK, CMD
Kathleen Hart Brumm

What does this Eb-en-e-zer mean, this rock which has a name?
Why do we eat a meal of lamb, strong herbs, and un-raised bread?
How is a nur-turing pre-sence in this wa-ter, bread, and wine?
Who are these, called by great I AM, who gives us each a role,

Or stones piled in the Jor-dan's bed which look like much the same?
And why would some-one take the cross which should be mine in-stead?
And how are we all gath-ered as one flawed yet faith-ful line?
who helps us to map out the Way by which we are made whole?

It means God brought us safe-ly here, we fol-lowed and be-lieved,
Be-cause Re-demp-tion passed this way, our lives have been re-stored
The Spi-rit, bold, mys-te-ri-ous, blows us where God has willed
These schol-ars call the church to learn, ex-tend sal-va-tion's reach.

and some-one gave her life to share the sto-ry you re-ceived.
and some-one gave his life to share the Good News of our Lord.
and peo-ple give their lives to share the power with which we're filled.
By grace, they give their lives to share what God gives them to teach.

Copyright © 2008 by Brummhart Publishing. All rights reserved. Used by permission.

Published Works of Donald J. Bruggink

Compiled by George Brown, Jr.

BOOKS

2004

Bruggink, Donald J. and Kim N. Baker. *By Grace Alone: Stories of the Reformed Church in America*. The Historical Series of the Reformed Church in America, no. 44. Donald J. Bruggink, general editor. Grand Rapids: Wm. B. Eerdmans, 2004.

1987

Esther, James R., and Donald J. Bruggink (eds.). *Worship the Lord*. Grand Rapids: Wm. B. Eerdmans, 1987.

1971

Bruggink, Donald J., and Carl H. Droppers. *When Faith Takes Form: Contemporary Churches of Architectural Integrity in America*. Grand Rapids: Wm. B. Eerdmans, 1971.

1965

Bruggink, Donald J., and Carl H. Droppers. *Christ and Architecture: Building Presbyterian/Reformed Churches*. Grand Rapids: Wm. B. Eerdmans, 1965.

1963

Bruggink, Donald J. (ed.). *Guilt, Grace, and Gratitude: A Commentary on the Heidelberg Catechism, Commemorating Its 400th Anniversary*. New York: Half Moon Press, 1963.

ESSAYS AND CHAPTERS IN BOOKS

2007

Bruggink, Donald J. "A Brief History of the Architecture of Reformed Churches in America." In *Liturgy Among the Thorns: Essays on Worship in the Reformed Church in America* edited by James Hart Brumm. The Historical Series of the Reformed Church in America, no. 57. Donald J. Bruggink, general editor. Grand Rapids: Wm. B. Eerdmans, 2007. pp. 91-99.

Bruggink, Donald J. "Extra-Canonical Tests for Church Membership and Ministry." In *A Goodly Heritage: Essays in Honor of the Reverend Dr. Elton J. Bruins at Eighty* edited by Jacob E. Nyenhuis. The Historical Series of the Reformed Church in America, no. 56. Donald J. Bruggink, general editor. Grand Rapids: Wm. B. Eerdmans, 2007. pp. 49-63.

1993

Bruggink, Donald J. "Reformed Worship." *The Complete Library of Christian Worship*, Volume III, *The Renewal of Sunday Worship*, edited by Robert E. Webber. Nashville: Star Song Publishing Group, 1993, pp. 180-83.

1992

Bruggink, Donald J. "Dutch Reformation." In *The Encyclopedia of the Reformed Faith*, edited by Donald K. McKim. Louisville: Westminster/John Knox Press, 1992, pp. 110-12.

Bruggink, Donald J. "Helvetic Confession, Second." In *The Encyclopedia of the Reformed Faith*, edited by Donald K. McKim. Louisville: Westminster/John Knox Press, 1992, pp. 169-71.

1983

Bruggink, Donald J. "Ecclesiastical Architecture in the Christian Reformed Church." In *Perspectives on the Christian Reformed Churches, Studies in Its History, Theology, and Ecumenicity*, edited by Peter De Klerk and Richard R. DeRidder. Grand Rapids: Baker Book House, 1983, pp. 35-52.

1971

Bruggink, Donald J. "Liturgy and Architecture." In *A Companion to the*

Liturgy, a Guide to Worship in the Reformed Church in America, edited by Garrett C. Roorda. New York: Half Moon Press, 1971, pp. 57-64.

1963

Bruggink, Donald J. "The Holy Sacraments." In *Guilt, Grace, and Gratitude: A Commentary on the Heidelberg Catechism, Commemorating Its 400th Anniversary*, edited by Donald J. Bruggink. New York: Half Moon Press, 1963, pp. 136-65.

ARTICLES

2001

Bruggink, Donald J. "Western Theological Seminary: The First Century 1866-1966," *Origins* 19, no. 1 (2001): 14-21.

1998

Bruggink, Donald J. "Revelation through Architecture." *Church Herald* 55, no. 8 (September, 1998): 29.

1997

Bruggink, Donald J. "A Symbol of Sacrifice." *Church Herald* 54, no. 4 (April, 1997): 20-23.

1995

Bruggink, Donald J. "Contemporary Context and the Biblical and Theological Roots of Reformed Worship." *Reformed Review* 48, no. 2 (Winter, 1994-1995): 77-90.

1991

Bruggink, Donald J. "Beginning the Second Century." *Reformed Review* 44, no. 3 (Spring, 1991): 185-202.

Bruggink, Donald J. "The Church in the USSR." *Faith and Form* 24 (Winter, 1990-91): 14-16.

1990

Bruggink, Donald J. "A Panel Discussion for Congregational Education" with Robert Rambusch, John Dillenberger, Donald Bruggink, Terry Eason, and Chip Reay. *Faith and Form* 23 (Winter, 1989-90): 41-44.

1989

Bruggink, Donald J. "More Than Just Furniture." *Reformed Worship*, no. 14 (Winter, 1989): 8-9.

Bruggink, Donald J. "Filioque and the Reformed Tradition." *Perspectives* 4, no. 8 (October, 1989): 8-10.

Bruggink, Donald J. "Preaching Uniforms: What to Wear in the Pulpit." *Reformed Worship*, no. 10 (Winter, 1988-1989): 7-9.

Bruggink, Donald J. "Being Faithful with the Apostles." *Church Herald* 46, no. 6 (June, 1989): 7.

Bruggink, Donald J. "Family Connections." *Church Herald* 46, no. 5 (May, 1989): 19.

Bruggink, Donald J. "Meeting the Needs of Others." *Church Herald* 46, no. 4 (April, 1989): 18.

1988

Bruggink, Donald J. "The Orthodox Orthodox: Liturgy, Tradition, and Ministry from a Calvinist Perspective." *Perspectives* 3, no. 9 (November, 1988): 6-8.

1987

Bruggink, Donald J. "IFRAA in Japan." *Faith and Form* 20 (Spring, 1987): 36-38.

Bruggink, Donald J. "Lived Fidelity to Christ." *Perspectives* 2, no. 5 (May, 1987), 11-13. This article was later published, with permission, by Faith and Order of the National Council of Churches of Christ in the USA.

1985

Bruggink, Donald J. "A Responsible Response." *Church Herald* 42, no. 19 (November 1, 1985): 13.

Bruggink, Donald J. "God Reveals Himself." *Church Herald* 42, no. 18 (October 18, 1985): 17.

Bruggink, Donald J. "Approaching God." *Church Herald* 42, no. 17 (October 4, 1985): 18.

Bruggink, Donald J. "The Worth of Worship." *Church Herald* 42, no. 16 (September 20, 1985): 9.

Bruggink, Donald J. "The RCA: Participating Separatists." *Church Herald* 42, no. 1 (June 7, 1985): 8-11.

Bruggink, Donald J. "IFRAA: Post-Conference European Seminar on Church Art and Architecture." *Faith and Form* 17 (Spring, 1985): 29-31.

1984

Bruggink, Donald J. "Together We Believe." *Church Herald* 41, no. 3 (February 3, 1984): 7.

1982

Bruggink, Donald J. "Interview with Donald J. Bruggink." *Your Church* 28, no. 5 (September/October, 1982): 8.

Bruggink, Donald J. "The Reformation of Liturgical Space." *Reformed Liturgy and Music* 16, no. 2 (February 2, 1982): 51-56.

1979

Bruggink, Donald J. "Theologies of Christian Thinkers." *Church Herald* 36, no. 10 (May 18, 1979): 21.

1978

Bruggink, Donald J. "The Limitations of Being 'Christian.'" Part 7 *Pioneer Christian Monthly* 29 (December, 1978): 16-17.

Bruggink, Donald J. "The Limitations of 'Doing It Right.'" Part 6 *Pioneer Christian Monthly* 29 (November, 1978): 8-9.

Bruggink, Donald J. "The Century of Church Growth—the Nineteenth." Part 5 *Pioneer Christian Monthly* 29 (October, 1978): 14-15.

Bruggink, Donald J. "Big Conflicts for a Little Church." Part 4 *Pioneer Christian Monthly* 29 (September, 1978): 12-13, 15.

Bruggink, Donald J. "The Problem of Polity, or How Do We Get a Minister?" Part 3 *Pioneer Christian Monthly* 29 (July/August, 1978): 6-7.

Bruggink, Donald J. "The Linguistic Limitations of the Dutch Church." Part 2 *Pioneer Christian Monthly* 29 (June, 1978): 9, 11.

Bruggink, Donald J. "350 Years of God's Grace, or the Actualization of an Impossibility." Part 1 *Pioneer Christian Monthly* 29 (May, 1978): 6-7.

Bruggink, Donald J. "The Limitations of Being a Christian." *Church Herald* 35, no. 7 (April 7, 1978): 14-15.

Bruggink, Donald J. "The Limitations of Doing It Right." *Church Herald* 35, no. 6 (March 10, 1978): 13-14.

Bruggink, Donald J. "The Century of Growth—The Nineteenth." *Church Herald* 35, no. 5 (March 10, 1978): 14-15.

Bruggink, Donald J. "Big Conflicts for a Little Church." *Church Herald* 35, no. 4 (February 24, 1978): 12-14.

Bruggink, Donald J. "Problems of Polity." *Church Herald* 35, no. 3 (February 10, 1978): 18-19.

Bruggink, Donald J. "The Linguistic Limitations of the Dutch Church." *Church Herald* 35, no. 2 (January 27, 1978):12-13.

Bruggink, Donald J. "Less Than 10,000 Hollanders," in the series, "350 Years of the Reformed Church in America." *Church Herald* 35, no. 1 (January 13, 1978): 4-5.

1976

Bruggink, Donald J. "General Synod Prayer." *Church Herald* 33, no. 15 (July 23, 1976): 15.

Bruggink, Donald J. "The Graffiti-Free Church." *Church Herald* 33, no. 3 (February 6, 1976): 6-7, 27.

1975

Bruggink, Donald J. "The Graffiti-Free Church." *Your Church* 21, no. 4 (July-August, 1975): 18, 23-25.

Bruggink, Donald J. "The Church Today: A Symposium." *Reformed Journal* 25, no. 2 (February, 1975): 10-27.

1974

Bruggink, Donald J. "Architecture for Total Ministry." *Your Church* 20, no. 6 (November/December, 1974): 6.

Bruggink, Donald J., and Kansfield, Norman J. "Worship." *Reformed Review* 27, no. 2 (Winter, 1974): 67-82.

Bruggink, Donald J. "A Treasure of Our Past." *Dutch Immigrant Society Magazine* 4, no. 4 (March, 1974).

1972

Bruggink, Donald J. "Contemporary Protestant Worship." *Faith and Form* 5 (Spring, 1972): 12, 25.

Bruggink, Donald J. "A Community of Faith." *Your Church* 18, no. 1 (January/February, 1972): 10, 11, 29-31.

1970

Bruggink, Donald J. "Differences within Our Church." *Church Herald* 27, no. 3 (January 16, 1970): 12-13.

Bruggink, Donald J. "Sociological Separation and Unity." *Reformed Review* 23, no. 2 (Winter, 1970): 106-121.

1968

Bruggink, Donald J. "Liturgy, Architecture, and Vatican II." *Reformed Review* 22, no.1 (S, 1968): 20, 45-50.

Bruggink, Donald J. "Introduction." *Your Church* 14, no. 2 (March/April, 1968): 6-8.

1967

Bruggink, Donald J. "Heresy in the Sanctuary." *Eternity Magazine* (April 1967): 22-25.

1966

Bruggink, Donald J. "The Historical Background of Theological Education." *Reformed Review* 19, no. 4 (May, 1966): 2-17.

Bruggink, Donald J. "A Witness to Faith." *Your Church* 12, no. 2 (March/April, 1966): 24-26, 52-55.

1961

Bruggink, Donald J. "Gaius." Sunday School Lesson Exposition for July 9. *Church Herald* 18, no. 30 (September 15, 1961): 20.

Bruggink, Donald J. "Titus." Sunday School Lesson Exposition for July 9. *Church Herald* 18, no. 29 (September 1, 1961): 22-23.

Bruggink, Donald J. "Aquila and Priscilla." Sunday School Lesson Exposition for July 9. *Church Herald* 18, no. 19 (September 1, 1961): 22.

Bruggink, Donald J. "Timothy." Sunday School Lesson Exposition for July 9. *Church Herald* 18, no. 28 (August 18, 1961): 22-23.

Bruggink, Donald J. "Lydia." Sunday School Lesson Exposition for July 9. *Church Herald* 18, no. 18 (August 18, 1961): 22.

Bruggink, Donald J. "Silas." Sunday School Lesson Exposition for July 9. *Church Herald* 18, no. 27 (August 4, 1961): 20-21.

Bruggink, Donald J. "John Mark." Sunday School Lesson Exposition for July 9. *Church Herald* 18, no. 27 (August 4, 1961): 20.

Bruggink, Donald J. "Dorcus, A Woman of Good Works." Sunday School Lesson Exposition for July 9. *Church Herald* 18, no. 26 (July 21, 1961): 20-21.

Bruggink, Donald J. "The Apostle Thomas." Sunday School Lesson Exposition for July 9. *Church Herald* 18, no. 26 (July 21, 1961): 20.

Bruggink, Donald J. "Mary and Martha, Friends of Jesus." Sunday School Lesson Exposition for July 9. *Church Herald* 18, no. 25 (July 7, 1961): 20-21.

Bruggink, Donald J. "Matthew the Converted Publican." Sunday School Lesson Exposition for July 9. *The Church Herald* 18, no. 25 (July 7, 1961): 20.

Bruggink, Donald J. "Andrew A Fisher of Men." Sunday School Lesson Exposition for July 9. *Church Herald* 18, no. 24 (June 23, 1961): 23.

Bruggink, Donald J. "Mary the Mother of Jesus." Sunday School Lesson Exposition for July 2. *The Church Herald* 18, no. 24 (June 23, 1961): 22.

Bruggink, Donald J. "Why Hast Thou Forsaken Me?" *Church Herald* 18, no. 8 (February 24, 1961): 12-13.

1959

Bruggink, Donald J. "Calvin and Federal Theology." *Reformed Review* 13, no. 1 (September, 1959): 15-22.

Bruggink, Donald J. "Calvin in Japan." *Reformed Review* 13, no. 1 (September, 1959): 51-52.

Bruggink, Donald J. "Speaking in Tongues." *Church Herald* 16, no. 17 (April 24, 1959): 12.

1958

Bruggink, Donald J. "Away in a Manger, No Crib for a Bed." *Church Herald* 15, no. 49 (December 19, 1958): 11.

1953

Bruggink, Donald J. "Christ and the Jehovah's Witnesses." *Western Seminary Bulletin* (May, 1953).

DOCTORAL DISSERTATION

Bruggink, Donald J. *The Theology of Thomas Boston, 1676-1732*. University of Edinburgh, 1956.

BOOK REVIEWS

2006

Bruggink, Donald J. Review of *What God Has Joined Together?* by David G. Myers. San Franciscio: HarperSanFrancisco, 2005. In *Reformed Review* online 59, no. 2 (Winter 2005-2006): 250-51.

2000

Bruggink, Donald J. Review of *Clash of Gods*, by Thomas F. Matthews. Princeton: Princeton University Press, 1993. In *Reformed Review* 54, no. 1 (Autumn, 2000): 60-61.

Bruggink, Donald J. Review of *Seeing Beyond the Word*, by Raymond A. Metzer. Grand Rapids: Wm. B. Eerdmans, 1999. In *Reformed Review* 54, no. 1 (Autumn, 2000), 71.

1988

Bruggink, Donald J. Review of *Byzantine Liturgy*, by Hans-Joachim Schulz. New York: Pueblo, 1986. In *Calvin Theological Journal* 23, no. 1 (April, 1988): 123.

Bruggink, Donald J. Review of *The New Westminster Dictionary of Liturgy and Worship*. Philadelphia: Westminster Press, 1986. In *Reformed Worship*, no. 6 (Winter, 1987-1988): 46.

1972

Bruggink, Donald J. Review of *New Forms of Worship*, by James F. White. In *Reformed Review* 25, no. 2 (Winter, 1972): 103-104.

1971

Bruggink, Donald J. Review of *Early Netherlandish Triptychs: A Study in Patronage*, by Shirley Neilsen Blum. Berkeley: University of California Press, 1969. In *Church History* 40, no. 2 (June, 1971): 217.

1969

Bruggink, Donald J. Review of *Modern Architecture and Christian Celebration*, No. 18, *Ecumenical Studies in Worship*, by Frâedâeric DeBuyst. Richmond: John Knox Press, 1968. In *Reformed Review* 23, no. 1 (Fall, 1969): 38-39.

Bruggink, Donald J. Review of *The Early Church,* No. 1, *The Pelican History of the Church,* by Henry Chadwick. Grand Rapids: Wm. B. Eerdmans, 1969. In *Reformed Review* 23, no. 1 (Fall, 1969): 40.

1961

Bruggink, Donald J. Review of *The Westminster Confession for Today: A Contemporary Interpretation,* by Georg Stuart Hendry. Richmond: John Knox, 1960. In *Reformed Review* 14, no. 4 (May, 1961): 52.

1960

Bruggink, Donald J. Review of *John Calvin: The Man and His Ethics,* by Georgia Elma Harkness. New York: Abingdon, 1958. In *Reformed Review* 13, no. 4 (May, 1960): 55-56.

1958

Bruggink, Donald J. Review of *The Gospel of the Incarnation,* by George Stuart Hendry. Philadelphia: Westminster, 1958. In *Reformed Review* 12, no. 1 (Spring, 1958): 51-53.

THE HISTORICAL SERIES OF THE REFORMED CHURCH IN AMERICA

Donald J. Bruggink, general editor. All volumes published in Grand Rapids by William B. Eerdmans unless otherwise noted. Listed below in order of publication.

Harmelink, Herman III. *Ecumenism and the Reformed Church.* 1968.

Bruins, Elton J. *The Americanization of a Congregation: A History of the Third Reformed Church of Holland, Michigan.* 1970.[1]

Van Ess, Dorothy F. *Pioneers in the Arab World.* 1974.

Van Hoeven, James W. (ed.) *Piety and Patriotism: Bicentennial Studies of the Reformed Church in America, 1776-1976.* 1976.

Van Hoeven, James W. *A Study and Discussion Guide for* Piety and Patriotism *Including Questions for Certification as a Bicentennial Scholar in Reformed Church History, 1776-1976.* 1976.

---

[1] A second edition was published in 1995.

De Jong, Gerald F. *The Dutch Reformed Church in the American Colonies.* 1978.[2]

Vandenberge, Peter N. *Historical Directory of the Reformed Church in America, 1628-1978.* 1978.

Schuppert, Mildred W. *A Digest and Index of the Minutes of the General Synod of the Reformed Church in America, 1958-1977.* 1979.

Schuppert, Mildred W. *A Digest and Index of the Minutes of the General Synod of the Reformed Church in America, 1906-1957.* 1982.

De Jong, Gerald F. *From Strength to Strength: A History of Northwestern 1882-1982.* 1982.

Dykstra, D. Ivan. *B.D.: A Biography of My Father, the Late Reverend B.D. Dykstra.* 1982.

Dalenberg, Cornelia. *Sharifa.* 1982.

Beardslee, John W. III (ed.) *Vision from the Hill: Selections from the Works of Faculty & Alumni, published on the Bicentennial of the New Brunswick Theological Seminary.* 1984.

Hageman, Howard G. *Two Centuries Plus: The Story of New Brunswick Seminary.* 1984.

Hoff, Marvin D. *The Reformed Church in America: Structures for Mission.* 1985.

Cook, James I. (ed.) *The Church Speaks: Papers of the Commission on Theology Reformed Church in America 1959-1984.* 1985.

Van Hoeven, James W. (ed.) *Word and World: Reformed Theology in America.* 1986.

Ten Zythoff, Gerrit J. *Sources of Secession: The Netherlands Hervormde Kerk on the Eve of the Dutch Immigration to the Midwest.* 1987.

Van Wylen, Gordon J. *Vision for a Christian College: Essays by Gordon J. Van Wylen, President of Hope College, 1972-1987.* Ed. Harry Boonstra. 1988.

Klunder, Jack D., and Gasero, Russell L. (eds.) *Servant Gladly: Essays in Honor of John W. Beardslee III.* 1989.

[2] Reprinted with a new cover design in 2008.

Boersma, Jeanette. *Grace in the Gulf: The Autobiography of Jeanette Boersma, Missionary Nurse in Iraq and the Sultanate of Oman.* 1991.

Brouwer, Arie R. *Ecumenical Testimony.* 1991.

De Jong, Gerald F. *The Reformed Church in China 1842 - 1951.* 1992.

Gasero, Russell L. (ed.) *Historical Directory of the Reformed Church in America 1628-1992.* 1992.

Meeter, Daniel J. *Meeting Each Other In Doctrine, Liturgy, and Government: The Bicentennial of the Celebration of the Constitution of the Reformed Church in America.* 1993.

Janssen, Allan J. *Gathered at Albany.* 1995.

Bruins, Elton J. *The Americanization of a Congregation*, 2nd ed. 1995.

Mast, Gregg A. *In Remembrance and Hope: The Ministry and Vision of Howard G. Hageman.* 1998.

Gasero, Russell L. (ed.) *Historical Directory of the Reformed Church in America: 1628-1992.* 1992.

Venema, Janny (trans. and ed.). *Deacons' Accounts 1652-1674: First Dutch Reformed Church of Beverwijck/Albany, New York.* 1998.

Swart, Morrell F. *The Call of Africa: The Reformed Church in America Mission in the Sub-Shara, 1948-1998.* 1998.

Scudder, Lewis R. III, *The Arabian Mission's Story: In Search of Abraham's Other Son.* 1998.

House, Renée S., and John W. Coakley, eds. *Patterns and Portraits: Women in the History of the Reformed Church in America.* 1999.

Bruins, Elton J., and Robert P. Swierenga. *Family Quarrels in the Dutch Reformed Churches of the 19th Century.* The Pillar Church Sesquicentennial Lectures. 1999.

Janssen, Allan J. *Constitutional Theology: Notes on the* Book of Church Order *of the Reformed Church in America.* 2000.

Mast, Gregg A. (ed.). *Raising the Dead: Sermons of Howard G. Hageman.* 2000.

Brumm, James Hart, ed. *Equipping the Saints: The Synod of New York, 1800-2000*. 2000.

Beeke, Joel R. (ed.). *Forerunner of the Great Awakening: Sermons by Theodorus Jacobus Frelinghuysen (1691-1747)*. 2000.

Gasero, Russell L. (ed.). *Historical Directory of the Reformed Church in America 1628-2000*. 2001.

Heideman, Eugene P. *From Mission to Church: The Reformed Church in America Mission to India*. 2001.

Boonstra, Henry. *Our School: Calvin College and the Christian Reformed Church*. 2001.

Cook, James I. (ed.). *The Church Speaks*, Vol. 2, *Papers of the Commission on Theology Reformed Church in America 1985-2000*. 2002.

Coakley, John W. (ed.). *Concord Makes Strength: Essays in Reformed Ecumenism*. 2002.

Swierenga, Robert P. *Dutch Chicago: A History of the Hollanders in the Windy City*. 2002.

Armerding, Paul L. *Doctors for the Kingdom: The Work of the American Mission Hospitals in the Kingdom of Saudi Arabia 1913-1955*. Foreword by Ravi K. Zacharias. 2003.

Bruggink, Donald J. and Kim N. Baker. *By Grace Alone: Stories of the Reformed Church in America*. 2004.

Durkee, June Potter. *Travels of an American Girl*. 2004.

Kansfield, Mary L. *Letters to Hazel: Ministry within the Women's Board of Foreign Missions of the Reformed Church in America*. 2004.

Stellingwerff, Johan. *Iowa Letters: Dutch Immigrants on the American Frontier*. Ed. Robert P. Swierenga, trans. Walter Lagerwey. 2004.

Kennedy, James C., and Caroline J. Simon. *Can Hope Endure? A Historical Case Study in Christian Higher Education*. 2005.

Swierenga, Robert P. *Elim: A Chicago Christian School and Life-Training Center for the Disabled*. 2005.

Koopman, LeRoy. *Taking the Jesus Road: The Ministry of the Reformed Church in America Among Native Americans*. 2005.

Blei, Karel. *The Netherlands Reformed Church 1571-2005*. Trans. Allan J. Janssen. 2006.

Sheeres, Janet Sjaarda. *Son of Succession: Douwe J. Vander Werp*. 2006.

Janssen, Allan J. *Kingdom, Office, and Church: A Study of A.A. van Ruler's Doctrine of Ecclesiastical Office*. Trans. Allan J. Janssen. 2006.

Smidt, Corwin, Donald Luidens, James Penning, and Roger Nemeth. *Divided by a Common Heritage: The Christian Reformed Church and the Reformed Church in America at the Beginning of the New Millennium*. 2006.

De Jong, James A. *Henry J. Kuiper: Shaping the Christian Reformed Church, 1907-1962*. 2007.

Nyenhuis, Jacob E. (ed.). *A Goodly Heritage: Essays in Honor of the Reverend Dr. Elton J. Bruins at Eighty*. 2007.

Brumm, James Hart. (ed.). *Liturgy among the Thorns: Essays on Worship in the Reformed Church in America*. 2007.

Swierenga, Robert P. and William Van Appledorn (eds.). *Old Wing Mission: Cultural Interchange as Chronicled by George and Arvilla Smith in their Work with Chief Wakazoo's Ottawa Band on the West Michigan Frontier*. Published in cooperation with the Van Raalte Institute. 2008.

Brown, George Jr. (ed.). *Herman J. Ridder: Contextual Preacher and President*. 2008.

Brumm, James Hart (ed.). *Tools for Understanding: Essays in Honor of Donald J. Bruggink*. 2009.

Hoff, Marvin D. *Chinese Theological Education*. 2009.

EDITED BOUND VOLUMES OF STUDENT RESEARCH PAPERS

The Western Christendom Travel Seminar Papers, 1967, Vol. 1

The Western Christendom Travel Seminar Papers, 1967, Vol. 2

The Western Christendom Travel Seminar Papers, 1969

The Western Christendom Travel Seminar Papers, 1973

The Western Christendom Travel Seminar Papers, 1975

The Western Christendom Travel Seminar Papers, 1977

The Impact of John Calvin on France, Switzerland, Germany, and the Netherlands: Seminar Papers, 1978

The Western Christendom Travel Seminar Papers, 1979

Paul to Justinian Seminar Papers, 1980

The Western Christendom Travel Seminar Papers, 1981

The Cities of St. Paul: Seminar Papers, 1982

Rome: City of Peter and Paul: Western Christendom Travel Seminar Papers, 1983

The Cities of St. Paul: Seminar Papers, 1984

Rome: City of Peter and Paul: Seminar Papers, 1985

The Huguenots: Seminar Papers, 1986

Rome: City of Peter and Paul: Seminar Papers, 1987

The Cities of St. Paul: Seminar Papers, 1988

Rome: City of Peter and Paul: Seminar Papers, 1989

The Cities of Paul and John: Seminar Papers, 1990

Rome: City of Peter and Paul: Seminar Papers, 1991

The Cities of Paul and John: Seminar Papers, 1992

Rome: City of Peter and Paul: The Western Christendom Travel Seminar Papers, 1993

The Cities of Paul and John: Seminar Papers, 1994

Rome: City of Peter and Paul: Seminar Papers, 1995

The Cities of Paul and John: Seminar Papers, 1996

Rome: City of Peter and Paul: Seminar Papers, 1997

The Cities of Paul and John: Seminar Papers, 1998

Rome: City of Peter and Paul: The Western Christendom Travel Seminar Papers, 1999

Index

Abeel, John, 173n96
Abraham, 194, 241
Academij Seminarium, 162
Adam, 232, 240
Addams, Jane, 98n96
Afscheiding, 210, 214
Ahlstrom, Sydney E., *A Religious History of the American People*, 19
Albany, Particular Synod of, 38
Alexander, Archibald, 197
Althaus, Paul, *The Theology of Martin Luther*, 299n14
Ambrose, 153, 168n82
American Academy in Rome, Italy, xxviii
American Association of Theological Schools, 35-36, 53
American Reformed Church, Orange City, 41
American Society for Church History, 10n25
American University in Cairo, 42

Americanization of a Congregation, The, xliii
Amsterdam, Classis of, 117, 161, 163, 164, 190, 204
Amsterdam, Dam Square, 252
Amsterdam, Free University, 34, 296
Anderson, Marian, 85n52
Andover Theological Seminary, 197
Anselm, 297n10, 314-15
Anselm, *Cur Deus Homo?* 298, 299
Aquinas, Thomas, 149-53, 153n33, 154n37, 185
Architectural Forum, xxx
Articles of Dort, 278-79
Articles of Union, 163, 165, 204-205
Athanasius, 154n37, 301
Atonement, The (Hughes), 307n38
Atonement and the Sacraments, The (Paul), 297n10, 299n14, 304, 315n68, 317n77
Augustine of Hippo, 153, 168n82, 236n5, 270

Aulén, Gustaf, 298-99
Austin College, 42, 43
Austin Presbyterian Theological Seminary, 43-44, 50, 54, 64

Baillie, D.M., *God Was In Christ*, 299n16
Baker, Kim Nathan, 134
Barth, Karl, 256n2, 281-83, 296n3
Basil the Great, 154n37
Baslika Vierzenheilegan, Bavaria, xli
Bast, Henry, 31, 33-34, 180
Bay View Reading Club, 79, 95n88
Beach, Myrtle, 84n49
Beardslee, Frances Davis, 67-109
Beardslee, John Walter, Jr., 68-69, 68n2, 70, 71n10, 83, 85n51, 100-101
Beardslee, John Walter, Sr., 70, 75n21, 83, 101, 212, 212n35
Beardslee, John Walter, III, 10, 122
Beardslee, Sarah, 70, 74, 75n21, 83, 108
Beardslee, William Armitage, 70
Bechtel, Carol, 32, 143
Beck, T. Romeyn, 77
Belgic Confession, 160, 170, 248-53, 260, 285
Benson, Robert, 171
Berg, Joseph, 21
Berkouwer, G.C., *The Work of Christ*, 301n19
Bertolino, Dianne, 32
Bertsch, Olive, 97, 98n95
Bethany Reformed Church, Grand Rapids, 34
Beza, Theodor, 169n82
Bi-Level Multi-Site Program, xli, 221-25
Billings, J. Todd, *Calvin, Participation, and the Gift*, 301n20, 317n77
Blocher, Henri, 297, 302, 316
Board of Domestic Missions, RCA, 209
Board of Theological Education, RCA, 183-84, 220-21, 223, 225-26
Boelkins, Dawn, 32
Boniface VIII, 153-54, 160
Bonnet, Gisbert, 197

Boot, Florence M., 84n49
Boston, Thomas, xxxiv
Boyle, John F., 149
Boys, Mary, 44
Bradford, John M., 174n96
Brauer, Jerald C., 19n52
Brink, Emily, 289-91
Brodhead, J. Romeyn, 121, 125
Brodhead, Jacob, 198n28
Broek, Dirk, 76, 213
Brook, J.V.K., 303n26
Brouwer, Arie R., 135, 223-24, 286-87
Brower, John I., 119
Brown, George, Jr., 287-88
Brown, Joanne Carlson, 298n12
Bruggink, Donald J., 4, 21, 26 f., 29-30, 32-33, 53, 112, 114, 124-25, 128, 130, 133, 137, 142, 295; *Christ and Architecture*, xx; *When Faith Takes Form*, xx
Bruggink, Erma VanRoekel, xxixn7, xxx, xlv
Bruins, Elton, xliii, 21, 128n1, 136
Brumm, James Hart, 194n15
Brunner, Emil, 301n19
Bucer, Martin, 29, 157
Bullinger, Heinrich, 264
Burgess, Warren, 59
Burggraaff, Winfield, xliii, 36
Burns, Lucy, 93

Caird, George, 244n12
Callicles, 258, 258n31
Calvin, John, 29, 155-58, 164, 169, 185, 251n6, 253-54, 263-64, 267-71, 274-75, 275n48, 290-92, 295-319; *Institutes of the Christian Religion*, 155
Calvin, Origins and Development of His Religious Thought (Wendel), 296n5
Calvin College, 41
Calvin Institute for Christian Worship, 289
Calvin's Christology (Edmondson), 297
Calvin's Doctrine of the Work of Christ (Jansen), 296-97, 312
Calvin's Perspective on the Exultation of

Index   343

Christ (Hoogland), 296
Canons of Dort, 160
Carroll, Jackson, 68n1
Catherine of Sienna, 154n37
Catt, Carrie Chapman, 94
Cedar Grove, Wisconsin, xxi, xxix-xxx, xxxv, xxxvii
Centennial Discourses of the Reformed Church in America, 111, 167n79
Central College, xii, xxvii, xxx-xxxi, 33, 39, 295
Central Reformed Church, Grand Rapids, xli, 223
Century Club, 72, 82-84, 108
Chase, Steven, 4n2
Chautauqua, 79
Chicago, Particular Synod of, 73n13, 215
Chicago, University of, 42, 69
Chicago Manual of Style, The, 131
Christ and Architecture (Bruggink and Droppers), xx, xliii
Christ in Our Place (Van Buren), 295, 297
Christian Faith and Life Community, 45-50, 57, 63
Christian Intelligencer, 121, 215
Christian Reformed Church, 103n111, 214, 289
Church Herald, 39, 56-57, 128, 288
Church of England, 278
Church Order of Dort, 158-60
Clark, Mrs. O.H., 97
Clark, Wade, 68n1
Coakley, John W., 38n26, 167n79
Coburn, Mrs. C.C., 88
Coetus-conferentie controversy, 162-63, 204-205
Cole, Richard, 288
Collegiate Church of the City of New York, 170, 172, 190, 193, 205
Collegiate Suffrage Association, 72n11
Colorado Springs Police Department, 61, 63
Colorado Springs Sun, 61
Columbia University, 44, 171, 184, 205

Commissioned pastors, 227-28
Commission on Christian Worship, RCA, 183, 229, 288
Commission on Church Order, RCA, 183, 186
Commission on History, RCA, xiii, xv-xvi, xviii, xlv, 122, 123-24, 125, 229
Commission on the Revision of the Liturgy, RCA, 283
Commission on Theology, RCA, xliii, 182, 186-87
Committee on Ecclesiastical Office and Ministry, 183
Committee on Education, 218-19
Committee on History and Research, RCA, 122
Committee on Professorate and Theological Seminaries, 219-20
Committee on the Revision of the Constitution, RCA, 181
Committee on Theological Education, 221
Condict, Ira, 174n96
Congregational Union, 93
Constitution of 1833, 174
Cook, James I., 225
Cornell College, Iowa, 68n3
Corwin, Edward Tanjore, xxviii, 21, 111, 121-22, 125, 160
Cotton, John, 274
Covenant Life Curriculum, 37, 50, 56, 58-59, 64
Crane, Caroline Bartlett, 95, 107
Crawford, Dan, 83
Crispell, Charles, 212
Crispell, Cornelius E., 175, 217
Cross of Jesus, The (Morris), 299n15
Cuyler, Cornelius, 198n28

Daughters of the American Revolution, 72, 84-87, 99, 105, 108
Da Vinci Code, The, 235n4
De Christologie van Calvin (Emmen), 296
De Cock, Henrik, 210
DeGruchy, John W., 292

Dehn, Anna, 100
De Hope, 5, 212-13
DeJong, Eberdine, xxix, xlv
DeJong, Gary, xxix, xxixn5
De Jong, James A., 129n1
de Knijff, H.W., 254-55
De Merrell, Iantha Aldrich, 101, 105, 107
Dendy, Marshall C., 50
Denny, James, 308n39
De Witt, John, 198n26
De Witt, Thomas, 118-19, 121, 125, 174, 209
Diekema, Mary Alcott, 108
Digest and Index of the Minutes of the General Synod, A (Schuppert) xlivn34
Doctor Ecclesiae, 153-54
Dolientie, 249
Dominice, Max, *L'humanité de Jesus d'après Calvin*, 296
Doremus, Sarah, 136
Dort, Great Synod of, 158, 160, 169, 185, 202
Dort, Synod of, I (1576), 158
Dosker, Henry E., 3-4, 5ff, 6n7, 9, 12-14 ff., 23, 28, 30, 214, 216; *Outline Studies in Ecclesiastical History*, 16
Dostoyevsky, Fyodor, 298
Doumergue, Émile, 280
Dragt, Gordon, xxxviii
Droppers, Carl, xxx; *Christ and Architecture*, xx; *When Faith Takes Form*, xx
Droppers, Oliver, xxx, xxxn8
Dubbink, Gerrit H., 24-25
Duffy, Ada, 84n49
Dulles, Avery, 151
Dutch American Genealogist, 116
Dykstra, Craig, 166
Dyrness, William, 264

Eames, Charles and Ray, xlii
Eastminster Presbyterian Church, Grand Rapids, 57, 60
Ecclesiastical Ordinances, 156-57, 168n81
Ecumenism and the Reformed Church, xliii

Edinburgh, University of, xxvii, xxxiii-xxxv, 32
Edmondson, Stephen, 297n7, 309n44, 312, 312n54, 317, 317n77; *Calvin's Christology*, 297
Edwards, Jonathan, 274-75
Eelman, James C., 284-85
Eenigenburg, Elton Marshall, xxxviii, xxxviiin22, 3-4, 19, 27, 31, 36, 51, 53, 58, 222
Eerdmans, William B. Publishing Company, xv
Eglise et Liturgie, 282-83
Embden, Synod of, 158
Emmen, E., *De Christologie van Calvin*, 296
Englund, Harold N., xxxv, xxxvn19, xxxix, 31, 44n45, 51
Enlightenment, the, 251
Erasmus Hall, 171, 172
Erasmus of Rotterdam, 270
Eusebius, 21, 312n53
Eve, 240
Explanatory Articles, 167-70, 173
Ezra, 239

Faculté Libre de Theologie Evangélique, 297
Fairchild, Roy, 58
Faith and Order conferences, 282
Fall, the, 238
Fatio, Olivier, 297n10
Federal Union, Reformed Church in America and German Reformed Church, 19
First Presbyterian Church, Sherman, Texas, 42
First Reformed Church in Cedar Grove, xxix
Fisher, George Park, 9
Flowers, Charles, 99
Folkert, Morris, 283-84
Fordham Manor Reformed Church, xxviii, xxxv-xxxvii, xlv, 32, 229
Forsyth, P.T., 308n38
Franklin, William, 206
Freke, Timothy, 235n4
Frelinghuysen, Theodore, 203, 205-206
Froleigh, Solomon, 173, 192

Fuller Theological Seminary, 225
Fundamental Articles, 161-62

Gandy, Peter, 235n4
Gasero, Russell, 111, 133, 137; *Historical Directory of the Reformed Church in America*, xxvii, 124
Gateway United Presbyterian Church, Colorado Springs, 62
Geertz, Clifford, 256-57
General Federation of Women's Clubs, 80-81
General Program Council, 116, 221, 223
General Synod Council, 116
General Synod Executive Committee, 183, 220-21
General Synod of the Reformed Church in America, xx, 10, 36, 100, 116-19, 142, 170-80, 183, 186-87, 189-90, 194, 201, 214, 226-27, 279, 283
General Synod Professors Task Force, 141-42
Geneva Catechism, 300
Genne, Bill, 58
George, Timothy, 314-15; *Theology of the Reformers*, 297n10
Gereformeerde, 249
Gerrod, Ruby, 84n49
Gilmore, Christine Van Raalte, 105, 107
Gilmore, Richard C., 107
Gogol, Nikolai, 298
Gohlke, Mrs. W.J., 101
Gonzalez, Justo, 20n53
Goulooze, William, 3-4, 5n4, 8, 13, 33
Gowdy, Elsie, 97, 98n95
Graham, William, xxxiv
Grand Haven Daily, 88
Grand Rapids Police Department, 54
Greeley, Andrew, 127
Gregory I, 153
Gregory of Nazianzen, 154n37
Groningen, University of, 197, 282
Groome, Thomas, 44
Grosse Pointe Memorial Church, 60
Guillabaud, H.E., *Why the Cross?* 296n2
Guilt, Grace, and Gratitude, xliii
Gunn, Alexander, 193, 194, 194n15, 195n19

Hackensack, Classis of, 165n71
Hageman, Howard, 201, 219-20, 224, 280-81
Hall, Anna M., 84n49
Hall, Charles A.M., *With the Spirit's Sword*, 299n14
Hall, David W., 297
Hamilton, Alexander, 84
Hamilton, Elizabeth Schuyler, 84
Hamilton, Mrs. C.B., 94
Harmelink, Herman, III, xliii
Harrington, Lilla Marie, 84n49
Hase, Charles, 8
Healy, Nicholas A., 149-50
Heidelberg Catechism, xxxviii, 7, 158, 160
Heideman, Eugene, xxxi, 295
Heinen, Charlotte M., 55
Helm, Paul, 306; *John Calvin's Ideas*, 296n5
Hemmerlein, Felix, 269
Henderlite, Rachel, 36, 50, 57
Herformde Kerk, 210
Hertzog, Anna, 175
Hertzog, Peter, Theological Hall, 175
Hesselink, I. John, xxxi, 224
Hester, David C., 37
Hill, Charles E., 297
Historical Directory of the Reformed Church in America (Vandenberge, Gasero), xxvii, xliv, 124
Historical Highlights, 116
Historical Series of the Reformed Church in America, xii, xv-xvi, xviii, xxi, xliii-xlv, 21, 124, 128, 130, 133
Hoff, Marvin D., xliv, xlivn32
Hoffman, Marsha, 128
Holbrook, Joseph, xxxii, xxxiin16
Holifield, E. Brooks D., 10n25
Holland, Classis of, 73n13
Holland, Michigan, xxxv, xxxvii, 67-104
Holland City News, 101

Holland Classical Union, 72, 78-79, 107
Holland Daily Sentinel, 88, 90n67, 94, 96n90, 97-98, 103
Holland Equal Suffrage Club, 107
Holland High School, 106
Hoogland, Marvin P., *Calvin's Perspective on the Exultation of Christ*, 296
Hope Church, 73, 75, 77-78, 83, 85, 107
Hope Church Ladies' Aid Society, 72-74, 105
Hope Church Ladies' Missionary Society, 72, 74-78, 105
Hope College, xix, 39, 67-69, 71n10, 97, 107-108, 175, 208-212
House, Renée S., 38n26
Hughes, Thomas Hywell, *The Atonement*, 307n38
Hunter, A. Mitchell, *The Teaching of Calvin*, 296n5
Huyck, Jan, 160

Iconoclasts, 270-72
Iliff School of Theology, 62
Institutes of the Christian Religion (Calvin), 155
International Journal of Religious Education, 56
Irenaeus of Lyons, 235n4
Iron Mountain, 116
Israel, 191

James, Frank A., III, 297
James, M. Stephen, 179
Jamison, Wallace, 221
Jansen, John F., *Calvin's Doctrine of the Work of Christ*, 296-97, 312
Janssen, Allan J., 135
Janssen, Paul, 289
Jellema, Bill, xxxv
Jerome, 153, 168n82
John Calvin's Ideas (Helm), 296n5
John Chrysostom, 154n37
John Paul II, 153n33
Johnson, Arthur, 283-84
Jones, Laverne, 100
Joosten, Lynne, 287

Kaiser, Christopher B., 4n2
Kansfield, Mary L., 38, 136n11
Kansfield, Norman J., xx, xl, 33, 123
Keillor, Garrison, xxix, xxxiiin17
Kemper Military College, 41
Kent County Department of Social Welfare, 54
Kent County Juvenile Court, 54
Kierkegaard, Søren, 290
Knox, John, 280
Kollen, Martha Diekema, 105, 108
Kolyn, Matthew, 3-4, 7
Koopman, LeRoy, 136n10
Koops, Hugh, xxxix
Kooy, Vernon, 39
Kraemer, Charles E.S., 36
Krahe, Charles, Jr., 281
Krankenbezoekers, 160, 202
Krol, Sebastiaan Jansz, 160
Kruithof, Bastian, xxxv, xxxvn18
Kurtz, Johann Heinrich, 5, 5n6, 8
Kuyper, Abraham, 17, 17n46, 249-50, 260, 280
Kuyper, Cornelius, xxixn6
Kuyper, Lester Jacob, xxxi, xxxin15, xlv, 31, 64, 223

Labagh, Peter, 174n96
Landwehr, Louise, 105, 107
Latini, Theresa, 32
Laverman, Bruce, 54, 58
Leader, 101n111
Lescaze, William, xxx
Lewis, C.S., 244n10
Lewis, W. Jack, 46
L'humanité de Jesus d'après Calvin (Dominice), 296
Lillback, Peter, 297
Lipmann, Walter, 184
Liturgy and Psalms, 283
Liturgy of the Reformed Church in America, 28-29
Livingston, Henry, 172n93
Livingston, John Henry, 139, 143, 163, 165, 167-75, 189-200, 204, 206-207
Locke, John, 191
LOGOS, 61
Lubbers, Brent Douglas, 42, 61n105, 62-63

Lubbers, Clark Edward, 42, 60
Lubbers, Egbert Edward, 41-43
Lubbers, Elaine, xxxix, 31-65
Lubbers, Jill Claire, 42, 60
Lubbers, Paul Jeffrey, 42
Ludlow, Gabriel, 194, 200
Ludlow, John, 174, 198, 198n26
Luidens, Donald, 129n1
Luther, Martin, 271, 299, 303n26
Lynn, Robert W., 36

MacLeod, Meri, 32
Manual of the Reformed Church in America, xxviii
Maodush-Pitzer, Diane, 32
Marble Collegiate Church, 75
Marty, Martin E., 19n52
Masonic Lodge, 214
Mast, Gregg, 291-92
Matthews, Joe, 48-49
Mattison, Robin D., 32
McBride, Laura, 84n49
McBride, Mrs. Charles, 94-95
McCord, James I., 44
McDonagh, Elizabeth, 92n78
McLean, Ida Sears, 84, 84n49
Meeter, Daniel, 169n82, 194n15
Menenga, George H., xxxi, xxxin12
Mercersburg Movement, 276-78, 283
Meyer, Andrew, 39
Meyer, Hermanus, 164n69, 167, 173n94
Michaelius, Johannes, 160-61, 202-203
Michigan, University of, 60, 95n88
Michigan Equal Suffrage Association, 72, 87-105, 108
Michigan Federation of Women's Clubs, 80, 93
Michigan Suffragist, 93
Middleburg, Synod of, 158
Midrash, 144
Miller, Glenn T., 40-41
Ministerial Formation Coordinating Agency, 226-28
Mishnah, 144
Moncrief, John W., 7
Moerdyk, Peter, 10
Moerdyk, William, 211

Montgomery, Classis of, 38
Moravian Church, 36
Morris, Leon, *The Cross of Jesus*, 299n15
Mozley, J.K., 308n39
Mulder, Bernard J., xxxvii-xxxviii, xxxviin21, 56
Mulder, Edwin, xxxi, xxxin10
Mulder, John R., xxxi, xxxin11
Mutch, Carol, 227
Myconius, Oswald, 269

Nanes, Laura, xxx, xxxn9, xlv
National American Equal Suffrage Union, 93, 94
National Association of Evangelicals, 25
National Council of Churches, 25
Neal, Ava, 196
Neander, Augustus, 8, 22
Nelson, C. Ellis, 36-37, 44
Nelson, Marjorie, 64
Nemeth, Roger, 129n1
Nettinga, Siebe C., 3-4, 7-8, 15
Neumann, Balthasar, xlii
Nevin, John, 23, 276-78
New Amsterdam, 160-61
New Brunswick, Particular Synod of, 178
New Brunswick Theological Seminary, xviii, xxviii, 4, 39, 69n4, 100, 116, 120, 171-76, 196, 208, 210, 214, 217-26
New Brunswick Theological Seminary Board of Superintendents, 173, 178, 197-99, 220
New Jersey, Particular Synod of, 178
Newman, Albert Henry, *A Manual of Church History*, 8-9, 13
Newman, John Henry, 22-23
New Netherland, 160-61
New Women, 70-71
New York, Classis of, 170
New York and Philadelphia, Presbyterian Synod of, 166n71
New York Missionary Society, 192
New York State Assembly, 171
New York Times, 247

Niesel, Wilhelm, *The Theology of Calvin*, 296n5
Nietzsche, Friederich, 258
Noah, 238, 240
Noll, Mark, 19n52
North Holland, Synod of, 163, 165
North Park Church, Kalamazoo, 39
Northwestern Junior College, 41
Nykamp, Robert, xxxix

Occasional Papers (RCA Historical Society), 116
Oggel, Lillie Bright, 99, 105
Olson, Jeannine E., 156, 186
Ordination of women, 38-39
Ordination of Women, RCA Committee on the, 39
Orr, James, *The Progress of Dogma*, 24-25, 27
Osmer, Richard, 155, 187
Osterhaven, M. Eugene, xxxi, xxxin13, xxxvii-xxxviii, 6n8, 32, 296
Oude Kerk, Amsterdam, 274
Oudersluys, Richard C., xxxi, xxxin14, xlv, 32, 39, 53
Outline Studies in Ecclesiastical History (Dosker), 16
Overbeek, Karl, 54-55
Oxford Movement, 276

Palmer, Benjamin, 85
Pannier, J., 311-12
Paquier, Richard, 282-83
Paramus, Classis of, 219
Parker, T.H.L., 316
Parkway Presbyterian Church, Corpus Christi, 44-45, 57, 63
Partee, Charles, *The Theology of John Calvin*, 297
Paul (the apostle), 145-47, 187, 194, 232, 234, 241-42, 288
Paul, Alice, 93, 94n83
Paul, Robert S., *The Atonement and the Sacraments*, 297n10, 299n14, 304, 315n68, 317n77
Pelikan, Jaroslav, xl, xln24, 21n57, 27
Penning, James, 129n1
Perkins School of Theology, 48

Peter (the apostle), 234, 241
Peterson, Robert A., Jr., 305n28, 309n44, 312n54, 314-16, 316n69
Peterson, Robert A., Jr., *Calvin and the Atonement*, 297, 315n65
Phelps, Philip, Jr., 77, 212
Piet, John, xxxix, 32, 53
Pieters, Albertus, 5
Piety and Patriotism (VanHoeven), 111
Pioneers in the Arab World (Van Ess), xliii
Plato, 145, 259n31
Polman, A.D.R., 252-54
Ponstein, Lambert, 39
Post, Anna Coatsworth, 80, 95n88
Post, Kate Garrod, 88, 92n77, 95n88, 105
Post, Katherine, 81-82, 84, 84n49, 95-97, 98n95, 100, 105
Post, Richard H., 106
Pottersville Reformed Church, 287-88
Potts, Johann, 97n95
Presbyterian Church in the United States, 36, 39
Presbyterian Church in the United States, Board of Christian Education, 32, 36, 44, 50, 58, 63
Presbyterian School of Christian Education, 36
Price, H. Douglas, 92n78
Princeton College (Princeton University), 206
Princeton Theological Seminary, 50, 62, 197
Proclus, 143
Professor of theology, General Synod, xiii, 139, 141-187, 191-92
Progress of Dogma, The (Orr), 24-25, 27
Protestant Church of the Netherlands, 249
Pueblo, Presbytery of, 61
Puritans, 274
Putin, Vladimir, 247

Queens College, 193, 206-207
Queens College Board of Trustees, 173-74, 190
Quinius, Henry, 54

Ratmeyer, Una, 38n26
Ratzinger, Joseph Cardinal, 153n33
Rausch, Thomas, 151
Red Cross, 86, 99
Reformed Church Historical Society, 116, 125; *Occasional Papers*, 116
Reformed Church in America, 20-21, 26, 39-40, 67, 103n111, 121, 214, 228, 249, 278-80
Reformed Church in America, Board of Direction, 119, 178
Reformed Church in America, Board of Domestic Missions, 116
Reformed Church in America, Board of Education, xxxvii-xxxviii, 36, 56
Reformed Church in America, Board of World Mission, 63
Reformed Church in America, Women's Board for Foreign Mission, 38
Reformed Review, xx, xxviiin3, 29, 57
Reformed Worship, 289
Religious plays, 272
Revelation of John, 243, 254
Rich, Cynthia Holder, 32
Richmond Reformed Church, Grand Rapids, 34
Ridder, Herman J. ("Bud"), xl-xli, xlin25, xlii, 58, 143, 221-23
Ritzema, Johannes, 204-205
Rock, Stanley, xl
Romeyn, Dirck, 173, 192
Romeyn, James VanCampen, 173n96
Romeyn, Jeremiah, 173n96
Roosevelt School, Colorado Springs, 61
Rossman, Parker, 45-46, 49
Rottschaefer, Henry, 89n64
Routley, Erik, 288-89
Russian Orthodox Church, 247
Rutgers College, 210
Ryan, Blackie, 127

Sage, Gardner A., 120
Saint Mary's Hospital, Grand Rapids, 54
Saint Peter's Cathedral, Geneva, 268
Salthouse, Arlen, 288
"Saturday Night Live," 263

Schaff, Phillip, 8n18, 9, 23, 276-78
Schieffelin, Samuel B., 213
Schmidt, Corwin, 129n1
Schoonmaker, Jacob, 198n28
Schuller, Robert, xlv
Schuppert, Mildred, xl, xlivn34
Schureman, John, 174n96, 198n26
Schüssler-Fiorenza, Francis, 148, 152
Schuyler, Philip, 84n46
Scott, Charles, 77, 217
Scott, John R.W., 299n15
Scudder, William W., 176
Second Vatican Council, 25-26
Servetus, Michael, 251n6
Seth, 240
Shaw, Anna Howard, 94
Sheeres, Janet, 129n1
Sheldon, Henry C., 7, 9
Sherwood, Martha, 84n49
Sieckentroosters, 160, 202
Simmons College, 69
Slicker, Joe, 48
Smith, Thomas Gibson, 173n96
Socrates, 258n31
South Grand Rapids, Classis of, 59
Steffans, Nicholas M., 3-5ff., 6n9, 10-11, 14-16, 24n65, 28, 77, 213
Stellingwerff, John, 128n1
Stewart, Sonja M., 32
Strong, Thomas, 119
Stryker, Elise, 36
Sweet, Leonard, 289
Sweet, William Warren, 19
Swierenga, Robert P., 128n1, 136
Swift, Adeline Hinkley, 84n49

Table of Nations, 240-41
Taylor, Charles, 251
Taylor, Vincent, 298
Ten Clay, Henry J., 31, 51, 64
Texas, University of, 43, 46
Theological Education Agency, 225-26
Theology of Calvin, The (Niesel), 296n5
Theology of John Calvin, The (Partee), 297
Theology of the Reformers (George), 297n10
Theresa of Avila, 154n37
Thérèse of Lisieux, 154n37

Third Reformed Church, Holland, xlv, 229
Third Reformed Church, Pella, xxx
Third Reformed Church, Philadelphia, 175
Thistelthwaite, Susan, 40
Thomas, Derek W.H., 297, 301n20, 317n77
Thomas, Norman, 222
Torrance, Thomas, xxxiii, xlv
Tosephta, 144
Tower of Babel, 238, 240-41, 245
Traveler's Club, 69n4, 82
Travel Seminars, xli-ii
True Reformed Church, 173
Truss, Lynne, 131

Ulster, Classis of, 219
Unam Sanctum, 153
Union Theological Seminary, New York, 44
United Presbyterian Church in North America, 36
Utrecht, University of, 191, 204

Valkenburg, W.G.B.M., 150-51
Van Bunschooten, Elias, 195
Van Buren, Paul, 305n28, 309n44
Van Buren, Paul, *Christ in Our Place*, 295, 297
VandenBerge, Peter N., 179; *Historical Directory of the Reformed Church in America*, xliv
Vanderbilt, John, 171
Van der Leeuw, Gerardus, 282
Vander Lugt, Gerrit T., 39
Van der Muelen, Jacob, 212n35
Van der Veen, Charles, 212-13, 215-16
Van der Veen, Christian, 212n35
Van Dyk, Leanne, 32
Van Eck, Arthur O., 55-56
Van Ess, Dorothy, *Pioneers in the Arab World*, xliii
Van Ess, John, xliii
VanHoeven, James W., *Piety and Patriotism*, 111n2
Van Ostenburg, Gordon L., 143
Van Pelt, Daniel, 77

Van Raalte, Albertus C., 67, 107, 209-10
Van Raalte, Christina, 107
Van Raalte Institute, xii, xix, xxi
Van Rensselaer, Catherine, 84n47
VanRoekel, Gerritt, xxx
Van Ruler, A.A., 254-58, 259-61
Van Soest, Bert, 283-84
Van Syckle, Mrs. W.A., 95, 100
Varrick, Richard, 171
Vitterwijk, Henry, 212n35
von Mosheim, John Lawrence, 8, 8n16
Voskuil, Dennis, 4n2, 4n3
Vredenburgh, John Schureman, 174n96

"Waldensian theory," 21
Walker, Williston, xl, 9
Wallace, Ronald, 317n77, 317n79
Washington, Booker T., 81
Watt, Hugh, xxxiii, xlv
Watts, Isaac, 275, 275n48, 293
Weaver, J. Denny, *The Nonviolent Atonement*, 298n12
Weber, Otto, *Foundations of Dogmatics*, 312n53
Webster, Daniel, 81
Wellesley College, 69
Wellesley Hills Congregational Church, 68n3
Wendel, Francois, 306n33, 307, 317n77
Wendel, Francois, *Calvin, Origins and Development of His Religious Thought*, 296n5
Wesel, Synod of, 158
Westerhoff, John H., 44
Western Christendom Travel Seminar, 29-30
Western Michigan University, 60
Western State College, 61
Western Theological Seminary, xii, xix-xx, xxvii, xxxi-xxxiii, xxxvii-xlii, 3-31ff., 39, 42, 50-58, 63-65, 67, 70, 112, 123, 143, 175, 208, 216-26, 230
Western Theological Seminary Board of Trustees, 32n2, 142

Wheaton College, 297
Wheeler, Anna, 84n49, 85, 105, 108
Whelan, Anna, 97, 98n95
When Faith Takes Form (Bruggink and Droppers), xx
Whitman, Mrs. P.W., 100
Why the Cross? (Guillabaud), 296n2
Wilcock, Michael, 245n13
William of Orange, 251n5
Willis, E. David, *Calvin's Catholic Christology*, 296
Wilson, Peter, 171-72
Wilson, Woodrow, 92, 97
Winn, George Hinsdale, III, xxxvin20
With the Spirit's Sword (Hall), 299n14
Witvliet, John, 289
Women's Board of Foreign Missions, 71n9, 75, 77n36, 78, 108n125
Women's Christian Temperance Union, 67-68n1, 72n11, 79-80, 86, 92-93, 99
Women's Foreign Missionary Society, 76
Women's Literary Club, 72, 79-82, 86, 93-95, 95n88, 99, 107-108

Woodbridge, Samuel M., 4, 12, 21, 28
Woods, Leonard, 197
World Council of Churches, 25
Wren, Christopher, 275
Wright, Elliott, 36
Wright, Frank Lloyd, xxx
Wyckoff, D. Campbell, 50
Wyckoff, Isaac, 209
Wynn, J.C., 58

Yale Divinity School, 45
Yates, Anna, 84n49
Yates, Gertrude, 84n49
Yoemans, Grace, 98n95
Young, Frances M., 299
Young Men's/Women's Christian Association, 68n1, 72n11

Zachman, Randall, 305-306
Ziegler, Jesse, 53
Ziggy, 113
Zikmund, Barbara Brown, 68n1
Zwemer, Sara Winter, 71n10
Zwingli, Huldrich, 263-67, 269-71, 291